MANAGING LOCAL GOVERNMENT FOR IMPROVED PERFORMANCE

A Practical Approach

After working for nearly three years to improve the performance of the government of Flint, Michigan—and discovering that there was no comprehensive work on the subject of local-government management to refer to—Brian Rapp and Frank M. Patitucci felt a personal as well as a professional need to write a book that would help them understand their successes and failures, and that would help others do a better job in similar situations. The result, this book, is unique both in its approach and in its presentation.

The authors, establishing a conceptual framework within which to understand their subject, use Flint as a case city to examine the practical impact of factors affecting city government, and they indicate the major standards and criteria that should be applied in evaluating that impact.

Although they recognize that within each city there are unique conditions that make a blanket prescription impossible, the authors are nevertheless convinced that many individuals both in and out of government can do something to improve the performance of their city government, and they have set out to help these individuals understand, in the most concrete terms possible, how they might go about it.

Brian Rapp served as city manager of Flint, Michigan, from 1971 to 1974 and is currently assistant county manager of Santa Clara County, California. He has also worked as an associate at McKinsey and Company, a management consulting firm, and in 1970 he was selected as a Presidential Executive Interchange Fellow. Frank M. Patitucci was both director of community development and director of finance in Flint. He has worked in the private sector as a financial and management analyst for TRW, Inc., and as a management consultant for ICF Incorporated, and is now president of the California State Housing Finance Agency.

MANAGING LOCAL GOVERNMENT FOR IMPROVED PERFORMANCE

A Practical Approach

Brian W. Rapp
Frank M. Patitucci

with a Foreword by
Elliot L. Richardson

Westview Press | Boulder, Colorado

Copyright © 1977 by Brian W. Rapp and Frank M. Patitucci

Published in 1977 in the United States of America by
  Westview Press, Inc.
  1898 Flatiron Court
  Boulder, Colorado 80301
  Frederick A. Praeger, Publisher and Editorial Director

Library of Congress Cataloging in Publication Data
Rapp, Brian W
  Managing local government for improved performance.
  Bibliography: p.
  1. Municipal government—United States.
2. Flint, Mich.—Politics and government. I. Patitucci,
Frank M., joint author. II. Title.
JS331.R27   352'.008'0973   76-25240
ISBN 0-89158-121-9

Printed and bound in the United States of America

To Merton and Elizabeth
B.W.R.

To Serena and Anna
F.M.P.

CONTENTS

FIGURES

EXHIBITS

FOREWORD

William Hazlett has observed that "man is the only animal that laughs and weeps; for he is the only animal that is struck by the difference between what things are and what they ought to be." As public managers, Brian Rapp and Frank Patitucci have experienced first-hand the difference between what local governments are doing to meet human and community needs and what they could achieve through better management. In this timely volume, they examine ways to close the gap between local governments' actual and potential performance.

Government has become a hotly debated topic during this decade for many of the reasons that make this study important. In a real sense, it is the performance of local governments that will determine the success of efforts to decentralize our federal system. Reversing the flow of power to Washington, however, will always be difficult. A prerequisite is to convince Congress and the Executive Branch that 39,000 town halls, city halls, and county buildings can be managed to serve the people effectively.

When citizen confidence and trust in government at all levels are tenuous, the quality of local-government performance is vital to the attitudes of individual citizens. Once citizens come to feel that they cannot trust the local officials to whom they have delegated responsibility for their common concerns, free representative self-government is made impossible. Trust and confidence in local-government institutions grow increasingly important as greater numbers of individuals become dependent on local government for essential services ranging from housing and health services to fire protection and transportation.

As the costs of local-government services outrun increases in available revenue, local-government officials across the country face a painful dilemma: increased taxes or reduced levels of service. For local officials the critical question is not *whether* to strive for better management in local government but *how* to achieve it. A vast amount of research and analysis has been devoted to factors affecting the performance of private business; there has also been considerable attention to the performance of the federal government, and to some extent state governments. Local-government performance, meanwhile, has not received its due share of critical examination. By responding to this need, Rapp and Patitucci have made a major contribution.

Five significant factors distinguish this book.

Of primary importance is the emphasis on process. The authors do not prescribe simplistic solutions for problems like crime, poor housing, or inadequate health care. They do, however, scrutinize the process that local officials traditionally pursue in efforts to resolve problems in a community. The book focuses on the ways in which local-government officials decide what needs to be done within a community and on how they plan to achieve their goals with the resources that are available.

The book is analytical and diagnostic—not descriptive. Recognizing the vast differences that separate Beverly Hills from Newark, the authors have provided the reader with a framework for developing a strategy that can improve the performance of any government and make it responsible to unique local conditions. They have developed an analytical tool that will help practitioners, students, and citizens alike in understanding how to cope with the circumstances they find in their own communities. Their book provides a launching pad for those who want to make their local governments more responsive and effective.

The volume contains a comprehensive examination of concrete cases. In addition to discussions of municipal unions, the civil service, government organization, financial practice, and managerial incentives, the reader will find analyses of the impact on a local government of the media, the judiciary, and private-interest groups. This consideration of internal and external factors, and their interrelationships, sets this work apart from more conventional studies.

The book is modeled on real government. The authors apply their analytical framework to an actual city government, thereby allowing the reader to understand the practical nature of the barriers impeding improved performance and the difficulty of removing them. The ninety-five "mini-cases" that illustrate the study of Flint, Michigan, provide a window into management at the local level. The fact that the authors were not only actors in the Flint situation, but have since rebounded to important public sector positions, increases the book's credibility and attests to its practical value.

Finally, the book defines public management as an important discipline separate and distinct from political science or public administration. Traditional wisdom has it that politicians establish public policy and administrators carry it out. Those who work in local government have come to recognize the inconsistency and obsolescence of this notion. They understand that politics and administration overlap in virtually all local governments. Deciding what to do and getting it done are inseparable parts of the process of public management.

Many kinds of readers will benefit from this book. For government practitioners at all levels, it furnishes a valuable starting point for the development of a performance-improvement strategy. For students who intend to work in local government, it offers a revealing account of what goes on in the real world of the public sector as opposed to the cloistered halls of academia. For citizens, it provides a useful lesson in understanding what takes place in local government and how they can influence it. For all these reasons, it should be read, contemplated, and translated into action.

ELLIOT L. RICHARDSON
MAY 1977

PREFACE

Many counties, cities, and other local governments are not working well. The garbage is rarely collected on schedule, citizens are mugged in broad daylight, schools are not teaching children to read, potholes in the streets seem to multiply, striking policemen break the law they were sworn to enforce, legislators admit to rigging zoning cases, traffic congestion makes driving an ordeal, no one at city hall will answer a simple question—the list goes on and on. Underlying this record of inadequate performance is a growing fiscal perversity: as local-government performance decreases, taxes increase. Taxpayers are demanding to know what their tax dollars are buying, but few local-government officials have answers for them. Increasingly, the media as well as individual citizens are attributing poor performance to poor management.

What is local-government performance? How is it related to the process of management? What factors affect the management process in a local government? What can be done to make this process work better? This book examines these questions.

The subject of local-government performance became important to us in late 1971, when we accepted the positions of city manager and community-development director in the city of Flint, Michigan. For each of us, the decision to pursue a public-management career at the local level reflected a disillusionment with the ability of the federal government to solve local problems. It also reflected a desire to work at that level of government most responsible for getting things done; in short, to be where the action was. We wanted to be among those local officials who would test the validity of the assumption on which the theory of the New Federalism was based: that local governments should and could assume a greater role in our federal system.

We began our jobs in Flint with the firm belief that with hard work, fact-based analysis, and a willingness to act on convictions we could improve the ability of a city government to get things done. We assumed that significant progress would be made in satisfying community needs if a local government were run more like a private business. We believed that others cared as much as we did about making local government work better. Three sobering years later, having lost more battles than we had won, we left Flint with a greater appreciation for the enormity of the task involved in managing the many separate businesses that comprise a local government.

From our experience in Flint, subsequent research, and discussions with local-government practitioners throughout the country, we have reached a number of conclusions that we believe are relevant to the improvement of local-government performance. The most important is that improving the way in which things are done (process) is critical to improving what gets done (performance). Regardless of whether a local government decides to clean up the environment, increase access to public transportation, reduce crime, or improve the quality of housing, the ability to get it done depends in large measure on the quality of the management process employed. The ability to reduce crime may depend on the quality of police-officer training; improving the quality of transit service may turn on the skill with which labor relations are administered; the provision of adequate low-cost housing may be significantly impaired by financial practices imposed on local government by the federal or state government.

In addition, we have concluded that:

- Most economic, social, and physical problems within a community can be solved best at the local level, yet most local governments do not have the capacity to use available resources in a manner that will produce the desired results.
- The conditions that affect the ability of local-government officials to get things done are most often unique to the specific community; general prescriptions about how to solve urban problems and improve the performance of all local governments are not generally applicable.
- Although local-government officials can learn much from their private-sector counterparts, a local government cannot be managed exactly as a private business is managed.
- Many individuals, working within and outside a local government, affect its performance; these individuals and the institutions they represent must be considered and involved in taking actions to improve performance.
- There are no quick solutions or easy answers to the challenge of making local governments work better. It is a long-term undertaking that must recognize the interplay between political and bureaucratic forces, between citizen demands and financial realities, between management responsibilities and employee rights, and between local prerogatives and state and national priorities.

Our experience in Flint was enhanced by a course we taught at the University of Michigan–Flint entitled "Managing Urban Change." Teaching forced us to think more rigorously about the barriers that prevented Flint's city government from achieving higher levels of performance and to be more precise in extracting conclusions from our experience. In large part, the material we assembled for the course provided the foundation for this book.

We believe that this book fills a gap in the literature concerning the practice of public management. Prior to our departure for Flint, we tried to find material in bookstores and libraries which would be useful to us in our new jobs. We found that, although much had been written about local government, very little had been written that would guide us while working as management officials in local government. We could not find a single book that addressed, in a comprehensive and practical manner, the question that was foremost in our minds: what should we take into account in trying to manage Flint's city government? In the classroom, we confronted the same problem. We found nothing in the literature related to local government which would give our students a comprehensive framework for understanding the ability to manage, or which would give them a practical view of what it is like to work and function within a local government.

This, then, is the book we wanted to read before assuming our jobs in Flint. It is also the book we wanted to assign to our students. It is the book we will refer to associates who ask, "What did you learn from your experience in Flint?"

We have tried to write a book that will be useful to practitioners, students, and citizens. We have not attempted to describe every element in the landscape of local government; instead, we have tried to fashion a tool that will enable readers to cope with the particular landscapes they find in their communities. We have tried to write a book that is practical. Because the substance of this book is based on experience, it provides a window into the reality of conditions within local governments. Finally, we have tried to write a book that is comprehensive, one that addresses both the internal and the external factors that affect the ability of local-government officials to get things done. We are as much concerned with how private-interest groups, newspapers, and the judicial system affect performance as we are with a city charter or a budgeting system. In summary, we have tried to organize and present the material in a way that will make it most useful—as a text, as a reference source, or as an accurate account of day-to-day life within a local government.

We hope that this book will enable its readers to better understand both the magnitude of the barriers that impede efforts to improve local-government performance and the potential for constructive change which can be realized through better management. Above all, we hope that this book will communicate the excitement and satisfaction that can be obtained by becoming involved in efforts to achieve a better quality of life for all citizens.

BRIAN W. RAPP
FRANK M. PATITUCCI

ACKNOWLEDGMENTS

The purpose of most acknowledgments is to give credit to those who made a book possible while at the same time absolving them of all blame for its contents. Ours is no exception.

Dave Brunell made the journey to Flint possible. Francis Limmer, Paul Visser, and other members of Flint's City Council (Jerry Yurk, Gordon Suber, Doug Philpot, Fred Tucker, and Sandy Applegate) made our stay in Flint enjoyable and rewarding. We owe a debt of gratitude to these individuals and to many other friends both within and outside city government.

Writing a first book, like making love for the first time, leaves one reasonably uncertain about the outcome until the end of the experience. We are, therefore, in debt to those who saw what this book could be and encouraged us to produce it. Dick Darman's conceptual clarity and Jeff Mayer's insight and attention to literary detail have left their mark throughout this book. Scott Fossler's encouragement and perceptive criticism significantly strengthened the final product. Above all, we are indebted to Merton H. Rapp, who from the beginning said it could be done.

To Bill Moran, Dick Wilberg, Ward McAllister, Clark Tibbets, Alden Briscoe, and Lynn Corson we offer our sincere thanks. We are also indebted to Governor John Gilligan, Steve McConahey, John Steinhart, John Mudd, John Russell, Don Borut, Steve Freeman, Don Haider, George Barbour, Jan Lodal, Mick Seidl, Judy Barbour, and Richard Rose for their special contributions.

Institutions as well as friends helped make this book a reality. We are especially grateful to James H. Billington, director of the Woodrow Wilson International Center for Scholars, and to Elliot Richardson, who enabled a local-government practitioner to spend a year in Romanesque splendor exchanging ideas with a distinguished group of Fellows. We are also grateful to the Mott Foundation, which provided some of the funding, and to the Stanford University Graduate School of Business for stretching its institutional boundaries to encompass this project.

A list of those who helped convert our illegible scribble into manuscript form would fill several pages. To all those who put up with countless revisions and the ill humor that often accompanied them, we offer a special note of thanks. To one person— Mary Hunter Vanbragt—a thank you is not enough. Without her help there would be no book. Thanks also go to our friend and early editor, Flip Caldwell.

We are also grateful to Lynne Rienner, Ann Williams, and the entire staff at Westview Press for converting our final manuscript into a book. This book profited immeasurably from Lynne's guidance and editorial support. She has perfected the art of literary midwifery. Finally, we are indebted to Fred Praeger, who convinced us that it is possible for a publishing house to care about its authors.

To our families, who suffered most throughout this literary ordeal, we have one thing to say: This is the last time!

B.W.R.
F.M.P.

MANAGING LOCAL GOVERNMENT FOR IMPROVED PERFORMANCE

A Practical Approach

INTRODUCTION

Performance and the Management Process

What now has to be learned is to manage service institutions for performance.
Peter Drucker
Management

During the 1960s, many observers of government were disillusioned by the repeated failures of innovative public programs to achieve their goals. . . . Very often, what appeared to be bold and excellent ideas did not produce the promised results after they were enacted. . . . These difficulties are rooted in an earlier view of public affairs that separated the problem of policy analysis from the task of implementation and administration.
Derek Bok
Harvard University

Local government is a public business. It consumes resources, provides vital services, and is managed by elected and appointed officials. Like private corporations, it can and should be managed for performance. The critical problem facing local governments is not, as many claim, a lack of resources; it is an inability to use existing resources efficiently and effectively in meeting legitimate demands for public services.

To manage a local government for improved performance, we must first take into account its unique combination of characteristics. Local governments are legal entities created by states: their decisions have the force of law within specified geographic areas. Local governments are part of an intergovernmental system: they share responsibility with other levels of government for the provision of many public services. Local governments are continually exposed to public scrutiny: the way something is done is often as important as what is done. The owners of the business of local government are also its customers: citizens can obtain from their local government what they want and are willing to pay for.

In addition, local governments consist of many different and complex businesses: these range from sewer construction, fire protection, and garbage collection to housing management, health care, and transportation. Local governments provide essential services, many of them (fire protection and

3

water supply) in response to immediate and urgent needs. Local governments are monopolistic: they need not compete to provide public goods and services. Finally, revenue received by local governments is generally unrelated to results produced: citizens are taxed regardless of their judgment about the quality and quantity of municipal services they receive.

Perhaps the most important characteristic of local government is the lack of accepted and quantifiable criteria for measuring its performance. Without such standards, it is extremely difficult, if not impossible, for citizens to determine if the business of local government is being performed well or poorly. Citizens concerned about the performance of a local government cannot find the measurement equivalent of games won and lost, earnings per share, or return on invested capital. Unlike an athletic team or a private business, a local government has few accepted measures that permit citizens to objectively monitor its performance.

In the absence of clear measures of performance, it is easy to understand why many county and city governments have been allowed to drift from crisis to crisis, caused by internal and external forces that were not anticipated while there was still time to consider alternative ways of coping with them. In the absence of accepted standards of performance, citizens have watched helplessly as local governments have mushroomed in size, assuming responsibilities without developing the management skills or using the management tools that are necessary to exercise such responsibilities.

More important, the inability to measure the performance of a local government makes it difficult to examine the benefits that can be derived from alternative improvements. Without standards of performance, it would be difficult to evaluate the potential benefits of a proposed corporate merger or to determine whether a football team had been wise in trading a star running back. Similarly, without accepted performance measures it is difficult to determine whether programs designed to strengthen the way in which a local government is managed have actually resulted in improved performance.

Despite this difficulty, the central thesis of this book is that improving the way in which local governments get desired things done (*process*) is critical to improving what gets done (*performance*). Before examining the relationship between process and performance, it is important to agree on the meaning of each term.

What is performance?

The performance of any institution, public or private, is related to the business in which that institution is engaged. More precisely, performance is related to the degree to which desired ends have been achieved at least cost. Because a local government is in business to provide services that satisfy the needs of individual citizens, we define the performance of local government as *the extent to which public officials in a community are able to achieve stated economic, social, or environmental conditions with a minimum expenditure of resources.* By "stated economic, social, or environmental conditions" we mean the conditions within a community that citizens, through their elected representatives, have indicated they want their local government to achieve. By "resources" we refer to the manpower, time, capital, and dollars available for expenditure by public officials.

Performance has two dimensions: effectiveness and efficiency. Performance is *effective* according to the degree to which a stated community condition is achieved or maintained. For example, if public officials determine that by 1980 a mass-transit system will be in operation, and if this condition is subsequently achieved, performance may be considered "effective." Performance is *efficient* depending on the quantity of resources expended in the effort to achieve a desired condition. For example, if a city completed the mass-transit system by 1980 as planned by spending $1 billion more than was anticipated or warranted, performance would be considered "effective" but "inefficient." Optimal government performance, therefore, must combine effectiveness with efficiency.

In recent years productivity improvement has become a focus of attention in many cities and counties. Productivity does not equal performance as we have defined it. Productivity explains the relationship between results produced by a government activity and the resources used in their production. For example, the productivity of a waste-collection crew can be related to the tons of garbage collected per crew-day; the productivity of a housing inspection activity, to the number of houses inspected per person-day. Productivity is a measure of efficiency, not of effectiveness. Increased productivity is necessary but not sufficient to ensure improved performance.

Local-government performance must be related to changes in community conditions, not solely to the results produced by government activities. One would hardly give a waste-collection crew high marks for performance if it increased the tons of garbage it collected each day and yet left the streets littered with paper and debris. Nor would one consider the housing inspection activity effective if homeowners and landlords did not correct housing code violations. As Figure 1 illustrates, the performance of police activities is ultimately measured by the safety and security of citizens within the community (a desired community condition), not by the number of arrests made or the miles of streets patrolled (the direct results of police-department activities). The challenge facing local-government managers is that of strengthening the relationship between the results government produces and, presumably, can control and actual community conditions.

What is the management process?

A local government, in its attempts to satisfy the economic, social, and environmental needs within a community, implicitly or explicitly follows a process. We refer to this as the *management process*. Simply stated, the management process is *the way in which public officials decide what to do and get it done.** The management process refers to the way in which public officials translate community needs into community objectives; develop strategies and programs to achieve those objectives with available resources; implement the programs, producing desired results with budgeted resources; and evaluate results, making adjustments as necessary.

The management process consists of three major phases: planning, implementation, and evaluation. These phases are interrelated and overlapping, but each is sufficiently distinct to warrant separate analysis. The management process in explained in Exhibit 1.

The management process is a common denominator in the undertaking of many activities. Take, for example, a family outing to the beach. This effort calls for careful planning (where to go, when to get there, how much food to take); determined implementation (getting the kids into the car, finding the right beach, deciding whether naps can be skipped, and fighting the traffic to get home); and thoughtful evaluation (deciding whether the day's joys outweighed its headaches and whether the family should attempt to repeat the outing the following week). Depending on the nature of the

---

* The literature about local government, urban management, public administration, political science, and related fields contains a variety of terms which are used differently by different authors. To ensure accurate communication, we define key terms—such as goals, objectives, policies, efficiency, effectiveness, performance, productivity, and the like—in the text. A complete glossary of terms is presented on page 385.

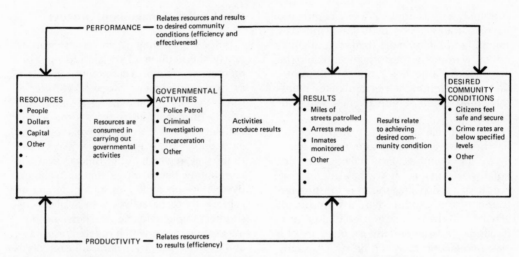

Figure 1. The relationship of performance to the achievement of desired community conditions.

endeavor, the management process is more or less evident and important. It is not likely that we would think about it as a distinct process in relationship to a family outing. But in carrying out the business of local government, it demands our separate attention.

The importance of improving the management process

Many individual solutions have been advanced as the answer to the question: how can we improve the performance of our local government? Some argue that improving the quality of elected officials is the key factor in improving performance. Others counter that conversion to the city-manager or strong-mayor form of government is the critical determinant. Still others contend that the crucial issue is whether local governments have made use of advanced management tools, hired trained management personnel, or applied sophisticated technology to urban problems. A few even propound, albeit timidly, that local-government performance could be improved if new federal programs were developed to replace the old ones that have failed.

Public-affairs literature is filled with claims that the quality of life within a county or a city could be significantly improved if only a specific urban problem (housing, health, education, income maintenance) were solved. Thus, argue some social scientists and politicians, the vicious circle of urban deprivation would be broken and a series of reinforcing improvements in the quality of life would be set in motion.

Perhaps the most often mentioned single solution to the problems faced by local government is "more money!" Mayors and local-government officials are fond of saying each year at budget time that the only thing impeding their ability to improve performance is the lack of this one resource. On a more pessimistic note, some contend that domestic problems will never be solved and government performance will never be improved. This view is based on the observation that improvements are always accompanied by an equivalent or greater increase in the level of public expectations, thereby guaranteeing a gap between expected performance and reality.

In this book we advance the proposition that improving the management process will improve the performance of local govern-

EXHIBIT 1

The Three Interrelated Phases of the Management Process

The management process in local government should consist of three phases: planning, implementation, and evaluation.

Planning, the first phase, involves four steps: (1) determining what to do—the translation of community needs into community objectives, (2) determining how to do it—the definition of the means (programs, strategies, projects) required to achieve stated objectives, (3) assigning responsible managers—the identification of those who will be held accountable for carrying out the programs, and (4) allocating resources—the development of a budget for each program and for each responsible manager.

Each step is critical to successful planning. The most critical step, however, is the establishment of community objectives—the end result of community planning. To be useful, these objectives should meet four requirements. First, they should be explicit. They should be written down and communicated throughout the community as well as throughout agencies and departments of local government. Second, community objectives should be easily understood, so that citizens have a basis for holding their elected leaders accountable. Third, objectives should be achievable by a specified date. They should not represent "pie-in-the-sky" desires that raise expectations that cannot be met. Finally, community objectives must be capable of being measured, so that it is clear when achievement has, or has not, been realized.

Determining what to do within a community has little or no value unless public officials also determine how they are going to get it done, who is going to do it, and whether there are sufficient resources available to do it. The annual budget is the means of doing this. The budget is the most important document of a local government because it bridges the gap between planning and implementation.

Implementation, the second phase of the management process, addresses how we will get done what we have decided to do. A local government budget should represent a series of contracts wherein responsible managers agree to produce specified results with budgeted resources. Implementation is the process of executing these contracts. Accordingly, it involves organizing (coordinating people, functions, and activities), staffing (putting the right people in the right jobs), determining productivity standards (identifying the results that should be obtained per unit of resource consumed), and supervising and controlling work (directing day-to-day activity to ensure that resources are spent and results are produced according to plan).

Evaluation, the final phase of the management process, is related to both implementation and planning and asks: Did we do what we said we would do? Were results produced and resources consumed as planned? To the extent that they were not, what modifications should be made? In short, evaluation is the process of relating what was intended to be done to what was actually done, and initiating changes to reflect new circumstances.

ment. We do not, however, suggest that better management is the only answer. Improving the process by which a local government is managed will not guarantee improved performance. There is no immutable law that says: if you improve the way in which things are done, they will be done better. Because an athletic team trains more intelligently than its rival does not mean that it will win more games. There is no guarantee that if a family plans its vacation in advance its members will have a better time than those in a family that rejects planning. A private business noted for the excellence of its management-training programs will not necessarily outperform its competitors. Similarly, there is no guarantee that a local government that improves its budgeting system, modernizes its city charter, and develops equitable collective-bargaining procedures will improve the quality of life within the community. There is, however, in each of these examples a consistent hypothesis: if we improve the way we do things, it is probable that the things we do will be improved. Strengthening the management process increases the probability that more will get done with available resources than otherwise would be the case.

Peter Drucker, a thoughtful writer on subjects related to business performance and management, has most clearly articulated the proposition that the performance of public and private institutions can be improved by strengthening the process by which they are managed.[1] Regardless of what an institution decides to do, success depends, in large part, on the management process that is employed to do it. There are countless examples in our highly technological society of engineers and inventors who have discovered and developed new pro-

ducts only to see their businesses fail despite the potential market value. This happens because performance depends on more than having a good product; it also depends on the ability to market successfully, the quality of the people employed, the capacity to finance operations, and the efficiency of the production process. In short, successful performance depends as much on the quality of the management process as on the potential value of the product. Perhaps the most dramatic illustration of this point is recounted by Alfred P. Sloan in his book *My Years with General Motors*. In this work Sloan describes William C. Durant, the person who put together General Motors: "Mr. Durant was a great man with a great weakness—he could create but not administer. . . . That he should have conceived a General Motors and been unable in the long run to bring it off . . . is a tragic chapter of American industrial history."[2]

Public policy and the management process

Understanding the management process in local government serves to integrate politics (the process of determining public policy) with public administration (the process of producing results). The view advanced by Woodrow Wilson and other progressive reformers that there should be a rigid separation between politics and administration does not reflect the reality of the decision-making process within most local governments. In his 1974 "Report to the Board of Overseers," Derek Bok, president of Harvard University, forcefully stated the need to integrate politics with public administration. In this report Bok called for a new generation of

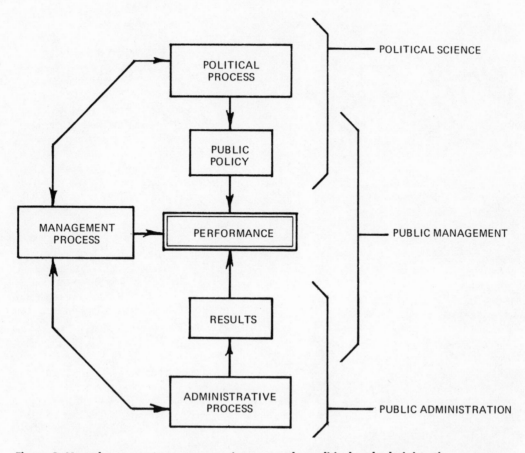

Figure 2. How the management process integrates the political and administrative processes.

public officials who would serve in responsible government positions armed with a better understanding of how politics and administration interact in the formulation and implementation of public policy.

Focusing on performance as it is related to the management process satisfies this need. As Figure 2 illustrates, the management process links the political process to the administrative process. By focusing on performance, the management process integrates public policy with administrative results, bringing political science and public administration together in the study of public management.

Part I
A framework for understanding managing for performance

In the past we could afford to view local government primarily in political terms: that is, as the resolver of conflicts between competing demands and interests within the community. This reflected the fact that local governments provided a minimum of services; they were caretakers and maintainers, not developers or innovators. Today this is not the case. Because local governments are responsible for the delivery of a growing range of services directly related to the quality of life citizens experience, the importance of improving performance has increased. The necessity of managing local government for improved performance is the subject of Chapter 1.

Given the importance of improving local-government performance, it is tempting to conclude that a local government should be managed like a private business. Certainly, the key factors for successfully managing a private business are applicable to a local government; however, they cannot be transferred directly. Chapter 2 examines the reasons for this.

Chapter 3 presents a conceptual framework designed to help practitioners, public and private leaders, citizens, and students better understand what affects the performance of a local government and what they can do about it. This framework enables us to examine the major internal and external factors that affect the process of getting things done and provides a structure for the analysis in Part II.

CHAPTER 1

Improving Local-Government Performance

The most compelling reason for Congress to reenact revenue sharing is quite simple and quite painful: The failure to do so will result for an absolute certainty in either substantial cuts in police protection, fire protection and other essential local services, or in substantial increases in local property taxes.

Pete Wilson
Mayor of San Diego

We have no alternative but to raise taxes or cut costs and services.

Abraham Beame
Mayor of New York City

In 1971, President Richard M. Nixon heralded the beginning of the "New American Revolution"—a revolution that was dedicated, in part, to the return of power and resources to the people. This peaceful revolution promised to give federally collected revenues back to state and local governments without federal "strings," to be spent to meet locally determined needs in accordance with locally determined policies and priorities. The guiding philosophy of this revolution was labeled New Federalism; its cardinal tactic was revenue sharing.

The president proclaimed that this experiment in federalism would close the gap between the world of promise and that of performance. Through revenue sharing, he declared, the need for heavier property and sales taxes would be reduced, new job opportunities would be created, and competition between domestic programs and de-

fense needs would be reduced. The president further claimed that revenue sharing would allow every individual to find a "sense of participation in government," produce a "laboratory for modern government," strengthen the federal government by allowing federal officials to "focus on those matters which ought to be handled at the federal level," and ensure that local officials could be "held accountable for their stewardship of all public funds." Responding to the pleas of local officials, Nixon proclaimed that if local governments were given the tools they needed they could "finish the job."[1]

Fulfillment of these promises rested on one critical assumption: that cities, as well as other units of local government, had the capacity to use unrestricted funds in an efficient and responsive manner. In short, the president assumed that local govern-

13

ments had the ability to get the job done.

It is surprising that few in the vanguard of Nixon's "New American Revolution" recognized that it was the lack of management capacity within local government which in part had contributed to the inability of many Great Society programs to achieve their intended results. The Great Society programs represented the most significant direct federal intervention in the solution of social and economic problems in our nation's history. Yet under these programs federal bureaucrats could only determine procedures, set standards, devise required reports, and withhold funds in the event of failure to comply with established regulations. Federal personnel did not directly train the unskilled, teach ghetto children to read, rehabilitate urban neighborhoods, build health centers, or validate police entrance exams. Local-government officials were responsible for doing these things. Local officials could not be bypassed in implementing programs to improve the quality of urban life.

In reviewing the record of the Great Society programs, Eli Ginzberg and Robert Solow concluded that a major cause of the gap between promise and performance was the inability of local governments to carry out their responsibilities. "It is clear," Ginzberg and Solow argued, "that the best-conceived federal programs will falter or fail if the agencies charged with implementing them lack initiative or competence. And the sorry fact is that *most state and local governments—with some notable exceptions—are poorly structured and poorly staffed to carry out new and innovative tasks. They have a hard time even meeting their routine commitments." [Authors' italics.][2] It is somewhat ironic that the policy of New Federalism was based on an assumption about the management capacity of local governments which had been called into question by the very Great Society programs this policy was designed to replace.

We are all decentralists now

It is still too early to draw definite conclusions about the success or failure of New Federalism and its principal program, revenue sharing.* The record is incomplete. One fact, however, is indisputable: revenue sharing has not alleviated the fiscal crisis which many cities and counties were experiencing at the time of its passage. In 1971 county supervisors, mayors, council members, and other local officials argued vigorously that without increased federal funds (revenue sharing) they would be forced to finance growing operating deficits by raising local taxes, cutting municipal services, or both. Five years later, as Congress considered the renewal of revenue sharing, it found that this program had done little to mute the cry for more money. Today we continually read or hear public statements that local governments are dependent on revenue sharing to finance the delivery of basic municipal services. Yet, even with this federal source of funds an increasing number of local governments are not able to balance their municipal budgets. For these public officials the short-term alternatives are bleak: either increase revenue, by raising taxes or obtaining increased state and federal subsidies, or drastically decrease costs, with a corresponding reduction in the quantity and the quality of municipal services.

---

* We do not distinguish between general and special revenue sharing. Both programs involve the transfer of federal revenues to states and localities. The principal difference between them is that special revenue sharing restricts the use of money to broadly defined purposes: community development, transportation, economic development; general revenue sharing has no effective restrictions. Special revenue sharing may be distinguished from bloc grants in that the latter require matching funds from recipient state and local governments.

The growing financial crises facing many of our nation's counties and cities in the mid-1970s, combined with the growing evidence that revenue sharing had not been used to finance new initiatives, served to discredit the policy of New Federalism. In the main, revenue sharing was used to pay the increased costs of providing traditional maintenance services. Instead of allowing a county or city to initiate new programs to meet needs, it financed the growing costs of existing programs. Reviewing the record, Congress in 1975 and 1976 debated a critical issue of national public policy: should the federal government move back in the centralist direction of the Great Society programs, which were characterized by categorical grants and significant federal involvement in the affairs of local government? Should the federal government tell local officials what they should do and how they should do it? Or should the federal government continue to decentralize power and authority, giving local officials greater autonomy, financial resoures, and decision-making responsibility?

For most local-government practitioners, the answer was obvious. If the Great Society programs accomplished nothing else, they demonstrated that massive federal intervention does not guarantee success in solving major urban problems. Because each locality experiences urban problems differently, "single solution" programs administered uniformly throughout the country are not effective. In simple terms, Congress cannot serve as the nation's city council.

In many respects, the outcome of the centralist-decentralist debate by 1975 was moot. As Irvin Kristol noted, "We are all decentralists now." Few people disagreed with the argument that local-government officials were better able to assess local needs, set priorities, allocate funds, and achieve results than were distant federal bureaucrats. Most people agreed that New

Federalism had forced accountability closer to the people and, in the process, eliminated some of the federal red tape that had impeded the successful implementation of earlier programs. It is interesting to note that during the presidential primaries and election of 1976 not one presidential aspirant seriously attacked the basic premises underlying New Federalism. Despite the possibility that local governments might be incompetent or might not spend federal resources in accordance with national priorities, no presidential candidate found it in his political interest to argue for a reversal in the flow of power and money from Washington to the local level.

Responsibility rests with local governments

Whether or not we have all become decentralists, the fact remains that the capacity of local government to manage local programs for performance is the key factor in implementing either Great Society (centralized) or New Federalist (decentralized) programs. Furthermore, after reviewing the history of the past two decades, one conclusion bears repeating: Congress cannot act as the nation's city council. Strengthening the management process within local governments cannot be accomplished from Washington. Performance will be improved only if local officials assume this responsibility themselves. National policies, be they centralist or decentralist, cannot take into account the vast differences in condition and character of nearly 40,000 units of local government. Local individuals, both within and outside of local government, must assume the responsibility for the way in which their own local government invests and expends its resources to satisfy community needs.

As local officials and local citizens turn to the difficult challenge of managing their governments for better performance, it must be recognized that, in the short term, some may have few options available to them. Like Mayor Abraham Beame of New York, many local-government officials have no alternative but to increase taxes or decrease costs. In the longer term, however, all local governments have a third alternative: they can improve their capacity to use available resources more efficiently and effectively.

The stakes are high

As recently as a decade ago, the necessity of improving the performance of local government was not widely perceived. Today this is no longer the case. During the past decade the business of local government has changed dramatically. Today, in addition to being a "housekeeper" responsible primarily for maintenance functions (the construction and repair of roads, street cleaning, garbage collection and disposal, leaf and snow removal, public safety, and the like), local governments are expected to be agents of change. Today, problems in the areas of air pollution, health care, mass transit, and energy conservation are all the responsibility of local governments. These responsibilities, combined with the growing interdependence among federal, state, and local governments, have exacerbated the consequences of poor government performance.

The economic impact of local government is also great and becoming greater. From 1965 to 1974, local-government expenditures increased 153 percent. By fiscal year 1974, they accounted for 10 percent of the gross national product, double the percentage in fiscal year 1955. Local-government expenditures increased from $26.2 billion in 1953 to $140.4 billion in 1974—a fivefold increase.

Local government is also growing as an employer. In 1974, 11 out of every 100 people in the civilian work force were employed by local government, as compared to only about 6 out of every 100 in 1955. The role of local government within the national economic picture is thus expanding. Historically, economic growth has depended primarily on the performance of the private sector. As the production of goods and services by government increases in proportion to total economic activity, maintenance of continued economic growth will depend increasingly on improving the performance of government in general and of local government in particular.

Another reason for concern with local-government performance is the growing level of citizen discontent.[3] Upset about rising governmental expenditures that require ever-increasing taxes, and angered by the fact that few local-government officials can tell them what their tax dollars actually buy, citizens are rebelling. They are turning down bond issues,[4] defeating incumbents, and electing candidates who promise to hold the line against increased costs and higher taxes. As citizens' discontent increases at the same time that their perceived ability to do someting about it decreases, the result is a growing sense of alienation and apathy—major enemies of a democratic system of government.

Increased responsibility, increased economic significance, and greater citizen discontent are persuasive arguments for an active strategy to improve the performance of local government. Local officials, as well as the citizens to whom they are accountable, must address the difficult but important question: how can we manage our local government for improved performance?

CHAPTER 2

Managing Local Government
as a Public Business

If only they could run city government the way they run General Motors.
Anonymous

It is tempting to those engaged in efforts to improve the performance of a local government to look toward what would appear to be a simple solution: manage local government as if it were a private business.

It is true that many of the management techniques used in a private business are transferable to a public business. These techniques should be transferred more often and more rapidly than they have been in the past. But, as we have pointed out, the "business" of local government has certain characteristics that are not found in most private businesses. To understand what affects the management process in local government, it is necessary to understand how it is different from private enterprise.

Lack of performance imperatives

In private business, success in the marketplace determines the viability of an enterprise. Consumers' decisions to select one product over another collectively determine whether a business can earn sufficient re-

venue to cover its costs and produce a reasonable profit. If it cannot, it ceases to exist.

The existence of a local government, unlike that of a private business, is not solely dependent on satisfying its customers, nor is the revenue collected by a local government based on consumer choices related to the worth of a product or a service. A government's revenue is, in fact, based on a level of taxation that was politically acceptable at the time tax rates were established. The criteria for determining revenue are thus political, not economic. Peter Drucker, in his book *Management,* points out:

Businesses, other than monopolies, are paid by satisfying the customer. They are paid only when they produce what the customer wants and what he is willing to exchange his purchasing power for. Satisfaction of the customer is, therefore, the basis for assuring performance and results in the business.

Service institutions [local governments], by contrast, are typically paid out of a budget allocation. This means that they are not paid for by what the

17

taxpayer and the customer mean by results and performance. Their revenues are allocated from a general revenue stream which is not tied to what they are doing but obtained by tax levy or tribute.[1]

Freedom from performance imperatives is explained, in part, by the fact that local government is a monopoly responsible for the provision of essential public services. Citizens cannot in the short run postpone the consumption of many government services, such as fire and police protection; nor can they make substitutions for others, such as water supply, garbage removal, and sewage disposal. Moreover, a local government is responsible for producing certain "public goods" that can be provided only on a collective basis. Public goods, unlike the products of a private business, satisfy a collective need that the political process has determined should be satisfied, but which would not be satisfied by a free-enterprise system. These include such services as street construction and repair, public transportation, and park development.

These differences have important implications for the conduct of the public-management process. In public business there is no externally imposed discipline or incentive to produce more and better services with fewer resources. Without competition there is no way to establish the relative, or marginal, value of a good or service; thus there is no incentive to curtail nonproductive activities. There is no incentive to reallocate scarce resources from marginally valuable services to services that represent greater value to county or city residents and users. There is no way to determine when to cease providing a particular service and allocate those resources to the provision of another service. This may explain why government programs, once started, are rarely terminated: while at the same time we see the products of private business come and go from the shelves of our favorite stores.

The fact that revenue is received regardless of the quality or the quantity of results produced eliminates a critical check on performance. Because of this, external groups, such as the communications media, special interests, private citizens, and even the judiciary, are often the only substitutes for the marketplace as constraints on negative government performance.

Lack of performance measures

In private businesses there are generally accepted measures of performance. In addition to the time-honored "bottom-line" measure of profit, there are such other useful measures as volume of sales, sales growth, earnings per share, stock price, and return on investment. Different people (stockholders, managers, division heads) may use different measures at different times for different purposes. For each user, there is not always complete agreement on any one measure. In general, however, the language of private-sector decision making is quantitative, and is clear enough so that groups of investors or managers can usually decide which measures are most useful in determining success or failure.

This is not the case in local government. There is little agreement about which measures of performance, if any, tell political leaders, managers, and citizens whether their local government is succeeding or failing. Even though local government may be viewed as a business, its decision-making environment, in contrast to that of a private business, is political, not economic. In a private business, economic measures provide common denominators for making management decisions; in a public business, there are no such common denominators.

The absence of accepted performance measures in local government has two principal causes. First, the overall purpose of local government is intangible and unclear:

it may be perceived differently by different people. Second, political leaders are often resistant to the establishment of measures that can be used by their constituents to hold them accountable.

The implications of managing a business in which there is little ability to measure success or failure (and, in some cases, little desire to do so) are considerable. The absence of accepted performance measures makes it extremely difficult to establish achievable objectives, which, in turn, are the basis for setting priorities, allocating scarce resources, organizing personnel, and evaluating program implementation. Without accepted performance measures, it is difficult to determine which investment—more police, more street cleaners, or more garbage collectors—will provide citizens with the highest return on their tax dollar. When objectives are not clear and measures do not exist to evaluate them, means tend to become more important than ends, style replaces substance, and preoccupation with procedure replaces a willingness to face up to and make tough decisions.

Moreover, the inability to measure government performance makes it more difficult to evaluate objectively the performance of government personnel. The absence of accepted performance measures makes it difficult to translate organizational objectives into personal objectives, a fact that often results in a situation in which personal objectives are in conflict with organizational objectives. For example, if a mayor believes that citizens cannot really measure how well a city government is performing, he or she may place a higher priority on personal ends (e.g., running for higher office) than on community ends. The inability to measure governmental performance has led also to a proliferation of personnel systems in which promotion and compensation tend to be based on the size of a department's budget, the number of people supervised, or the length of government service, rather than on

the quality of results produced. This makes the task of managing people considerably more difficult.

The absence of performance measures makes it difficult, as well, for citizens to recognize the gap between what a local government could produce (optimum performance) and what it does produce (actual performance), and to compare the performance of one city or county government with that of another. Citizens have no objective basis on which to compare their expectations with reality.

Greater constraints on the management process

The stockholders of a private enterprise usually are more interested in the results achieved by the organization than in the means used to achieve them. Most private businesses establish policies that govern the actions of managers and employees, but such policies generally place far fewer limitations on their actions than is the case in a public business. In government, *how* things are done often has greater impact on public confidence and attitudes than *what* is done. Political leaders are thus inclined to take a short-term view that places greater emphasis on means than on ends, with the selection of means dictated more by prospects of political return than by those of impact on performance. For example, a mayor may find it to his or her political advantage to give in to a demand for higher retirement benefits by a public employees' union without considering the long-term costs of doing so.

This emphasis on means, not ends, is reflected in higher costs and in the establishment of cumbersome procedures for carrying out government business. When managers and employees are rewarded for *how* they do things rather than for *what* they do, it is exceedingly difficult to motivate them to be concerned with the quality or quantity of public services.

Conflicting incentives among participants in the management process

A private business involves four groups of participants in the management process: stockholders, directors, managers, and labor. The basic division of incentives is usually between the first three groups, loosely termed management, and the fourth group, labor. In a private concern, the interest of stockholders, directors, and managers are generally the same: they all want to maximize profit—the difference between revenue and costs. Labor is a cost in the production process, and therefore is an element which management tries to limit. Labor groups, on the other hand, want to ensure that employees are properly rewarded for the services they provide; thus they resist efforts to reduce costs of labor. At the same time, labor benefits from good economic performance and recognizes that poor performance may mean fewer jobs and tougher contract negotiations. Therefore, to some extent, all participants involved in a private business have a common incentive to improve and maintain the performance of that business.

Local government also has four groups of participants: citizens, political representatives, municipal managers, and labor. In this model, there is no reason for alliances among participants based on common incentives related to performance. Labor has the same basic incentive it has in private business—to ensure proper compensation for its members. Managers, however, do not necessarily have the same incentive as political representatives (the elected board of directors that usually hires them). In fact, managers may have incentives that are more closely related to those of labor: they may be more interested in protecting their jobs from exploitation by politicians than they are in improving or maintaining performance. Citizens (stockholders), too, may not have the same motivation as their political representatives. Politicians may be more interested in retaining office or aspiring to higher office than in finding ways to deliver better-quality services to their constituency.

Different, often conflicting, incentives among major participants in local government may be attributable to a number of factors. First, the absence of performance imperatives makes it more difficult to establish a basis for relating personal compensation to performance. Second, because the revenue received by a local government is independent of the quantity or quality of results produced, there is no incentive for political leaders, municipal managers, or public employees to be concerned about how their actions (or inactions) affect performance.

When there are no consistent incentives linking the interests of political leaders, citizens, and municipal managers, there is less willingness to delegate to managers the authority required to achieve a satisfactory level of performance and greater hesitancy on the part of managers to take risks and explore innovations. Shifting incentives and alliances among participants in the management process also make it harder to attract and retain competent managers. When the responsibilities of a manager are unclear and the requisite political support uncertain, and when the rewards do not compensate for the difficulties, the job becomes less attractive. Finally, in local government, labor may be the *only* participant motivated by consistent incentives over time. This can significantly enhance labor's ability to pursue its narrow interests—possibly at the expense of governmental performance.

Fragmentation of executive authority

In private business, a chief executive officer is usually responsible for the conduct of the management process and the performance of the organization. Some corporate decisions require the approval or consent of the board of directors or of a management committee, but their involvement in administrative decision making is generally minimal.

In local government this is not the case. The division of power does not end with separation of the executive and the legislative branches; there is usually further fragmentation of authority and responsibility within the executive branch. Most city or county governments, by charter or state law, create numerous decision-making authorities which are independent or semi-independent of the chief executive—and of the legislature, for that matter. These bodies—which include planning commissions, elected city department heads, park and recreation boards, transportation authorities, and the like—play active roles in the conduct of the management process. Each fragmentation of executive responsibility can have an adverse effect on the ability of local governments to get things done. Not only does fragmentation lengthen the decision-making process and create duplications of effort, both of which can be very costly, but it also leaves citizens without a clear basis for determining where the "buck" stops, and whom to hold accountable for governmental performance.

Roles played by nonprofessionals

In local government a number of important jobs in the management process are performed by nonprofessionals. For example, civil-service commissions made up of citizens who lack professional personnel training may be responsible for making decisions about recruitment, hiring, promotion, and firing. Similarly, planning commissions composed of private individuals may make capital-investment decisions without necessarily having the expertise to do so. In contrast, nonprofessionals do not make major decisions in most private businesses.

The involvement of nonprofessionals in local government can be explained, in large part, by three traditional legacies: the town meeting, where citizens could meet and confer about municipal decisions; the fear of concentrated political power and the abuses it might foster; and the democratic belief that public decision making is within the competence of the common citizen. Nonprofessional involvement in the management of local government continues at a high level because most citizens do not appreciate the complexity of local government and the difficulty of managing it effectively.

The participation of nonprofessionals in the government decision-making process often causes major delays in making routine decisions and, more important, uninformed decisions. When facing complex and highly political decisions, nonprofessionals often place total reliance on special interests with whom they are associated or whom they feel obligated to represent. In short, the role of nonprofessionals complicates the conduct of the management process in local government.

In summary, managing a city government as a private business will not automatically improve its performance. Because of the significant differences between public and private businesses, you cannot "run city government the way they run General Motors" or any other private business. This is not to say that lessons learned in the private sector cannot be transferred to the public sector. To the contrary, within the limits described in this chapter, strategies and means of improving performance in private business can and should be applied to local government. But the need still exists for a conceptual framework, tailored to the specific characteristics and conditions of local government, that will help us understand what affects its performance and what can be done about it.

CHAPTER 3

Analyzing the Performance of a
Local Government

The task of setting a policy for strengthening public management is saddled with . . . a lack of conceptual clarity about the elements of public management and thus the proper focus for capacity building programs.
1975 Report of Special Committee on Policy Management Assistance,
Office of Management and Budget

Efforts to improve the performance of local government are severely hampered by the lack of a framework within which to analyze the factors that affect the process of managing local government. In Chapter 2, we pointed out the significant differences between the management of public and private businesses. Because the key factors for success in managing a private business cannot be extrapolated to a public business without significant adjustment, there is a need to develop an analytic framework, tailored to the specific characteristics of local government, that will enable government officials, public and private leaders, students, and citizens to understand what affects the performance of local government and to do something about it. The purpose of this chapter is to present such a framework.

Factors that affect the performance of local government

If we are interested in improving our health, we can generate a list of the critical factors that affect it—for example, family history, diet, weight, smoking, exercise, alcohol consumption, tension, sleeping habits. Similarly, if we are interested in improving the performance of local government, we will want to identify the critical factors that affect it. In short, we must determine how to unravel the interrelated web of forces that affect the ability of public officials to use available resources to get things done.

To do this we have developed an analytic framework—a way to look at local government—which will facilitate an understanding of the environment within which a local government must perform and the forces that affect its management. This framework should help public officials, private citizens, and students identify the most promising opportunities to strengthen the management process and thereby improve performance.

The framework we have developed is relatively simple. It consists of twelve factors that affect the process of management within local governments and therefore affect its performance. Figure 3 and Exhibit 2 present

23

INTERNAL FACTORS

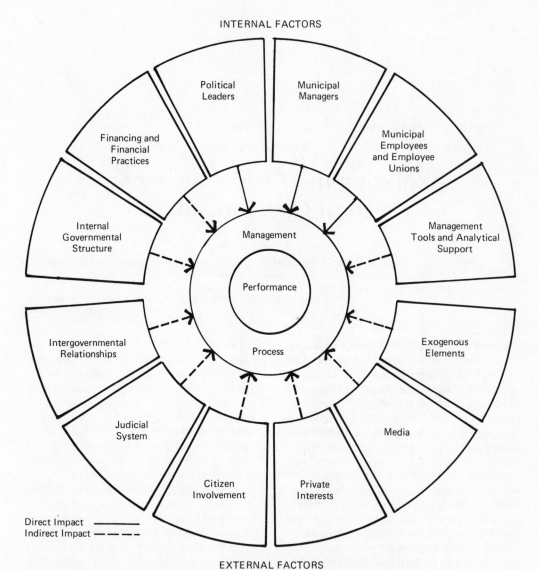

EXTERNAL FACTORS

Figure 3. Twelve factors affecting the performance of a local government.

the framework and define each factor.

The primary purpose of any model or analytical tool is to simplify reality. Invariably, some will conclude that what has been lost through simplification is *the* critical element. No model can include all variables or all elements of conceivable interest, or it would cease to be a model and thus cease to be useful. Moreover, the necessity of em-

phasizing certain variables or factors renders all models value-laden. Ours is no exception.

Three criteria were used in determining the factors that affect the management process in a local government. First, each factor had to be sufficiently distinct to warrant separate attention. We felt, for example, that it was not possible to separate "employee unions" from "municipal employees." Second, each factor had to have a significant impact on the management process. After considerable debate, for example, we included the judiciary as a separate factor because of the growing impact judicial decisions have on the way a local government conducts its business. Third, each factor had to make sense to practitioners as a separate area of study and potential improvement. We reviewed this framework with a number of practitioners in order to test the usefulness of our factor designations.

Each of the factors, except "exogenous elements," is examined and studied in detail in a separate chapter in Part II. The impact of exogenous elements—including natural disasters (earthquakes, floods) and national economic swings—varies so greatly that a generalized discussion would be of little diagnostic or analytical value. The purpose of including this factor in the framework is to point out that in some cases local-government performance may improve or deteriorate independently of other factors. The potential importance of the unexpected cannot be discounted.

Characteristics and classifications of factors

There are a number of ways to classify these twelve factors so as to enhance our understanding of each factor and illuminate their interrelationships. The first and most important classification is to designate factors as internal or external. *Internal factors* are those which exist within the legal, political, and administrative structure of local government. *External factors* exist outside this structure. Exhibit 2 shows how factors break down into these two classifications.

We can then classify internal and external factors by the ways in which they affect performance. A factor may have a *direct* impact on the way in which local government officials decide what to do and their ability to get it done. For example, political leaders and municipal managers make deci-

sions that directly affect how resources are used to achieve community objectives. In most cases, their decisions are final. Their impact, therefore, is direct.

Alternatively, a factor may have an *indirect* impact on performance, in that it affects other factors. The media, for example, do not directly make decisions that determine what a local government does or how it does it. Nevertheless, the media are extremely important because they can have a significant indirect effect on the decisions of political leaders, municipal managers, and even public employees.

A third way to classify the twelve factors is as follows:

People-related Factors
• Political leaders
• Municipal managers
• Municipal employees and their unions

Management Systems
• Management tools and analytical assistance
• Financing and financial practices

Structure
• Internal government structure
• Intergovernmental relationships
• Judicial system

Interest Groups
• Private interests
• Media
• Citizen involvement

Other
• Exogenous elements

Here factors are placed into five categories according to the nature of each factor. In this classification, the term *people-related factors* describes the decision makers who have a major impact on the performance of local government. *Management systems* is a classification for the tools used by these actors in carrying out their responsibilities. *Structure* and *interest groups* refer to struc-

---

EXHIBIT 2

Factors That Affect the Performance of a Local Government

Internal Factors

Political leaders include both elected local officials and citizens who are appointed to independent boards, commissions, and authorities.

Municipal managers are appointed, full-time professional personnel who have significant management responsibilities, as determined by the number of employees they supervise, the funds they control, or the importance of their functions.

Municipal employees and *municipal employee unions* are local government employees who are not categorized as political leaders or public managers. Many of them are members of unions or associations that represent them in the collective-bargaining process.

Managements tools and *analytical support* are terms that refer to the methods, systems, and devices used to generate and interpret the information required by political leaders, municipal managers, and citizens in order to make informed public decisions.

Financing and *financial practices* are the ways in which local governments obtain financial resources and control and restrict their use.

Internal governmental structure consists of the formal (legal) relationships among individuals and functions of local government, as established by city and county charters, state legislation, and administrative regulations.

(continued)

---

tural, political, legal, and human constraints on the ways in which governmental actors use available tools to achieve performance.

As is the case with any classification scheme, there are difficult judgments to be made. It can be argued, for example, that citizens should be classified as actors in the process of managing local government. Whether one classifies this factor as a constraint or as an actor depends primarily on how one views the role of citizens in the management process. Additionally, some may consider the judicial system a people-related factor, reflecting the view that judges are people, elected or appointed through the political process, who make decisions that affect the way in which local governments carry out public business. Again, the proper classification depends on how one views the role of the judicial system relative to the executive and legislative functions carried out by the other two branches of government. On balance, where a factor is placed is not as important as understanding

EXHIBIT 2 (cont'd)

External Factors

Intergovernmental relationships is the term used to indicate the assignment of responsibilities to and the conduct of functions by levels of government, and the relationships among these levels.

Citizen involvement is the process of providing all residents of a local government a full and equal opportunity to influence those government decisions that affect the quality of their lives.

The media are private organizations and individuals engaged in the collection and dissemination of news and public information. Generally, the media consists of newspapers, television stations, radio stations, and periodicals.

Private-interest groups are civic associations, banks or branches of larger banks, consumer organizations, foundations, universities, private corporations, associations of local business executives, and other profit-making organizations and institutions that have the power to influence the decisions of public officials.

The judicial system is that branch of government entrusted with the responsibilities of interpreting constitutions, laws, charters, and other legislation, and of resolving differences among levels and branches of government.

Exogenous elements are external forces and conditions, such as geography, location, chance, natural disasters, and the like, that may affect the ability of public officials to get things done within a local government or which may constrain the potential for improving its performance.

the reason for placing it there.

In developing this framework, we used and discarded a variety of different classification schemes, many of which were interesting from a purely analytical point of view. In the end, we concluded that the most important prerequisite for understanding this framework is understanding the individual factors, and that different classification schemes are useful merely to the extent that they improve this understanding. Therefore, except for classifying factors as internal or external and indicating whether their impact is direct or indirect, the classifications and characteristics described here are used only within individual chapters to help explain an individual factor.

Relative importance of factors

In reviewing this framework with local-government practitioners, professors, students, and citizens, the question continually arose, "Aren't certain factors more important than others?" The answer to this question is, "It all depends!" The importance of any factor depends primarily on local conditions that affect performance. In some cities political leaders and management tools may be most important. In a neighboring city, however, these factors may be relatively less important because their impact on the management process is less significant. In short, it is the application of the internal and external factors to a specific local government that provides the basis for determining their relative importance. Part II examines how this can be done.

Part II
Applying
the framework

In Part II, we apply the analytic framework developed in Part I to a "case" city. We need to examine each factor in a realistic setting in order to demonstrate how this analytical framework may be used to identify specific opportunities to improve the management process on which performance depends.

Each chapter of Part II examines a specific internal or external factor within the analytic framework. They all employ a common format. The first section of each chapter examines the importance of a factor and how it directly or indirectly affects the capacity of public officials to manage a local government. The second section sets forth a series of criteria that may be used to evaluate how that factor affects the process of getting things done within a specific local government. Recognizing that local governments vary widely in size, structure, and population, the evaluation criteria included in each chapter are presented, not as a definitive list of *the* requirements to be met by all local governments, but rather as a beginning—a first approximation—which should be examined and modified in the light of the unique circumstances within each local government.

The third section of each factor chapter represents a case study, that of Flint, Michigan. Within that section we examine actual conditions in Flint and analyze their causes and consequences. The final section of each of these chapters completes the case analysis with a discussion of opportunities for strengthening the impact of each factor on the management process.

CHAPTER 4

The Case City: Flint, Michigan

Flint: GM's mark of excellence.
Richard Hébert

Flint is an unusual city. In addition to being the birthplace of General Motors, it has an active private sector that still resides within the city, an energetic and exceptionally able congressman,* a large number of federal programs (Model Cities, urban-renewal, public housing), a college and cultural center unparalleled among cities of its size, three institutions of higher learning, and a strong industrial base. The United Auto Workers was founded in Flint. The city is also the home and general beneficiary of the Mott Foundation, one of the country's largest private foundations.

We did not select Flint as our "case" city because it is either typical or atypical of local governments throughout the country. We selected it for one simple reason: we worked there and therefore know and understand it better than any other local government. As a result, it is the most appropriate city for us to use in demonstrating how

to apply the analytic framework we described in Chapter 3.

Background

Flint is located some seventy miles northwest of Detroit (see Figure 4) and covers a thirty-two-square-mile area. It is Michigan's third-largest city, with a population in 1970 of 193,000. In 1819 Jacob Smith, Flint's first settler, built his cabin on the bank of the river that gives the city its name. In the three decades following its incorporation as a city in 1855, Flint was the center of a vast lumbering area that extended throughout central Michigan. At the high point of lumber industry activity, some 90 million board-feet of pine was sawed in Flint in one year. The lumber industry stimulated the development of rail and road connections with major centers in the Midwest.

After the supply of available pine was exhausted in the late 1870s, economic activity in Flint turned to carriage and wagon making. By the turn of the century, Flint was known as the Vehicle City. In 1900, some

---

* Don Riegle, Flint's congressman at the time this book was written, was elected in 1976 to serve in the U.S. Senate.

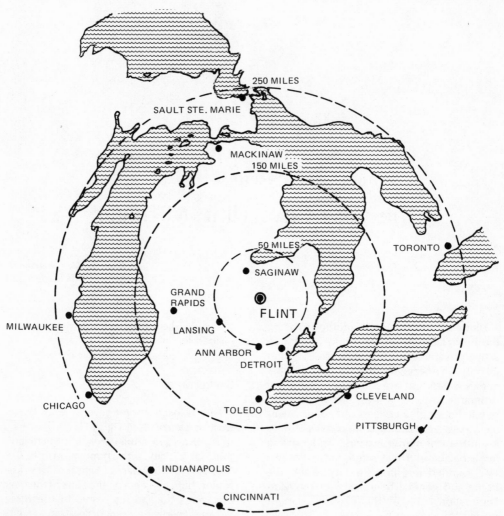

Figure 4. Flint's location within the Great Lakes Region.

100,000 horse-drawn vehicles were made in Flint, roughly eight times the population. The Durant-Dort Carriage Company—started in 1886 by William C. Durant and his partner, J. Dallas Dort, with $2,000 they had borrowed from a local bank—produced more than half of Flint's carriages. Durant-Dort was at that point the largest carriage company in the world. In 1904 Durant took over the Buick Motor Company, then a very small company making motorized carriages and capitalized at a value of about $75,000. By

1908, 8,000 Buicks made in Flint had been sold throughout the country, making Buick the best-selling automobile in the world.[1]

Building on Buick's success, Durant incorporated General Motors on September 16, 1908, and made Flint its home. One of GM's first acquisitions was 49 percent of the stock of the Weston-Mott Company, then the world's largest axle maker. Thus the two forces that were to shape the history of Flint in the twentieth century—General Motors and C. S. Mott—were joined.

Flint today

Flint in 1977 remains a blue-collar company town, the largest company town in the country. The primary consequence of its dependence on General Motors and on the automobile industry is that it has prospered and suffered as the national economy has prospered and suffered. It is not an exaggeration to say that when the national economy sneezes, Flint catches a cold. In mid-1975 the recession then gripping the nation produced in Flint an unemployment rate in excess of 15 percent.

Of course, Flint has benefited as well as suffered from its marriage to General Motors. Many of the positive economic, social, and environmental conditions in Flint are directly attributable to the influence of GM. In addition to being the home of Buick (all Flint police cars are Buicks), Flint hosts four Chevrolet plants (the city has the world's largest concentration of Chevrolet workers), a major division of AC Spark Plug, and more than forty smaller facilities that supply GM with everything from aerials and radios to auto wax.

High per-capita ownership of cars, a massive freeway construction program, easy credit for private homes, and a perennially high hourly wage rate combined to make suburbanization a phenomenon in the Flint area long before it appeared elsewhere. In the decade of the 1960s, population in the Flint metropolitan area increased by almost 25 percent, while the population of Flint proper declined by 2 percent. Today Flint is ringed by suburban towns and shopping centers that have taken their toll of downtown retail business. Local merchants hope that completion of an expanded University of Michigan campus in the center of the city will revitalize the downtown retail area and bring, as one businessman put it, "pennies from heaven." There are those, however, who believe that downtown Flint is destined to become a financial and professional center, with retail business decentralized in suburban malls.

Today, Flint is more than GM's "mark of excellence." It is also the home of the Mott Foundation, formed in the mid-twenties and dedicated, by virtue of C. S. Mott's personal interest, to making Flint a model city. Flint is the birthplace of the community school—a facility used throughout the year by all residents of the community for athletics, adult education, special classes, and almost anything else eight or more people desire to do. It is estimated that since 1935 the Mott Foundation has spent over $45 million to improve education in Flint.

The Mott Foundation was the catalyst that made possible the development of Flint's college and cultural complex, which includes a community college, a planetarium, an art center, a music center, a theater, a library, a four-tiered opera house, and an automotive museum. The fact that this complex is underutilized points to the lack of social diversification within the city. In 1973, the Mott Foundation and its president, Harding Mott, were primarily responsible for persuading the University of Michigan to expand its Flint campus on a new site located in the center of the city along the banks of the Flint River.

To ensure a complete understanding of conditions in Flint, and to enable the reader to compare these conditions with those that exist in other cities of comparable size and characteristics, we have included as an appendix a profile of conditions in Flint. This profile is organized into eleven categories (called urban conditions) which together provide a description of the quality of life in Flint. These categories include housing, physical environment, safety, health, justice, education, leisure time, transportation, standard of living, citizen participation, and general government.

With a better understanding of Flint's conditions and characteristics, we can now turn to an examination of ways to improve the performance of its city government.

CHAPTER 5

Political Leaders

Now, as never before, the American city has need for the personal qualities of strong democratic leadership. Given the difficulties and delays involved in administrative reorganization or institutional change, the best hope for the city, in the short run, lies in this powerful instrument.

President's Riot Commission, 1968

Leadership is the quality of making people go where they do not want to go and like it.
President Harry S Truman

The performance of any institution depends primarily on the quality of the people who work within that institution. People—not laws, charters, computer systems, or organizational structures—determine the quality of government performance. People make the decisions that determine the quality and the quantity of services citizens receive through the expenditure of their tax dollars. Improving the performance of local government, therefore, requires improving the capabilities of the people who work for it. The message contained in the President's 1968 Riot Commission Report is as applicable today as it was then: the best hope for our cities, as well as for other local units of government, is the development of effective political leaders.

Political leaders are those individuals who are elected to represent the interests of their constituents in deciding what a local government should do and how it should do it.

County supervisors, members of the city council, town aldermen, elected mayors—these leaders are ultimately responsible to citizens for the way in which resources are used to satisfy community needs. We also include in our definition of political leaders those individuals who are appointed by elected representatives to serve on boards and commissions, such as planning commissions, housing commissions, or mass-transportation boards. These individuals often play major roles in determining community objectives and allocating public resources.

Besides merely translating the desires of their constituents into public decisions, political leaders must exercise leadership. Leadership is an intangible quality. One way to understand its nature is to examine the adjectives that we use to describe those we judge to be leaders. We think of these people as imaginative, courageous, candid, charismatic, intelligent, and self-confident.

Alternatively, we describe people who lack leadership qualities as reactionary, myopic, apathetic, or fearful of change. Perhaps Harry Truman's quote best captures the essence of leadership—getting people to do something they didn't want to do and making them like it.

Impact on Process and Performance

Political leaders, unlike the municipal managers they appoint, are directly accountable to the public for the performance of a local government. If citizens become upset with the way the parks are maintained, angry about the existence of massage parlors in residential neighborhoods, or frustrated by their inability to call city hall and receive a direct answer to a simple question, their ultimate recourse is the ballot box. Perhaps the clearest indicator of how citizens evaluate government performance is whether they reelect their political representatives. Political leaders who forget that their jobs depend on the consent of the people for whom they govern often find themselves seeking new careers.

County supervisors, city council members, and elected mayors are *directly* responsible for each phase of the management process— planning, implementation, and evaluation. They are responsible for assessing and prioritizing a community's economic, social, and environmental needs; deciding what specific community objectives can be achieved to satisfy the highest-priority needs; allocating available resources to accomplish these objectives; and making sure that expected results are produced on schedule, within budgeted resources.

The traditional notion that there is a rigid separation between politics and administration is invalid. Political leaders must work closely with their appointed managers in directing each phase of the management process. Woodrow Wilson's often-quoted statements that "administration lies outside the sphere of politics" and that "administrative questions are not political questions" ignore the reality of life within a local government.[1] In any county or city, elected mayors or members of the legislative body continually make decisions that affect the way government operations are administered. In approving budgets and budget adjustments, ratifying labor contracts, authorizing purchases over a certain value, approving professional contracts, and making personnel decisions, political leaders play a major role in the day-to-day administration of local government. We do not find in local governments an absolute separation between politics and management; rather we find a situation in which political leaders and municipal managers work together to manage the public business. While political leaders are directly accountable to the public for the process of managing a local government, they share responsibility with municipal managers for the conduct of this process.

Political leaders not only affect government performance directly, they also affect it indirectly by strengthening or weakening the impact of other factors on performance. For example, political leaders are able to help or hinder the ability of managers to do their jobs. They appoint managers who are responsible for implementing their policies and programs. Their support and the degree to which they delegate administrative responsibility will determine, in large measure, how well these managers perform. Moreover, the relationship between political leaders and municipal employees can have a major bearing on performance. If political leaders allow municipal employees or their unions to make "end runs" around responsible managers, performance may suffer.

Political leaders can indirectly affect performance by encouraging private interests, especially the media, and citizens to participate more actively in the decision-making process. They can also play a major role in determining the nature of intergovernmental relationships at the local, state, and national levels. In short, political leaders can affect the impact of all other factors on the way in which a local government performs its business.

Criteria for Evaluation

The ability of political leaders to manage a local government for performance depends, in large part, on their relationships to municipal managers and municipal employees, the adequacy of management tools, the responsiveness of government structure, and the involvement of external groups. These are the subjects of later chapters. In this chapter we are concerned with the ability and the motivation of public leaders themselves. The following criteria provide a starting point for identifying ways to improve the impact of political leaders on performance:

Do elected officials demonstrate the willingness to lead? Most political leaders are well aware of the political maxim that the most ineffective leader is the one who is not reelected. There is, therefore, a political incentive to respond exclusively to short-term considerations calculated to satisfy those groups upon whose support electoral success depends. The responsibility of elective office, however, involves the necessity to lead rather than to follow. This question examines whether political leaders have the willingness and the capacity to persuade their constituents to sacrifice individual interests for community interests, regardless of the perceived political consequences.

Are political leaders able to translate community needs into community objectives? Political leaders who are willing to actively lead efforts to improve their community, rather than simply following the dictates of political expediency, must identify community needs and translate them into measurable objectives which provide a basis for determining government performance in satisfying these needs.

Are political leaders willing to delegate to municipal managers authority and responsibility for achieving community objectives? Political leaders are elected to represent the interests of their constituents in the resolution of conflicting views about what the community should do and how it should do it. Once this has been resolved and community objectives have been established, political leaders alone are accountable to the public for achieving them. This does not mean, however, that political leaders should assume the day-to-day tasks of government. The job of achieving these objectives should be delegated to managers, who must be provided with requisite political support to do their jobs.

Do political leaders have the ability to marshal the external support and resources that will achieve community objectives? Achievement of community objectives in many cases depends on the ability of political leaders to convince representatives of the media, public-interest groups, business executives, labor leaders, and other external groups and individuals to support or finance required programs and initiatives.

Can political leaders gain and maintain the respect and confidence of the people they represent? Respect for elected political leaders is a prerequisite for the maintenance of a democratic system. Political leaders who by their actions prove unworthy of citizen confidence help to stimulate apathy and alienation in the citizenry. This produces a vicious circle: incompetent political leaders produce apathetic citizens who do not vote or participate in the affairs of their government, in turn producing incompetent leaders. Thus, it is important to ask: are political leaders unentangled in conflicts of interest which could cause citizens to question their motivation?

Conditions in Flint

In 1971 the City Council was the most important political body in Flint. It consisted of nine members, each elected from a separate ward of the city (each ward contained approximately the same number of citizens). Council elections were held every two years. At its first meeting the newly elected council elected one of its members to serve as mayor. The council was responsible for appointing the four top administrative officials of the city: the city manager, the director of finance, the city attorney, and the city clerk. It also made appointments to numerous boards and commissions. The governmental structure of Flint is analyzed in greater detail in Chapter 10.

Members of the Flint City Council and their political appointees have had the single most important impact on the performance of that city's government. In November 1970, Flint voters elected what many city hall observers considered to be an extremely competent council. Two lawyers, an architect, three businessmen, and two General Motors supervisors gave this council a professional image that contrasted sharply with that of prior councils. In the words of the new mayor, the council elected in 1970 dedicated itself to "getting the city of Flint moving ahead," or, as one new member of the council put it, "bringing Flint city government into the twentieth century."

This council served for three years.* Many in Flint, including the editors of the local newspaper, concluded that more was achieved in this three-year period than in any like period in the past. By the council election of November 1973, Flint was "moving ahead"—a fact that was primarily attributable to the council's leadership. As the *Flint Journal* noted in summarizing the perfor-

mance of this council: "In terms of moving Flint off dead center, where it gathered dust for so many years, the outgoing council performed an extremely valuable service. For the first time in memory, there is a real sense of momentum from city hall—for which [the council] can take credit."

Change is never achieved easily. The initiatives taken and the actions supported by the 1970 council alienated a number of political interest groups, primarily municipal employee unions. When in 1973 three council members decided for personal reasons that they would not seek reelection and two incumbents were defeated in the primary, the city's municipal unions seized the opportunity to elect a council more sympathetic to their views.

The primary concern of the council elected in the fall of 1973 appeared to be political survival, not improved performance. The actions of each council member to maintain good relations with the constituency in his or her ward were substituted for what had been a relatively conscientious effort by the previous council to consider the needs of the entire city. In justification of their own actions, the new council members were quick to point out that it was the incumbents' lack of attention to their wards that made them politically vulnerable and eventually resulted in the loss of their jobs.

At the new council's first meeting in November 1973, an insurance executive and former administrative assistant to Flint's congressman was selected by his fellow council members to serve as mayor. From that point on, this council was able to agree on very little else. Split racially, ideologically, and politically, this nine-person committee— charged with both executive and legislative responsibilities in the city—was unable to match or continue the record of the past council. By 1974 the city that had been "moving ahead" appeared to have come to an abrupt stop.

---

* In 1970 the Michigan legislature passed a law allowing cities to hold council elections in odd-numbered years. Accordingly, Flint's City Council elected to extend its term one full year.

EXHIBIT 3

What Is the Cost of a City Council Seat?

In announcing his decision not to seek reelection to the city council in November 1973, a prominent Flint attorney explained that in 1972 alone he had lost over $40,000 in income as a result of serving on the council. He estimated that a conscientious council member spent a minimum of twenty hours per week on council business, for which he or she received a maximum of $600, or $10 a meeting for up to five meetings a month. This, he pointed out, amounted to about $1.67 per hour, assuming a two-week vacation each year.

Debate over the salaries of Flint's council members had raged for decades. Many argued that compensation for council members should reflect the total time they work for the city, not just the time they spend at council meetings. Others pointed out that compensation for political leaders should be high enough to attract qualified candidates but should not be so high as to produce an erosion of public confidence. There were, of course, those who felt that council members should receive no compensation, thereby ensuring that political leadership would remain in the hands of a qualified "elite" who could afford to serve without pay.

This situation was partially resolved in 1973, when the city's Compensation Commission voted to pay council members a salary of $5,000 a year, plus $25 a meeting for up to 100 meetings. Although some citizens voiced violent objections, most were sympathetic to the pay increase. A few felt the salary level was still insufficient to attract qualified people.

Willingness and ability to lead

The exercise of political leadership, in the words of Irving Kristol, "involves taking the long view rather than the short one, studying issues rather than striking postures about them, and above all, making hard, controversial, and frequently unpopular decisions that are in the public interest." Traditionally, people with leadership qualities had not run for the council in Flint for a number of reasons. Foremost among these was the negative image associated with being a member of the council. Decades of do-nothing, corruption-tinged councils had tended to produce a self-fulfilling prophecy: qualified people did not run for council seats because of the council's negative reputation; therefore, unqualified people ran and won, thus substantiating the initial judgment. Moreover, negative public expectations about council actions resulted in intense, often derogatory publicity. Most people were not willing to subject themselves to such treatment. In contrast, the city's Board of Education was considered a more desirable body on which to serve because its politics were both less intense and less public.

A second reason that qualified individuals did not seek council seats, as Exhibit 3 suggests, was that they believed they would not be adequately compensated for their time.

Many qualified individuals could not afford to serve on the council. And, surprisingly, serving on the council was not a stepping-stone to higher office; generally, a seat on the council was a dead-end political job. The most ambitious—and, often, most quali-fied—politicians ran for other offices, gener-ally at the state or federal level.

A third reason involves the city charter. Ward elections, nonpartisan ballots, and a two-year term of office combined to pro-duce a situation in which even the most effective political leaders found it difficult to get anything done. Because each council member represented only one-ninth of the city, no one had a political incentive to worry about citywide problems or issues. Further-more, nonpartisan elections discouraged any organized attempts to find promising candidates who could be persuaded to seek council seats with the guaranteed support of established organizations.

The fact that the *entire* council had to run for reelection every two years resulted in high political turnover—another disincen-tive for able people to seek a council posi-tion. It was difficult to assemble at least five candidates (a council majority) who shared similar views on the city's problems and their solutions to run as a slate. As a result, the power of a few well-established individuals, usually representing old-line city departments and municipal unions, was greatly increased.

A final reason that qualified people did not run for council seats was the fact that pri-vate-interest groups did not encourage do-ing so. Historically, General Motors, the United Auto Workers, the Mott Foundation, and other major private interests had paid little attention to local politics and to the need for competence in city government. These groups were powerful enough to ob-tain what they wanted when they wanted it from whoever was elected; as a result, they had little incentive to ensure that the best-qualified people served on the council.

The 1970 council was an exception to the historical pattern. From the beginning of its term, this council exhibited a willingness to make tough decisions. The council members began by replacing the city manager of eight years, who they felt had become too closely allied with the bureaucracy. They followed this with many controversial and innovative decisions which, as Exhibit 4 suggests, result-ed in an impressive record of achievement. This group's capacity to lead was perhaps best demonstrated by its efforts to persuade the University of Michigan to move its Flint campus to a riverfront site in the heart of downtown (see Chapter 19). At least two members of this council may have lost re-election precisely because of the kind of leadership they exhibited—they moved too far out in front of their constituencies.

In seeking an explanation for the lack of leadership on the 1973 council, it is interest-ing to note how several members of this council viewed themselves. In conversations with the city manager in 1973, one council member described leadership as "the ability to know where your constituents are going and the capacity to get out in front of them." Another put his view of leadership in one word: "Survival!" A third supported this by adding, "The worst leader is the one who is not there." Another warned the manager not to oppose or contradict him publicly, because to do so would damage his credibili-ty and reputation with his constituency.

As the case presented in Exhibit 5 clearly shows, leadership, for certain members of the 1973 council, was the process of follow-ing what they perceived to be the dictates of their constituents, not of educating or guid-ing their constituents in the best interests of the city. The local newspaper best summar-ized the impact of the 1973 council's view of leadership when it noted, "The city has returned to politics as usual."

Willingness to set objectives

The common-sense observation "If you don't know where you are going before you start, you have no way of knowing when you

EXHIBIT 4

The Mayor Reviews an Exceptional Record

Delivering the first State of the City message in Flint's history, the mayor described the year 1972 as a "year of beginning for the city." In referring to the major council achievements during the previous year and a half, he said: "It's a question of pride. I want people to say in years to come that when I was mayor, a helluva lot of good things were done."

During its initial term, the 1970 council racked up the following accomplishments:

- allocated $6 million to assemble land for a downtown riverfront campus for the University of Michigan—Flint, thereby triggering development of a $60-million campus in the heart of the city;
- initiated a $7-million river beautification and flood-control project adjacent to the new university campus;
- obtained final approval from the Department of Housing and Urban Development of an urban-development program (one of the last such programs approved in the country) to develop a residential community across the river from the new campus;
- revitalized the urban-renewal program, culminating in a $1.2-million land sale to Buick for industrial development and a $560,000 bonus from HUD for outstanding performance;
- implemented a citywide demolition program to remove more than 1,000 vacant, dilapidated, once dangerous buildings throughout the city;
- passed a city ordinance requiring that all homes in Flint be brought up to code prior to sale, to be implemented in conjunction with a citywide code enforcement program;
- initiated a plan to place the city's airport and health departments on a metropolitan basis, thereby ensuring an adequate financial base;
- provided a $300,000 subsidy to reinstitute public bus service in Flint;
- created an office of citizen service within city hall;
- initiated the financing of a $50-million sewage-treatment and expansion plant;
- initiated a program to modernize management tools, including the development of a new master plan, a comprehensive budgeting system, a performance-reporting system, and an expanded data-processing capability.

Flint's mayor concluded: "In reviewing the performance of city government in 1972, one could point to many objectives that were not achieved. One could note that there still exists a major gap between what the city ought to be and what it is. But to suggest that this was not a successful year would miss the crucial point: 1972 was a year of beginning."

EXHIBIT 5

Telephone Calls Induce a Change of Heart

It was no secret that a number of council members had actively campaigned before the 1973 council elections on a promise to fire the city manager. Before acting on his promise, one of these newly elected councilmen spent a considerable amount of time with the city manager, viewing at first hand the problems in his ward and the way the city was organized to solve them. As a result, he developed second thoughts about firing the manager. In fact, less that three months after his election, he announced publicly at a council meeting that he had been wrong about the city manager and the administration. "The manager," he stated, "was acting in the best interest of the city and deserved the support of the council and the public." He added, "I don't know if I'll ever get reelected, but when I find out what appears to be the right thing to do, I will do it." The *Flint Journal*, in a subsequent editorial, hailed this speech as a rare act of leadership.

At the very next council meeting, however, this councilman totally reversed his position. He stated that during the preceding week he had received more than seventy-five calls criticizing his public statement. "Based on these calls," he said, "I have no choice but to oppose the manager."

To this councilman, leadership apparently had been reduced to a simple arithmetic function: Add up the "yes" and "no" telephone responses on any given issue, and whichever is greater determines your position.

---

get there" is extremely relevant to the management of local government. Setting objectives is imperative if citizens are to have a basis for evaluating government performance and the performance of elected and appointed officials. In the absence of clear and accepted measures of performance, it is critically important that a board of supervisors, city council, or elected mayor be willing to state precisely what they intend to achieve through the expenditure of tax dollars. Not only will such statements provide managers and employees with a sense of direction, they will make it easier for citizens to understand what their local government is doing. It is far easier, for example, to understand a police department that says it is

attempting to reduce response time for emergencies from fifteen minutes to five minutes than it is to understand a department that says it is dedicated to "making the community safe from crime."

Defining precise objectives may also help political leaders justify raising taxes or charging special users' fees. Politically, it is easier to persuade citizens to accept the necessity of a tax increase if the additional revenue can be related to a specific project or program (e.g., the development of a neighborhood park or the establishment of an emergency rescue unit). Most important, a willingness to set objectives focuses the attention of political leaders on the most important part of the management process—the determination of what local governments should do and how they should do it.

Neither the 1970 nor the 1973 city council in Flint fully accepted the need to establish community objectives as the basis for making resource-allocation decisions or informing citizens about what their tax dollars would buy. Most council decisions were made on an ad hoc basis. The name of the game was simple: assemble five votes on any given question and make a decision.

Both councils, however, took steps to change this approach. In early 1972 the council authorized funds to replace the city's sixteen-year-old existing master plan, which had never fully served to guide development decisions. The council indicated that a new master plan should assess development and maintenance needs within the principal neighborhoods of the city and then translate these needs into policies and programs that would shape future budgets and influence community-development decisions for both public and private agencies. The council, as Exhibit 6 shows, rejected the idea of polling citizens in order to determine the community's high-priority needs. The council did not feel that a citizens' poll should be part of the planning process.

The council did, however, establish a procedure for spending federal revenue-sharing funds which was based on a clear public statement of collective priorities. This procedure, described in Exhibit 7, included citizen groups in the revenue-sharing allocation process. Reaction to this process, as the following *Flint Journal* editorial suggests, was extremely favorable.

It is not the intent of the administration to permit every individual to sell a pet project, but to offer recognized sectors of the city government and private organizations with public projects an opportunity to state their cases.

If the fire department feels it would benefit by an additional rescue outfit it would have to show the need, set the costs, and suggest the continuing

costs; if the Flint Environmental Action Team thinks it has a claim on revenue-sharing money to help solve environmental problems, it would have to spell out how it proposed to do so and what it would cost.

It should be obvious there will not be enough money for everything every unit wants. But a process such as this does give promise of providing a more rational use of the city's resources. [2]

The council elected in 1973, like its predecessor, rejected the idea of using citizen surveys. This council did, however, agree to participate with the administration in a three-month orientation program. The purpose of this program, reviewed in Exhibit 8, was to examine community needs (economic, social, and physical), review the status of current programs and projects being implemented by the city to meet these needs, and identify and establish priorities for new initiatives that the council might undertake during its term of office. The ultimate product of the orientation was to be a "program of progress" that would indicate specifically what the new city council intended to do during its two-year term.

Unfortunately, short-term political considerations eroded the consensus that had been established during the orientation program. During its first year in office, the 1973 council retreated from a collective desire to set objectives and returned, instead, to the politically expedient process of satisfying ward complaints. Consideration of citywide needs were postponed as members of the council focused on special interests in their own wards. Consideration of community development programs was replaced by such issues as the allocation of space in the garage for council members' cars, the determination of whether members of the council should travel first class or second class, and the establishment of a schedule for mowing the weeds in each ward. The 1973 council returned to the political traditions that had characterized Flint councils prior to 1970.

EXHIBIT 6

Council Rejects Citizen Survey

"Quicky Poll Decides Pollsters Unneeded," read the *Flint Journal* headline. The article described the City Council's decision to veto a proposal to hire a professional public-opinion polling organization to learn how Flint residents wanted to spend the city's share of federal revenue-sharing funds.

The city manager had recommended investing $20,000 in finding out how citizens wanted to spend $20 million over a period of five years. The council disagreed. "Anyone who has campaigned knows where the priorities are," Flint's mayor stated. Another councilman added, "This poll proposal is a farce . . . it's passing the buck." Perhaps the most important reason for the council's rejection of this proposal was summarized by one council member who told the city manager that no politically astute politician would allow the public to determine community objectives that he could later be held accountable for achieving. He added, "A successful politician is someone who takes credit for the inevitable and avoids staking his political credibility on the possible."

Willingness to delegate responsibility and provide support to municipal managers

Having selected a destination and charted the best course for reaching it, it could be disastrous if a flight engineer with no specialized flight training decided that he or she also had the ability to fly the plane. In equal measure, it could be disastrous for a city council to decide, having charted a course for city government, approved appropriate programs, and allocated the required resources, that it had the skills and the ability to supervise the day-to-day decisions involved in getting the job done. Just as there is a special need for a pilot to get a plane to its destination, there is a need for professional managers to implement council-approved policies and programs.

Willingness to delegate responsibility for achieving community objectives does not imply a need to separate politics from administration. Such a separation, as we suggested earlier, is impossible. Political leaders and municipal managers interact in the process of managing a local government. Municipal managers help political leaders determine community objectives, and political leaders assist municipal managers in achieving them. What is required is not an absolute separation of political and administrative roles but a willingness on the part of a council to delegate its responsibility for the conduct of the management process while retaining accountability for the results produced by the process.

Council support may take different forms. In some cases, it may be necessary to develop new management tools and to hire people to use these tools. In other cases, it may be necessary to prevent public employee unions from going over the heads of responsible managers and taking their grievances

EXHIBIT 7

Council Gives Citizens a Role in Spending $4.7 Million of Revenue-Sharing Funds

The Flint City Council had a problem: how to spend $4.7 million of revenue-sharing funds during the next fiscal year.

Every manager in Flint had his own idea. The fire chief wanted to construct a new fire station; the police chief, a new communication system; and the director of public works, a new vehicle-maintenance area.

The council, however, had its own plans. The expenditure of revenue-sharing funds, the council indicated, would reflect its own ideas about priorities of community needs and would allow citizen groups full opportunity to influence final decisions. "Political rhetoric!" the critics charged. The council responded by implementing the following process:

First, each council member established the priorities for community needs in ten categories. This was done by taking 100 percentage points and allocating them to each community condition area, thereby reflecting relative priorities. "Education" was not considered in the list because the council had no responsibility for the condition of education within the community. Results from each councilman were tabulated and summarized into a total council profile.

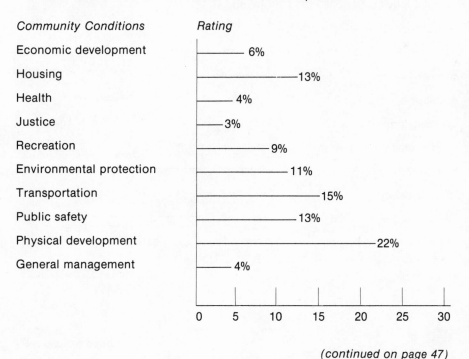

Community Conditions	Rating
Economic development	6%
Housing	13%
Health	4%
Justice	3%
Recreation	9%
Environmental protection	11%
Transportation	15%
Public safety	13%
Physical development	22%
General management	4%

(0 5 10 15 20 25 30)

(continued on page 47)

EXHIBIT 8

Council Develops Two-Year "Program of Progress"

Away from the ringing phones and the intrusion of private business, the newly elected city council met with top managers and the media at a retreat some thirty miles from Flint. The council's purpose was to spend an intensive two-day period trying to develop a program that would guide budget decisions and other actions during its two-year term of office.

In preparation for this retreat, the council completed a five-day review of all city operations. Department managers made presentations concerning the purposes of their respective operations, the services they provided, the policies and procedures adopted by the council that affected their departments and the status of major ongoing projects.

Based on an examination of current and projected conditions in Flint, as defined in the process of developing a new integrated master plan for the city, the 1973 council had developed its own priorities—which, as the following analysis suggests, were in sharp contrast to the priorities established by its predecessor.

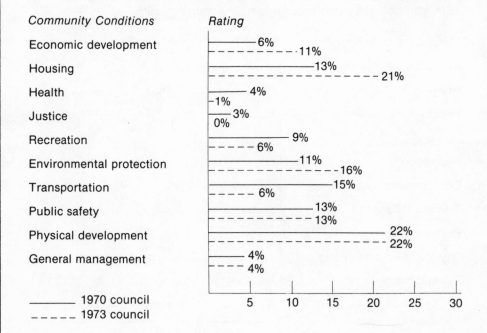

(continued on page 47)

EXHIBIT 7 (cont'd)

Then the revenue-sharing pie was divided according to the relative importance of each condition. For example, of the $2 million that would be available for discretionary expenditure in the first year, $260,000 (13 percent of the total) would go to housing projects, $80,000 (4 percent) for health projects, $180,000 for recreation projects, and so on.

Finally, the council encouraged every public and private institution in Flint to propose projects that would meet specific needs within each area. Each proposing agency had two opportunities to review its program or project with the city manager and a budget review committee. Altogether, 177 separate requests were submitted, exclusive of capital project requests, which were handled separately. Ultimately, the council appropriated $260,000 from the $2-million revenue-sharing allocation for seven projects sponsored by community organizations. The rest was allocated to city agencies.

EXHIBIT 8 (cont'd)

The council had then asked the city manager to develop alternative programs and projects that would address community needs within each category. Sixty-nine initiatives were prepared and presented to the council. Each recommended program indicated what results would be produced, the cost and time required to produce them, the manager who would be responsible, and how the program would be financed.

After all the presentations had been completed, each council member placed the sixty-nine programs in priority order by allocating 1,000 points among all those proposed. The seven projects receiving the highest-priority ratings became the principal items on the council's action agenda for the next two years.

---

directly to the council. It may be necessary at times to remove major impediments to increased productivity, such as antiquated city policies or unproductive employee incentive systems. Despite the public's growing concern about higher taxes, it may be necessary to fight for management salaries that are sufficient to attract and retain qualified people. Finally, it may be necessary for political leaders to create an atmosphere in which change and risk-taking are valued, not maligned. In short, political leaders can have a significant impact on the performance of local government if they provide their municipal managers with the right kind of support.

The 1970 City Council in Flint provided considerable support to the new city manager and his administration, primarily because it had hired him and because its political interest was closely tied to making his administration successful. In response, the manager treated the council as a decision-making body and provided council members with the information they needed to make informed decisions. For the first time, evaluation reports on major projects were presented to the council on a regular basis. This policy differed substantially from the way city managers had dealt with councils in the past.

A second reason underlying the 1970 council's willingness to delegate responsibility was that problems were being solved by the city staff which formerly had required the council's personal attention. For example, in the fall of 1971 the council created a special social programs committee to review management problems in the Department of Community Development. Involvement in these problems not only was time-consuming for council members, it also involved them in the operation of complex federal public-housing and urban-renewal programs. In the summer of 1972, the chairman of this committee announced that, because the new management of the department had resolved most of the problems that had necessitated the formation of his committee, it could now be disbanded. In his formal report to the council, he expressed his relief that the council was now letting the people who got paid to manage these programs do the actual managing.

The 1973 council was much less willing to delegate responsibility to the city manager. With the support of the municipal employee unions, a majority of the 1973 council had been elected with the understanding that they would fire, not support, the city manager. Attempts by the manager to obtain the support of the new council failed. An illustration of the 1973 council's unwillingness to delegate responsibility to managers is presented in Exhibit 9. Although in this case the council ultimately failed in its attempts to fire the community development director for properly doing his job, the ultimate negative impact on the morale of the managers in city hall was considerable.

Another indication of the 1973 council's unwillingness to delegate responsibility to managers was contained in a councilman's presentation to the Charter Revision Commission, which was holding hearings to consider alternative ways to revise Flint's city charter. The commission wanted civic and community leaders to present their ideas on how Flint's city government should be organized. The councilman's presentation is reviewed in Exhibit 10.

In summary, the councilman reflected his distrust of and lack of appreciation for professional managers by proposing an organization structure whereby elected council members would divide up the administration of various city departments. It is clear from his proposal that he would not support the delegation of authority and responsibility to professional managers.

The inability of the council to separate its responsibilities from those of municipal managers can be attributed primarily to the fact that, under Flint's city charter, the council was both the legislative and the executive body. Because a council member had to approve every purchase over $1,500, authorize every contract, and create every new position, the council was drawn into the day-to-day management process.

A second and equally important reason was the inability of managers to satisfy citizens' demands for service. For example, the inability of the Department of Public Works to carry out the city's mowing program on schedule resulted in a deluge of complaints to members of the council, who, in turn, were forced to immerse themselves in the operations of this program. In 1972, the council had become so involved in this program that it soon was determining which areas of the city would be mowed, the way in which they would be mowed, and the timing of each mowing. This involvement in day-to-day city operations would not have happend had managers done a better job in the first place.

A third reason that members of the 1973 council felt that they had to become involved in day-to-day municipal operations was expressed by a veteran council member this way: "It's the only way to get something

EXHIBIT 9

City Council Tries To Fire Community-Development Planner

In a ringing defense of planning, a *Flint Journal* editorial proclaimed that "to back off on solid land-use planning now would be comparable to driving to California with total reliance on a 1935 road map. Flint cannot afford to stray onto dead-end roads in its development during the remainder of the century." This editorial was occasioned by a City Council vote to abolish the position of community development planner—the only position responsible for citywide physical planning.

A number of reasons were cited for the attempted firing. Three councilmen stated that they wanted to save money (this position cost the city $11,000). Another councilman stated that what bothered him was that the city administration always accompanied requests for action with threats of what might happen if the council did not oblige them. Planning apparently meant an analysis of consequences, and this was bad. Others pointed out that Flint looked like hell, "proving" that there was no need for community-development planner. Finally, one councilman stated that a businessman, whom he refused to name, had told him that the city had enough administrators to run a city four times the size of Flint.

A large group of civic and community leaders gathered at a council meeting to protest the council's action. After firm statements by the city manager that he could not do his job without proper staff support, that such neighboring cities as Ann Arbor and Lansing spent two or three times more per capita on planning than did the city of Flint, and that there was clear environmental evidence that current conditions in Flint reflected the absence of planning, the council decided not to abolish the position.

Less than a month later, the community-development planner resigned. He noted in his letter of resignation that "Flint has at least as many detractors of reasonable, logical, and professional planning as it has supporters. The result is a status-quo planning effort." What he did not state was that the major reason behind the controversy over his position was his refusal to review zoning matters with certain members of the council before these matters became public at Planning Commission meetings.

done in your ward." Some council members felt that the only way they could get information about what the bureaucracy was doing was to intervene personally. As Exhibit 11 illustrates, certain council members argued that if they were denied an opportunity to intervene in daily operations they could not perform their political functions. Others responded by saying that this argument was nothing more than an excuse to justify spe-

EXHIBIT 10

More Power to the Politician

"I don't believe we need expertise to run the city of Flint—that's my main point."

Armed with multicolored charts, a prominent councilman recommended a new form of government to the Flint City Charter Revision Commission—a "strong mayor–strong council form of government," he called it.

The councilman's proposed structure would have established four commissions consisting of two council members each. These commissions would be responsible for all line and staff departments of the city. Both members of the council and the mayor would be employed on a full-time basis. The mayor would have no aides or administrators beneath him, but, with council approval, he could appoint the heads of four city departments and have responsibility for administering them directly. Council members would serve on all independent boards and commissions of the city. Further, all actions of the Civil Service Commission would have to be approved by the City Council.

The councilman stated that his purpose was "to create a balance of power and a division of authority." He added, "People that are elected should run the city; people not elected should not run the city."

In responding to questions about this proposal, he indicated that he personally felt most qualified to administer the police and fire divisions.

---

cial treatment. A newly elected councilwoman observed that there were certain councilmen who, because of personal friendship or political muscle, received better service in their wards. Supporting this view, Flint's mayor pointed out that certain department heads took special steps to provide increased levels of service in the wards of those council members who were most supportive of their operations.

It would be a mistake to underestimate the political difficulty of accepting public accountability for results while delegating responsibility for producing them. Developing an effective balance depends primarily on the level of trust that exists between political leaders and their appointed managers. In

Flint, perhaps the most important difference between the 1970 and 1973 councils was that the former trusted the managers it had hired to get the job done for them, while the latter did not.

Maintenance of citizen respect and confidence

"Who cares what happens in this city?" "They're all a bunch of crooks anyway!" These were often-repeated sentiments expressed by Flint citizens about their city government officials. Both statements reflected a lack of citizen respect for and confidence in Flint's City Council. Historically, the council

---

EXHIBIT 11

City Council Wants Right To Tell City Employees What To Do

Section 16 of the city charter stated explicitly, "Council members shall deal with the administrative branch of the city government solely through the city manager, except in the Departments of Law and Finance." Members of Flint's City Council disagreed with an interpretation of this section that obliged them to deal with city employees through the city manager's office.

Speaking for a majority of the council, one council member stated his case this way: "Just by virtue of the fact that I am elected as a councilman, do I give up my right as a citizen to get public information? All I want," he added, "is to be treated like any other citizen."

Was this councilman acting like just any other citizen when he called an employee in the Department of Community Development and asked him to prepare a special analysis on urban-renewal property in his ward? Was any council member just an ordinary citizen in levying requests upon city employees of any nature? This was the heart of the issue.

The city manager clearly stated that if each member of the council were in a position to request information and make work assignments for city employees, he could be accountable neither for the performance of these employees nor for the quality of the information the council received. In support of this position, one councilman pointed out that any council member who simply wanted information could obtain it like any other citizen without identifying himself as a member of the council. A councilwoman added, "I don't want to spend a year and a half romancing all the department heads so I can get the same level of service in my ward as other councilmen who have been around a long time and know everyone." She was referring to the fact that several councilmen spent a considerable portion of each day at city hall trying to obtain favored treatment for their respective wards.

By a vote of 6-3, the council voted to approve a resolution allowing them to contact city employees and levy information requests whenever they so desired.

---

had never commanded public respect or confidence. Monday council meetings, broadcast live on the radio, were often referred to as "The Comedy Hour," Flint's version of "Laugh-In," or "The Monday Night Fights." Derogatory stories about the intellectual capacity of council members were told throughout the city. One often-repeated story involved a councilman's public reaction to a colleague's remark about the famous fictional detective Sherlock Holmes. This particular member of the council, some-

EXHIBIT 12

Council Balks at Proposed Controls on Travel

Should a city council adopt policies concerning travel to out-of-town conferences? Flint's newspaper thought so. In an editorial, the *Flint Journal* noted that
the cost of council travel from December 1973 to August 1974 was 250 percent
higher than the total accumulated by the previous council during a similar period.
In addition, a number of citizens accused the council of taking useless junkets at
city expenses. These citizens pointed to the fact that during the previous five
months members of the council had traveled to San Juan (Puerto Rico), Las
Vegas, San Diego, San Francisco, Washington, Chicago, and several other
places.

Members of the council responded angrily. One councilman retorted, "We're
actually doing the taxpayer a favor by attending meetings. They're just not
reported that way." A black councilwoman reacted more vehemently, charging
that questions about council travel were part of a "racist plot." She added,
"Limitations on council travel are going up all over the country with one
purpose—to increase white control and limit the power of blacks and the poor."
The mayor disagreed; his view was that "trips funded by the city provide a gravy
train which my colleagues refuse to get off."

Flint's finance director was not as much concerned about where the council went
as he was about the policies governing their expenses. Traditionally, the finance
director approved all "actual and necessary" travel expenses—but, he explained,
"It is impossible to do this without an idea of what 'actual and necessary' means."

(continued)

what agitated by the reference, stated on the
radio that, as far as Sherlock "Homes" was
concerned, he wanted everyone to know
that he would not support any more public
housing projects in Flint.

Because of the lack of competence of
previous city councils, public respect for
council members in general was not high.
When a competent council was elected in
1970 with an honest desire to improve the
performance of city government, the public
did not trust it. In large part because of lack
of public respect, several members of this
council chose not to serve the city again in
1973.

The 1973 council also suffered from a lack
of public respect. In this case, however, the
council members themselves contributed
significantly to this condition. In reviewing
the 1973 council's performance after six
months in office, the *Flint Journal* noted:

A few more weeks like this one in Flint's city hall
and there may be a ground swell to do away with
municipal government altogether. Such is the
state of affairs that in some eyes anarchy must be
emerging as a practical alternative. If the public's
tolerance of political bickering isn't nearing its
limit, it should be.

EXHIBIT 12 (cont'd)

He noted that in the past "actual and necessary" had meant anything a council member wrote down on an expense statement. He added, "It is politically difficult to challenge the travel costs submitted by my employers. Therefore, I believe the council should adopt specific policies governing its own costs of travel."

The council complied with the finance director's request and reluctantly approved a $30-per-diem limit to cover all expenses except transportation, hotel accommodations, and registration fees. Any other expense that a councilman felt was "necessary" must be verified by receipts and approved by the rest of the council.

It did not take long for some council members to challenge the travel policies that they had adopted. A councilwoman stated that $30 a day for meals and other expenses wasn't enough to meet her health needs for special food. "I'd be dead within three or four hours if I ate bacon and eggs," she said. Others complained that, despite their $7,000-a-year salaries, they were paying travel costs out of their own pockets. One councilman stated, "It costs me every time I go somewhere."

The mayor, on the other hand, argued that travel policies had to be tightened, not loosened. He argued that the council should limit the number of council members attending any single conference, and that advances for travel should be withheld from any member who did not turn in his expense statements to the finance director. The mayor added, "Considering the budget cuts that have been made in city departments, we ought to be able to tighten our own belts."

His views did not prevail. The council voted to raise the per diem to $35 and to exempt taxi fares from this amount.

Flint's newspaper, as Exhibit 12 indicates, carefully scrutinized council actions. Citizens, too, watched the council. People throughout the city had long speculated that the votes of certain council members on important zoning decisions were based on bribes, payoffs, and other forms of influence peddling. Although neither speculations nor allegations about such activities had ever been substantiated, the critical point was that a large number of citizens *believed* that such things were part of the decision-making process at city hall. The incident described in Exhibit 13 helped substantiate these feelings.

An important consequence of the council's failure to maintain community respect was concisely stated by the president of the General Motors Institute in a letter to the newspaper: "If labor leaders or business executives wonder why General Motors is the only major corporation willing to gamble on the future of Flint, all they have to do is attend or listen on the radio to a meeting of the Flint City Council." In short, it was difficult to enhance the economic climate in Flint when people did not respect their elected political leaders or have faith in the latters' ability to deal with community problems.

EXHIBIT 13

Grand Jury Investigates Council Zoning Decision

On December 2, 1973, a headline in the *Flint Journal* read: "Did Bar Owners Influence Council Rezoning Refusal?" The accompanying article went on to say:

> A recent zoning decision by the Flint City Council may have been based largely on a consideration that had nothing to do with good land-use planning. There is evidence that a factor behind the council's denial Monday of a rezoning request was that a number of east-side restaurant and bar owners didn't want competition from a restaurant-bar whose owner wants to move his business.

If this allegation had been true, the council's action would have constituted a violation of the law.

The facts surrounding this allegation were these: In November 1973, the Planning Commission, with only five members in attendance (four were absent), voted 3–0 with two abstentions to deny a request to rezone an industrial property for

(continued)

Ability to marshal external support for the accomplishment of community objectives

Both the 1970 and the 1973 councils attempted to implement a number of development programs. Implementation of these programs depended, in large measure, on each council's ability to marshal external support and financial resources. The successful effort to relocate the University of Michigan–Flint campus (see Chapter 19) is a good example of how the 1970 City Council obtained external support and resources for a project the council felt was critical to the development of Flint.

The development of the St. John's Street Industrial Park was also a major objective of both the 1970 and the 1973 councils. The case presented in Exhibit 14 explains how Flint's mayor in 1973 was able to marshal the necessary external support and resources to initiate this project.

Opportunities for Improvement

By far the most important way in which Flint could improve the impact of political leaders on governmental performance would be to persuade qualified people to seek positions on the council or accept appointments to important boards and commissions. Until qualified individuals are elected or appointed to major policy-making positions within the city, improved performance will not be achieved or sustained.

Although improving compensation and providing better support services at city hall

EXHIBIT 13 (cont'd)

commercial use. The person making this request wanted to move his restaurant and bar to what he considered a more favorable location. The planning staff recommended approval of the requested rezoning, noting that it was entirely consistent with the city's master plan and adjacent land uses. The major objections to the rezoning came from bar and restaurant owners in the area, who admitted that they feared additional competition.

In January 1974, the members of the Planning Commission who were not present at the November meeting successfully placed this item back on the agenda. By a vote of 5–4 the commission reversed its earlier decision and permitted the requested rezoning.

At a subsequent meeting the council voted 6–3 not to accept the Planning Commission's latest decision. No reasons were advanced for the council's action.

Consequently, the proposer filed a lawsuit, claiming that the council's decision had been based on improper criteria. The grand jury began an investigation of the relationship between certain members of the Planning Commission, the council, and the bar owners in the area.

would provide some positive incentive for qualified people to seek council seats, these steps alone will not be enough. Persuading qualified citizens to accept the sacrifices of public service will require the active support of key individuals and groups in the community—people who recognize the impact political leaders can have on the quality of life in Flint. In the absence of political parties' involvement in city affairs, public and private leaders need to develop alternative mechanisms for selecting and supporting candidates. To this end, civic and community leaders might come together to form citizen-based coalitions capable of identifying and persuading qualified people to run for public office. If such a coalition were to pledge financial and organizational support, a qualified individual might be persuaded to seek political office. Such a coalition could have the organizational value of a political party without its partisan image. To be suc-

cessful, however, such a coalition should not place specific demands on those whom it supported. The primary criteria for support would have to be individual integrity and a willingness to face objectively the toughest public decisions.

A second way of improving positive political impact would be to increase citizen involvement in the decision-making process at city hall. If we believe that our system of government works, then we must believe that improving the quality of political leadership, in the long run, depends on educating the public about the impact political leaders can have on the community. To stimulate greater citizen involvement, the City Council should consider such actions as conducting periodic opinion polls, publishing summaries of City Council meetings and important commission or board meetings, publishing a periodic newsletter that would be sent to each home, opening all meetings to the public,

EXHIBIT 14

Mayor's Leadership Accelerates Industrial Development

In December 1973, the newly elected mayor of Flint announced that the completion of the St. John's Street Industrial Park was his highest-priority objective. This project had been stalled because of the cancellation of the federal urban-renewal program by the Nixon administraiton. Working with the council member whose ward encompassed the St. John's Street area and with the economic-development coordinator for the country, the mayor set out to obtain additional federal funding.

Earlier in 1973, the county economic-development coordinator, working with the city, had almost succeeded in obtaining a $1.6-million grant from the Economic Development Administration (EDA) to make infrastructural improvements (roads and sewers) to the area. The purpose of this grant was to enhance the marketability of the land for industrial purposes. Partly because of poor timing and lack of local political support, Flint did not get this grant.

Neither the economic-development coordinator nor the mayor was willing to take no for an answer. Taking advantage of his longtime friendship with Flint's congressman, the mayor launched a major campaign to obtain the EDA grant. After many months of negotiation, EDA finally agreed to provide the money if the city would come up with $1.6 million as its matching share.

Because the city's budget had no excess funds for development purposes, the mayor turned his attention to alternative sources. He began a series of negotiations with the Mott foundation, Flint's longtime benefactor. With the aid of the city manager, the mayor argued persuasively that this project represented an important investment in Flint's future. The foundation ultimately agreed to provide the $1.6-million matching share. In addition, it provided $200,000 more than was requested in order to launch other projects in what was called the Comprehensive Economic Development Program.

rotating the location of council meetings throughout the community, and holding council and commission meetings at night so that working citizens can attend.

The involvement of private institutions in Flint should also be encouraged. If General Motors, the Mott Foundation, the University of Michigan, and other private institutions recognize the importance of political leader-

ship, they should encourage their employees to become more involved in the political process. Participation on task forces, attendance at public hearings, acceptance of positions on key boards and commissions—these are all ways in which individuals from such organizations could become more involved in their city government. Moreover, private employers should encourage qualified individuals to seek these positions by adopting such policies as flexible work hours so that civic participation will not create severe hardship for an employee.

There is also a need in Flint to specify more precisely what the council plans to do with taxpayers' money. If citizens do not know what their elected political leaders are attempting to do, they have no basis for evaluating their performance. It is imperative that citizens, citizen groups, private interests, and all external forces exert pressure on Flint's council to state publicly the objectives council members are trying to achieve through the expenditure of public resources. This can be done through the press, public discussion, or public hearings on the annual budget. In each case, pressure must be placed on the council to explain the results each city department or agency plans to produce and at what cost. The loop can then be closed by reporting back what was actually done versus what was intended.

Flint's City Council has the responsibility to enact necessary legislation and to determine the policies and the programs that will best meet the high-priority needs of the city. This important role of the council, however, does not—or should not—extend to the conduct of the day-to-day operations of the city. Municipal managers and employees are hired to ensure that council policies and programs are implemented as planned. The council can thereby increase its own effectiveness by limiting its involvement to setting the direction and providing managers the necessary support to do their jobs well.

CHAPTER 6

Municipal Managers

Managing local government is where the action is. It requires the skills of a corporate executive, the sensitivity of a statesman, and the endurance of a long-distance runner. The demands are great, the expectations are high, and the pressures are intense. Yet, if we are to have local governments that are responsive to the needs of citizens, they must be managed by individuals who have the ability to operate in a fishbowl environment while creatively carrying out local-government policies and programs.

Mark Keane, Executive Director
International City Management Association

In any business, public or private, someone has to translate policies into action at the working level. This someone is the manager—a person with the experience, skills, and authority to make the day-to-day decisions and direct the activities that are necessary to ensure that the right things get done. The performance of a local government depends on the capabilities of municipal managers—those nonelected employees who, by virtue of the number of people they supervise, the amount of dollars they control, and the importance of the functions they administer, are responsible for the quality and quantity of municipal services. Positioned between elected political leaders and municipal employees, municipal managers face the difficult challenge of converting political desires into community realities.

Mark Keane, executive director of the International City Management Association, is right—public managers at all levels of government have tough jobs, and none has a

tougher job than one who manages a county, city, or other municipality. In contrast to the situation in the private sector, the job of a municipal manager is made more difficult by the lack of accepted performance measures that indicate whether city operations are succeeding or failing. While doing their jobs, municipal managers are heavily encumbered by legislative, financial, and administrative restrictions which limit their actions in areas generally considered the sole prerogative of managers. Such areas include the use of funds; the selection, promotion, and compensation of personnel; and the organization of employees and functions. In addition, conflicting incentives among elected officials, citizens, and professional managers often make it difficult to gain agreement on the ends to be achieved with public resources. The "fishbowl" nature of the job places added constraints on the process of achieving community objectives. Municipal managers must constantly be aware of the potential public and political reactions to decisions aimed at making government operations more productive. Finally, municipal managers usually must operate within a fragmented government structure in which responsibility for achieving results is shared among competing levels of government and among different agencies of the same government.

The difficulty of being a municipal manager is exceeded only by the importance of the job. The role of municipal managers has changed dramatically in the last decade, as the business of local government has changed. Responding to federal legislation (Great Society programs in the 1960s and revenue sharing in the 1970s) as well as to accelerating public demands for more and better services, local governments have been forced to assume responsibility for meeting the economic and social needs as well as the traditional physical needs of the community. This shift has placed new demands on the capabilities of municipal managers. Skills that were adequate to perform maintenance functions are not adequate to manage complex businesses providing services that range from transportation and health to housing and environmental protection.

Management—from first-line supervisors to the county executive, city manager, or elected mayor—generally represents about 10 percent of a local government's work force. Within this broad spectrum, it may be necessary to group managers according to their levels of responsibility within the organization. For example, one could identify executives (top-level managers and agency/department directors), administrators (line and staff division heads), managers and management staff (mid-level managers and management analysts), and supervisors.

In many local governments, the most critical need is to clearly identify those employees who are part of management; within this effort, the most difficult challenge is identifying first-line supervisors who exercise management responsibilities.

Supervisors have perhaps the most critical and least well-defined responsibilities within a local government. On behalf of management, supervisors exercise one or more of the following functions: employment, promotion, transfer, suspension, discharge, and adjudication of employee grievances. The exercise of these responsibilities requires using independent judgment. In the private sector, promotion from a nonsupervisory to a supervisory position is an important and well-defined step—an elevation to the first level of management. In the public sector, the distinction between the supervisor and those supervised is often unclear. The consequences of this lack of clarity are profound, as the next chapter on municipal employees and employee unions indicates.

Impact on Process and Performance

Municipal managers have both direct and indirect impact on what a local government decides to do and its success in getting it done. Each year, a legislative body (city council or board of supervisors) approves a budget that states implicitly or explicitly the results or services that will be provided during the fiscal year. In essence, the budget is a contract with the legislative body wherein responsible managers agree to produce specified results with a given amount of resources. In the implementation phase of the management process, municipal managers should be directly accountable for executing the terms of these budget contracts. The performance of government operations depends directly on their ability to do so.

Municipal managers have an indirect impact on the management process through the way in which they affect other factors. For example, municipal managers assist political leaders in the process of converting constituent demands and community needs into measurable objectives. After priorities have been established for community objectives, managers help political leaders determine the best means (programs and projects) for accomplishing these ends. Managers also play a critical role in the development of productive employees and in large part are responsible for maintaining an appropriate balance between union rights and management responsibilities.

Municipal managers affect the achievement of community objectives through their ability to develop and use advanced management tools and analytical assistance, their ability to increase the involvement of citizens and private-interest groups in the process of making government decisions, and their ability to inform and involve the media. Armed with patience and facts, managers can increase the ability of media reporters to cover public events and, in the process,

better educate the public.

Because of their pivotal role in each phase of the management process, municipal managers have the potential to compensate for the negative impact of other factors. If political leaders refuse to establish community objectives, municipal managers may develop an informal process for doing so. If financial practices are unduly restrictive, municipal managers may seek funding from other sources. If the internal structure of a local government impedes effective management, skilled professionals can find ways to work around the problem. And in the absence of adequate management tools, managers can marshal their own data-gathering and analytical capabilities so as to increase the probability that decisions will be based on accurate and complete information.

Criteria for Evaluation

Evaluating the capability of municipal managers involves an examination of (1) their competence; (2) their motivation; (3) the adequacy of the resources, both financial and human, at their disposal; (4) the quality of the management tools they use; and (5) the balance between the exercise of union rights and management prerogatives. In this chapter we examine the first two areas: competence and motivation. The other subjects are addressed in later chapters.

Competence

If municipal managers do not have the management skills required to administer important public activities and functions, the performance of a local government will suffer. It is difficult to evaluate the competence of municipal managers in the absence of clear measurements of how well municipal operations satisfy public needs or achieve operational objectives. For example, if we do not know what the police department is

expected to accomplish or how to measure it, it will be difficult to evaluate the management skills of the police chief. We can, however, apply a number of criteria in order to assess more effectively the level of competence of municipal managers:

Do municipal managers individually and collectively have the requisite management skills? Successful business performance—public or private—requires not only individual managers with highly developed management skills but also the development of a management team that collectively has the capacity to get things done. Evaluation of competence is focused on the skills of individual managers as well as on the aggregate skills of the management team that the chief executive is able to assemble.

Are municipal managers promoted on the basis of their abilities to perform in higher-level positions? If the performance of local governments is to be improved, municipal managers must be promoted primarily because of their abilities to perform in higher-level positions, not because of their abilities to perform well in their present jobs. Past performance should, of course, be a factor in making a promotion decision, but it should be of considerably less importance than projected performance in the new job. Evaluation of promotion procedures and of the influence of non-job-related factors on promotion decisions will clarify the extent to which managers are elevated to positions for which they are not qualified.

Are municipal managers provided opportunities to improve their management skills? No manager, private or public, ever reaches a level of complete competence. Skills constantly need to be sharpened and improved. Accordingly, the availability of management training, special education, and other skill-building programs is important in maintaining competent management. This question attempts to determine (1) the quantity and quality of management-training opportunities available to people at all levels of management and (2) the extent to which these opportunities heighten the awareness of management as a responsibility separate from the technical knowledge required to administer a particular activity.

Motivation

In many cases, municipal managers have the competence to administer their operations efficiently and effectively but lack the motivation to do so. Motivation, and what affects it, is a complex subject. There are no panaceas that will suddenly produce highly motivated managers. There are, however, a number of criteria that, if met, should improve the motivation of municipal managers to do a better job or at least remove negative influences on their motivation:

Do political leaders provide adequate support to municipal managers? If managers are to be motivated to get things done, political leaders must delegate responsibility and provide managers with the support required to (1) accomplish politically determined objectives, (2) supervise and control government functions and activities, and (3) conduct labor negotiations and administer negotiated contracts with municipal employees.

Do municipal managers know what they are expected to achieve, and can they be held accountable for their performance? If municipal managers do not know what results they are held accountable for producing, there will be little incentive for them to be productive. Therefore, it is necessary to examine the extent to which expected results are clearly established and communicated to all responsible managers. Furthermore, it is necessary to determine whether managers can be held accountable for producing these results. The latter requirement involves a determination of (1) the extent to which governmental structure ensures that managers are responsible to the chief executive for the quality of the performance, (2) the extent of a manager's control over the functions that affect the exercise of his responsibilities, and (3) the impact of civil service, union representation, and other such restrictions on a manager's control over the people who work for him or her.

Is the compensation of municipal managers based on performance? Managerial motivation in any business, private or public, is primarily related to the allocation of rewards and penalties based on demonstrated performance. In most cases, compensation is the critical motivator. If the compensation (including fringe benefits) of municipal managers does not fairly represent the responsibilities they discharge, and if compensation increases are not based on job performance, there will be little or no incentive, save personal pride, to make government operations more productive. This question attempts to determine whether compensation received by municipal managers is comparable to that paid to managers holding similar positions in other public and private organizations, and the extent to which compensation increases are related to job performance.

Are municipal managers residents of the community for which they have public responsibility? Considerable debate has surrounded the question of whether municipal employees will be motivated to do a better job if they live within the municipality that employs them. At minimum, municipal managers who make decisions that determine the quality and quantity of municipal services provided to citizens within the jurisdiction will be motivated if they personally experience the problems they are responsible for solving. A police captain, for example, probably will be more concerned about how his professional actions and decisions affect the safety of local residents if he and his family are among those residents.

Do municipal managers view themselves as professionals? Perhaps the most important motivator in the public sector is whether a manager views himself as a professional. Municipal managers must operate between two often-conflicting forces: a political body that is often uninterested in the consequences of its actions, and a bureaucracy that is often unresponsive, if not antagonistic, to management initiatives. A sense of professionalism combined with a desire and a will to manage allows a manager to maintain a proper relationship between these two forces.

Conditions in Flint

The parallel in private industry to the circumstances facing many local governments is often referred to as a "turnaround situation." Sophisticated investors, trying to maximize their return on investment, are always looking for companies that in the past had been successful, profitable, and produced high-quality products, but which of late have been falling behind the competition in product quality, service to customers, and profitability. The key to picking a potential turnaround is knowing the assets of the company, both tangible and intangible, and then deciding how better management could make these assets more profitable.

Many a county and city throughout the country represents a potential turnaround in that it has all the assets, tangible and intangible, to ensure that citizens will receive the highest possible return from an investment of their tax dollars. Taking advantage of these assets depends in large measure on the competence and motivation of municipal managers who can be attracted to the challenge.

Flint, in 1971, represented a turnaround situation primarily because the majority of the managers did not have the capacity to capitalize on the city's extensive assets or to use its resources most productively. There were two main causes: (1) managers lacked

the management skills necessary to administer complex businesses, and (2) managers were not motivated to use the skills they did have or to develop skills they lacked.

Managerial competence

In Flint, most municipal managers—from the city manager to field supervisors—did not have the management skills required to administer a $55 million-a-year public corporation made up of complex, highly varied municipal businesses. This lack of management skills may be attributed, in large part, to what is commonly referred to as the Peter Principle—the observation that because a person can perform one job well he will be promoted to another job he *cannot* perform, and there he will stay. In Flint the Peter Principle created a situation in which able technicians had over the years been promoted to management positions for which, in many cases, they did not have the skills—and there they stayed.

The term *technical skills* refers to specialized knowledge in a particular function or discipline, e.g., traffic engineering. The term *management skills*, on the other hand, refers to the abilities to integrate functions and people into a coordinated operation, to identify what needs to be done, and to get it done with the resources available. In short, management skills allow the execution of all phases of the management process—planning, implementation, and evaluation. A good manager (the director of community development) may be a good technician (land-use planner), but a good technician (a doctor or criminal investigator) may not necessarily be a good manager (director of health or police chief).

In 1972, the majority of municipal managers in Flint were technicians, not managers. Both the police chief and the fire chief had worked their way up from the entry-level positions of policeman and fireman. In fact, civil service rules prohibited lateral entry into either of these services. For the most part, civil service examinations tested technical knowledge rather than managerial skills. Therefore, it was not surprising to find that an engineer managed the Department of Public Works, a doctor managed the Department of Public Health, a former recreation leader managed the Department of Parks and Recreation, a city planner managed the Department of Community Development, an accountant managed the Finance Department, and a lawyer managed the Legal Department. Together, these departments spent more than $30 million of taxpayers' money in fiscal year 1973. Yet, the people responsible for managing them had had little formal management education or training.

This is not to say that all of these people were bad managers. The fire chief, for one, was able to recognize that his position required management skills. On his own he developed and practiced them. But this was the exception, not the rule.

Four additional factors contributed to a lack of managerial competence. First, the lack of clear measures of performance for city operations made it difficult to distinguish managerial competency from incompetency. Incompetent managers were under little pressure to improve their managerial skills because there was little risk that poor performance would be recognized and, if it were, little or no risk that one's job or compensation would be affected.

A second factor was civil service. In Flint, managers—from field supervisors to the city manager—did not select, promote, or compensate those who worked for them. These functions, normally the prerogative of a manager, were the responsibility of an independent Civil Service Commission.

Civil service procedures (as Exhibit 15 indicates) did not provide a suitable means for filling top-management positions with candidates who had requisite management skills or for assembling a competent management team. Subjective and imprecise oral examinations were used to fill most management positions. Subjectivity is unavoidable; but in these cases it was exercised, not by the appointing authority who was responsible for the performance of the person who would fill the job, but by a three-member examination board that usually had no direct interest or involvement in the position. The manager's discretion in selection was limited according to how the position was to be filled. If a position was to be filled on an "open competitive" basis, the manager could select from the top three scorers—the "rule of three." If the position was to be filled on a "promotional" basis, the manager had two options: (1) select the highest scorer—the "rule of one," or (2) leave the position vacant for a year. In either case, a fully qualified candidate who had made a bad impression on any one of the three panelists in an oral exam could be eliminated from final consideration for appointment. Most important, the person accountable for the job—the appointing authority—had little to say about it.

Another civil-service obstacle to strengthening management competence was that is was nearly impossible to dismiss a manager against his will. As the cases presented in Exhibit 16 suggest, managers could not be dismissed even for insubordination, disloyalty, or gross incompetence.

A third factor contributing to the absence

EXHIBIT 15

Independent Civil-Service Commissioners Fill Top-Management Positions

Director of Community Development

In 1972, the civil service director forwarded the names of three finalists for the position of community development director to the city manager. This officer reported to the city manager, and therefore the latter could pick one of the three top candidates to fill the position. This list was determined as follows: The Civil Service Commission decided, following the recommendation of the civil service director, that an oral examination would be the sole basis for selection. Civil service technicians, none of whom had any managerial experience themselves, reviewed applications and narrowed the more than sixty candidates to eight. Why eight? Because there are eight hours in a working day, and the civil service director had allotted one day for conducting oral examinations.

The city manager was permitted to suggest questions to be asked in the oral interviews, but the civil service director determined the final questions. The civil service director then selected three people to comprise an oral examination board: the director of community development from a neighboring city, a professor of urban studies from Detroit, and a professor of land-use planning from Michigan State University. None of the three was a resident of Flint, knew much about the city and its particular community development needs, or knew anything about the management needs of the Department of Community Development.

Forty-five-minute interviews were held with each candidate. At the completion of the examination, each oral board member assigned points to each candidate, using a number of criteria in the scoring system developed by the Civil Service Commission. The three top scores for this position were 93.96, 93.61, and 80.96. The city manager had to choose one of the top three candidates. He chose the top scorer, who was, by civil service standards, the best candidate—by .35 of 1 percent.

(continued on page 66)

of management skills and competent managers in Flint involved the power of municipal employee unions. Not only were all managers selected through civil-service procedures (except the four council appointees), but, with the exception of several department heads, they were also members of municipal employee unions or associations. The inclusion of middle managers in employee associations and nonsupervisory employee unions made it difficult to recruit and retain competent managers. On balance, Flint's managers wanted to remain insulated from outside competition, and, with the help of the Civil Service Commission and the courts, they were, for the most part, successful.

EXHIBIT 15 (cont'd)

Head of the Water Division

Another illustration of how civil service promoted managers occurred in 1973, when the head of the water division, an $8 million business within the Department of Public Works, retired. In this case, civil service determined that at least two people within the Department of Public Works (DPW) met minimum qualifications for this position. Therefore, a promotional examination would be given. People who did not work for the city and those who worked for other city departments, regardless of their skills and management competence, could not compete. Candidates were ranked according to the numerical results of their oral examinations. In accordance with the city charter, the city manager and the director of public works had to promote the person who received the highest numerical score or leave the position vacant for one year.

In this case, the person receiving the highest score had previously served as staff assistant to the director of public works and had no "line" management experience. Furthermore, despite exceptional willingness and energy, he had performed poorly on a number of previous assignments for the city manager. As a result, the city manager refused to allow the DPW director to fill the position. Subsequently, a new city manager, under extreme pressure from city unions and members of the City Council, reluctantly filled this position. The choice was difficult: either an important position had to remain vacant or a less than totally competent person would be appointed.

Deputy Director of Finance

In early May 1974, civil service announced that a promotional examination would be given in July to fill the position of deputy finance director and that seven employees within the finance department would be eligible to take it. This precipitated an outcry from a number of city employees who felt that qualified people from throughout the city government should be eligible to take the exam. Championing this cause, the director of finance appeared before the Civil Service

(continued)

In fairness to the municipal managers in Flint, it should be noted that a fourth cause of inadequate management skills was the absence of any appreciation of management as a necessary skill and of any training program to develop this skill. Prior to 1971, decision making within Flint's city government was highly centralized. The city manager had responsibility for making almost all major management decisions that affected munici-pal operations. Because he refused to delegate management responsibility, it made little sense to provide managers with special training or skill-development programs; therefore no management-training programs had been initiated. Efforts by the city manager from 1971 to 1974 to strengthen the skills of municipal managers were limited and produced unsatisfactory results. The council did not believe that a management-

EXHIBIT 15 (cont'd)

Commission and requested that the second-highest position in the department be filled on an interdepartmental rather than a departmental basis. The difference was important: departmental promotion meant that years of experience with the city were added to the exam score and that the "rule of one" applied (the person with the highest score automatically got the job); interdepartmental promotion did not give credit to years of experience and permitted the finance director to select one of the top three scorers.

At a Civil Service Commission meeting, the finance director told commissioners that he had requested in writing to see the criteria used to select the seven people deemed eligible by the civil-service director, but that these criteria had not been disclosed. The civil-service director responded that eligible candidates were selected by personnel technicians, who used their own judgment in determining which jobs constituted natural preparation for promotion to this position and which did not. The finance director disagreed vigorously with the conclusions of the personnel technicians, whose own civil-service classifications were several levels below that of the position being filled. He indicated that there were at least twenty people throughout the city whose finance and accounting experience qualified them to compete.

The director of finance also questioned the commissioners as to why the initial list had been prepared on May 7 but the examination had not been scheduled until July 19. The civil-service director replied that this delay was intended to accommodate the vacation schedule of one employee. The employee, as it turned out, also happened to be the president of the supervisors' union. The finance director told the commission, "It would seem that the overall requirements of the city are more important than the private schedule of an individual employee." To the civil-service director, he added, "Your actions can make or break a department . . . through your staff, you must serve the needs of city departments that are charged with serving the public rather than exclusively serving the needs of individual employees or organized employee groups."

By a vote of 2-1, the Civil Service Comission reversed its previous position and agreed to open competition to all city employees.

training program was necessary, and refused to approve funds in support of this objective.

Managerial motivation

If you invest your money to purchase the stock of a private corporation, you want to be sure that the company is run by able, highly motivated managers. As shareholders in your city government, should you be less concerned about the motivation of municipal managers? Regardless of your answer, the motivation of municipal managers has generally not been a subject of major interest in most counties and cities; this was certainly true in Flint.

One of the major reasons that municipal managers in Flint lacked the motivation to

---

EXHIBIT 16

It Is Almost Impossible To Fire a Civil Servant

The Purchasing Director

In October 1972, the city manager returned a tape recorder that he had borrowed from the city's purchasing director. He had borrowed the recorder to dictate his private record of issues and events at city hall. Inadvertently, he had left a partially recorded tape on the machine. When the purchasing director discovered the tape, he did not return it. Instead, he played it for a number of people at city hall. Among these was the president of the supervisors' union, which was currently involved in a lawsuit against the city protesting the manager's personnel policies. A number of those who heard the tape urged the purchasing director to return it. Disregarding this advice, he took the tape to the union's lawyer to see if anything that had been said on the tape could be used in the case against the city and the city manager.

When the city manager realized that he had left the tape on the machine, he asked that it be returned. The purchasing director refused. The next day the city manager fired him on grounds of insubordination and failure to return personal property. In his dismissal letter, the manager stated that in the absence of trust, neither he nor the city council could have confidence in the recommendations or actions of the purchasing director. A majority of the council stood firmly behind the manager.

The purchasing director appealed the case to the Civil Service Commission. Meanwhile, the president of the city employees' union announced that his union was considering mini-strikes during snowstorms to bring public attention to what he termed the "dictatorship" at city hall. He stated that consideration of such strikes had been stimulated by the firing of the purchasing director.

After a long evening of deliberation, the three-person Civil Service Commission reinstated the purchasing director, giving him a thirty-day suspension without pay. The commission found him guilty of insubordination and lack of discretion, but felt that the city manager's action was too severe.

The city manager replied that, denied the right to hire or fire top management personnel, it would be impossible for him to motivate or control those who reported to him. In the future, he said, neither the council nor members of the community could hold him accountable for the actions of his purchasing director.

(continued)

---

improve their management skills was the absence of political support from the City Council. This lack of support took many forms. Of particular significance was the council's unwillingness to approve needed staff positions. Executive managers, department directors, and division heads had virtually no staff support. As the case presented in Exhibit 17 reveals, attempts to persuade the council to provide the city manager with the

EXHIBIT 16 (cont'd)

The Real-Estate Division Supervisor

In April 1972, the director of community development fired the supervisor of the real-estate division, who was responsible for acquiring approximately $3 million in real estate annually to support the city's urban-renewal program and other city programs that required property acquisition. The director's reasons were several: The supervisor had purchased property for himself in an urban-renewal area in which he was purchasing property for the urban-renewal program. This constituted a potential conflict of interest that could jeopardize the city's contract with the federal agency that funded this program. In addition, the supervisor had violated the acquisition schedule agreed upon for the current fiscal year. He had purchased $67,000 worth of property that was not scheduled for acquisition until the following year, thereby forcing property owners scheduled for the current year to wait. Furthermore, one of the properties purchased a year early was owned by a family that planned to relocate into a home being sold to them by the supervisor's brother, a real-estate agent. The discharge paper filed with civil service also noted lesser reasons for dismissal, including failure to maintain adequate records, poor relationship with residents in the urban-renewal areas, and lack of dependability on the job.

The supervisor requested and was granted a hearing before the Civil Service Commission. On the day of the hearing, the director of community development was invited to a meeting with the president of the city employees' union, the attorney for this union, and the city attorney. In this meeting, the union president requested that the charges be dropped or, at minimum, that the supervisor—who did not belong to this union—be given only a short suspension. The union's interest in this matter, according to the union's president, was that the firing of any employee by a department head might have serious implications for other city employees. In view of union support for the supervisor and the Civil Service Commission's past record on firings, the union president told the director he did not have a very good chance of making the firing stick. The city attorney agreed and suggested that the supervisor agree to resign immediately, thereby permitting the community development director to withdraw the charges. After consultation and negotiation, the supervisor did agree to resign in three weeks, after using up his accumulated vacation time. The community development director, wanting only to rid his department of this employee, accepted the compromise as being the best he could obtain from the system.

basic staff support required to manage a major public business met with extreme political resistance. The council was reluctant to hire what one member termed "high-priced managers" at a time of budget tight-ness. Council members, on the whole, were unwilling or unable to educate their constituents concerning the value that an investment in staff support might represent in terms of better management of city resour-

EXHIBIT 17

Council Compromises on Top-Level Staff Positions

"City Council Approves Addition of Four Assistants for City Manager," read a headline in the February 15, 1972, *Flint Journal.* This headline was not quite accurate. The council had approved four positions that would make up a new Office of Planning, Budgeting, and Program Evaluation. This office would be headed by a deputy city manager responsible for integrating these staff functions and relating them to general city operations.

In justifying the establishment of these positions, the city manager argued that no one was responsible for planning, budgeting, or operations evaluation. The city's Planning Commission had one person responsible for reviewing zoning requests, the finance director had a staff assistant responsible for budget preparation, and no one was responsible for program evaluation. The manager noted that, according to the *International City Management Association Yearbook,* Flint had the lowest per-capita expenditure for planning of all cities of comparable size. He pointed out that inadequate planning in the past had cost the city a significant loss of revenue, and that this loss would continue in the future. He added that better analysis of programs could realize substantial savings by improving productivity. At minimum, the city would be less dependent on consultants. In summary, the city manager told the council, "A well-managed city must have the capacity to

(continued)

ces. Consequently, city managers operated without support in such areas as personnel management, budget preparation, program analysis, labor relations, and citizen service. Line managers had to perform these functions themselves, taking valuable time away from their other management responsibilities.

Union–management relations was another area where the council failed to provide municipal managers with the support they needed. The example presented in Exhibit 18 of union leaders demanding to negotiate directly with the council concerning the organization of the police department was not the exception but the rule. As the next chapter discusses in detail, the political pow-

er of municipal unions in Flint allowed union leaders to consistently make "end runs" to the council around the managers, whom the council had hired and whom they presumably held accountable for labor relations.

A second factor explaining the absence of motivation was the fact that municipal managers did not know, in most cases, what they were expected to produce. In 1971 the absence of a budgeting system that specified results to be produced for resources provided made it difficult to hold managers accountable for their performance (see Chapter 8). Moreover, managers were denied the satisfaction of knowing how well they were doing. Of course, managers knew they were responsible for performing certain

---

EXHIBIT 17 (cont'd)

plan ahead and evaluate program results. At present, Flint is not organized to perform these functions."

Reaction to the council's decision was not altogether positive. The city's finance director said that he did not believe any money was available for these positions and asked the council to wait until the annual budget was approved. Union leaders, representing general city employees as well as supervisors and middle managers, appeared at council and Civil Service Commission meetings to argue that these positions were not needed, but adding that if they were to be filled, civil service regulations should confine recruitment to existing city employees. Some members of the Planning Commission felt that their commission should be responsible for all planning. Finally, private citizens appeared before the council arguing that the city manager was trying to build an empire, and that prior city managers had gotten along well enough without staff assistance.

Reacting to public pressure and, in some cases, to their own doubts, the council asked the city manager not to fill these four positions until they had time to review their decision. "We're not saying we're backing down," the mayor stated, "but we're sending it back to committee for further discussion."

The *Flint Journal*, in a special editorial, counseled: "Government, like politics, is the art of compromise, and if such compromises are not always the best answers, they are sometimes the only possible ones." Heeding this advice, the council compromised on this issue. In mid-April it approved three instead of four positions, and requested the manager to fill two of the three from existing city personnel.

---

functions (collecting garbage, patrolling streets) or conducting certain activities (housing inspection, property acquisition), but specific target results within these functions and activities were not defined. As a result, managers did not know if they were to be held accountable for inspecting ten houses per day or two, picking up fifty tons of garbage per crew day or ten.

Fragmentation of authority, combined with civil-service and union power, also had a dampening effect on motivation. As Chapter 10 describes in detail, the executive branch of Flint's city government was highly fragmented. The city manager had no control over personnel, financial, or legal functions, nor did he have responsibility for parks and recreation, the airport, the city hospital, the bus system, or most other social services. As a result, the council could not hold the manager accountable for these functions. The manager, in turn, had little ability to hold his department heads accountable for their performance. The fire chief is a good example. The city manager could neither hire nor fire him, and his compensation was determined by civil service solely on the basis of seniority. Moreover, the fire chief belonged to the same union as the personnel he managed, creating little incentive on his part to make tough decisions to improve the quality of fire protection, especially if these efforts required personnel actions. To his personal credit, the fire chief, despite these obvious

EXHIBIT 18

City Unions Tell Council
How To Organize Police Division

If an ambitious patrolman in the Flint police division wanted to be chief, he could follow one of the two following promotional routes:

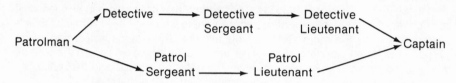

Both promotional sequences came together at the rank of captain, then proceeded to assistant chief, and finally to chief. (There was no lateral entry into the police division, so to become chief an employee had to start as a patrolman.)

In 1971, the administration proposed a plan to combine these two promotional routes as follows:

Patrolman ──────► Sergeant ──────► Lieutenant ──────► Captain

This, it was argued, would provide the police chief with greater flexibility in assigning supervisory personnel in order to satisfy changing needs in the area of investigation and patrol, ensure better-trained officers, and create a unified career ladder.

There was one problem: what would be done with the detectives? The manager and the police chief agreed that this classification should be abolished, and that as detectives retired or were promoted their positions would be deleted. The

(continued)

disincentives, consistently made tough management decisions—winning, in the process, the enmity of the firefighters' union.

Department heads suffered from the effects of this fragmentation of responsibility. The director of the Department of Community Development, for example, found it difficult to implement the urban-renewal program on schedule because the independent city attorney refused to provide the legal services necessary to move properties through the condemnation process.

A third factor explaining why managers had little incentive to increase their management skills was their compensation. A city cannot attract and motivate the most competent managers at levels of compensation below those that they could command in comparable positions in private or other public institutions in the area. Of course, not all compensation is monetary. Some cities can offer managers "environmental" compensation, providing desirable climate and recreational facilities, but most cities, like

---

EXHIBIT 18 (cont'd)

detectives did not disagree with this proposal. What they wanted was a raise in pay. Therefore, they filed a request with the Civil Service Commission that their classification be increased three levels to correspond with that of sergeants. This request was based on the belief on the part of the detectives that they were doing the same work as their supervisors. If the request was granted, each of the thirty-eight detectives would receive a raise of almost $1,600 in addition to the 7.2 percent increase in compensation they had recently received through the collective-bargaining process. Civil service granted the detectives' request.

Subsequently, the sergeants asked civil service to raise their classification two levels in order to maintain a separation between a supervisor (sergeant) and the people he supervised (former detectives). This would have raised the sergeant's salary an additional $2,500 per person. Civil service denied this request, and the sergeants filed a suit in circuit court to get the additional pay.

Next the Flint City Council got into the act: it refused to create the necessary positions in the budget to accommodate the civil-service decision to move the thirty-eight detectives to the level of sergeant. The council ruled that the detectives should remain detectives until they could prove they were performing the same duties as their supervisors. The detectives then filed suit in circuit court asking that the initial decision of civil service be upheld.

Meanwhile, the detectives and the sergeants began to put pressure on members of the council. This strategy was ultimately successful. Acting in direct opposition to the advice of its appointed managers, the council agreed to negotiate directly with the detectives and the sergeants over their desired salary raise. Ultimately, the council accepted the positions of both the detectives and the sergeants. The taxpayers paid the cost—more than $100,000 per year. The net result, in the words of the mayor who opposed the compromise: "It is now clear who is running the city of Flint—and it sure isn't the City Council or its appointed managers."

Flint, cannot. These cities must pay top dollar for top managers or settle for lower quality at less cost.

The compensation paid to Flint's non-civil-service executive managers (the city manager, the finance director, the city attorney) was not comparable to that paid similar executives in either the public or the private sector. Moreover, not only were executive managers paid less than their counterparts, they were paid less than the employees they supervised. This resulted from the fact that civil service determined compensation primarily on the basis of time on the job (seniority). Several department and division heads (director of public works, fire chief) and assistant department heads (assistant city attorney, assistant finance director) had been employed by the city for a considerable period of time, and their seniority was reflected in their compensation. Although the council had to both approve the civil-service pay structure and set the salaries of the city manager, the finance director, and the city attorney, the latter task was much more difficult politically than the former.

As Exhibit 19 illustrates, the 1973 City Council, at the urging of the finance director, adopted a new executive-compensation ordinance. This ordinance fixed the city manager's salary at 10 percent higher than that of the highest-paid employee he supervised and tied the salaries of the finance director and the city attorney to that received by the city manager. This change corrected the internal problem, but the fact remained that Flint's executive managers still were paid less than their counterparts in the private sector.

While it is difficult to compare the salaries of middle- and upper-level managers in Flint with those of comparable positions in the private sector, it is possible to examine the growth in compensation of municipal managers compared with that of general city employees. An analysis performed by the finance office indicated that during the period from 1964 to 1973 the salaries of average city employees, such as policemen or firemen, increased nearly 160 percent, while those of a middle manager (division head) and of a department director increased from 120 to 130 percent. During the same period, the salaries of the city manager and the finance director (after the increase described in Exhibit 19) increased 80 percent and 98 percent, respectively—about one-half the rate of increase for the employees they supervised.

Managers in Flint had no ability to relate compensation to performance. Managers' salaries were set by the City Council within the civil-service classification structure and could not be adjusted solely on the basis of performance. In addition, managers could only recommend to civil service that the initial pay level of a management position be increased in order to attract qualified personnel. This type of request was called a "discretionary salary increase," which meant that a person newly hired by the city would be paid at a level comparable to that of a person who had worked for the city in that

position for up to four years. For instance, in 1972 the top candidate for the position of traffic engineer held the same position in the neighboring city of Saginaw. The Civil Service Commission initially set a salary level for this position that was significantly lower than the salary the candidate received in that city. After four months of delay and argument, civil service finally agreed to raise the compensation level by assigning the four-year discretionary rate. This action enabled Flint to obtain the services of a qualified manager. Such accommodation to management was rare, despite the importance of compensation in attracting qualified managers.

In addition to seniority, civil service determined a manager's classification and thus the compensation he would receive on the basis of the number of people supervised and the size of the budgets controlled. This created a perverse situation in which a manager had a possible incentive to make conditions within the city worse, not better. For example, as crime increased within the city, the police chief could lobby for more men, a larger budget, and, ultimately, greater compensation for himself. If crime decreased, the case could be made that both the police chief's budget and the number of employees he supervised should be decreased, leaving no basis for requesting greater compensation and, in fact, creating a basis for recommending a decrease in compensation.

An illustration of this occurred in July 1973, when the city manager transferred eight stockkeepers from the Purchasing Department to the Department of Public Works. The purchasing director opposed the move and urged the city's unions to initiate a lawsuit blocking the manager from making this transfer. The motivation of the purchasing director was understandable: his civil-service classification, and hence his compensation, was based primarily on the number of people he supervised. Therefore, losing eight stockkeepers—almost a third of the employees he managed—could have resulted in a lower classification and a lower level of compensation. He had a direct incentive

EXHIBIT 19

Executive Managers Paid Less Than Employees They Supervise

Would you take a new job that involved significantly greater responsibilities, a pay cut of $1,000, and a situation in which your salary was less than those of the people you supervised? This is what the City Council inadvertently asked its new finance director to do.

In January 1973, the Flint City Council selected the city's director of community development to become the next director of finance. The director of finance was one of four positions reporting directly to the City Council. The day after he took office, an article appeared in the newspaper reporting that the new director of finance was taking a $1,000 pay cut by changing jobs.

This news surprised a number of people, especially the new director. According to his calculations, the salaries were approximately the same: $24,800. What he failed to realize was that the job change happened to correspond with the anniversary of his employment with the city. Under civil service rules, this automatically meant a $1,000 increase in the salary in the previous job. The director of finance job was not covered by civil service and did not benefit from automatic increases. The article further pointed out that a number of managerial employees in civil service jobs earned more than the council appointees to whom they were responsible.

The news article had also surprised the mayor, who said, frankly, that he was not aware of these facts. The director of finance prepared an analysis for the mayor proposing a change in executive salary structure. The table below presents the results of that analysis. It shows, among other things, that the four council-appointed officials (indicated in the table by an asterisk) earned less than the civil servants they supervised.

(continued on page 76)

to resist the change. The efficiency of the purchasing function and the storage and distribution function received very little consideration in this issue.

Another condition that affected the motivation of Flint's municipal managers was their place of residence. The charter demanded that the four executive managers appointed by the council live within Flint, but in 1974 almost 50 percent of the city's other managers lived outside the city limits.

This situation generated considerable concern on the part of citizens and citizens' groups, especially minorities, who believed that the people who were responsible for formulating and implementing public policies and programs should have to live with the consequences.

In December 1972, the city manager recommended to the council that all future division and department heads, in addition to council appointees, become residents of

EXHIBIT 19 (cont'd)

SALARIES OF MANAGERIAL PERSONNEL, CITY OF FLINT

Position	Salary	Supervisor
Administrator, hospital	$ 44,800	Hospital board of directors
Director, health	40,000+	City manager and county Board of Commissioners
Assistant administrator, hospital	30,500	Administrator, hospital
Director, public works	29,700	City manager
Director, community development	29,700	City manager
*City manager	28,000	City Council
Deputy city attorney	27,700	City attorney
Superintendent, water	27,700	Director, public works
Chief of police	27,300	City manager
Fire chief	26,900	City manager
Superintendent, parks and recreation	26,400	Park board
City engineer	25,200	Director, public works
City assessor	25,200	Finance director
City treasurer	25,200	Finance director
*City attorney	24,800	City Council
*Finance director	24,800	City Council
Director, nursing services	24,800	Administrator, hospital
Director, civil service	24,600	Civil Service Commission
Director, nursing school	22,000	Administrator, hospital
*City clerk	19,500	City Council

A second table compared the salaries of other positions considered comparable to that of the city manager. This comparison, showed that the Flint city manager was valued far less highly than the superintendent of the city's Board of Education, an organization approximately equivalent in size to the city government; the president of Genesee Community College; and the chancellor of the University of Michigan—Flint, both considerably smaller than city government. The manager's salary also compared unfavorable with those of city managers of nearby communities, all of which had less than half the population of Flint.

(continued)

the city within one year of their employment. Limiting the application of this policy to future management personnel ensured that existing employees, many of whom had made major financial commitments to their homes outside of the city, would not suffer unduly by a change in the employment rules. The manager also recommended that the civil service adopt a procedure that, all other things being equal, preference for promotion would be given to Flint residents. It was felt that this policy would provide an incentive for those managers who wanted to advance to higher levels to become residents of the city on their own accord. This policy was not intended to sacrifice competency for

EXHIBIT 19 (cont'd)

SALARIES OF NONCITY POSITIONS COMPARABLE TO CITY MANAGER

Position	Salary	Comments
Superintendent, Board of Education	$ 38,800	Three-year contract plus house
President, Genesee Community College	32,000	Multi-year contract plus house
Chancellor, UM-Flint	40,000+	Multi-year contract plus house
City manager, Ann Arbor	37,200	
City manager, Pontiac	34,600	
City manager, Saginaw	36,000	Contract
City manager, Midland	32,500	
City manager, Flint	28,000	

This analysis concluded with a recommended method for setting the salaries of the city manager and the other three appointed officials in relationship to the civil servants they supervised. The city manager's salary was to be set at 15 percent above that of the highest-paid department head he supervised; the director of finance and the city attorney's salaries would be set at 89 percent and the city clerk's at 70 percent of the city manager's salary.

The initial proposal was greeted unenthusiastically by the City Council. Privately, council members did not disagree with its logic, nor with the need to adjust appointed officials' salaries; they especially liked the idea that once this decision was made, future salary increases would no longer be the subject of public discussion. However, 1973 was an election year, and prospects for a tight budget were looming. The council was thus not in a mood to consider what was a politically unpopular subject (second only in unpopularity to the council's consideration of its own salaries). In mid-March, however, a compromise was reached to pay the manager 10 percent more than the department heads he supervised. The problem was resolved once and for all.

residency; rather, it was intended to add one additional criterion to other job-related criteria such as training, experience, and demonstrated performance. Neither the City Council nor the Civil Service Commission acted on this recommendation, which was opposed by the majority of Flint's employees and by all of the municipal employee unions.

A final condition affecting managerial motivation was a pervasive lack of professionalism. An illustration of this situation involved the chief of police. In November 1973, the police chief, acting as a private consultant, prepared a report for the Airport Commission outlining steps that it should take to make the city's airport more secure.

EXHIBIT 20

City Attorney Accuses City Manager of Stealing Official Documents

In May 1974, Flint's city manager was preparing to leave his position during the following month. He began the arduous task of putting his books, personal papers, newspaper clippings, and the like in order for ultimate shipment. Prior to departing on a two-day trip on city business, the city manager packed all of his boxes, put them in his car, and took them home.

No one was more surprised than the city manager when he learned by telephone that the city attorney—his professional colleague and legal counsel—had filed a complaint with the office of the county prosecutor suggesting that the city manager had illegally removed official books, papers, and records from his office. If true, this was a felony. The City Council members were equally surprised. The city attorney had never made this allegation to the city manager or to the council.

The Genesee County prosecutor reluctantly agreed to review this matter. After examining the situation, he concluded, "It is our unequivocal legal conclusion and judgment that the city manager has not violated the terms and provisions of the aforementioned statute." The prosecutor's opinion went on to state that the materials the city manager had taken were not official books, papers, or records. Moreover, to be in violation of the law required that such material be taken with the willful intent not to return it. No such intent had been alleged or proven. Furthermore, the prosecutor's opinion noted, until the city manager officially left office, he was free to take home anything he wanted.

An alert employee in the Finance Department questioned the nature of the $1,000 invoice submitted to pay the police chief in this private capacity. Preparing such a report as a private consultant represented a potentially serious conflict of interest, since the security of the airport was part of the job that the taxpayers of Flint were already paying the chief of police to perform. When confronted, the chief agreed to withdraw the invoice and absorb whatever costs had been incurred. As Exhibit 20 illustrates, this example was not an isolated occurrence.

Because municipal managers were insulated from accountability by civil service and by their participation in unions, there was little incentive to develop a strong sense of professionalism. Few managers perceived a responsibility to serve as an independent force between the highly political City Council and the highly unionized bureaucracy. Few saw a reason to inform the council of the consequences of their actions or to resist the encroachments of organized employees into areas of management responsibilities. There was no sense in Flint of a management team working in harmony to achieve community objectives that would make Flint a more desirable place to live and to work. Instead, there was a collection of individuals who, for

---

EXHIBIT 21

Council Grants Top Administrators First Written Employment Agreement in City's History

"Professionalism be damned!" a Flint councilman stated. "If you submit a resignation, whether you mean it or not, I'll accept it." This councilman was reacting to a decision by the city manager and the finance director to submit *pro forma* resignations to the newly elected City Council.

In a letter to the City Council members, five of whom were new and only one of whom had selected the present city manager, the administrators asked the council members to take ninety days to carefully consider what they wanted to do during their term of office and who they wanted to help them get it done. The letter stated, "As professional administrators, we feel an obligation to allow you complete freedom in selecting a management team that will be able to administer your policies and programs."

Both made it clear that they wanted to remain in their current positions, but only if the new City Council—several members of which had campaigned on the promise that they would fire the city manager and the finance director if elected—wanted them to stay. They indicated that this type of resignation was a standard procedure in many public and private businesses when the board of directors or policy-making body changed.

The finance director summarized the administrators' case by saying, "Administrators are caught between a bureaucracy, over which they have little control, and the council. Prior administrators chose the bureaucracy, and we choose the council. If the council doesn't choose us, we'll go."

In addition to an affirmation of support, the city manager and the finance director asked the council for an employment contract. Such a contract would allow the council to terminate their employment whenever they desired, but would require payment of severance pay if they chose to do so.

(continued on page 80)

---

the most part, came at eight and left at five and generally exhibited a "don't rock the boat" attitude. As one veteran city hall employee noted, "Professionalism just doesn't pay in city government."

Attempts by municipal managers to act in a professional manner were not supported by the City Council. In the example given in Exhibit 21, the premise underlying the city manager's and finance director's *pro forma* resignations and their request for an employment agreement was that professional managers must be willing to risk their jobs if necessary in order to be effective. When job security becomes more important than the quality of the job being done and the standards on which performance is based, the public interest is not served. The council's

EXHIBIT 21 (cont'd)

"Working on a week-to-week basis," the city manager observed, "makes it difficult to implement the council's programs." The manager argued that treading on the brink of instant unemployment did not induce confidence, and that if the bureaucracy did not know that the council was firmly behind its administrators, it would be extremely difficult to get things done.

Flint's mayor applauded the approach taken by the city's top administrators. He told two local service clubs, "The lack of a contract subjects them to week-by-week political pressures. If we can't give them a vote of confidence, they shouldn't be there. We're not going to get anything done."

A councilwoman echoed the mayor's sentiments. She told the City Council, "All the other city employees have contracts—even the City Council has a two-year contract." Other council members, however, were less supportive. Some felt it was a power play. Others indicated that the administrators should not be given contracts at all, but instead should be fired.

An important supporter of the employment contract was the UAW's political-action arm. The local press also supported the idea. In an editorial, the *Flint Journal* observed, "There can be no doubt that there is a sound basis for their contention that the present week-to-week arrangement, with its growing pressures, is no longer tolerable. Job security cannot be a top priority for those operating at the higher levels of management, particularly in government. But a reasonable freedom from job insecurity is essential, particularly in the professional management field."

Before the ninety days were up, the council, by a vote of 5–4, endorsed the principle of an employment agreement but referred the substance of an agreement to a three-member committee. In early February, Flint's city manager and finance director were offered a contract—of a sort. The city manager noted that this contract did little more than put into writing what had been past practice, but he told newspaper reporters, "No negotiated agreement is wholly satisfactory to either side." The finance director added, "What we've gained outweighs the negatives. We're not happy with some provisions of the contract, but these can be reviewed in the future."

response indicates that this kind of professionalism was not high on the list of qualities it wanted in its municipal managers.

The most important consequence of a situation in which municipal managers lack both adequate management skills and a motivation to use the skills they have is poor government performance. In the absence of clear measures of performance, it is difficult to identify the immediate consequences of poor management; in some instances, however, the results are inescapable. One Flint manager in 1972 ordered a work crew to wash down a city street without checking to see whether the temperature was below freezing. Within minutes the street, in the words of one observer, "looked like a giant ice-skating rink." Embarrassed, the manager

EXHIBIT 22

Public-Works Crew Repaves Vacated Street

"Probably a half-dozen people should have picked it up," said the director of Flint's Department of Public Works (DPW). He was attempting to explain how one of his crews had managed to repave a stretch of a city street which had been vacated the previous year. The purpose of vacating the street was to permit the Buick Motor Division to construct a new personnel building, partly utilizing the vacated street.

The DPW director explained that the resurfacing of the street had been scheduled for the previous year, but that the program for that year had not been completed. He further explained that the previous year's list of unfinished resurfacings had been added to the current list, and that there was no system to monitor changes in the status of streets to be resurfaced. He did not indicate why the streets scheduled for repaving in the earlier year had not been completed.

The director pointed out that his department had a budget of more than $20 million annually and was responsible for services ranging from water supply and traffic engineering to a municipal garage and all commercial and housing inspections. It was extremely difficult, he added, to control such a diverse range of services.

quickly sent out salt crews to melt the ice. Another Flint manager was responsible for demolishing by mistake the home of a seventy-seven-year-old grandmother. And, as the story presented in Exhibit 22 recounts, still another ordered a city street to be paved—only to find out later that it had been vacated a year earlier.

Despite the lack of positive incentives, there were examples of superior management performance in Flint. Exhibit 23 indicates in dramatic fashion how good management "turned around" conditions within the Department of Community Development. The credit for this turnaround is primarily due to the former director, an urban planner, who had had the courage to admit that he lacked the skills required to manage a complex business with a $10 million annual budget. The city benefited immeasurably

from his honesty and courage in stepping down to let a more qualified person take his place. Unfortunately, few managers in Flint had the same sense of personal integrity.

As the community-development story indicates, the absence of adequate management skills resulted in an inability to manage federally funded development programs. A history of mismanagement caused the city of Flint considerable embarrassment and created an extremely negative image with federal departments, especially HUD. Prior to assuming his position in December 1971, Flint's new city manager called HUD's Detroit area office to inquire about the status of Flint's eight urban-renewal programs as well as its public-housing program. He was told that Flint's management of housing programs was the worst in Michigan and possibly the worst in the entire Midwest region. Whether or not

EXHIBIT 23

Better Management Can Make a Difference

It seemed unbelievable. The Department of Housing and Urban Development was giving Flint $560,000 more than it had requested for the next fiscal year. What was more unbelievable was that it was doing so in recognition of significant improvement in performance during the last fiscal year.

To understand just how unbelievable this was requires a brief review of the department's history. In 1971, when the new director of community development assumed his position, the department had serious management problems. The Housing Commission, which advised the department on public-housing policy, had threatened a mass resignation over its frustration with the management of public housing. One commissioner stated, "A lack of professionalism and finesse permeates this department." The council had transferred responsibility for program finance and accounting to the finance director because of its fear that the Community Development Department was mismanaging funds. A citizens' group representing an urban-renewal area had retained an attorney and was petitioning for a full-scale investigation of the department. They alleged gross nonperformance and threatened litigation if the council failed to act. A just-completed management consultant's report indicated that the department had no control over the activities it performed and had established ambitious goals it did not have the capacity to achieve. The city's application for annual funding had not been approved by HUD because the city and the department lacked an acceptable affirmative action program. Last, and most important, the department had been unable to spend $3.5 (or 25 percent) of the $13.5 million it had received in federal funds over the past three years. In response to these and other problems, the City Council had launched a full-scale investigation of the department.

Reacting to this crisis, the new director of community development made a number of changes in the department. First, an acceptable affirmative action program was prepared and fiscal-year funding was obtained from HUD. Then, the department was reorganized to pinpoint project as well as functional responsibility, something the previous structure did not do. Project managers were designated to be responsible for the specific requirements of each project area and to

(continued)

this was true may be debatable; the critical point is that HUD officials believed it. As a result, Flint experienced chronic difficulty in gaining approval for federal funding.

The importance of improving management skills and managerial motivation was underscored by Flint's congressman, who in 1974 noted that

in two years Flint has gained a capacity to control its destiny, and federal officials in Washington have confidence in the city's ability to manage

EXHIBIT 23 (cont'd)

communicate with the project residents. Third, department personnel were shifted (to the extent permitted by civil service) in an attempt to match job requirements with personal skills. Fourth, a series of meetings was held with the City Council, the Public Housing Commission, the citizen district councils that represented the urban-renewal area residents, and HUD representatives for the purpose of exchanging information concerning departmental improvements. Next, in order to control program activity, a performance and financial-control system was developed and implemented. Sixth, major private interests in the community were enlisted to participate in the redevelopment activities: the University of Michigan agreed to relocate its campus in the heart of an urban-renewal area; the Buick Motor Division and two local trucking firms agreed to purchase the land within a proposed industrial park, which previously had been unsuccessful in attracting investors.

Last, the new director recognized that one of the major problems with the urban-renewal program was that it had promised more than could be delivered. As a result, he recommended concentration of resources on "target areas"—defined as areas that could be developed within a five-year period, given realistic estimates of funding. This meant that only one-fifth of what had been planned for the program would be completed in five years. After a long and difficult debate, the council and area residents accepted this approach as being the only realistic option. As one citizen put it, "Perhaps now the Department of Community Development has stopped lying to us."

The results of these changes were significant and measurable. The level of confidence of residents of urban-renewal areas rose appreciably. Complaints to the City Council, though not completely eliminated, were reduced significantly. The council discontinued its investigation, and HUD approved the city's 1972 budget request earlier than the budget had ever been approved. Moreover, the city was able to spend all the money it received during the next fiscal year, and as a result was awarded $560,000 more for the following year than it had initially requested.

In 1971 the city's eight urban-renewal projects covered approximately 3,000 acres of the city and affected almost 35,000 residents. It was estimated that it would cost approximately $200 million ($60 million, city; $140 million, federal government) to complete these projects. At current funding levels, this would take almost fifty years.

---

itself. . . . Flint's improved reputation in Washington has enhanced the city's ability to tap money sources there. There is a lot of competition among cities for federal money, and cities that are perceived as being well managed stand a better chance to get federal money.[1]

The unionization of middle managers and supervisory personnel was another consequence of a situation in which managers were neither compensated nor rewarded. In 1972 middle managers formed their own employee association so that they could bargain collectively for better compensation and working conditions. Their motivation appeared to stem from two sources: on the one hand, they were tired of being treated in the same category as general employees; on the other hand, they wanted to protect their gains. Many of them realized that they had been promoted by civil service to jobs they were not fully equipped to perform. Therefore, an employee association (a euphemism for a union) might better protect them against potential action by a city manager or the City Council.

Members of the Association of Middle Managers continued to refer to themselves as managers, although at the bargaining table this definition was often unclear. In 1973, for example, this association—which included the supervisor of the water division (the director of an $8 million business), the waste-collection supervisor (the director of a $1.5 million business), the city treasurer, the city assessor, and other important management personnel—demanded that its members be paid for overtime. The line between general employees and managers had indeed been blurred.

Perhaps the most important consequence of the absence of management skills in Flint was the necessity to use management skills from the private sector. This was done in three ways: (1) the establishment of special task forces, (2) the use of management consultants, and (3) the development of contracts with the private sector for the delivery of some municipal services.

In 1971, the mayor created a special task force to develop a plan for the resumption of bus service in Flint. This service had been suspended ten months earlier because of the bankruptcy of the private bus company. Similarly, in 1972, the mayor selected a number of the city's foremost computer experts to serve on a data-processing task force. The purpose of this effort was to help the city develop a five-year plan to improve its data-processing capability. As a result of their efforts, the City Council ultimately adopted a $5 million program to develop

and install a new data-processing system, a testament to the quality of the work performed by this task force.

Historically, the city of Flint had not used management consultants wisely. This situation reflected the fact that in most cases the work to be done by consultants was not properly defined prior to the initiation of the project. As a result, it was never clear whether the consultant had performed the task as envisioned or whether the city had gotten an inferior product. After 1971, the City Council adopted a procedure of specifying, in detailed terms, the products to be produced by each consultant prior to the initiation of work. In most cases, city personnel were assigned to work with the consultants to ensure that the expertise gained in preparing particular products did not leave with the consultants. In this manner, the city was able to extract maximum value from the consultants and, in the process, compensate for the absence of internal management skills.

On balance, Flint was not successful in negotiating private-sector contracts for the delivery of municipal services. The city's major effort in this area, however, was successful. As the case presented in Exhibit 24 describes, the city successfully contracted with the private sector for the provision of all legal services, replacing a staff of seven assistant city attorneys.

In other areas, the idea of "privatizing" city services was raised but discarded. In 1972, the city manager was asked by the City Council to analyze the possibility of contracting with the private sector for vehicle-maintenance, waste-collection, and building-maintenance services. This trial balloon had barely lifted before it was punctured by a barrage of union objections. Union leaders threatened slowdowns, walkouts, and even a strike if this idea was considered prior to full negotiations with all affected employee groups. Attempts to explain that this effort was exploratory were lost in the emotions that this issue raised with the rank-and-file employees and their representatives.

The civil-service director was equally op-

EXHIBIT 24

City Uses Private Attorneys—For a While

The city's first major effort to contract with the private sector for the provision of services formerly provided by city employees occurred in a most unlikely area—the city attorney's office.

The city attorney, hired by the new City Council in 1971, faced a very difficult situation. The four senior assistant attorneys (there were seven in total) were both ineffective and, because of civil service, unremovable. As Flint's mayor stated, "The taxpayers are not getting their money's worth as far as the city's attorneys are concerned."

The city attorney had almost no power to deal with this situation. Because of civil service rules, he could not lay off the senior assistants until he had laid off those assistants who had been most recently hired. He couldn't do this because the latter were doing most of the work. He couldn't fire the incompetents because incompetency was difficult to prove and civil service did not recognize it as grounds for dismissal. In September 1972, in near-desperation, the city attorney proposed to the council that all seven assistant city attorneys be eliminated from his budget on the grounds of economic inefficiency. The city attorney argued that if he were allowed to use his entire budget to obtain legal services from the private sector, he could handle the same caseload while saving almost $50,000 a year—roughly one-fourth his budget.

Primarily because two attorneys served on the City Council, this request was approved. The action was generally accepted by the public as a step toward more effective city government. While the proposed budget saving did not materialize, the quality of legal representation increased dramatically. As one private attorney put it, "After the council's action, we actually had to do our homework in arguing a case against the city."

The assistant city attorneys, who had formed a union only a month before their dismissal, appealed their case to the Michigan Employment Relations Commission (MERC), charging the city with an unfair labor practice. In addition, they filed a lawsuit against the city seeking to ban the hiring of private lawyers. After almost two years of argumentation, MERC upheld the assistant city attorneys' position and ordered the city to reinstate them with back pay. A circuit court ruling reached the same conclusion. Both judgments were appealed to the Michigan Court of Appeals.

This apparent success in the "privatization" of a city service was short-lived. In April 1974, the Michigan Supreme Court refused to hear an appeal of the lower-court ruling against the city. Consequently, the city had to pay the difference between the money the assistant city attorneys actually earned during their absence from the city and the money they would have earned with the city, and hire back those who wanted to return.

posed. He stated that, in accordance with civil-service rules and regulations, the city was prohibited from contracting with the private sector for any service that existing city employees could provide, and he suggested that the idea be dropped. Department heads were openly skeptical and some were critical. The director of public works, the department responsible for the services mentioned by the council, was extremely negative. Using waste collection as an example, he argued that a private contractor would quote an unreasonably low bid, obtain the city's business, wait until the city had sold its equipment and transferred its employees, and then drastically increase its price. In his judgment, privatization would lead to an increase, not a decrease, in the cost of these services. The city, he contended, was providing services as cheaply as possible. He pointed out that the city collected garbage at roughly 25 cents per household per week, and that this could not be duplicated by any private contractor.

The most significant question about privatization was raised by a member of the council who asked whether the city had the ability to compare the costs of private versus public provision of specific services. Lacking a cost-accounting system, the city actually was *not* able to determine the full costs of providing city services. For example, the waste-collection cost figure used by the public works director did not include capital costs (trucks and other equipment), the value of space used in municipal buildings, the cost of city overhead services (financial and personnel support services), fringe benefits (budgeted centrally), or an allocation of departmental overhead costs. The cost estimates included only the direct costs of labor and materials— hardly an appropriate basis for comparisons with private-sector service costs.

The net result of union opposition to privatization was a council decision to discontinue consideration of the idea, pending the development of better information about city services. Union pressure, restrictive civil service regulations, lack of accurate cost information, and lack of an analytical staff capable of presenting alternative ways to implement such a program combined to kill the idea at its inception.

Perhaps the most far-reaching proposal to use private-sector skills in Flint to compensate for the lack of management expertise and motivation within the city was set forth in a report prepared for the Mott Foundation in 1974. This study was based on the premise that the city did not have managers with the skills needed to successfully administer the following community-development projects:

- construction of the University of Michigan–Flint campus (estimated development cost $60 million)
- development of a new residential community in an urban-renewal project area adjacent to the new campus (estimated development cost $30 million)
- completion of a river-beautification and flood-control project in the center of the city adjacent to both the new campus and the urban-renewal project area (estimated development cost $10 million)
- development of an industrial park in an urban-renewal area (estimated development cost $80 million)
- completion of a major freeway through the heart of the city (estimated development cost $40 million)

Given the hiring constraints imposed by civil service, the inability to pay competitive salaries, and the uncertainties posed by charter revision, the probability of attracting qualified managers within the city to administer these projects seemed low. In response to this situation, the Mott Foundation commissioned a study to examine the feasibility of incorporating a nonprofit development company with which the city would contract for the management of these projects. The absence of private-sector leadership and the reluctance of city officials to lose control over development projects combined to defeat this idea.

Opportunities for Improvement

Nothing is more important to the successful performance of a local government than the will to manage. Marvin Bower, the former managing director of McKinsey and Company and a man whose career has paralleled the development of the management-consulting profession, emphasized the importance of the will to manage in this manner:

The key to corporate success is a leader with a strong will to manage, who inspires and requires able people to work purposely and effectively through simple and traditional managing processes that are integrated into a management program or system tailored to the nature and the environment of the business. [2]

Although Bower was writing primarily about managers in private corporations, the will to manage is no less important in a public business.

The will to manage depends on one critical factor: a manager who views himself as a manager. Without this perception, the will to manage has little meaning. In most cases, this requirement was not met in Flint. Many managers did not view themselves as professionals, distinct from the employees they supervised and responsible to the City Council for using available resources to achieve community objectives. The steps that could be taken to change this condition in Flint are summarized as follows:

Prepare a management directory. After developing criteria for determining who is and who is not a manager, the city should compile a directory of employees who are recognized as part of management. This directory, organized according to line and staff departments, would include the name of each manager, his job title, and his work telephone number. This directory should be distributed to all managers and to external organizations that interact with city departments. Recognition as managers should provide a positive stimulus to managers at all

levels. Development of a management directory, however, might have the greatest impact at the supervisory level, in that supervisors (in title) who do not have management responsibilities would be identified and their job titles and descriptions amended to coincide with their actual responsibilities.

Develop a management-compensation plan related to managerial performance. Once managers have been identified as a separate employment group, the city should develop a compensation formula that would accomplish three objectives:

- Provide managers with salaries and fringe-benefit packages comparable to those received by private-sector managers with similar responsibilities.
- Allow managers to select the form of indirect compensation that best meets their individual needs. For instance, a manager with nine children may wish to have more health-insurance coverage instead of increased vacation time. A comparable manager may wish the opposite: more vacation time and less health coverage. Having determined the dollar value of each indirect benefit and the total dollar value each management group member will be allowed, the individual manager should be given the flexibility to select the indirect benefits that suit his or her particular needs.
- Establish a mechanism (e.g., an annual bonus system) for recognizing and rewarding superior performance by individual managers. This recognition would be in the form of increased compensation.

In some instances nonmonetary forms of compensation may be an acceptable substitute for direct monetary compensation. Therefore, in conjunction with the development of a revised compensation plan, a system should be developed whereby the council and the city manager publicly recognize and give credit for superior performance by managers throughout city government.

Terminate union representation for identified managers. Once managers have been clearly identified and rewarded by appropriate compensation, a basis will have been established for removing them from union representation. Ideally, this will be accomplished by managers themselves, as they recognize their professional status and realize that they need not be organized to receive adequate compensation for their performance.

Provide executive managers with employment contracts. Recognition and appreciation of management should start at the top. Therefore, the council should develop employment agreements with all the managers it appoints, thereby providing a clear statement of the political support that will be afforded to its management team. Such contracts need not be more costly, in terms of salary or fringe benefits, than a noncontract arrangement.

Even if managers in Flint truly have a will to manage municipal operations for performance, they may need to improve their capacity to do so. Contrary to the old maxim, where there is a will there is not always a way. Other actions must be taken. Changes in personnel policies and procedures (such as actively recruiting managers with demonstrated management skills, allowing executive managers discretion in filling all top-management positions, basing promotions primarily on assessments of ability to perform in higher-level management positions, and providing managers with discretion in terminating employment on the basis of poor performance) are discussed in the next chapter. The use of advanced management tools, the establishment of improved financial practices, and the development of a more responsive government structure can also improve managerial competence. These factors are discussed in subsequent chapters. Here we address four specific opportunities for improving the skills of managers in Flint: (1) improved management training, (2) ex-change of managers with comparable local governments, (3) exchange of managers with private corporations, and (4) contracts with the private sector for the delivery of municipal services.

Develop and implement a management-training program. A management-training program (which should be mandatory for all managers) should be structured around the major elements of the management process. Stressing the difference between technical skills and management skills, this program would reinforce the will to manage and develop practical tools for translating intent into effective action. Wherever possible, management training should be conducted in the manager's work environment, thereby ensuring that the constraints under which he normally operates are taken into consideration. This type of training program could draw on the considerable resources available from the University of Michigan, the General Motors Institute, and the Mott Community College. To achieve maximum success, training opportunities should be supplemented by career planning and counseling services, so that managers know what skills they need to develop and why.

Develop a local-government management exchange program. Development of management skills through sharing practical experience could be accomplished by a program in which Flint's managers exchanged positions with comparable managers in other local governments in the state. For example, the deputy city manager for operations could spend a month in Grand Rapids, a city of similar size, while his counterpart worked in the city of Flint. By exposing managers to different operational methods and problem-solving techniques, skills and experience could be broadened and motivation improved.

Develop a private-sector management exchange program. In the short run, improving the performance of Flint's city government would be facilitated by taking advantage of external management skills. The City Council should continue its efforts to develop an executive interchange program with General Motors. Such a program would encourage General Motors to permit its management personnel to take leaves of absence for specified periods of time in order to work for the city of Flint on public-sector problems. In some instances, the program could work the other way, placing municipal managers in management positions within General Motors. Exchanging managers not only would improve management skills, it would also improve relationships between the city and its most important corporate citizen.

Develop a "privatization" program. Entering into contracts with private-sector institutions for the delivery of specific public services—the privatization of city services—offers an excellent opportunity to take advantage of external management skills and meet the imperatives imposed by growing financial constraints. In the long run, use of the private sector may be the most economical way to provide high-quality services.

The difficulty of designing and implementing a privatization program should not be underestimated, especially in view of the fact that unions are certain to be opposed to such a program. The city would need an analytical staff with the capacity to (1) prepare "full-cost" analyses of selected city services, (2) identify performance measures for these services, (3) compare city performance against that achieved by the private sector, and (4) recommend services eligible for a privatization program. Without adequate staff support and information, the council will not have a basis for successfully implementing such a program.

In order to determine which services are eligible for privatization, some key questions should be considered:

- Is the activity potentially eligible for "privatization" separable from other government activities?
- Are citizens sensitive to the way in which the service is provided?
- Can performance measures for the service

be quantified?
- Is there a demonstrated inability of the city to deliver the service efficiently or effectively?
- Is there proven capability to perform the service in the private sector?
- Do private-sector institutions have a particular advantage in the delivery of the service because of economies of scale or specialization?
- Is the service one for which the city has difficulty recruiting (at comparable salaries) a cadre of professionals and experts?
- Is the bureaucratic mode of operation an impediment to successfully implementing the program?
- Is the program or service one in which time is a critical factor?
- Is technology for the program changing rapidly?

Once eligible services have been selected, the city has a number of options for converting them to private delivery. The city could (1) leave the provision of required services to the private market without intervention or regulation, (2) require residents to acquire a service but leave its provision to the private sector, (3) control the private provision of services through franchises, permits, or limitations on profits or fees, (4) contract with a private supplier for the provision of a total service, (5) contract with a private supplier for partial service delivery in specified geographical areas, (6) stimulate the private sector to take desired actions through tax incentives or incentive payments.

Having selected services eligible for privatization and the most appropriate way of achieving this end, the city must determine whether a significant savings to the taxpayer can be realized. This estimate should be based on a careful consideration of comparative costs. In many cases, privatization would require laying off or transferring city employees. In some cases, equipment would need to be sold or transferred and detailed control procedures instituted. Such efforts would not be justified unless the benefits of privatization were significant.

Finally, successful privatization of services depends on developing a contract that will adequately control the performance of a private supplier and protect the interests of the city. Such a contract should be based on clear performance standards and should establish precise targets that can be monitored by the city. Both penalties for poor performance and incentives for good performance must be included. Monitoring and evaluating an established contract—and periodically checking with citizens to ensure that the quality of services has not eroded—

are necessary procedures in the successful implementation of such a program.

Taking advantage of these opportunities would not be easy, but the benefits of doing so would be considerable. As Fred Malik, former deputy director of the U.S. Office of Management and Budget, has observed, "Public management is the toughest job in the country. The stakes are so high and the demands are so constant that public purposes can be achieved only if our organizations are managed by able, prepared, and committed people."

CHAPTER 7

Municipal Employees and Employee Unions

Public employees—civil service professionals, clerical workers, blue-collar laborers, you name it—are the people who make a city run, not the politicians, the political appointees, and the high-priced consultants.

Jerry Wurf
President, American Federation of State and County and Municipal Employees

The issue boils down to whether elected officials or public employees are going to manage the city's business.

Wes Uhlman
Mayor of Seattle

Local government is a labor-intensive business in which the delivery of goods and services is dependent on municipal employees—those who work in nonmanagerial positions. Unlike other labor-intensive activities such as agriculture, opportunities to substitute capital equipment for manpower in local government are extremely limited. This fact adds force to Jerry Wurf's conclusion that municipal employees are "the people who make a city run."

The role of municipal employees within city governments has changed dramatically during the past century. In the late nineteenth and early twentieth centuries, municipal employees often represented pawns in a political process in which successful political candidates replaced existing employees with their own political supporters, or "ward heelers." Local government jobs—the spoils of political victory—were distributed not

only at top-management or appointive levels (department and division heads) but also at the rank-and-file levels (street cleaners, firemen, garbage workers, policemen, and the like). As a result, county or city government employment was often temporary and was based on the vicissitudes of the political process.

The civil-service reform movement attempted to end the spoils system. Under civil service, employees are supposed to be hired, promoted, and compensated on the basis of their individual merit, not their political allegiance. This system was designed to ensure that the best-qualified people received government jobs, thereby providing greater continuity of employment as well as more uniform and competent delivery of municipal services. To guard against the "corrupting" influence of politics, most civil-service systems were established on an autonomous basis, outside the control of elected officials. Because of the severity of prior political abuses, few citizens disagreed with the progressive objectives of early civil-service reforms. Consequently, most city and county governments, especially the larger and older ones, operate today under some form of civil-service system.

Unfortunately, instead of improving the quality of services by providing security for municipal employees, civil service has often had the opposite effect. Under many civil-service systems, positions are filled on the basis of written examinations that attempt, but very often fail, to measure performance; promotions occur only from within the system as existing employees are shielded from outside competition; compensation increases are automatic—based on time served, not on demonstrated performance; and employees cannot be disciplined without following an arduous, time-consuming process. By blurring the link between employee productivity and decisions related to hiring, promotion, compensation, and discipline, civil-service systems have almost eliminated the very principle of merit that led to their creation.[1] In short, civil service in many cities has become a meritless system in which existing employees are protected from objective evaluation and competition in the same manner that political ward heelers were once protected from public accountability by the politicians they helped elect. Civil service in the 1970s may represent a spoils system in reverse.

More significant than civil-service systems are municipal employee unions. Public employee unions may have a more profound effect on the performance of local government than any other single factor. Building on the success of private-sector unions, and responding to new legislation permitting or requiring collective bargaining, membership in municipal unions and employee associations has expanded dramatically during the past few years. A total of 3.8 million, or 56 percent, of all full-time local government employees belonged to employee organiza-

tions in October 1974. This figure represented a 12.1 percent increase since October 1972.[2] During the same two-year period, the number of full-time government employees increased by only 7 percent.

More important than the growth in municipal union membership is the dramatic growth in union power. Contrary to the opinion of many observers, municipal employee unions are not carbon copies of their private-sector counterparts. Unlike most private businesses, city government is a monopoly that produces many services which are essential to the safety and welfare of the community. Hence, municipal unions have unique power derived from their ability to withhold the delivery of such services. If General Motors stops producing automobiles because of an employee strike, a consumer may buy a Ford, repair his old car, buy a used car, or use public transportation. If public employees go on strike, a citizen cannot find a substitute supply of water or postpone the need for fire-suppression services.

In a private business, the power of employee unions to affect performance is balanced by the interests of managers, directors, stockholders, and, to some extent, labor itself. All have a common interest in maintaining a viable business that will generate reasonable profits on which jobs and improved terms and conditions of employment depend. In the private sector, management and labor attempt to negotiate a favorable division of a given amount of resources obtained from the marketplace. Both sides know that what one party gains, the other loses, and that both parties must live with the consequences. Both know that if decisions reached at the bargaining table damage the ability of the business to perform successfully, both sides can ultimately lose.

Municipal union leaders, on the other hand, know that the existence of the business of city government and the revenue it receives are not dependent on performance. The amount of resources over which labor and management negotiate is not determined by competitive market forces. If mu-

nicipal employee unions are able to negotiate more money than a county or city has
available, the taxpayer will be asked to pick
up the difference. Local government and
union officials do not bargain with their own
money, hence they do not face a "win-lose"
situation. Both sides may "win," at the expense of the taxpayer.

The political power of municipal employee unions constitutes the most important difference between public and private
unions. Unlike private-sector unions, municipal unions can marshal the necessary resources—money, manpower, and votes—to
determine who will be their employers. In
essence, municipal unions have the power to
elect the very people who, in turn, determine their wages and working conditions. In
many cities, the balance among competing
political interest groups—the essential basis
of a democratic political system—can be altered by municipal unions whose vested interests give them a disproportionate share of
political power.

Until recently, public officials did not actively attempt to counter the growing power
of municipal unions. During the economically prosperous sixties and early seventies,
public officials, threatened with labor unrest
and the political consequences of holding
the line against excessive union demands,
could afford to buy labor off with generous
contract settlements while at the same time
avoiding the necessity of increasing taxes.
Most cities had an expanding tax base; federal and state funds were bountiful. The crunch
came in the early and mid-seventies, when
local governments began to feel the powerful impact of inflation, recession, and

the limitations of the federal budget. As revenues leveled off and costs continued to increase, public officials realized that they
could no longer afford to treat municipal
employees in the manner to which the latter
had become accustomed. Not only was there
insufficient revenue to meet expanding employee demands, in some cases there was not
enough money to meet the terms of contracts already negotiated.

Relying on their political clout and on the
threat of withholding essential services, municipal employee unions in several major cities have displayed an unwillingness to moderate their demands. This, in turn, has led
many large-city mayors, like Wes Uhlman, to
wonder who is running city hall—the
unions or the elected political leaders?

There is no doubt that the power and influence of municipal unions in cities, counties,
and other units of local government has affected the way in which the public's business
is conducted. The impact of this power has in
some cases led to an erosion of management's ability to assure adequate service delivery and has escalated the costs of operating government. These developments are
not, however, due solely to the actions of
municipal employee unions. The imbalance
between the exercise of management responsibilities and the exercise of union rights
is as much the result of weak public management as it is of strong municipal employee
organizations. The quality of local-government performance in the long run depends
directly on the extent to which a balance between union rights and management responsibilities can be achieved and maintained.

Impact on Process and Performance

This book is concerned with the process
whereby public officials determine what
should be done within a community to meet
high-priority needs and how to get these
things done at least cost. We have called this

the *management process.* No factor has a
greater impact on this process than municipal employees, individually or collectively.
Municipal employees directly affect the
quantity and the quality of city services and

the amount of resources available to provide these services. They also can have an indirect impact on the capacity of public officials to improve productivity.

First and foremost, public employees—not political leaders or municipal managers—are directly responsible for the delivery of public goods and services to the customers of city government: its residents and users. It is a firefighter, not the mayor, who puts out a fire; it is a water repairman, not a member of the city council, who repairs a broken water main; it is a nurse, not the city manager or the director of health, who inoculates citizens against infectious disease. Municipal employees not only affect the quantity of services provided (the number of houses inspected or the tons of garbage collected), they also affect the quality with which they are provided. Often, the way in which a service is provided is more important to citizens than the actual service itself. A police officer who is rude and insulting in the process of writing a traffic ticket may be damaging rather than protecting the public welfare.

The second direct impact of municipal employees is on the budget. In most local governments, labor costs account for 60 to 80 percent of total operating costs. Primarily because of the power of municipal unions, the budgetary impact of municipal employees has increased substantially in the last decade. Increasing labor costs have caused operating expenses to increase, in many cases, two to three times faster than operating revenue. This, in turn, has forced public officials to increase taxes, find new sources of revenue, or use up prior reserves, while maintaining the same level of services.

Traditionally, municipal employees were not paid as well as their private-sector counterparts because they enjoyed near-absolute job security and early retirement with adequate pensions. During the last decade, however, this situation has changed. With no decrease in job security, the total compensation (wages, salaries, and fringe benefits) paid to municipal employees has increased

dramatically and now exceeds, in many instances, that paid for comparable positions in the private sector.[3]

Ironically, the growing power of municipal unions may have an impact on the level of employment that a county or city is capable of sustaining. Because municipal employee unions in many cases have contributed to increasing the cost of government significantly faster than operating revenues have grown, public officials have been forced to balance municipal budgets by restricting expansion of the work force or, in some cases, reducing the work force through attrition or even layoffs. This employment impact was noted by California's Governor Edmund G. Brown, Jr., in his reaction to the first strike by police and firemen in San Francisco's history. Governor Brown put it this way: "If the salaries of municipal employees go beyond a reasonable level, then people are going to be either laid off or not replaced. Work forces will get smaller, working conditions will get more difficult, and unemployment will increase."[4] The Governor failed to point out that a decrease in employment, in the absence of significant increases in employee productivity, will also tend to diminish the quality and quantity of city services.

Municipal employees can have an indirect impact on government performance through their effect on the capacity of public officials to manage city government. Reflecting on the "old days" before municipal unions became involved in the process of managing cities, Frederick O'R. Hayes, former budget director of the city of New York, wrote:

It was a far easier world for public managers when decisions on employee compensation and benefits could be made unilaterally, subject only to the approval of the legislative body. And, perhaps more important, the capacity to realize managerial objectives was far greater when management still had managerial prerogatives, when work load, work organization, and working conditions were determined, not negotiated.[5]

Increasingly, municipal unions have demanded the right to negotiate in areas that, by almost any definition, are considered management prerogatives. Generally unconstrained by federal, state, or local laws that define what is and what is not a bargainable issue, municipal employee unions have demanded the right to negotiate hiring, promotion, and disciplinary policies and procedures. Increasingly, municipal unions want the right to determine what is a "fair" work load or work assignment (e.g., case loads for social workers, class size for teachers, manning of patrol cars for police officers). Such developments are having a major impact on the ability of public managers to get things done. As David Stanley put it: "A whole new ball game has started since unions in the public sector have begun to operate in areas traditionally reserved to management."[6]

One unanticipated and somewhat ironic impact of the growing power of municipal unions is that public officials are becoming more aware of themselves as managers instead of as simply bureaucratic caretakers. Improving the productivity of a city work force depends, in many instances, on the ability to change work rules and to better allocate resources (dollars and people) to accomplish desired results. The fact the public officials can no longer unilaterally make these decisions underlines the importance of developing able municipal managers and electing competent political leaders who have the capacity to manage the business of local government under new and more challenging conditions.

Criteria for Evaluation

An evaluation of the impact of municipal employees on the capacity of a local government to get things done must address three areas: employee competence, employee motivation, and the extent to which a proper balance exists between management responsibilities and union rights.

Employee competence

The productivity of municipal employees cannot be improved if positions are filled by persons who lack the competence to perform the jobs for which they are paid. Evaluating the competence of municipal employees, however, is both a difficult and (in the absence of established work standards and productivity measures) an extremely subjective exercise. At minimum, the following evaluation criteria should prove useful in establishing a basis for determining the extent to which municipal employees are competent:

Are the best-qualified people able to compete for all government positions on an equal basis without artificially created barriers? Theoretically, every position within a local government would be filled with the best-qualified person available. Therefore, it is necessary to determine whether the best-qualified people are encouraged to compete for local government positions, whether competition for positions is arbitrarily limited to existing employees, and whether other arbitrary barriers have been erected which prevent certain applicants from seeking or obtaining local government jobs.

Are tests for local government positions job-related? Most municipal employees obtain employment by passing a written test. This question examines whether (1) the results of such tests provide a valid indication of how applicants will perform on the jobs for which they are being tested, and (2) discrimination based on race, sex, age, religion, or cultural background is reflected in testing policies and procedures.

Are promotion decisions job-related? Promotions should be based on both past performance in a present job and predicted performance in the new job. Answering this question requires an examination of (1) the extent to which employees are promoted to positions beyond their abilities to perform competently and (2) the extent to which arbitrary criteria, such as longevity of employment, enter into the promotion decision.

Are educational and training opportunities available? Employee competence can be significantly enhanced through the development of educational and training programs. This question examines whether such programs are conducted and the extent to which employees have an opportunity to take advantage of them. A complete answer would also require an analysis of whether counseling is provided, so that employees understand the educational and training opportunities that could have the greatest impact on their career development.

Employee motivation

An employee may have the competence to do a job productively but lack the will to do so. Therefore, evaluating the extent to which a city's work force is motivated to become more productive is critical to any effort to evaluate the impact of municipal employees on performance.

Many factors can affect employee motivation. To some extent, an employee who knows the results he is expected to produce and knows that he will be evaluated and rewarded based on them will be motivated to become more productive. Other motivating factors are suggested by the following questions:

Do employees have reasonable job security? Proper motivation results in part from the knowledge that tenure is immune from arbitrary political consideration. We must examine, therefore, whether employees are reasonably secure from undue political or other arbitrary influences.

Is employee compensation equitable and based on job performance? The total compensation received by municipal employees should be comparable to that paid to people in similar positions in both the public and the private sector. Equally important, work standards and productivity targets should be used in the process of evaluating employees' job performance, and job performance should be the basis for allocating rewards and penalties.

Are employees adequately supervised? Employee motivation and ultimate productivity will be only as good as first-line supervision. This question calls for an examination of the quality of supervision and the extent to which supervisors are concerned with and effective in motivating employees.

Do employees have opportunities to advance commensurate with their interests and skills? Most positions within a local government should be filled through the promotion of existing employees. This policy serves to boost morale and to motivate employees to develop their own capabilities. Promotion, however, should not be automatic. Promotional sequences (often called career ladders) should be developed for municipal employees. Furthermore, employees should be provided educational and training opportunities to allow advancement along established career paths as quickly as interest, ability, and openings permit.

Is there a fair and timely procedure for handling employee grievances? An equitable grievance-resolution procedure will ensure that employees spend their time worrying about today's job instead of yesterday's complaints. The grievance procedure should be fair, and it should expeditiously resolve disagreements in the implementation of policy, employee contracts, and bargaining agreements. Such a procedure should cover all employees, resolve issues quickly, require a minimum of paperwork and time on the part of both employees and managers, and produce binding decisions.

Are employees satisfied with their jobs? Traditionally, it has been assumed that job satisfaction is solely a function of compensation and working conditions. Increasingly, however, it is clear that employee motivation to become more productive is based as much on the nature of the job as on the compensation paid for it. Answering this question involves an examination of the extent to which employees feel that their jobs are challenging and provide them with a sense of self-worth.

Balance between management responsibilities and union rights

In those local governments where municipal employee unions have obtained the exclusive right to bargain for employees concerning the terms and conditions of their employment, it is critical to the development of a productive work force that an appropriate balance be maintained between the exercise of management responsibilities and the protection of union and employee rights. Asking the following questions should be helpful in evaluating the nature of this balance:

Is union representation limited to nonmanagement personnel? There is no reason why management personnel, from supervisors up to the chief executive, should feel a necessity to participate in a union in order to ensure job security or to receive compensation that reflects responsibility and performance. Answering this question, therefore, necessitates an examination of whether supervisors and other management personnel are represented by a municipal union. To the extent that they are, are they in different bargaining units from the employees they supervise? If not, does this condition impair the exercise of supervisory responsibilities?

Is management's responsibility for collective bargaining clearly established and professionally administered? Fragmentation and diffusion of management authority within local governments has made it difficult for both unions and the public to know whom to hold accountable for the results of the collective-bargaining process. This question determines whether municipal managers "pass the buck," refusing to assume respon-

sibility for their roles in the collective-bargaining process. Are municipal unions able to make "end runs" to the legislative body (the board of supervisors or the city council), thereby circumventing the bargaining process? Is there a clear determination of who represents management at the bargaining table and who is in a position to make final contract decisions? Is this person professionally qualified to exercise such responsibility?

Is the scope of bargaining clearly established? If the concept of "hours, wages, and working conditions" is to have meaning in the collective-bargaining process, then each must be clearly defined. It is therefore necessary to examine whether federal, state, or local laws have established criteria that may be used in determining which issues are subject to bilateral agreement by labor and management through collective bargaining.

Is the length of the negotiation process defined, and is the contractual period of reasonable length? Defining the length of the negotiation process is in the interests of both labor and management. It is also in the interests of labor and management that a contractual obligation be fixed for a long enough period (minimum: two years) so as to permit efficient administration. This question examines the extent to which time constraints on the collective-bargaining process reduce the high costs of continuous negotiations.

Does management develop a strategy prior to the initiation of the collective-bargaining process? Too often, management's role at the collective-bargaining table is reactive. It is therefore necessary to ask if management officials have determined what they want to obtain from the collective-bargaining process. Have they prepared a formal statement of their objectives prior to the initiation of the process? Furthermore, does management have the ability to develop quickly reasoned counterproposals to the union demands advanced during the collective-bargaining process?

Are both public officials and union leaders accountable for the consequences of an im-

passe situation? If citizens know whom to hold accountable for the consequences of an impasse situation, the probability of such a situation arising is reduced. This question examines how impasse situations are resolved within the labor-relations process. Are strikes permitted? Are third parties brought in to resolve disputes?

Is management prepared to continue government services in the event of an employee strike or work stoppage? It is critical that municipal managers understand how to maintain essential government services in the event of a strike. This question asks if management officials have a "strike plan" that defines precisely how the local government will operate in the event of a strike (or other form of work stoppage).

Are negotiated union contracts adequately administered? Labor relations can be significantly improved if negotiated contracts are administered intelligently. This question examines whether the management personnel responsible for the implementation of union contracts are adequately trained and prepared to administer negotiated contracts. Do managers receive training in the content and potential management implications of negotiated contracts? Do local governments centrally record and monitor the resolution of grievances, thereby ensuring that managers and employees throughout the local government profit from the results of grievance resolutions?

Conditions in Flint

Flint is a union town. Therefore, it is not surprising to find that municipal employees and their unions have had a significant impact on the performance of its city government. In the balance of this chapter, we examine this impact and conclude with a list of opportunities for improving government performance by altering the role of municipal employees and their unions.

Employee competence and motivation

Because managers are responsible for selecting, promoting, rewarding, and penalizing employees, they are ultimately responsible for increasing employee productivity. In carrying out this responsibility, authority for personnel development and management is usually delegated to a personnel department reporting to the chief executive. This department is responsible for hiring, testing, selection, and promotion procedures; education and training programs; and evaluation and grievance practices.

In 1974 Flint did not have such a personnel department. In its place was an independent civil-service system. Our analysis here begins

with a review of how this civil service evolved, how it was initially structured, and why this structure was a major impediment to the development of competent and motivated employees.

In 1935, Flint's charter (adopted in 1929) was amended to incorporate a civil-service system. This amendment gave an independent civil-service commission and its staff the responsibility for examining, hiring, classifying, and promoting all employees; determining appropriate pay levels for all job classifications; determining the rules for suspension and dismissal of all employees; protecting employees against undue political influence; and guaranteeing general employee rights and benefits. Under this system only four positions remained exempt from civil service. These were the direct appointees of the City Council: the city manager, the director of finance, the city attorney, and the city clerk.

The rules and regulations governing the conduct of civil service were extremely detailed and complex, filling almost 20 percent of the 130-page city charter. To administer the system, a three-person Civil Service Commission was established. One commissioner was appointed by the City Council, one by the city hospital board of directors, and one by the Board of Education.[7] The commission, in turn, appointed a director, who supervised a staff which by 1974 consisted of thirteen people. In terms of responsibilities, the civil-service director was comparable to a personnel administrator, yet he was totally independent of the city manager, the mayor, and the City Council. He could be removed only by the Civil Service Commission, and then only if "reasonable cause" were demonstrated in a public hearing.

In essence, Flint's City Council and city manager had no control over the administration of the city's personnel policies and procedures. Imagine the difficulty a manager would face in running a business that was forced to operate under the following constraints:

Recruitment was closed. All positions in Flint, from street sweeper to the director of public works, were filled by an existing employee if at least two employees wanted the job and if civil service determined that they both met minimum qualifications. This restriction made it virtually impossible for the city manager, department heads, or division supervisors to recruit the best-qualified personnel available. In short, managers in Flint had almost no control over the skills and competence of the employees under their supervision. When civil service did allow open recruitment, its efforts were minimal. Advertisements were placed in trade journals and in the local newspaper. No attempt was made by civil service to actively seek the best-qualified person. If a manager wanted to recruit a highly qualified person, he had to do it himself, and then there was no guarantee that the person would be hired.

Examinations were invalid. In 1974, the city hired employees solely on the basis of the results of civil-service-administered examinations. If civil service determined that only people within a department were eligible to compete for a vacancy, the appointing authority had to promote the person who finished first on the civil-service test, regard-

less of whatever special knowledge, experience, or aptitudes other candidates might have. This was called the "rule of one." If civil service determined that employees from more than one city department or from outside the city could compete for a vacancy, the appointing authority had to select one of the top three highest scorers on the civil-service exam—the "rule of three." An appointing authority who felt that none of the top three finalists was qualified to fill a vacancy had two options: he could do nothing, leaving the position vacant for at least one year; or he could fill it with a person he felt was unqualified.

These rules placed a heavy burden on the accuracy and validity of civil-service testing. The civil-service staff's faith in its presumably objective testing system often led to bizarre results. Civil-service tests were graded to the second decimal place—implying a testing accuracy that simply did not exist. It was not uncommon to have a hundredth of a point separating top scores on a particular test. A person who scored 96.35 would be judged qualified, while a person who scored 96.34 would not. More important, after scores were recorded to this level of detail, additional points were awarded to certain candidates on the basis of factors that were related neither to the job nor to the competence of the applicant. For example, if an applicant was a veteran, five points was automatically added to the final score. In addition, an applicant could receive one point for every year of "relevant" experience with the city, as determined by civil-service technicians. In order to make the top-three cutoff, a new employee who was not a veteran had to score ten to twenty points more on a civil-service test than his or her competition to be judged qualified for the position.

If the written-test scores, years of city service, and military experience were accurate predictors of performance on the job, such a system would be acceptable. This is not the case. No graduate school would select entrants solely on the basis of entrance exami-

EXHIBIT 25

Sex, Height, Education, and Cultural Background Often Determined Who Could Work for the City of Flint

Could *you* get a job with the city of Flint? If you are a woman, less than five-feet-seven-inches tall, a high-school dropout, or a person who grew up in a central city ghetto, the answer until recently would probably have been—no!

In April 1972, a woman who had completed fifty-five semester hours of college study in a police-administration program applied to the Civil Service Commission to fill one of twenty-two patrol officer positions funded by the Emergency Employment Act. The civil service staff refused to give her an application, saying that the Civil Service Commission had determined that "male sex was a bona-fide occupational qualification of the position of patrol officer." The woman subsequently filed a lawsuit in federal district court. A year later, the Civil Service Commission, complying with a court order, was required to remove the sex barrier to employment as a police officer.

During the same period, the city of Flint was also recruiting for firefighters. A Spanish-American student who had recently completed the requirements for a baccalaureate degree contacted the city's Equal Opportunity Office and expressed interest in applying for a firefighter position. He indicated that there might be a problem with his application because he was only five-feet six- and one-half-inches tall and weighed 142 pounds. The civil service had determined that the minimum entrance requirements for a firefighter position were a height of five feet seven inches and a weight of 150 pounds. Accompanied by the equal opportunity director, the young man was measured by the civil service office with his shoes on and recorded an acceptable height of five feet seven inches. After a lengthy debate, civil service officials decided that the applicant could not be measured with shoes on (despite the fact that most firefighters wore shoes when

(continued)

nation scores or years of military service, nor would a business hire employees solely on the basis of their college grades. Many factors must be used in reaching an educated guess concerning which candidate would perform best in a given job. The most critical factor in this determination, and the factor purposely excluded by Flint's civil service, is the judgment of the manager who would be accountable for the performance of the se-lected employee.

Civil-service tests for several entry-level positions (e.g., patrol officers, firefighters, waste collectors) were eventually proven in-valid; that is, they did not adequately predict the ability of applicants to do the job. More-over, as the examples presented in Exhibit 25 indicate, civil service often discriminated against certain applicants on the basis of race, cultural background, age, and sex.

EXHIBIT 25 (cont'd)

fighting fires). His application was rejected. Under the threat of a court order, the Civil Service Commission abolished the height and weight requirements a year later.

In 1973, a woman applied to the Civil Service Commission for the position of telephone operator. With three and one-half years of experience as a telephone operator with Michigan Bell, she felt qualified for the job and optimistic that she would receive it. Her application was rejected by civil service because she did not meet the minimum entrance requirement of "high-school diploma or equivalent." Following her mother's death, the applicant had quit high school midway through her senior year to help her father care for her younger brothers and sisters. The Civil Service Commission recommended that she take the high-school equivalency test given by the Board of Education; she did so, and passed. This certification, however, did not reach civil service before the application period for the job she wanted had closed; hence, she was not considered. A subsequent Civil Service Commission study of the validity of the high-school education requirement resulted in its removal for most positions of this type.

The Civil Service Commission, under pressure to develop examinations that tested the capacity of applicants to perform on the job, developed a number of performance tests. One of the earliest performance tests was administered for the position of forestry caretaker—a nonsupervising position responsible for cutting brush, limbing trees, and performing other related maintenance functions. A key part of the examination consisted of a large sheet of plywood to which had been affixed various tools used by forestry caretakers. Applicants were then asked to identify each tool and tell how it was used. Test results showed that a disproportionate number of blacks failed the test. An inquiry revealed that most of the blacks taking this test had had no prior experience with the tools displayed in the examination. As one applicant put it, "I don't know the difference between a pruning saw, a pole saw, and a bow saw, but I know how to saw." Other, more experienced applicants admitted that the tools displayed in the test were known to them by different names. Cultural background, not ability to do the job, appeared to be a primary reason for failure.

The results of this discrimination on minority employment were startling. In October 1971, the minority population in Flint exceeded 30 percent; yet, the city employed only 1 black firefighter out of a total of 185. Only 10 black patrolmen were employed out of 151 patrol officers. In fact, in the 118-year history of the Flint police division, only 26 black officers had been employed, and none had been promoted above the rank of patrolman. As of January 1974, only 11 percent of the 545 permanent employees in the Department of Public Works were of minority status. Of the 1,802 people who worked for the city of Flint, only 12.2 percent represented minorities. These were not impressive figures, yet they represented a 25-percent increase in minority employment from the previous two years.

During this period affirmative action was a

EXHIBIT 26

*White Police Officers Strike over
Promotion of Black Officers*

Early in 1973, a circuit court decision ruled that the civil service promotional test for the position of police sergeant was not valid—it was not relevant to the job. The city was enjoined from giving any promotional tests until a valid exam could be prepared. As vacancies in the sergeantcy ranks occurred the need for adequate supervision of patrolmen increased. Therefore, in April 1973, the police chief promoted sixteen patrolmen, on a provisional basis, to the position of sergeant. Two of these sixteen were black—the first promotions of black officers in the division's history. The two black officers involved had been on the force for more than five years and had demonstrated superior ability, according to their superiors. One officer, in fact, had scored higher on the previous civil service test than other white officers who, because of seniority, were promoted ahead of him. The chief made it clear, however, that these promotions were temporary and that all eligible officers would eventually take a validated exam to secure permanent promotion.

The reactions to these promotions were swift. Off-duty policemen and their supporters began to picket city hall, protesting what they described as a lowering of the standards of the police division. Picketers marched around city hall for three days. Although spokesmen for the police claimed that these protests were not racially motivated, few observers agreed. A press release by the sergeants'

(continued)

major priority of the City Council, but gains were hard to achieve. As the case presented in Exhibit 26 indicates, efforts to promote minority employment in Flint city government were resisted by existing employees and their unions and inhibited by the difficulty in validating civil-service examinations.

Another difficulty with the testing procedure in Flint concerned the length of time it took civil service to complete the examination process and actually hire or promote an employee. Usually, three to five months were required. In one case, involving the selection of a budget analyst, the process took civil service eight months. The system was geared to serve existing city employees. Jobs filled by promotion took the least amount of time to fill; jobs requiring open competition took the longest.

Promotions were not related to job performance. Promotions in Flint were based primarily on test scores, seniority, and other factors—not on merit. Promotions were not based on predicted performance in a higher-level position nor even on demonstrated performance in an existing position. Instead, they were based on examinations that in many cases had been proven to be inadequate predictors of performance.

The role of managers in the promotion

EXHIBIT 26 (cont'd)

and lieutenants' union read, in part, "The racially motivated advancement of two police officers is an outrage to the sense of right and decency. The glaring disregard for competence, experience, and leadership quality in deference to a minority quota is a disservice to the community and the Flint police division." The picketing police spokesmen threatened an epidemic of "blue flu." For a period of time they stopped giving traffic tickets. Nevertheless, city officials held firm.

The newspaper asked in an editorial that "the extremists in the [police division] back away from confrontation tactics and thereby avoid what threatens to develop into one of the most unpleasant and regrettable situations Flint has faced in many years." When the city manager agreed to make all possible effort to complete the development of a valid exam within ninety days, the striking officers ended their picketing. Eventually a valid exam was completed and the promotions were made. None of those promoted was a member of a minority.

At the height of this emotional issue, a City Council meeting was held. A large majority of the white police officers attended with their families. A lawyer, hired to be their spokesman, gave an impassioned speech condemning the actions of the City Council, the city manager, and the press. He received a rousing ovation from the police and their supporters in the audience. The irony of this situation became apparent less than three months later when the same auditorium was filled with blacks from Flint's north end protesting the police shooting of a black youth. The shooting pushed the city perilously close to the brink of racial confrontation. It is speculation, but if one or two of the six patrolmen involved in this incident had been black, the problem and the danger it represented to the community might have been significantly reduced.

process was minimal. Each employee had a personnel record which contained evaluations by all previous supervisors. These were seldom used in evaluating personnel for promotion. In 1974 the Civil Service Commission went so far as to preclude past performance from having any weight in an evaluation, thus requiring complete emphasis on test scores, years of service, and veteran preference.

Education and training opportunities were nonexistent. Flint's city government had no formal training program for its employees. Some departments paid tuition costs for courses that they determined to be job-

related, with a reimbursement ceiling of $100 per semester. This policy, however, was not uniform and affected very few employees. Departments made no attempt to counsel employees concerning which courses were most relevant if they wanted to advance to higher positions within a department. Furthermore, employees could not be released from their jobs to complete educational requirements or receive special skill training. Civil service played no role in the education and training of employees.

Tenure and compensation decisions were unrelated to job performance. In Flint most employees received tenure after six months on the job. Firing an employee was a virtual impossibility. Incompetence was not grounds for dismissal. As long as an employee did not commit a crime or blatantly demonstrate incompetence by an overt or costly act, continued employment with the city was guaranteed.

The city's compensation plan, administered by the civil service, often created arbitrary and inequitable situations. The plan allocated pay levels to each job classification through a quasi-scientific process that worked like this: a civil-service technician, who seldom had personal knowledge of the job being analyzed, would evaluate the job on the basis of eight presumably objective criteria. Within each criterion the technician's evaluation would be equated with a numerical score. The total of the eight scores then produced a total score for the position which could then be related directly to a salary level. In essence, this system depended upon the subjective evaluation of a civil-service technician. More often than not, the recommended salary did not reflect the relative importance of the job within the organization, the qualifications of the person who would perform the job, or the salary level required to recruit and retain the best-qualified person.

Once the level of compensation had been determined, salary increases were automatic and were totally unrelated to performance. Moreover, an employee could get extra compensation increases by successfully persuading civil service to "reallocate" his or her job. A reallocation could be initiated by either the appointing authority or the employee. Usually it was the employee, supported by union representatives, who made the request. Following such a request, an employee would attempt to persuade a civil-service technician that his or her job had become more difficult or had changed significantly since the last time it was evaluated; it therefore deserved more points within one of the eight evaluation criteria. If the technician could not be persuaded, the employee or the union could appeal directly to the Civil Service Commission.

In 1972, for example, the sanitation workers—who had just negotiated a new contract with management giving them a 5.1 percent increase in compensation—went to civil service and demanded a reallocation. They argued that their jobs were now riskier because some sanitation workers were driving larger trucks. Furthermore, they argued, their jobs were now harder because there had been a 10-percent increase in garbage collected during 1973 with no corresponding increase in men or equipment. They reasoned that they were being asked to work harder and should be compensated for it.

The sanitation workers' objective was to obtain enough extra points to raise the classification of their jobs from level 15 to level 16, resulting in an additional 6-percent increase in pay on top of that previously negotiated. The city manager, with the backing of the City Council, urged the civil-service director, over whom neither had control, to deny the reallocation request. This case was finally resolved when the deputy city manager developed and negotiated a program that related the future compensation of the sanitation workers to their performance on the job. The case presented in Exhibit 27 provides a poignant example of how relating performance to compensation can stimulate employee motivation.

Evaluation and supervision were inadequate. Flint did not have a personnel-evaluation system that measured employee performance against established standards. In its place was a crude employee service-rating form which was typically ignored by both employees and managers because it was not used by civil service in determining promotions or compensation.* This system

---

* The city charter stated that an employee had to receive a "satisfactory" rating to receive an annual salary raise. However, this rating would be filed after the time at which the annual increment was given. Rarely was anything less than a "satisfactory" rating given—unless, of course, one wanted to develop the paperwork to eventually try to fire an employee.

EXHIBIT 27

Sanitation Workers Substantially Increase Productivity

After receiving a 5.1-percent increase in annual compensation negotiated by their union, the sanitation workers requested that civil service reallocate their job classification, giving them an additional 6-percent increase in compensation. Civil service refused, and in August 1973, the sanitation workers began a citywide slowdown.

The deputy city manager, who was concerned about the excessive overtime in the sanitation division, the large number of uncompleted collection routes, and the increasing citizen complaints about the quality of waste collection, negotiated an agreement with the sanitation workers. This agreement provided that, if unscheduled overtime was reduced by at least 37 percent, all waste collectors would be given an $.08 per-hour pay increase or a productivity bonus equal to half of the overtime savings, whichever was greater. Furthermore, all crews could go home when their routes were finished. The amount of shared savings would be reduced, however, if collection standards were not met.

The results of this program were dramatic:

- Total overtime in fiscal year 1974 was reduced 44 percent from the total of the previous year and 37 percent from the average of the past three years. By December 1974, all nonscheduled overtime had been eliminated.
- The average time to complete a collection route (all routes had been balanced to equalize the number of stops per route) was reduced from ten hours to six, giving the sanitation workers two free hours paid by the city.
- After paying all bonuses, annual savings to the city was approximately $17,000.
- Waste collectors received a bonus of $17,780 in the first year, or $261 per person, exceeding the compensation increase they would have been awarded by a civil service reallocation.
- The tons of garbage collected per man hour increased 8 percent in fiscal year 1974.
- No reduction in the quality of waste-collection service was observed during the first year. Because garbage was on the streets for less time and collection was more predictable, many felt that the cleanliness of the city had increased.
- Absenteeism and waste-collection injuries declined substantially in the first year of this program and the morale of waste collectors, according to their union leaders, increased dramatically.

The details of this case are recounted in *Tying City Pay to Performance,* a special report published by the Labor-Management Relations Service (LMRS) of the National League of Cities, National Association of Counties, and U.S. Conference of Mayors (Washington, D.C., December 1974).

worked as follows: each appointing authority completed a performance evaluation form every six months and sent it to civil service. The only part of this form requiring completion was a box that had to be checked to indicate whether, in the judgment of the appointing authority, the employee's performance was outstanding, good, satisfactory, questionable, or unsatisfactory. Only if an unsatisfactory rating were given did the appointing authority have to explain his rating on the form and to the employee. As a result, almost all rating sheets showed performance as satisfactory or better, and almost never did a supervisor or manager discuss the employee's performance.

Given the nature of the selection, discipline, and compensation procedures administered by civil service, it is not surprising to find that supervision in Flint was often inadequate. It was virtually impossible for a supervisor or a manager, at any level, to effectively motivate or control employees. This lack of control over rewards and penalties, combined with a total absence of supervisory training programs, made it extremely difficult to develop effective first-line supervisors.

Opportunities for advancement were inadequate. Attempts in Flint to develop "career ladders," or promotional sequences, for municipal employees had not been successful. In 1974, civil service showed little interest in developing a career-ladder program. Civil-service personnel were unwilling to review job descriptions to determine if the descriptions adequately reflected current job needs or, at minimum, accurately reflected jobs actually being performed. Furthermore, the City Council refused to appropriate funds for the development of employee-training programs that would have made a career-ladder program meaningful. Employees, on the other hand, did not take advantage of the limited tuition-reimbursement program that some departments offered. Apparently they were not confident that investing their own time and

money in preparing for more responsible, higher-paying jobs would be rewarded.

Grievance-administration procedures were ineffective. Civil service also played a major role in the grievance-administration process. General employees in 1974 had two separate grievance procedures available to them—an appeal to the Civil Service Commission or an appeal through their union or association. In many cases, employees were able to use both procedures. Moreover, grievance decisions were not binding. Decisions by the Civil Service Commission could be appealed in some cases to the City Council and in all cases to the courts. Because the city lacked a personnel department, managers had to take valuable time away from their other responsibilities to prepare and argue their own cases in grievance hearings. Because of inadequate preparation and lack of specialized staff assistance, most managers did not represent their positions well. Finally, no central records were maintained to record the resolution of particular grievances. As a result, managers throughout city government continually repeated errors in the interpretation and administration of negotiated contracts.

On balance, the personnel policies and procedures administered by civil service served to insulate Flint's employees from the consequences of their performance—good or bad. Because competence was not a critical factor in getting hired, being promoted, or receiving additional compensation, there were few incentives for employees to strengthen their individual skills and hence to improve their productivity. As a result, many employees used their energies to promote municipal unions or to perform second jobs. In 1973 the fire chief estimated that more than 60 percent of Flint's firefighters had second jobs.

The consequences of a low level of motivation among employees were compounded by the fact that many employees had been promoted to jobs they were not competent to perform. This forced many of them to expend their energies protecting their gains rather than doing their jobs better. Younger, more able employees often left city employment because time in a job (seniority) was more important to advancement than merit or performance. As one departing employee put it, "When years in the job are more important than performance on the job, it's time to move on." In sum, Flint's civil service was a major barrier to the development of competent, highly motivated municipal employees.

It is unfair, however, to lay all employee problems in Flint at the doorstep of civil service. The City Council shares the responsibility. The council consistently had been unwilling to take actions to strengthen personnel management. From 1972 to 1975 the council refused to create an office of personnel management that would be responsible for those personnel functions not assigned to civil service by the city charter. These functions included labor relations, personnel evaluation, position control, employee training and development, equal opportunity compliance, employee safety and medical services, workers' compensation, and employee benefits.

Managers had also done very little to develop and implement programs that would motivate employees to become more productive or to improve their skills. Because civil service insulated Flint's managers from accountability as completely as it did nonsupervising employees, there was no incentive to break out of the complacency that marked the boundaries of city government employment. Most important, supervisors lacked an identification as managers and were often more strongly allied with the people they supervised than with management. As a result, contracts were not enforced, performance targets were not established, and work was rarely controlled. By 1974, supervisors and municipal employees were relying almost exclusively on employee unions to provide them with adequate terms and conditions of employment. The vital link be-

tween managers and their employees—the relationship on which improved productivity depends—had been severed.

An imbalance between management responsibilities and union rights

In Flint, the imbalance between management's exercise of its responsibilities and municipal employee unions' exercise of their rights was as much a product of weak management as it was of strong unions. Flint's municipal managers in 1974 appeared to be neither able nor willing to control the expanding ambitions of city unions and their leaders. In the face of the unions' growing political power, municipal managers had few incentives to resist union encroachment of their prerogatives. The result, in the words of a newspaper editor, was that "Flint [was] run from the bottom up by employees and their unions instead of from the top down by elected officials."

By 1974 Flint's city government was almost completely unionized. Of the 1,870 employees who worked for the city, all but 39 were represented by a union or employee association (see Exhibit 28). In addition to general employees and all uniformed personnel, union representation included supervisors, division heads, nurses, and even the city's attorneys. The fact that most managers and professionals felt it necessary to unionize in order to obtain equitable terms and conditions of employment provides a clear indication of the municipal unions' power as well as the manner in which city government officials had treated managers in the past. All unionized employees in Flint were also protected by civil service.

Union representation was not limited to nonmanagement personnel. Supervisors in Flint not only belonged to municipal unions, in many cases they belonged to the same unions as the people they supervised. In the police and fire divisions the situation was most extreme. In the fire division, the fire-

EXHIBIT 28

Only 2.1 Percent of Flint City Government Employees Were Not Represented by a Union

UNION EMPLOYEES	NUMBER	PERCENTAGE OF ALL CITY EMPLOYEES
General, nonuniformed employees (Local 1600)	1,113	59.5
Supervisory employees (Local 1799)	67	3.6
Middle management (Unit II)	14	0.7
Uniformed policemen		
Patrolmen	302	16.1
Sergeants	34	1.8
Lieutenants	8	0.5
Captains and Assistant Captains	6	0.3
Uniformed firefighters (IAFF Local 352)	265	14.2
Public-health nurses	22	1.2
TOTAL	1,831	97.9
NON-UNION (EXEMPT) EMPLOYEES	39	2.1
TOTAL CITY EMPLOYMENT	1,870	100.0

Statistics as of December 6, 1974.

fighters' association (IAFF) represented all 265 employees, including the chief. The union dictated how all positions would be filled. An agreement between civil service and IAFF Local 352 provided that union officials would determine who was eligible to compete for promotions within the fire division. In the police division, separate bargaining units (called associations) represented each respective rank. The cooperation between these units was so complete, however, that in effect one departmental union represented all employees.

The quality of supervision need not suffer

just because a supervisor and his employees belong to the same bargaining unit within the same union. A supervisor who bargains on the same side of the table and makes the same working-condition and fringe-benefit demands as his employees may, in fact, be able to exert managerial control over these employees during the workday. But there are certainly strong incentives working the other way. Exhibit 29 illustrates what can happen when supervisors and the people they supervise are in the same union. The fact that one bargaining unit represented both the sergeants and the patrolmen they supervised had been a cause of concern to public officials. When the union president admitted that in certain instances sergeants had failed to exercise their supervisory responsibilities because they were upset with a City Council decision affecting a patrol officer, this fear was substantiated. If a productive work force depends on the quality of first-line supervision, there was real reason to question the productivity of Flint's police force.

This situation was by no means limited to the uniformed services. The general employees' union included a large number of supervisors within its ranks, as well. In 1972, the president of Local 1600 (which represented the largest number of city employees) explained to the new city manager that supervisory personnel were in local unions because there was very little difference between the jobs performed by general employees and those performed by their supervisors. "After all," he pointed out, "they are both doing the same work."

This was precisely the problem. A large percentage of Flint's work force was operating without adequate supervision, primarily because first-line supervisors were not properly trained and did not recognize that they had taken on different responsibilities when they became supervisors. Supervisors' identification with nonsupervisory employees was strengthened by the fact that civil-service job descriptions did not clearly identify or give ample credit for management re-

sponsibilities. In addition, the general employees' union, by virtue of its power with civil service and the fact that supervisory positions were rarely filled from outside the ranks of city employees, played a major role in determining who would become supervisors. Hence, it was not surprising that supervisors in Flint exercised very little meaningful supervision.

Management's responsibility in collective bargaining was unclear, and negotiations were not professionally administered. Not only did the City Council in Flint fail to set limits on the collective-bargaining period or develop a basis for determining bargainable issues, it also refused to hire a professional labor-relations administrator to negotiate and manage nine separate union contracts. In December 1974 these contracts covered 1,831 employees and accounted for, in salaries alone, about $27 million of taxpayers' funds. From 1965 to 1972 the city manager personally negotiated all union contracts, with intermittent help from department heads and the civil-service director.

In 1972 the City Council designated the new city attorney as its labor-relations negotiator because of his previous experience in this area. (The city attorney, who was independent of the city manager, was directly responsible for only six city employees.) Because of mounting legal responsibilities, he did not have sufficient time to devote to labor relations. As a result, both the city's legal work and its labor relations suffered. Moreover, neither the city attorney nor the city manager had sufficient staff to administer negotiated contracts. Hence, there was no central administration of contracts, no centralized resolution of grievances, and no dissemination of information concerning the nature of grievance resolutions. As a result, on numerous occasions the same grievance was repeated over and over in separate departments; managers did not learn from each other's experiences.

The scope of collective bargaining was unclear. A major cause of the seemingly endless nature of the collective-bargaining pro-

EXHIBIT 29

Police Sergeants Threaten To Abandon Their Supervisory Responsibilities

Has a policeman ever hit you in the face with a flashlight? A Flint resident claimed that he was so treated in December 1970 following a high-speed car chase in which he tried to escape from pursuing Flint police officers. This person claimed that several officers smashed his face into the hood of his car and that one officer hit him in the face with his flashlight. Because state law removes the city from liability in such cases, the resident sued the police officer for brutality and won. A jury ruled that the police officer should pay $1,100 in damages.

The City Council had an unwritten policy whereby the city would pay the legal expenses of any city employee who, *acting within the scope of his duties,* took actions that later were the cause of court-awarded damages. Accordingly, the police officer asked the council to pay the $1,100 in damages as well as approximately $900 in legal fees.

The City Council, in a 5–4 vote, said no. The majority felt that the police officer had acted negligently and outside the scope of his duties and consequently should not be paid. They cited the court's ruling as uncontestable proof of that fact. They further pointed out that if police officers knew that the City Council would pay for any damages awarded in police brutality cases, there would be no incentive to control the use of force in making arrests.

The council members in the minority were outraged. "We have to give our police officers some leeway," said one councilman. Another councilman said that he wanted the council and the community to support their police officers because they have to face "hopped-up, gun-toting teen-agers."

Reacting to the council's refusal to pay the convicted officer's bills, the president of the Teamsters' Union (representing the patrol officers) stated publicly that, at the right moment, patrolmen would show their united dissatisfaction with the council's action. He promised a "surprise work stoppage." He went on to say that patrolmen would refuse to act on some complaints unless ordered to do so by their supervisors, the sergeants, *who were represented by the same local.*

In fact, the Teamster president indicated, in one case—involving a suspected drunk—a sergeant had declined to take responsibility and the case was not pursued. In another case, involving a house disturbance, a sergeant refused to order the proper investigation.

The threat was clear: If the council did not change its stand, the quality of police supervision would decline and the public would suffer. It appeared that the control of police services was out of the hands of Flint's elected public officials.

cess was the fact that in Flint no limit was placed on the range of bargainable issues. Michigan's Public Employment Relations Act, which permitted the formation of municipal-employee unions, did not define or provide criteria with which to determine what was and what was not a bargainable issue. As a result, any demand that municipal employees wanted to make was advanced under the banner of a "working condition," a legitimate subject of collective bargaining. (The case presented in Exhibit 30 suggests the breadth of the union's definition of a "working condition.") From 1964 to 1974 Flint's municipal unions had become accustomed to negotiating such "working conditions" as hiring and selection policies, promotion and performance evaluation procedures, disciplinary measures, work assignment procedures, and the rights of management to contract with the private sector.

No limit was placed on the collective-bargaining period. No attempt was made by Flint's government officials to limit the duration of the collective-bargaining process. Since contracts were always made retroactive to the start of the fiscal year covered by the contract, union leaders had no incentive to limit the negotiation period. The fact that union leaders were paid a full salary to sit in negotiation sessions was surely an incentive to extend the negotiation period as long as possible. As a result, it was not atypical for contract negotiations to begin some months before the end of a contract year and continue several months into the next contract year. Since most contracts were only one year in length, this produced almost year-round negotiations. From 1971 through 1974 the average time required to complete the negotiation of a contract was approximately eight months.

Management did not develop a negotiation strategy. Flint's public officials failed to develop a list of the objectives they wanted to achieve in the collective-bargaining process. Management's posture was continually reactive. Instead of beginning the collective-bargaining process with a statement of the changes management would like to negotiate with labor, management officials were content to react to a list of union demands. Consequently, the labor-negotiation process was focused solely on what municipal unions wanted for their employees, not on what management wanted or needed to do their jobs better.

Neither employee unions nor management was accountable to the public for the results of the collective-bargaining process. The 1965 Michigan law that allows public employees to form unions also expressly prohibits strikes. In Flint, this provision was often violated in principle, if not in fact. Work stoppages and slowdowns—cases of the "blue flu"—were common.

More important, the courts in Flint refused to enforce the law prohibiting general strikes. In the summer of 1973, the teachers' union in Flint went on strike after failing to negotiate an acceptable contract with the Board of Education. A local attorney filed a suit seeking an injunction against the strike. The presiding judge refused to grant the injunction, despite the fact that the union was in clear violation of the law.

In Flint, most impasse situations were resolved by an arbitration process outside the control of both parties at the negotiation table. For arbitration purposes, union and management generally selected one representative each, and these in turn selected a third person who would ultimately make the arbitration decision. In essence, binding arbitration removed control of public decisions from the City Council, the public's elected representatives, and placed it in the hands of a third party who was not directly responsible to the public. The certainty of arbitration removed the incentives for union or management representatives to settle tough issues in the collective-bargaining process. As a result, public officials and municipal employee unions were less accountable to the public for the results of the collective-bargaining process.

The city had no "strike plan." In Flint, the threat of a strike by municipal employees was

EXHIBIT 30

Unions Veto Adoption of Policy and Procedures Manual

Imagine a $60-million business operating without any formal policies or procedures to govern its conduct. This was the case in Flint in 1971.

Disturbed by the absence of a policies and procedures manual, the new city manager began in 1972 to assemble, prepare, and disseminate written policies and procedures covering subjects ranging from the mowing of weeds and the removal of snow to the use of parking lots and city telephones. In January 1974, a formal policies and procedures manual was finally compiled. It contained all operating, financial, and personnel policies and procedures that had been promulgated to that date. The purpose of the manual was, in the words of the deputy city manager for operations, "to standardize the ad hoc, seat-of-the-pants management that existed in the past."

Because the City Council plays a major role in the execution of many city policies, this manual was submitted for its review. Formal adoption, however, was not necessary, since the document contained little that was new; it merely pulled together in one place that which previously had been contained in ordinances, council resolutions, departmental memos, actions of boards and commissions, union contracts, etc.

The city's employee union and the patrolmen's association demanded that *all* the policies and procedures contained within this manual be negotiated with the unions, regardless of the fact that a majority of them had been in effect for years without generating a single grievance.

The president of the general employees' union claimed that the manual violated employees' working conditions and their right to collective bargaining. Speaking before the council, he stated that the city administration was antiunion, and said he was appalled and ashamed that Flint, a labor town, would tolerate such an administration. He went on to charge the council with allowing city administrators to control them, and accused some council members of being "election-day friends of labor." He challenged taxpayers to get control of Flint back into the hands of Flint people. Ironically, none of the union leaders who spoke before the council lived within the city limits.

The union could have filed a grievance, claiming that specific terms of its current contract had been violated, but it did not. Instead, it filed an unfair labor practice charge with the Michigan Employment Relations Commission and launched a political attack on the City Council. Over strenuous opposition by the city manager and the finance director, the City Council agreed to negotiate the policies and procedures manual with the city unions.

Eventually, the council refused to formally adopt any policies and procedures, but did not prohibit their use by the administration in governing the conduct of city business.

an especially effective tactic in the hands of employee unions. A strike by almost any of the city's bargaining units could virtually close down city government. The city had absolutely no contingency plan for a strike situation, and everyone knew it. This was the case, not because no one had ever thought of preparing a strike plan, but because it was not clear what purpose a strike plan would serve when everyone, except a handful of top-management personnel, was in a union.

Contract administration was inadequate. After a contract was finally negotiated, it was months before copies of the contract were printed and distributed to responsible managers. Interpretations and guidelines for its implementation were never prepared. No attempt was made to educate or advise management personnel about potential problems within the terms and between the lines of newly negotiated contracts. This lack of guidance often led to misunderstandings about the proper interpretation of contract language. As a result, many grievances had to be heard and resolved which could have been handled in some other way.

Recent developments in such cities as San Francisco, Seattle, and New York suggest that conditions in Flint are far from unique. There is little question that a major challenge facing public officials in every city during the 1970s is how to employ the talents and energies of municipal employees in a more productive manner, so that both the employees and the public will benefit. To develop a basis for meeting this challenge, it is necessary to examine the causes and consequences of the conditions that existed in Flint.

The principal cause of the imbalance of power in Flint was the power of municipal unions to affect the election of members of the City Council. The city was divided into nine wards, each of which elected a council member. Commanding critical political resources—money, manpower, and votes— municipal unions in Flint were able to elect many of *their* candidates to the council. This situation, combined with the fact that the city

manager, director of finance, and city attorney served at the pleasure of five votes of the City Council, explains why municipal managers were not eager to contest union power. If a council member wanted to keep his or her council seat, or a manager his or her job, union demands had to be satisfied, as the case presented in Exhibit 31 attests. It is not surprising to find that from 1965 to 1974 public officials in Flint figuratively "gave away the store," allowing city unions to consume a larger and larger percentage of the operating budget and to assume an increasing role in the management of the city.

The fact that Flint was the birthplace of the United Auto Workers (UAW) also serves to explain the power of municipal employee unions. The UAW, organized in 1935, successfully carried out in Flint the first major strike against General Motors. As a result, Flint became known as a "labor town." This labor-consciousness spilled over to Flint's public employees. In the 1960s, UAW– negotiated benefits constituted a check list for city unions. By the early 1970s, however, the situation had been reversed: the terms and conditions of employment enjoyed by city unions could have served as a check list for the UAW. For example, the UAW had long sought a "thirty and out" contract provision allowing retirement after thirty years. By 1974, most municipal employees in Flint could retire after twenty-five years and some after twenty-two years. The most-recent city union demands were "twenty and out."

A third explanation of union power in Flint was the fact that the city in the late sixties and early seventies had a surplus of funds with which to "buy" labor peace. This surplus was partly the result of an act passed by the Michigan legislature which allowed cities with populations of less than 1 million to levy a 1- percent income tax on residents and a .5- percent income tax on nonresidents who worked in the city. From 1964 to 1974, most of this revenue was used to pay the cost of increased compensation of city employees. During this period, city employment increased 43 percent while average compensa-

EXHIBIT 31

City Council Reinstates Employees Who Paved the Parking Lot of a Friend's Bar

At a council meeting in October 1973, a council member informed his counterparts that a city work crew had been observed paving the parking lot of a private bar—on city time with city supplies and equipment. The deputy city manager informed him that this allegation had already been investigated and that the employees and their supervisors denied the charge. The city attorney said that if the allegation were true, it could be a felony.

Two days later, four city water division employees were fired after they admitted using one-and-a-half tons of city asphalt to patch holes in the parking lot of a friend's bar. The employees explained that at the end of the workday they were instructed to dump leftover asphalt in a specific place. Instead, they took the remaining asphalt to their friend's bar and helped him patch his parking lot. (Ironically, the asphalt used was the incorrect type for that kind of job.)

The city manager explained that the severity of the disciplinary action was due to both the seriousness of the offense and the fact that the employees had tried to cover it up. The four men involved appealed the action to the Civil Service Commission under provisions of the city charter. Three of the four employees also appealed to the City Council under the Michigan Veterans Preference Act of 1897. The president of the local union stated that the employees should not have been fired because they were following established practice. He could not, however, explain why, if this were true, the employees denied their involvement when initially asked. He did say that if the City Council and the manager had not become involved, making it a political issue, these employees would not have been fired.

The Civil Service Commission upheld the disciplinary action. This surprised many observers, especially the unions; because the commission usually sided with city employees when there was any doubt concerning the justification of management's motives.

One month later, the entire City Council stood for reelection. The general city employees' union endorsed nine council candidates. Each supported candidate was given funds by the union. Six were elected.

Three weeks after the election, the City Council voted 6–2 to reinstate the four men who were fired and to give them three weeks' back pay. The effect was to give the men, retroactively, a thirty-day suspension.

The president of the Civil Service Commission strongly criticized the council for reinstating the men who had been fired, saying, "The spoils system [has] returned to Flint in a completely new form." He went on to say, "A sad situation exists when city employees can use the political environment to bypass the bodies established to control personnel."

tion for municipal employees increased 145 percent.

The power of municipal employee unions in Flint was also enhanced by the fragmentation of management authority, a condition created by the city charter. Unions were able to play off civil service against city department heads and agency administrators, increasing their own power and benefits in the process. It was not uncommon for unions to negotiate compensation increases through the collective-bargaining process and then go to civil service to obtain additional compensation through reallocation of job levels. This often set off a domino effect that soon involved a large number of related employee classifications and an even larger number of employees. The unbudgeted costs of reallocations in 1973 approached $100,000 in annual wages and salaries.

City unions also benefited from the rapid turnover of political leaders, since an entirely new council was elected every two years. Union leadership, on the other hand, remained relatively constant. Few political leaders in Flint had the knowledge to match that of an experienced union leader who was also a longtime city employee.

The political realities that prevented the City Council from acting as a countervailing force against the power of city unions was mirrored in other political bodies as well. Michigan legislators, many of whom were dependent on union votes, continually passed legislation that strengthened public employee unions. In 1974 agency-shop legislation was passed, while repeated attempts to amend the Public Employment Relations Act to more clearly define bargainable issues or establish criteria for union membership were resisted successfully. The courts also tended to support city unions. In 1973, a Flint circuit-court decision ruled that municipal employee unions could participate in City Council elections despite the fact that a provision of the city charter expressly prohibited such activity. The fact that city unions were active in supporting the campaigns of circuit-court judges partially explains this decision.

The major consequence of excessive union power in Flint was the inability of municipal managers to control the increasing costs of city services. With labor costs constituting almost 80 percent of Flint's operating budget and increasing at roughly 9 percent per year, and with revenue increasing at only 3 percent, the city was gradually forced to consume the large surplus created by the passage of income-tax legislation in 1965. By 1972 this surplus was exhausted. Only the advent of revenue sharing kept the city from undergoing a severe financial crisis. And by 1974 it was apparent that not even revenue-sharing funds would be sufficient during the next few years to pay the increasing costs of municipal employees.

Municipal unions in Flint exercised a virtual veto power over the implementation of many city programs. For example, in 1973 the City Council wanted to develop a narcotics control program that would involve the assignment of plainclothes patrolmen, primarily black officers, to narcotics undercover work. The patrolmen assigned would have received an increase in compensation, in view of the increased hazards of the assignment. The patrolmen's union refused to allow this program to be implemented unless the remaining 260 patrolmen in the same classification received the same salary increase, with no additional work.

Another example involved the city's affirmative action program. Union opposition to this was so profound that after two years of concentrated effort marked by more than sixteen lawsuits, total minority employment was still only 12.2 percent in a city with a minority population in 1974 of more than 30 percent. Finally, as the cases presented in this chapter have suggested, union power was so pervasive that union leaders could dictate who would work for the city, the policies and procedures under which they would work, the kind of supervision they would receive, and the level of service they would provide the public.

As the power of municipal employee unions increased, the power of the city manager, as well as that of other municipal managers, decreased. Managers had fewer and fewer options available to them in carrying out council policies. To illustrate this point, in 1973 the City Council asked the city manager to examine ways to decrease the city's operating costs without reducing overall levels of service. One suggested alternative involved using private contractors for the maintenance and repair of city vehicles. The municipal garage had long been considered, even by employees, the most inefficient operation in the city, and an independent study of garage operations, completed in 1971, concluded that the cost of vehicle maintenance and repair could be reduced by as much as 50 percent if this service were obtained from the private sector on a contractual basis. Union reaction against even the consideration of this idea was so vehement that the City Council quickly instructed the city manager to postpone further study.

Another consequence of the municipal unions' power in Flint was the inability of public officials to discontinue ongoing programs after they had become obsolete or could no longer be afforded. Typically, this occurred in programs initially funded by federal grants for which the city was required to pick up the full cost at the end of the grant period. In nearly all such cases the council, cognizant of the political consequences of laying off existing employees, voted to continue the old program regardless of current need, past performance, or cost. As a result, Flint's bureaucracy continued to grow as new programs were added to old ones. None was discontinued.

A final consequence of the extensive power of city unions in Flint was the city's inability to attract and retain competent managers. After two years of debate, a full-time labor relations director was finally hired in January 1975. Seven days after he arrived, he resigned from the job, stating that the power of civil service and the influence of municipal employee unions made successful labor relations and personnel management impossible. He noted in leaving that Flint's personnel system was too fragmented, its civil-service system too powerful, and its municipal employee unions' influence with the City Council too pervasive. "The system has grown up over a long time," he said, "and it will take a long time to change it. For now, the city's labor relations are not in good shape."

Opportunities for Improvement

After reviewing conditions in Flint, it is clear that common sense, not sophisticated analysis, is the primary requirement for identifying opportunities to improve employee competence and motivation. Furthermore, major changes, not fine tuning, are required if the productivity of Flint's work force is to be improved.

Heading the list of obvious improvement opportunities is the development of a personnel department responsible to the chief executive and responsive to the council.[8] This department would be responsible for implementing a system based on merit, not on political patronage or seniority. It would attempt to ensure that the best-qualified individuals were hired and promoted, that compensation was based on demonstrated job performance, and that unsatisfactory performance would be dealt with in a fair and equitable manner.

The first order of business for the new personnel department would be the elimination of restrictive personnel policies and procedures. Among others, the following changes should be considered:

- Ensure open competition for all positions not contained in an established promotional sequence.
- Develop an active recruiting capability that would stress individual qualifications,

past experience, and specific job requirements.

- Use written examinations only when they are proven to serve as a valid predictor of performance in the job to be filled.
- Score examinations on an "excellent-pass-fail" basis, abandoning the pseudoscientific procedure of scoring tests to the second decimal point.
- Allow municipal managers an opportunity to select employees from a list of qualified candidates, all of whom have met established qualifications, abandoning the "rule of one" and the "rule of three."
- Establish probation periods based on the importance of the job.
- Develop a performance-evaluation system for all employees which is based, to the extent possible, on the use of established productivity measures and other measures of job performance.
- Base promotion decisions primarily on predicted ability in the new job and secondarily on actual performance in the old one; eliminate special promotion credits for seniority and veteran status.
- Base compensation decisions on individual performance; if a "base" compensation is determined for a group of employees, make bonuses a function of individual performance.

To guard against the potential abuse of power by elected or appointed executives, a personnel review board should be established with the sole function of considering alleged abuses to the merit system. After carefully weighing all the evidence presented, this board would make public recommendations to the City Council.

A personnel system that recognizes and rewards demonstrated merit should be supported by education and training programs that would allow employees to advance within the personnel system according to their interests and capabilities. Job counseling, career planning, tuition reimbursement, and on-the-job as well as off-site training should all be part of a personnel develop-

ment program that is tailored to the needs and responsibilities of employees.

It is less clear what can or should be done to make jobs more satisfying to the employees who perform them. Opportunities to make individual jobs more satisfying include such innovations as flexible time programs that allow personal scheduling of the workday within an established time range, job enrichment plans that provide employees with greater responsibility and permit them to see how the results of their jobs are related to the achievement of broader objectives, and management-employee committees that ensure that employees have opportunities to suggest improvements concerning the way in which government functions and activities are carried out.

The need to reduce the excessive power of Flint's employee unions, thereby bringing into balance the exercise of union rights and management responsibilities, is equally obvious. Several possible ways of doing this from the standpoint of municipal managers were discussed in the previous chapter. Additional suggestions include the following:

- Eliminate situations in which managers are in the same bargaining unit as the employees for which they are responsible.
- Develop an office of labor relations under a professional director who has clearly established responsibilities.
- Improve access to important information concerning labor relations. A network of informed individuals within the state of Michigan should be developed, and efforts should be made to improve information gathering about what comparable jurisdictions are paying municipal employees for comparable kinds of work and how labor-management issues are being resolved.
- Intensify efforts to define, in negotiated contracts, in local ordinances, and in state law, criteria for determining what is and what is not a bargainable issue.
- Establish a specific period of time within which the collective-bargaining process is

to be completed and negotiated contracts
are to be signed. This period should be
closely integrated with the budgetary process, so that the discipline of considering
how negotiated benefits will be financed
will be brought to the bargaining process.
Contracts, where possible, should be negotiated for multiple years with appropriate "reopener" clauses based on
specified conditions.

- Explore the feasibility of developing multijurisdictional bargaining with the Board of
Education and other agencies in Genesee
County. Multijurisdictional bargaining
would ensure that professional labor-rela-
tion skills would be brought to bear on the
negotiation and administration of contracts.

- Develop a set of management objectives
and a strategy for their accomplishment
prior to the initiation of the collective-bargaining process. The negotiation plan
should be reviewed with all top-level managers to ensure that it is practical and feasible.

- Adopt policies and procedures governing
City Council's relationship with unions
and union representatives during the collective-bargaining process. The ability of
unions to make "end runs" around designated council representatives must be curtailed.

- Develop the analytic capacity to understand and communicate the full cost of all
union proposals and counterproposals. In
the short run, this involves the assignment
of cost analysts to the collective-bargaining team. In the long run, this process requires the development of analytical tools
that will ensure rapid and accurate analysis
of and response to union demands.

- Prepare a "strike plan" and train municipal
managers so that essential services will be
continued in the event of a work stoppage

or an employee strike.

- Grant legally to municipal employee
unions the right to strike except in those
instances where a danger to the health or
safety of the community can be clearly
demonstrated. Binding arbitration should
be limited to those instances where strikes
have been prohibited by statute or injunction. If third-party arbitrators are used,
they should be selected on a random basis
rather than by participants.

- Develop a centralized grievance-control
system that would ensure that all municipal managers are informed of the nature
and resolution of grievances that may affect their own operations.

- Provide all municipal managers with proper instruction concerning the nature of negotiated contracts and potential problems
they may face in implementing them.

In view of the political power of city unions
and the increasing demands by citizens to
know how their tax dollars are being spent,
consideration should be given to opening
negotiating sessions to media reporters. This
would ensure that the public had a basis for
holding both labor and management
accountable for how city revenues are being
spent, and would educate both citizens and
the media about the collective-bargaining
process and its impact on management and
performance.

Unlocking the potential of municipal employees is central to strengthening the management process in local government. Improving performance depends heavily on
finding better ways of using the talents and
energies of employees. This is perhaps management's most challenging opportunity
and its most important responsibility in improving the performance of any local government.

CHAPTER 8

Management Tools

Man is a tool-using animal. . . . Without tools he is nothing; with tools he is all.
Thomas Carlyle

The use of sophisticated tools is a primary characteristic that distinguishes man from the rest of the animal kingdom. Tools extend the reaches of our mental and physical capabilities. Anthropologists study the tools used by a society as a means of evaluating the level of its development. Generally, the more advanced the tools, the more advanced the society.

This same observation could be made of both private and public institutions. The more advanced the management tools used by a private corporation or a public agency, the more advanced the institution. Applying this standard of development, local governments do not fare very well. As a rule, they have not made use of the advanced management tools that are regularly used by many private and other public institutions.

There is a basic reason why the private sector makes better use of management tools than the public sector: competition. Advanced management tools provide a competitive edge. Consider, for example, the airline industry. Even in this partially regulated industry, competition is intense as each airline attempts to provide the most attractive mix of services and schedules. As a result,

airlines raced each other to automate their reservation services, placing a computer terminal in front of every reservation clerk and providing customer access to a vast array of flight data. One large, government-owned airline would not have had the same incentive.

In the public sector, citizens do not have a choice between two or more agencies offering similar services. In local government, politics, not competition, is the motivating force behind the introduction of change. The challenge, then, is to make the use of advanced management tools good politics for the monopolies of government. The first step, however, is to determine which management tools local governments should be using.

In this chapter, the term *management tools* refers to the methods, systems, and devices used by political leaders and municipal managers to carry out the work of government. We believe that six management tools should be in place if a local government is to have the potential for improved performance: (1) an integrated planning process, (2) a comprehensive budgeting process, (3) a systematic performance-measurement system, (4) a responsive organizational structure, (5) a modern data-processing system, and (6) an adequate level of analytical support.

While each of these tools is distinct, each is closely related to the others. The fact that we discuss them in parallel, however, does not mean they are of equal importance—a budgeting system, for example, is significantly more important than a data-processing system. Nonetheless, they should be considered and used together in order to have the greatest possible impact on performance.

The common focus for all these tools is the management process—planning, implementing, and evaluating. An integrated planning process and a comprehensive budgeting system together contribute to the completion of the planning phase. A responsive organizational structure is related most directly to implementation. A performance-measurement system primarily supports the evaluation phase. A modern data-processing system and an adequate analytical effort support all three phases of the management process.

Impact on Process and Performance

Management tools provide information that political leaders, municipal managers, public employees, and citizens need in order to make informed decisions about community needs, define alternative ways to satisfy these needs, and evaluate the success with which an alternative is implemented. Better tools should result in better public decisions. Better tools should be good politics. With better information, politicians should be able to talk more knowledgeably about the nature of community problems and more realistically about what local government can do to solve them. At the same time, better information can be threatening to politicians. If advanced management tools provide information that is precise and easily understood, opportunities for emotional appeals are reduced and decisions made on purely political grounds are more easily identified.

Without accurate and timely information, managers cannot manage. Of course, decisions can be made without good information. If resources are plentiful and public scrutiny is absent, it may be of little consequence that decisions do not result in the most service provided for each tax dollar expended. If this is not the case, then advanced management tools and the information they generate may be a prerequisite for

a manager's keeping his job. Yet these very management tools can pose a threat to some managers. As a result of the information they provide, managers can be held more accountable for their performance—a threatening situation for some.

Information generated through advanced management tools also affects the way in which public employees work within the management process. Because the majority of public employees are concerned about the quality of their work and want to gain a sense of satisfaction from a job properly carried out, information that allows them to compare actual results with planned results is essential and desirable. Moreover, information that enables employees to see how their activities and functions fit into broader strategies to achieve community objectives can be an important factor in improving employee motivation. Of course, better information and increased accountability may be a threat to employees, as well as to managers and political leaders.

Advanced management tools and better information are prerequisites for meaningful citizen involvement in the process of government. Without accurate and timely information, citizens and community leaders are unable to understand what their government is doing for them and thereby contribute fully to the decision-making process. Moreover, advanced management tools allow media reporters access to information that permits them to analyze and evaluate how well a local government is performing, thus greatly facilitating efforts to inform the public.

Criteria for Evaluation

Improving the quality of each management tool will strengthen the ability of government officials to manage a local government for improved performance. Conversely, antiquated management tools can severely impede improvement efforts. This section describes six basic management tools and presents for each a number of evaluation criteria.

The planning process

The term *planning* refers to the process of developing realistic community objectives toward which the activities and resources of local government, as well as other public and private institutions within a community, are directed, and determining how these objectives will be achieved.

However one views the desirability of change, it is inevitable. Individuals will continue to seek better homes, higher-paying jobs, improved education, and more efficient forms of transportation; corporations will continue to seek greater growth and larger profits. In combination, these activities may produce positive opportunities or negative consequences for the community. The purpose of planning is to consider alternative ways to avoid the negative consequences while taking advantage of the opportunities.

The focus of planning should be the individual citizen. Too many plans address geographic areas or urban functions, as if these were the most important considerations within the community. Citizens—both individual and corporate—make up our counties, cities, and other local units of government. The quality of life enjoyed by these residents is what planning is all about.

The following criteria can be applied to a particular planning process and to its principal product—a master plan—in order to identify opportunities for improvement:

Is the plan realistic? If a plan is to guide change, it must indicate not only what is desirable but also what is possible, given available resources. Therefore, a master plan must contain objectives that are measurable and achievable within a reasonable period of time, indicate how programs and projects will achieve community objectives, and explain how much each program will cost, how it will be financed, and who will be responsible for its implementation. In short, the planning process must be linked to resource allocation and managerial accountability; available resources and the ability to carry out the plan should be the principal constraints in its development.

Is the plan comprehensive? If the focus of planning is the individual and corporate citizen, then a plan that is complete must address the full range of conditions that affect the quality of life all citizens experience. The planning process must recognize the inseparability and interrelationship of human, economic, social, and environmental conditions. One cannot be considered without the others.

Does the plan consider unique community conditions? Human economic, social, and environmental needs are not uniformly felt by all citizens within a county or city. If a plan is to serve as a tool to guide change toward desired ends, it must reflect the unique needs of individual neighborhoods and the citizens who reside within them. A master plan should be geographically decentralized. Different maintenance and growth strategies should be developed to meet the different needs of different parts of a community.

Is the planning process integrated with related functions? If those who are responsible for developing a city or a county plan do not work closely with those who are responsible for preparing the annual budget, implementing approved programs, and evaluating program results, planning will not be complete. Planning cannot take place in a vacuum, isolated from other steps in the management process. In answering this question, it is necessary to determine whether the planning staff works closely with the budget and evaluation staff. Are operating managers involved in the planning process? Do planners report to the executive who, in turn, is responsible to the electorate or to elected officials for carrying out the plan?

Does the planning process bring together essential public and private interests? Improving the quality of life for individual citizens cannot be accomplished solely by governments, nor can needs be satisfied entirely by the private sector in the free-market system. If needs are to be met, the planning process, conducted by government, must bring public and private interests together in a combined effort to solve community problems and satisfy community needs. It is, therefore, essential that those responsible for developing a community master plan work closely with other public and private institutions that can affect the conditions reflected in the plan.

Are citizens involved in the planning process? If a plan is to gain the political and community support required for its implementation, the process by which it is prepared must be open to all those affected by it. A master plan is intended to affect community conditions; it is intended to affect the lives of individual and corporate citizens. Therefore, it cannot be prepared in bureaucratic back rooms or a consultant's ivory tower. All too frequently, a finished plan is revealed to the public at a legislative meeting in a way that implies that the plan is complete and ready for ratification. This won't work. The process of developing a community plan must include continuous consultation with those who will be affected by it. Accordingly, citizens should have an opportunity to express their views and interests throughout the development of a county or city master plan.

Is the final master plan understandable? It is critical that citizens whose lives will be affected by the contents of a master plan be able to read and understand it. The master plan must be clearly written, understandable, and readily available to all citizens.

Is the master plan continuously updated to reflect changing conditions? A plan must be a working document that affects the day-to-day operations of a local government, or it is not a plan. It is therefore essential that a plan be updated as often as necessary to reflect changing conditions. This question examines whether the planning process provides for a periodic review of key assumptions, demographic data, and unanticipated events that may affect the actions initiated by the plan.

The budgeting system

A *budgeting system* is the single most important management tool in any business, public or private. A *budget* is a financial and operational plan for a particular period of time (generally one year). Simply stated, budgeting relates planned resource expenditures directly to the results these expenditures are expected to achieve and to responsible managers. Budgeting is part of the planning process. These functions cannot be separated: budgeting is planning.

Local-government budgeting involves considerable conflict. In addition to conflict about the selection of community objectives (what government should do), conflict centers on the selection of the most appropriate means to achieve these objectives. Conflict is enhanced by the absence of objective measures that enable government officials or the public to assess clearly the effectiveness of past programs in achieving community objectives. The results of the budgetary conflict are eventually captured in one document—an annual budget.

The following evaluation criteria represent conditions that a budget process should meet if it is to serve local-government officials as an effective management tool:

Is the budgeting process integrated with the planning process? Budgeting is part of the planning process. The development of community objectives serves to integrate planning and budgeting. The budget, and the process that produced it, must be compatible with a local government's master plan.

Is the budget comprehensive? A budget cannot include some governmental funds and not others, nor can it include some governmental activities and not others. A budget must incorporate expected revenue and planned expenditures for *all* funds and *all* activities. This question asks whether all resources (people, money, equipment, capital) are identified and allocated in the annual budget.

Are resources related both to results and to responsible managers? In essence, a budget represents a contract wherein responsible managers indicate the results they will produce with specified resources (dollars, people, equipment). This contract creates a realistic basis for holding managers accountable for their performance. This question examines whether responsible managers are identified for each government program, activity, or organizational element. Have the results these managers intend to produce been clearly stated? Are resources clearly identified, and can they be related to intended results? In short, is the budgeting process tied to managers within the organization structure and to a performance-measurement system?

Does the budget reflect the future consequences of current budget decisions? To ensure well-informed decisions, a budget should be related to past and projected resource expenditures. The "thin edge of the wedge" describes the bureaucratic ploy of advancing a project that requires few dollars in the first year but becomes very expensive in later years. This question examines whether a budget shows the future implications of budget-year expenditures (the "fat edge of the wedge"). Does it present adequate historical expenditure levels, so that current resource-allocation proposals are placed in appropriate perspective?

Is the budget understandable and usable? A budget should meet a variety of needs and lend itself to a large number of uses. Accordingly, a budget must be able to be understood by the general public and be used by different users for different purposes. The budget must be prepared in sufficient detail so as to permit expenditure control by financial officials as well as provide information in a way that will facilitate decision making by the legislative body and operating managers.

A performance-measurement system

A *performance-measurement system* is a tool that permits political leaders, municipal managers, and the public to compare what a local government says it will do with what it actually does, in terms of the services it provides, the output it produces, and the results it achieves. In short, a performance-measurement system facilitates an evaluation of how much a local government produces and how well it performs.

Performance measurement has long been an indispensable part of the successful operation of private business. It has not, however, been widely used in local governments—perhaps because in the latter there are few common denominators of overall performance, such as return on investment, earnings per share, or stock price. Nevertheless, it is imperative that local governments develop and evolve better measures of their performance.

Local-government performance can be

measured at different levels. One such level is overall *governmental performance*—defined as the ability of a local government to achieve community objectives with a minimum expenditure of resources. This was the subject of Part I. Another level is *operational performance*—defined as the ability of organizational units within a local government to produce specific results with a minimum expenditure of resources. While overall government performance is measured in terms of the attainment of a general condition within the community (the level of public safety as measured by crime compared to a target rate), operational performance is measured in terms of the operating results produced by an organizational unit (the number of miles of street actually patrolled during peak crime periods, compared to a target for this activity). Community objectives, of course, must be related to organizational objectives. In essence, the following relationship should hold: given specific assumptions, if organizational objectives are achieved, maximum progress will be made toward the attainment of community objectives. While measuring the achievement of certain community conditions (such as public safety) is extremely difficult, it is less difficult to measure performance at the operational level.

A performance-measurement system is crucial to the successful conduct of the management process. In concert with a budgeting system, a performance-measurement system contributes to planning by helping determine what can be done, to implementing by relating day-to-day actions to results, and to evaluating by providing the basis for determining the effectiveness or the efficiency of government activity.

The following criteria may be used to evaluate the quality of a performance-measurement system as a management tool:

Does the performance-measurement system establish performance standards and targets for all government operations? A performance-measurement system should incorporate measures for each government operation, recognizing that, in most instances, one or two measures may provide a sufficient basis for measuring performance. This question examines whether measures have been developed for each government operation, and whether all departments and agencies relate the results of their work to the resources they consume in producing it. Further, this question asks if measures are reevaluated periodically to ensure that they are motivating the appropriate organizational behavior.

Is the performance-measurement system integrated with planning, budgeting, and control systems? A performance-measurement system should be integrated with both the master plan and the budget. It should provide information to government officials, as well as the general public, about progress in the achievement of community objectives and the degree to which organizational results are being achieved. This question examines whether a performance-measurement system is integrated with accounting and financial reporting systems in the control of day-to-day operations; whether managers are able to compare actual results against those planned; and whether public officials can monitor progress in the attainment of community objectives.

Is performance-measurement information used by a wide variety of people? Performance data, like budget data, must serve a variety of users. In answering this question, we must examine whether measurement data are summarized and aggregated so that they are of use and of interest to the general public. We must examine whether performance-measurement data are provided in sufficient detail for use by municipal managers in exercising operational control. Further, we must examine whether performance data are provided to top management and legislative officials for their use in evaluating the performance of government departments as well as the progress made in achieving community objectives. Data should be provided in a manner that reflects geographic differences within neighborhoods or special districts. Finally, this question examines whether the performance-measurement and reporting system in use is flexible and capable of being changed as community needs and the ability of government operations to achieve them change.

Organizational structure

Organizational structure—defined as the relationships among people, functions, and activities within the executive branch of government—is a management tool.* An important management principle, too-often ignored in both public and private corporations, is that "organization follows people, and people follow strategy." In other words, an organizational structure should not be developed until the objectives of the organization have been defined, a strategy for their attainment has been developed, and people who will be responsible for implementing the strategy have been selected. In this sense, the structure of an organization is very much a management tool: it assists managers in carrying out strategies to accomplish the objectives of an organization.

Local governments that begin with organization, as many city and county charters require, begin at the wrong end of this sequence. What results is the necessity of first finding people who fit an established organizational structure and then limiting the development of strategies to what these individuals, constrained by a rigid organization, are capable of carrying out. Reversing the "strategy→ people →structure" sequence reduces the potential for local-government officials to improve performance.

---

* This reference to "organizational structure" differs from "local government structure" as discussed in Chapter 10. In that chapter the word *structure* refers to the allocation of legislative, executive, and judicial powers to branches and agencies of government as well as to individuals elected or appointed to positions of responsibility.

The following criteria provide a useful beginning in evaluating the impact of organizational structure on the management process:

Does the organizational structure capitalize on the strengths of present personnel? People, not organizational structures, produce results and deliver services. Organizational structure should enhance the ability of individuals to carry out their responsibilities. This question examines whether managers have the authority to organize people in a way that uses their strengths and minimizes their weaknesses.

Does the organizational structure clearly define responsibility and authority for achieving objectives? The purpose of an organization and of the people who comprise it is to achieve community and operational objectives. Answering this question, therefore, involves an examination of whether an organization reflects these objectives; whether duties and responsibilities of personnel are clearly defined and lines of authority clearly established, thereby ensuring accountability for performance. Further, this question asks whether responsible managers have the authority required to exercise the obligations imposed upon them.

Does the organizational structure provide managers with a reasonable span of control? The complexity and diversity of government operations will determine the appropriate span of control a municipal manager can handle. Managing a number of similar activities may permit a broad span of control; conversely, managing vastly different activities may require a narrow span of control. Answering this question involves a determination of whether public managers have an appropriate mix and number of people reporting to them and whether similar functions and activities are combined organizationally in a way that ensures that they will be properly managed.

Does the organizational structure facilitate delegation of authority and responsibility to the lowest level where it can be exercised well? The manager who is closest to the actual job being performed should have sufficient authority and responsibility to get it done. The responsibility and authority for achieving specified results should be delegated to operating managers, who, in turn, should be held accountable for their performance.

Is the organizational structure flexible? If organization follows the development of objectives and of a strategy to achieve them, it must therefore change as objectives and strategies change. This question examines whether an organizational structure is flexible and can be changed without undue effort and time. To what extent does a city charter define an organizational structure, thereby making change impossible without a vote of the people?

A data-processing system

Data processing is an important tool for use in strengthening the management process. In the thirty years since the development of the first "electrical computing machine," the use of electronic data processing has increased significantly in almost every public and private organization. Electronic data processing (EDP) has become an indispensable management tool, not only because electronic equipment can now record and process data, make calculations, and print reports faster and more accurately than humans can, but also because EDP can provide new information in a form and with a timeliness that was heretofore impossible.

In this chapter we emphasize the management uses of data processing and the impact of data-processing support on the management process. The following criteria may be used to evaluate the way in which a data-processing system serves government officials as a management tool:

Is data-processing support available to all departments of a local government? Data processing is a staff function that must be provided to all departments of a local government. Data processing should not be

monopolized by one department, such as finance or engineering. This question examines whether all departments have equal access to EDP support.

Is the data-processing function centralized at the appropriate level? The data-processing function should be assigned to that level of a local government organization where (1) data can be made most easily available for multiple purposes and users and (2) analytical talent is available to serve all users within government departments and agencies. These requirements must be met while ensuring responsiveness to users.

Is the data-processing plan based on government-wide user needs? A data-processing plan should reflect governmentwide needs and priorities. To ensure that multiple uses and users are properly served by a centralized data-processing organization demands a careful evaluation of user needs and hardware constraints. It is important also that the data-processing plan take advantage of the systems and knowledge other local governments have developed and acquired.

Is the data-processing system designed to be flexible? A data-processing system must be flexible and easily changed to meet changing management requirements. This question, therefore, examines whether each data-processing system is maintained in a way that best serves different users, makes most efficient use of existing equipment, and can be modified to meet changing user needs.

Analytical assistance

We include a discussion of *analytical assistance* here to underline the point that without expert analysts the most advanced management tools will have little or no impact on the management process. The ability of analysts, therefore, is an essential tool.

Analysts, both within and outside local government, are responsible for analyzing and presenting the information generated by management tools in a manner that will facilitate its use in the decision-making process. Analysts do not directly provide services to citizens, nor are they responsible for major line and staff functions. Rather, they are technical experts in such areas as policy analysis, budgeting, performance evaluation, and data processing. They provide essential support to political leaders and municipal managers. In evaluating the quality of analytical assistance, the following criteria should be considered:

Is the existing analytical staff adequate both in skills and in number? Management tools depend on analysts for their value. This question examines whether a local government has sufficient analysts with the requisite skills to design, operate, and apply management tools to the decision-making needs of government and public officials. Are staff analysts capable of improving the quality of decisions made by municipal managers and political leaders?

Are consultants and other outside experts used appropriately? In the absence of adequate skills within a local government, consultants should be used to help produce specified products. A local government should use consultants to augment its analytical staff and to compensate for the absence of requisite skills. Local-government staff members should work closely with consultant project teams to ensure that knowledge gained in producing each product is not lost when the consultants are through. This question examines whether consultants are properly used, thereby ensuring a basis for determining whether they have produced what a local government wanted.

Is analytical assistance provided at appropriate organizational levels? Each branch of local government requires analytical support to improve the decision-making process. The legislative body as well as the executive branch should have the requisite analytical support to perform its function adequately. Further, this question examines whether major executive departments have the requisite analytical support to manage their diverse operations.

Conditions in Flint

The planning process

In 1972 two plans affected the city of Flint: the 1960 Flint Master Plan and the Genesee County Land Use and Transportation Plan. The first had been prepared in 1958 (primarily on the basis of data from the 1950 census), submitted to the Flint Planning Commission in 1960, and adopted by that commission in 1965. The zoning ordinance it recommended was not adopted by the City Council until 1968. By the time the plan itself was adopted by the council, seven years after it had been prepared, it was already obsolete.

The Genesee County Land Use and Transportation Plan, a more recent product, was completed by the staff of the County Planning Commission in 1971. This plan dealt with the long-range land-use and transportation needs of the county to the year 1990. Although adopted by the County Planning Commission and the County Board of Supervisors, this plan was not adopted by any unit of local government within the county, including the city of Flint.

Both plans contained a considerable amount of interesting historical data and projections of potential land usage. The first plan was too old to be relevant to the problems and issues of the 1970s. The newer plan dealt with a geographic area that was so large, and with a time period so far in the future, that political leaders found it easy to postpone consideration of the issues it raised. Neither plan was useful as a decision-making tool.

In 1972 the City Council, reacting to the inadequacy of Flint's master plan, initiated a three-year program to completely revise both the plan and the planning process. The discussion that follows concentrates on an evaluation of the 1960 Flint Master Plan. In 1974 this was still the city's officially adopted master plan; it is typical of such plans in effect in many other cities throughout the country.

Flint's 1960 master plan was not comprehensive. The plan's main focus was on land use and transportation; economic and population characteristics of the community were analyzed only to the extent that they affected land use and transportation. In addition to land use, the major subject areas of the plan were zoning, streets, parking facilities, transit systems, parks, housing, and the central business district. The conclusions of the plan centered on land-use controls, transportation improvements, zoning-ordinance changes, and a capital-improvement program. The plan also contained a few very specific recommendations, such as those calling for the removal of railroad tracks in the downtown area, an urban-renewal program for one particularly blighted section of the city, and the future combination of local parks and school grounds into unified park-school complexes.

In the foreword to the 1960 plan, the consultants who prepared it stated:

It is the purpose of the master plan to aid and to serve as a guide for the city government, public and semi-public agencies, institutions, private developers—all who have a part in building the community—in the planning and coordinating of buildings, facilities, and services, with a view of producing an orderly, well-functioning and attractive community in which to live and which can be operated and maintained efficiently and economically.

This excerpt reflects the historical bias of city planners toward the physical environment—an approach to city planning based on the theory that improving the phsyical environment will somehow solve the complex human and economic problems of a community. It is also based on the pragmatic realization that the physical environment is all that cities traditionally have been able to control. Such a view is still prevalent in many local governments. Changing this view is a slow process, hindered by the fact that state and local legislation has isolated physical and transportation planning at the local level through the creation of planning commissions and planning agencies which are required to concentrate on these areas.

Conspicuously absent from traditional city planning has been a consideration of the human, social, and economic factors that affect the quality of life within the community. Granted, these factors are reflected in the physical environment, and more and more so-called comprehensive planners are taking them into account in preparing city master plans. Nevertheless, a plan that is primarily directed at the physical environment tends to view economic, human, and social conditions as constraints, not as ends in themselves. This tendency creates an inadequate basis for making decisions about total needs. In Flint, a truly comprehensive master plan would have addressed the improvement of local education, health care, and water and air quality; a reduction in the rate of violent crime; and the provision of ample opportunities for gainful employment. These were not addressed in the 1960 Flint Master Plan.

A major deficiency in the 1960 Master Plan was its failure to consider the need for economic diversification. At the time the plan was prepared, more than 50 percent of the work force in Flint was employed directly by the General Motors Corporation. Its almost complete dependence on GM made the community extremely vulnerable to the ups and downs of the national economy and of the automobile industry. This is not to say that Flint did not benefit from the automobile industry. It did. There was a time, however, in the history of Flint, when diversification of the local economy would have been in the long-range interests of both the community and General Motors.

One such time was the year 1960. The city in 1958 had undergone a major recession as a result of a slump in the sales of GM cars and trucks. Surprisingly, this problem was not addressed by the city planners. The 1960 Master Plan avoids any discussion of the issue and performs no analysis concerning the need for economic diversification. In 1974–1975, unemployment rates in Flint exceeded 15 percent, a condition created by a national recession and a decline in automobile demand. Better planning might not have solved this problem, but it certainly might have lessened its impact.

The master plan was not integrated with other management functions. The schedule followed by the Planning Commission and the City Council in adopting this plan is indicative of how remote it was from the actual day-to-day operations and decisions of city government. This plan sat on the shelf for five years between the time it was approved by the Planning Commission and the time it was adopted by the City Council. During that period five city budgets were adopted and carried out. During the same period, the Michigan Department of Transportation planned an entire freeway system through the city of Flint which almost totally disregarded the transportation element in the master plan. Freeway routes were determined through negotiations among the political forces in the Flint community, the Department of Public Works, and the State Transportation Department. Old, stable neighborhoods were destroyed and recreational areas were affected adversely. These were problems that good planning, even simple physical planning, should have avoided. In 1974, the freeway system through Flint was still not complete. Most delays were directly due to problems created by irresponsible decisions made at the time the original routes were chosen.

The master plan was not integrated with the budgeting system. The plan did not even include a forecast of its impact on city expenditures. There were no cost estimates for meeting any of the plan's recommendations; there was no indication of how the planners felt their few specific recommendations

would be implemented. The planners were totally unconstrained by financial or operational limitations. It is hard to imagine a private business surviving very long if its planning efforts were conducted without being subject to the discipline of financial or operational constraints. In Flint, few, if any, resource-allocation decisions were affected by this plan.

The plan was not realistic, nor was it dynamic. The following recommendation is typical of the plan's content: "Additional park space is needed in this neighborhood and should be developed adjacent to the elementary school." It was not clear if this recommendation was achievable (maybe the school was surrounded by intense development); nor was it measurable (the plan did not specify the number of acres of park that should be developed). The recommendation was clearly not time-specific (there was no target date for its completion), and there was no indication of who should be accountable for accomplishing the recommendation if it were adopted. Even if the park were built, citizens would not know if it was the park that had been planned. If after ten years, a park had not been built, no one could fault the plan or those implementing it. In short, there was no way to judge whether the plan was realistic because, in almost all cases, its recommendations were not specific enough for anyone to determine exactly what was intended.

A plan that took five years to be adopted can hardly be considered dynamic. The 1960 plan, adopted in 1965, was never updated during the thirteen years following its preparation.

There was little citizen or private-interest involvement in the preparation of the 1960 plan. Of course, the city conformed to planning legislation which required a series of public hearings prior to the adoption of the plan. However, if distribution of the plan after its adoption can be used as an indication of interest and involvement, we can conclude that citizens and community leaders were not very interested in the planning process. Of the 1,000 copies that the city had printed for distribution, more than half were still available for the asking at city hall ten years later. In the early 1970s, the planning office stopped charging $4 a copy and began to distribute it free. There were still few takers.

There are many reasons why Flint did not have an adequate planning process or an adequate master plan, and these reasons are not unique to Flint. Few cities today plan in a way that meets the criteria outlined above. A primary reason for this is that prior to the 1960s and early 1970s, local governments were not much concerned about the human, social, and economic problems that affected the quality of life of their residents. Cities, and counties, were primarily responsible for housekeeping and maintenance functions. Economic development and improvement of human and social conditions were considered either out of the purview of government altogether or the responsibility of the state or federal government.

The 1950s, when the Flint plan was produced, was a period of growth. Most cities measured their success, or "progress," by increases in population, the dollar value of new construction, or other growth statistics. Local-government officials showed little concern for how people lived within the community.

Another problem with master plans such as Flint's is that they are prepared primarily by planning technicians. Flint's plan, like most other city plans, was produced by a consulting firm staffed primarily by engineers, architects, and land-use planners. Their training reflected experience in the physical environment, with streets, bridges, freeways. It is not surprising that physical considerations were given priority over human, social, and economic considerations.

The costs of this kind of planning are high. One need only look at the physical environment of Flint to see that the 1960 plan has had little positive effect on the quality of the city's physical environment, and even less effect

on the quality of life enjoyed by Flint citizens. In fact, Dort Highway, a boulevard that stretches the length of Flint's east side, was used in one major urban planning textbook as a classic example of poor land-use planning.

The budgeting system

Prior to 1972, Flint had what is commonly called a line-item budget.* This budget was prepared annually by the director of finance. Its primary purpose was to ensure responsible fiscal administration and control. It did not, however, meet any of the criteria listed earlier in this chapter.

Flint's budget in 1971 was not comprehensive. The budget did not include all city funds or all the activities performed by city government, but instead focused primarily on the general fund, which accounted for expenditures financed from locally collected income and property taxes. Some funds did not even appear in the budget. For example, there was no budget for the Public Improvement Fund, from which the city made all of its capital appropriations. Some city departments, such as the Department of Community Development, had completely separate budgets that were approved on a cycle different from that of the city's general fund budget. Because most city departments and agencies spent money from a variety of funds, it was impossible under this system to examine the total budget of a particular department or organization within a department.

Flint's line-item budget did not contain all the resources controlled by the city. Although dollars were accounted for in infinite

---

* A *line-item budget* presents budgeted items at their lowest level of detail. For example, it would show a separate line for salaries, one for each item of fringe benefits, one for each item of supplies, etc. Each municipal activity might have twenty or thirty detailed budget lines.

detail—literally to the penny—personnel were not. Personnel costs were shown in this budget as line items within the funds from which salaries were paid. However, some employees were paid entirely from funds which did not appear in the city budget, or which showed up only partially. The equipment allocated to a particular department to perform its activities was not identified in the budget unless a new piece of equipment was to be purchased in the budget year or unless the department had to rent equipment during the budget year.

The budget was not coordinated with the planning process. This situation reflected the fact that the city effectively had no planning process. Since Flint's master plan was out of date and the county plan had not been adopted by the city, neither of these had any impact on budget decisions.

Flint's budget in 1971 did not compare resources with results. It made no attempt to relate expenditures proposed in the budget to what was to be accomplished with these resources. The old budget broke down costs by activity—the kind of work performed. For instance, "garbage collection and disposal" was an activity. However, the budget did not indicate the level of output each activity was supposed to produce in the budget year or whether one or more organizations performed the same activity. This was even true of the most easily measured items, such as the number of tons of garbage to be collected.

In addition, it was impossible to determine, even within one fund, the total cost of conducting a particular activity. The city budgeted a number of expenditures centrally, even though the expense resulted from an activity that occurred within a specific department. For instance, all of the fringe benefits for city employees were budgeted centrally, while base salaries were budgeted by activity. In many cases, fringe benefits amounted to more than 30 percent of base salaries. Such a procedure severely handicapped efforts to calculate and estimate the true cost of city activities, much less relate such costs to output.

The old budget did not relate resources to responsible managers. The budget was organized by fund, not by organization. Where a department was funded by only the general fund, the responsibility of the manager was clear. The situation in most city departments, however, was not so simple. Some departments, such as Public Works, were financed by as many as six different funds. As a test of the adequacy of the city's budgeting and financial-management systems, the director of public works was asked in 1972 what the total annual expenditures of his department were from all funds. His answer: approximately $30 million. Next, the department's accountant was asked the same question. His answer: approximately $20 million. Next, the city engineer, who was also the deputy director of the department, was asked. His answer: $10 million. As it turned out, the two top administrators were wrong and the department's accountant was right. The purpose of this exercise was not to prove who was right or wrong, but rather to demonstrate that the city's budget system did not pinpoint organizational responsibility and accountability.

The budget was not related to future expenditures. The budget presented expenditures by line item for the current year and the two preceding fiscal years; however, it did not estimate or forecast expenditures beyond the budgeted fiscal-year period. Thus, it was impossible to determine the future impact of current expenditures. The "thin edge of the wedge" problem could not be identified.

Flint's budget was difficult to understand and use. The city had one budget document that ran about 1,000 pages. Each page contained a list of line-item expenditures within a particular activity. Each line item had four entries: one each for the two previous years, one for the current year, and one for the budget year; and all of the figures were carried to two decimal places. This approach gave the illusion of precision and accuracy. The document, however, was almost useless to managers and members of the council. The only people who completely understood and could use the document were the Finance Department employees and accountants.

If such a document was not understandable to those who were expected to use it in making important budget decisions, it certainly was not understandable or useful to the average citizen, who had much less time, energy, and motivation to study it. In strict accordance with the city charter, however, a copy of this document was placed on file with the city clerk for public examination. Needless to say, it was rarely examined. Except for information that was reported through the media, no other budget information was provided to the public.

The city had such an inadequate budgeting system for a number of reasons. For one, political leaders had not demanded a better system. Past city councils simply did not use the budget as a decision-making tool. The short two-year term of a council member did not permit the luxury of trying to alter the city budget to reflect new priorities and directions. The common approach was for a council member—or, better, a bloc of five council members—to develop a few pet projects for their term of office. At budgeting time they would ensure that these projects were included in the budget; all other budget decisions were left to the administration. Moreover, because all new personnel positions (even though the budget called for them) had to come back before the council during the fiscal year for approval and because all significant purchases (those over $1,500) had to come back before the council on an item-by-item basis for a second approval, there was little need to spend time and energy on the budgeting process. All important decisions would come back for a second review.

Administrators showed little more interest in improving the budgeting system. Most city administrators depended more on their "gut" feelings about what was going on than they did on documented evidence. Civil service and union protection at all levels, combined with the policy of internal promotions, left managers with little incentive to push for change. Moreover, most managers felt that the less the council knew about what was going on in city hall, the better. Therefore, there was little motivation on the part of management to provide information that could be easily understood and acted upon by the City Council or the public. In fact, soon after a new city manager arrived at city hall in late 1971, the finance director, who had spent more than 25 years in Flint city government, told him that the more information the City Council had, the more dangerous it could become. The implication of his advice was to keep them in the dark.

Another reason for the lack of a good budgeting system was that the city did not have the personnel to support a better system. It is hard to imagine that a city responsible for spending $55 million a year had virtually no budget staff, but this was the case in Flint. In 1971, one person in the Finance Department was responsible for preparing the entire city budget. As a result, his job consisted of no more than compiling and collating submissions from departments. There was little analysis and review of departmental requests. Moreover, there was no data-processing support for the budgeting effort, and no one individual (other than each department head) was responsible for the budget in each department. In short, budgeting was a grossly neglected process.

The last explanation for the state of the city's budgeting system was that prior to 1972 the city did not face serious financial problems. Since the passage of a city income tax in 1965, there had been no need to increase taxes and only one instance of curtailment of services for financial reasons. During this period the city accumulated substantial surpluses. Apparently, past administrations had seen to it that there was ample money for the pet projects of key council members and ample funds to satisfy union demands for salary increases. As long as these objectives could be accomplished, there was no pressing need to improve control over other funds spent by the city.

One of the consequences of this kind of budgeting system was that the goods and services provided by the city probably cost more than they should have. (We use the word "probably" because, ironically, the inadequacy of the budgeting system makes it impossible to prove the assertion that such a system encouraged higher costs.) Knowing the costs of services is the first step in controlling costs. When the full cost of a service is unknown and when there is no system that records what a manager intends to do, there is no force working against the tendency to increase staff and budgets without corresponding improvements in services.

What can be more easily documented is that Flint's budgeting system encouraged the delivery of substandard levels of service. Because managers were not accountable for producing specific results during the budget year, they had little or no incentive to produce maximum services from the resources that were available. The most blatant example of this occurred in the Department of Public Works, which was responsible for the city's flood-control program. Exhibit 32 fully explains the circumstances that resulted from this lack of budgetary control. Because no flood-control budget had been established and used as the basis for controlling the annual expenditure of funds required to complete each phase of the work, the city suddenly found that there were no funds left to complete the last two phases of the project. The result was the necessity to appropriate more funds to complete the project.

Another consequence of Flint's inadequate budgeting system was that the city was unable to implement any form of productivity-improvement program—an effort to get more output from a given level of resources or the same output from fewer resources. Productivity improvements are based on the ability to measure output per unit of input. The budget system in Flint did not provide for this kind of measurement.

Last, Flint's old budgeting system made it

impossible to reflect community priorities in the budget process. The City Council was limited to a "bottom up" approach to reviewing the budget, reflecting the way it had been prepared. This meant that the council had to go through the budget fund by fund, activity by activity, and line item by line item. Because data could not be assembled in programmatic or organizational formats, it was impossible for the City Council to view the entire budget as a whole, examine major parts of it, or make resource-allocation decisions that cut across program areas or departments. Moreover, because budgets were prepared by each department, each line item from the previous year was automatically included, with this year's increment added to it. Any attempt by the City Council to shift priorities was strongly resisted by the bureaucracy.

For these and other reasons the City Council and the city manager in 1972 initiated an effort to develop a new budgeting system. The nature and scope of this effort are related in Chapter 18.

A performance-measurement system

Prior to 1972, the city of Flint did not measure the performance of its government operations. The only document that regularly contained performance-related information was the charter-mandated annual activity report. But this report *did not provide or monitor performance targets, nor was it related to planning, budgeting, or control systems.* It was produced by each department at the end of a calendar year and presented statistics on a broad range of departmental activities. Each department prepared its own report, each in its own format, with no central guidance or summarization. Activity reports were submitted by each department at the end of March each year. The manager's staff simply stapled these together and distributed the report to the council, placing a copy on file in the clerk's office for public examination. Be-

EXHIBIT 32

No Control over Flood Control

In July and August of 1972, the city manager was assembling a capital-improvement program to be recommended to the City Council. One of the high-priority recommendations of the Department of Public Works was a $171,000 appropriation to complete the third phase of a four-phase flood-control program for the Flint River. The city manager was told that the Army Corps of Engineers was prepared to commence work immediately but that the city needed additional funding in order to fulfill its commitments.

Upon further questioning and investigation, the city manager learned the following facts: A program to prevent flooding along a two-mile stretch of the Flint River through downtown Flint had been proposed nearly fifteen years before. In the early 1960s, a specific program was adopted by the Army Corps of Engineers and the city. In 1962 the city appropriated $1,250,000 as its share of the four-phase project. $800,000 of this amount came from a bond issue. The city's share of flood control consisted of providing 1 percent of the project costs, acquiring the land needed to make the improvements, and making modifications to the utilities at the construction sites. With the $1,250,000 appropriation, a flood-control account was established within the Public Improvement Fund. No budgets were established to control the project within this account. There were no separate controls over the costs of each phase of the project or over the activities of land acquisition, utility modification, or cash contribution.

After a number of delays, work on the first two phases began in October 1966 and was completed in 1970. In 1968 the City Council adopted an urban-renewal plan for the downtown area. This plan incorporated a beautification scheme for the river which was in conflict with the Army Corps of Engineers' plan for a concrete trapezoidal ditch. As a result, this section was extracted from the original plan so that it could receive special treatment after the remainder of the flood-control work had been completed.

By 1971 project funds had been totally depleted; yet the city needed an unknown amount of additional funds to meet its obligations to the Corps of Engineers. The city thus appropriated another $300,000 to the project in 1971. Now, in 1972, another $171,000 was needed in order to cover the city's share of the third phase of the project and permit the Army Corps of Engineers to commence construction again.

The city manager agreed to recommend that $171,000 be appropriated from the Public Improvement Fund to meet the city's commitment. However, in doing so, he asked what those responsible for this project intended to use as the source of funds for the city's portion of the remaining—and possibly most expensive—phase of the project. To this question there was no satisfactory answer.

cause the activity report was prepared looking back to the prior calendar year (January–December) and the budget was prepared looking forward to the next fiscal year (July–June), the report had little relationship to and absolutely no impact on the resource-allocation process. It was not possible to relate planned resource expenditures to planned results.

The annual activity report was not widely used. Few, if any, citizens ever asked to look at it. Government officials seldom referred to it even though it contained some extremely valuable, though inconsistent, information concerning the past performance of certain departments. If the useful information had been separated from the vast array of irrelevant data, provided in a more timely manner on a fiscal-year basis, and related to the budget, the city would have had the rudiments of a performance-measurement system. As it was, these data were collected for the sake of data collection and only because the charter required it.

The monthly budget status report was the only performance-related report to which managers referred. This was an accounting report, modified to include budget data. It contained actual versus budgeted expenditure data for selected city activities and funds. This report did not really measure performance; it provided only financial data, and in most cases it did not include all monies being spent by a division or a department. The budget status report was limited to accounting for General Fund expenditures, even though these represented less than half of total city funds. Departments that were funded from other sources were not provided budget status information unless they developed and operated their own reporting systems.

There are a number of reasons why Flint did not have a performance-measurement and reporting system. First, the ability and necessity to consistently measure performance is a fairly new development in city government, even though efforts to do this date back to the 1930s. The nature of local government has changed dramatically in the past two decades. When local governments provided a minimum of maintenance-type services it was easy to evalute performance by firsthand experience. But today local governments are providing a wide range of complex services. It is now difficult for citizens, chief executives, and legislative bodies to follow and evaluate all of the activities performed by a local government.

Another reason for the absence of performance-measurement systems is that, like most of us, political leaders, municipal managers, and public employees would prefer not to have their performance evaluated if they can avoid it. It is hardly an original insight into human behavior to suggest that those who work in a highly politicized environment would prefer not to have to state exactly what they intend to do and then be held accountable for doing it. This was certainly true in Flint. In one instance, a proposal that the City Council conduct a citywide poll to determine citizen views on the quality of city services was soundly defeated by an 8–1 vote: the council would do its own evaluating, according to its own criteria.

A final reason for the absence of a performance-measurement system in Flint is that neither the public nor the media demanded better information about the performance of their local government on a continuing basis. Only when the city grossly neglected to provide a service did anyone, including the press, become concerned about the quantity and quality of such services. Historically, citizens in Flint demanded little from their city government.

The lack of a performance-measurement system affects the quality of budget decisions, employee morale, and the future financial health of the government. It is hard enough to make intelligent resource-allocation decisions when good information is available; it is impossible to make good decisions when there is no information available. How, for example, can a city council decide whether to invest scarce tax dollars in extra patrol cars or in extra garbage trucks if it has no estimates of what an extra patrol car will produce in terms of crimes prevented or of what an additional garbage truck will produce in terms of additional levels of cleanliness achieved? Without this type of performance data, there is no quantitative basis on which to make budget decisions. As a result, resources are allocated in an uninformed, often uneconomic manner, resulting in higher-than-necessary costs.

Low employee morale and poor supervision throughout the city of Flint could be attributed in part to a lack of clarity concerning what employees and supervisors were supposed to do. It is difficult to obtain satisfaction from doing a job well if it is not clear what one is supposed to do. Furthermore, the absence of performance-related information made it impossible to explore with employees, supervisors, and middle managers ways of relating their compensation to the quality or quantity of work they produced. Such personnel actions as promotions or suspensions were thus based on arbitrary criteria rather than on objective measures of performance.

Finally, the lack of a performance-measurement system reduces the ability to project the future financial consequences of present operations. If you cannot relate the results of current activities to the resources being consumed in their production, it is impossible to examine future resource needs under various service-delivery assumptions. The lack of a performance-measurement system thus reinforced the day-to-day crisis management that pervaded city government in Flint.

In 1973 and 1974 an effort was undertaken to establish performance measurements for each organizational unit. Targets were set and a reporting system was put in place. Chapter 18 discusses the implementation of this system.

Organizational structure

The organizational structure of Flint's city government in 1972 met few of the criteria presented in this chapter. This was true primarily because of constraints imposed by the city charter. Problems related to the old city charter and efforts to resolve them are explained in Chapter 10. In this chapter we describe not only the charter's role but also the roles of other factors in preventing the development of a responsive organizational structure.

Because the charter prescribed in great detail the organizational structure for departments and divisions, it was virtually impossible for council members or their appointed managers to organize city government in a manner that would best accomplish community objectives. Moreover, because of organizational rigidity, it was difficult to take advantage of demonstrated managerial skills. An example of the latter problem involved the city's equal opportunity director. This manager was extremely competent and had clearly demonstrated an ability to undertake greater responsibility than that required to administer the three-person equal opportunity office. By late 1973, the equal opportunity office had reached a point at which its functions, though troublesome, were under control. The office was staffed with capable personnel, and most activities were carried out routinely. Therefore, its director was able to assume increased responsibilities within the organization. However, as Exhibit 33 indicates, a combination of civil-service resistance, union power, and organizational rigidity denied him the opportunity to do so.

Flint's organizational structure did not assign responsibility clearly. A close examination of the city's organizational structure in 1972 revealed that it (1) made no distinction between line and staff responsibilities and (2) contained little or no justification for the array of departments, divisions, and sections scattered throughout city government. This picture was further confused when one closely examined the organizational structure within a single department. For example, the Flint health director reported to both the city manager and the county commissioners; in fact, he was paid by both

EXHIBIT 33

City Manager Unable To Capitalize on Skills of Top Administrator

"Union claims city aide filling uncreated post"—this was Channel 12's featured news story on the night of July 11, 1973. The television reporter explained that the president of Local 1600 had accused the equal opportunity director of performing the duties of a personnel director, even though such a position had not been created by the City Council.

When interviewed, the city manager admitted that this charge was absolutely true. He explained that a number of major personnel responsibilities were not being handled properly, to the detriment of Flint's citizens and its city employees. No one, the city manager noted, was responsible for employee career-ladder development that would eliminate dead-end jobs within city hall; no one was responsible for personnel evaluation procedures that would ensure that a consistent set of personnel policies and procedures was enforced throughout the city; and no one was responsible for implementing negotiated union contracts, resolving grievances, and administering fringe-benefit programs. Most important, no one was responsible for monitoring personnel decisions to ensure that they were in compliance with the approved budget. The city manager indicated that the equal opportunity director had volunteered to assume some of these responsibilities at no increase in pay and that he, the city manager, had jumped at the chance to take advantage of the skills of such an able manager.

Opposition to this move was not confined to the unions. The civil service director, apparently sensing an intrusion onto his turf, sent the city manager a memo requesting that the additional duties assigned to the equal opportunity director be rescinded. He claimed that these duties had been allocated to the civil service director by the city charter and could not be assumed by the city manager. The civil service director admitted that the functions listed by the manager were not being performed, but said he felt this reflected a lack of staff and budget for the Civil Service Department which could be remedied by appropriate City Council action.

The city unions, however, were most adamantly opposed to this new assignment. They filed a lawsuit requesting the court to order that the equal opportunity director be required to work solely within his existing job classification. Their motivation, in part, stemmed from past conflicts with this person, who had advocated a strong affirmative-action program for the city which the unions had strenuously opposed. Of greater importance to their action, however, was an apparent desire to block the city manager from establishing a centralized

(continued on page 138)

EXHIBIT 33 (cont'd)

personnel-management function. Such a development would undercut their ability to wheel and deal in a highly fragmented system in which the potential was great for playing one party off against the other.

The unions withdrew their lawsuit when they realized that the tactic of working out of classification was one which many from their own ranks used to increase the compensation of a particular class of employees. Even though they decided not to pursue the matter in court, they did continue to pursue it politically. Key union personnel lobbied prounion members of the City Council, demanding that the city manager restrict the equal opportunity director to his former duties. The council, reacting to this pressure, forced the manager to rescind his action.

---

governmental bodies. In addition, he had major responsibilities to the state of Michigan. The costs of his department were shared by city and county. The health director stated on many occasions that he wore so many hats that he never knew which one he was wearing at any one time. This greatly reduced his ability to perform any of his jobs adequately.

Organizational authority was not allocated commensurate with responsibility. This was a serious problem in Flint. For instance, the city manager, under the city charter, was designated the chief executive officer. Yet he did not have organizational control over finance, personnel, labor negotiations, or legal services. Without management control of these functions, it was difficult for him to exercise full executive control over government operations. The city manager in Flint could not hire or fire those managers who reported to him; he did not even hire his own personal secretary. In essence, he was a coordinator of some operating departments. He did not have the authority required to exercise the executive responsibility implied by the charter or by his title.

Many managers within Flint's city government had an excessive span of control. Even though the city manager did not have authority over every department, he was personally responsible for fifteen different functions that reported directly to him,

including community development, health, police, fire, purchasing, public works, and equal opportunity. The finance director had ten separate functions reporting to him; the director of public works, thirteen. The range of their responsibilities made it difficult for these managers to have a complete grasp of the issues affecting the delivery of a broad spectrum of services. The public works director, for example, had to be knowledgeable in areas ranging from garbage collection, sewage treatment, water supply, and street construction to housing inspections, traffic engineering, and environmental control. The breadth of this responsibility would tax the abilities of even the best-trained manager.

The review of Flint's organization also revealed that authority and responsibility were not delegated to the most appropriate level. For example, the city manager was defined by the city charter as the director of public safety. The Department of Public Safety was a charter-created department made up of the police and fire divisions. Repeated attempts to have this responsibility assigned to a specific individual who had the requisite background and training to perform this function proved unsuccessful. To accomplish this would have required that the language in the city charter be changed by a vote of the people. This proposed change was also resisted vehemently by the police and fire chiefs, uniformed employee unions, and civil service.

Legal services provides an example of the lack of flexibility in the city's organization structure. Providing the city's legal services was the responsibility of the city attorney, an independent council appointee who directly supervised all attorneys hired by the city. Yet many city departments, such as the Department of Community Development, had sufficient legal problems or pending lawsuits to keep more than one full-time attorney busy. Under the city charter, however, neither the city manager nor department heads could assign attorneys to these tasks or employ attorneys on their staffs. Each department had to compete with other departments and with the city attorney's own priorities in getting the part-time attention of an assistant city attorney.

Similar functions and activities were not combined and managed at an appropriate level. The city had three separate inspection operations, fire, health, and building, each with a staff of inspectors. Because each staff of inspectors followed a separate schedule and no internal coordination existed, there was nothing to prevent an inspector from each of the three areas from arriving to check out the same premises on three consecutive days—or on the same day. Another example of inadequate organization of similar functions was found in the area of equipment repair and maintenance. Four divisions and departments (police, fire, public works, and parks and recreation) had their own garages to repair vehicles and equipment. There was no need for the city to operate four garages; three of them had only one or two mechanics, and they all repaired similar equipment.

There were many reasons for the deficiencies in Flint's organizational structure. As we indicated initially, many of the problems resulted from the outdated city charter. Although the charter was a major cause of organizational rigidities in Flint, it should be noted that the old charter reflected the conventional wisdom of much of the public and the press. The view that power within a

city government should be dispersed to the greatest extent possible was the basis on which the 1929 charter was developed, and this view was still prevalent in 1972. This approach, however, is contrary to the concept of giving an individual manager the requisite authority and the proper tools to get things done. Granted, authority can be abused if the individual in the position of authority chooses to abuse it. But such abuse is not a structural problem, it is a personnel problem. In such cases, one should concentrate on changing the individual in the job rather than changing the organizational structure to accommodate the lowest common denominator of employee. Designing a structure to ensure that power will never be abused will also ensure that very little is ever accomplished.

Another cause of Flint's poor organizational structure was the attitude of the city's management personnel, most of whom had come up through the ranks. Their exposure to concepts of organization and of organizational behavior was limited. They did not appreciate the role of organization in getting things done. They accepted the structure within which they had advanced with little concern for its adequacy. Furthermore, some managers evidenced a considerable amount of bureaucratic inertia and resistance to change. Managers operating in independent departments protected their own turf. The concept of an overall city organization attempting to achieve common ends was threatening and hence rarely supported by these managers. Since compensation and promotion decisions had little to do with demonstrated performance, most upper- and middle-level managers were happy to stay where they were, maintaining the status quo and putting in their time until the next promotion.

The civil-service system was significant in shaping Flint's organizational structure. Civil service was responsible for the establishment of job classifications for all positions in city government. Most organizational changes required changes in job classification. The civil service director systematically resisted changes that threatened to disrupt the mix and relationship of job classifications. In this respect, the tail wagged the dog. The civil-service system—which in theory was responsible for ensuring that people were paid commensurate with their responsibilities and that job classifications reflected the work being done—in effect determined what work people would do and how the city would be organized to do it. This organizational responsibility was clearly not in the scope of civil service, even under the old city charter, yet most managers had acquiesced to this state of affairs.

City unions had a virtual veto power over organizational change. This power was derived not only from the unions' political role in Flint but also from the strong support they received from the Civil Service Commission and the courts for their claim that even the most minor organizational change constituted an alteration in "working conditions" and was therefore a negotiable issue. The desire to "negotiate" organizational changes was evident not only in general city employee unions, which were primarily nonsupervisory, but also in the supervisors' and middle-management unions. This situation meant that any organizational change required not only the formal support of the City Council and the Civil Service Commission but also the informal support of middle-level managers, general employees, and the unions that represented them. An example of the time, energy and dollar costs associated with making relatively minor organizational changes is presented in Exhibit 18, Chapter 6. This exhibit discusses a two-year effort to eliminate the rank of detective within the police division.

An inadequate organizational structure can seriously impede efforts to improve government performance. The organizational structure in Flint affected the morale and the motivation of city employees and municipal managers because it created and reinforced inequities in both work load and compensation. Many highly qualified individuals were unable to assume greater responsibilities, while others, less competent, remained in positions of major responsibility. Poor organizational structure also resulted in higher costs for the performance of municipal functions. The most elementary analysis showed that it made little sense for the city to operate three separate inspection functions and four separate garage maintenance facilities. The taxpayer paid the bill for these bureaucratic extras. Given these organizational problems, it was clear that organizational change in Flint represented a significant opportunity to improve performance.

Data processing

In 1972 Flint's data-processing system did not serve as an effective management tool for most city departments. This function, located in and to some extent captive of the Finance Department, served primarily as a finance and accounting tool. The systems applications in 1972 were primarily oriented toward such clerical functions as treasury accounting, account distribution, and payroll. Indirectly, these systems served other departments, because all finance, accounting, and payroll activities were centralized. Yet, few systems directly supported the independent activities of other city departments and agencies.

The data-processing function was not centralized at the appropriate level. Theoretically, there was centralized control of the data-processing function, since the Finance Department was a central function serving all departments. The advantages of a centralized system, however, were not realized, because the needs of operating departments were always considered secondary to those of the Finance Department. Moreover, the city's electronic data-processing equipment in 1972 was obsolete. The electronic technology of the equipment was more than ten years old. The industry by 1972 had advanced rapidly but the city had not. The city's computer had the ability to perform a large number of clerical-type processing functions but it had little capability to retrieve and display, rapidly and efficiently, different information for different users.

The city had no plan for data-systems development. EDP systems in 1972 were developed on an ad hoc basis and were determined primarily by the needs of the Finance Department and by the ability of potential user departments to pay for systems development. The lack of available time on the equipment, the lack of skilled personnel available to develop new systems, and the inability of user departments to pay for systems development were the constraints placed on the full use of data processing to meet the needs of city departments.

There was no plan to replace inadequate computer equipment. The original equipment-purchase decision was made in the early 1960s on the basis of the manufacturer's claims about its capabilities rather than on an analysis of the long-term needs of the city and the appropriate equipment required to meet them. At that time, the director of finance determined that the proposed EDP system would satisfy the clerical needs of the Finance Department, and he was probably correct. However, ten years later this equipment was totally inadequate to meet almost any definition of current needs. Yet there was no plan for the acquisition of replacement equipment.

The systems in operation were not flexible. All systems operating in Flint in 1972 had been developed within very restricted limitations. The computer's programming language and configuration were not widely used by other cities or by private industry. As a result, Flint's systems were not flexible. By 1972, most of them had been patched and changed so many times that they could no longer be modified: each required a complete overhaul or redesign.

One of the causes of these problems was that the data-processing division of the Department of Finance operated as an "intra-governmental service" organization. This meant that the division did not receive direct

appropriations from the city budget; rather, it sold its services to other divisions of the Finance Department and to other departments. In other words, all departments of the city had to pay the costs of systems design, development, and operation out of their own budget appropriations. This approach to financing data processing turned out to be a major deterrent to the development of new systems, inasmuch as department managers chose to use budget funds for what they judged to be more pressing needs.

These conditions were exacerbated by a lack of forward planning on the part of the city's management and secondarily by the structure of city government. Most efforts of managers in Flint's city government were oriented to resolving day-to-day problems. Few managers had the time, willingness, or ability to look into the future and assess the implications of data processing on their operations. This, combined with the fact that the Finance Department was, by charter, totally independent of the city manager and of other city departments, produced a situation in which its computer was used primarily as a high-priced adding machine by the Finance Department.

The inability to properly use electronic data processing had a negative impact on performance. In 1972 the city still performed the bulk of its clerical functions manually, which resulted in higher costs in personnel, time, and accuracy. Since many clerical functions were not automated, the possibility that EDP might become a tool of management had not yet been considered. These circumstances encouraged management decisions based on subjective intuition rather than on objective information.

Analytical assistance

Prior to 1972, the top management of the city had virtually no analytical support. The city manager and the City Council, who were responsible for a public business that expended more than $50 million a year in

serving nearly 200,000 people, had no independent analytical staff and depended entirely on personal knowledge or city departments for information on which to base their
decisions. In the past, this had not bothered
managers, who in nearly all cases had
worked in the city for many years. Each knew
pretty much what the others were doing, and
their focus, like the council's, was on day-to-
day problems and operations. Therefore, the
absence of an analytical staff was not considered a problem.

In addition to the lack of analytical support
at the top levels of management, most city
departments did not have adequate internal
analytical support. The director of finance,
for example, had only one budget and research analyst to prepare the annual budget
and to perform special financial analyses.
The Planning Commission had a staff of
one—a "city planner" whose primary responsibility was to process zoning requests.
The police division had a small staff that was
primarily responsible for monitoring and
applying for federal law-enforcement grants.
The Department of Community Development had a small planning staff, responsible
only for preparing urban-renewal plans and
submitting required documents to the Department of Housing and Urban Development. The community development staff

support was the most extensive in the city,
mainly because the federal government was
paying the bill. Last, the Department of Public Works, which spent more than $20 million
of taxpayers' funds annually, had no staff
support except that provided by the engineering office and a two-person accounting
division.

In summary, what little analytical staff
support existed was at the departmental
level, and even at that level it was inadequate. As a result, nobody in the city had the
responsibility for looking forward, anticipating problems, and identifying ways of improving the way the city conducted its business. No one had responsibility for analyzing
existing operations and recommending improvement opportunities; no one was responsible for providing information that
would assist the City Council in making
better-informed decisions.

Soon after taking his job in 1971, the city
manager realized that, before a plan could
be put together to improve city services or to
develop more advanced management tools,
he had to assemble an analytical staff. An
initial review of the existing management
and staff personnel convinced him that the
required analytical skill, in the short run,
would have to come from outside the existing organization.

Opportunities for Improvement

In 1972 the city launched a comprehensive
management-improvement program consisting of two separate but related components: one focused on improving the quality
of community planning, encompassing
issues both internal and external to city government; the other focused on improving
the internal management of city government.

The first component, the development of
an integrated planning system, created a
framework within which all programs for
community betterment could be catego-

rized according to the purposes they addressed. This framework was intended as a
basis for interagency coordination of related
programs and program accountability. The
second component included a comprehensive budgeting system and a performance-
measurement system supported by automated data-processing. This program, together
with the efforts to reorganize city government and obtain analytical support, was
intended to improve the quality of decision-
making information available to the City
Council and top-level managers. Thus, it was

hoped, a basis for holding department managers accountable would be established and governmental performance would be improved. The efforts to initiate and develop these management tools are discussed in more detail in Chapter 18.

The purpose of this section is to briefly answer the question: what is the next step after identifying and initiating the development of new management tools? In many ways, the answer to this question is more important than the determination of what new tools to develop. Major benefits from management tools do not accrue immediately; they accrue over time as people become accustomed to the use of these tools and as the tools are adjusted to serve the particular needs of an organization. Just as one does not become a proficient cabinetmaker with the purchase of the newest-model rotary saw, city-government officials do not become proficient decision makers just because they have new planning, budgeting, or data-processing systems available. Management tools result in better decisions only if they are adapted to the particular conditions within a city government and only if government officials properly use the information these tools provide. Management tools are intended to focus the attention of political leaders, municipal managers, and municipal employees on doing the right things—but tools alone cannot do the job.

By the end of 1974 most of the management tools discussed in this chapter were in use in Flint. Specific community objectives had been incorporated into the budgeting system. Managers were actively involved in both the determination of appropriate performance measures for their cost centers and the establishment of performance targets against which they would be held accountable. Despite a reduction in funds and political support, a data-processing plan was being implemented. New EDP systems had been designed, a new computer system had been leased, and the Finance Department was in the process of modifying existing systems.

The area of organization structure was in the greatest flux. In November 1974, the citizens of Flint adopted a new city charter and with it a new form of government. The mayor now plays a major role in determining how the executive branch of government is to be organized. Citizens can hold a chief executive accountable for the performance of all government operations.

The challenge posed by the new charter to Flint's elected political leaders was concisely stated by one prominent Flint citizen when he told a large gathering, "The tone for continued poor government could be set by a mayor who continues political hackism and management by activity rather than management by results." In short, the degree to which the new management tools developed in Flint would be used to improve the performance of city government was dependent on the actions of those elected to supervise their use.

CHAPTER 9

Financing and Financial Practices

Somehow modern accounting just never infiltrated city government. I do not understand how the city has functioned for the last 300 years.

Kenneth S. Axelson
Deputy Mayor, New York City

Except for bond issues, few citizens have an opportunity to know the relationships or make or express a choice between cost, as represented by taxes, and service. . . . Apparently the overriding objective of many of our political representatives and governmental servants is to keep it this way and to confuse, not clarify those relationships. . . . We should advocate much more detailed analysis and publication of programs, unit costs of services, and recipients of tax revenue and of their comparison with other communities.

Charles P. Bowen, Jr., Chairman
Booz, Allen, and Hamilton

In assessing the reasons underlying New York City's financial crisis, many observers overlooked or underestimated the importance of accounting and financial-management systems. Typically, the crisis was attributed to the extravagant promises of politicians, the excessive demands of city unions, or the exodus of the corporate tax base from the city. However, as Ken Axelson discovered when he became deputy mayor, the absence of timely and accurate financial information had made it almost impossible to anticipate the nature and scope of New York's financial crisis or to do anything about it until it was too late. In this way, financial practices contributed to the crisis and exacerbated its severity.

In the wake of the New York City experience, financial institutions that hold munic-

ipal bonds, accounting and finance professionals, state and federal legislators, and citizens throughout the country have asked themselves whether what happened in New York could also happen to their local governments. The standard response has been, "No—New York City is unique; it couldn't happen here!" Certainly, the precise events and circumstances that resulted in near-bankruptcy for New York will not occur in other cities and counties. Yet, as Charles Bowen points out, the financial information necessary to make such determinations is not generally available to investors, analysts, or the public in a way that would permit this question to be answered conclusively. Unfortunately, the same financial and accounting practices that concealed New York City's crises are employed today in many other

145

counties and cities, similarly concealing potential major fiscal problems.

This chapter examines how the financing and financial practices of a local government affects its performance. For this purpose, *financing* and *financial practices* are defined as the way in which local governments obtain financial resources and restrict, record, and account for their use.

Financial practices are derived from a number of sources: city charters; state, local, and federal legislation; administrative regulations; and pronouncements by the financial and accounting professions. The primary and traditional purpose of municipal financial practices is to ensure that the public's tax dollar is spent (or not spent) in the way legislators, or the electorate, have deemed appropriate through legislation. This concern, which can be called *custodianship*, has dictated the format and content of the financial information that is available to most local-government managers, political leaders, and citizens. However, finance and accounting practices designed to establish an audit trail that traces monies from receipts to expenditures are not necessarily kinds of practices that provide decision makers with the information they should have to make responsible public decisions. The provision of financial information to support the decision-making needs of managers, political leaders has not received adequate attention in the public sector.

Many consider budgeting a financial function. True, budgeting does have a financial dimension; but it should consist of more than the allocation of financial resources. Budgeting, properly carried out, is the allocation of *all* resources available to a local government: people, dollars, equipment, time, and capital. Budgeting is where the management process and the political process come together, and where planning and implementation meet. Budgeting is the process that reflects decisions at the highest level of public policymaking. It is therefore carried out at the highest levels of management within a local government, involving the chief executive officer, legislative officials, appointed boards and commissions, and the public.

Financing and financial practices, on the other hand, are generally considered the domain of the financial manager, usually a director of finance. Unfortunately, they often do not command much attention from the chief executive or the legislative body unless serious problems arise, as they did in New York City.

Impact on Process and Performance

Like management tools, financial practices by themselves do not have a direct impact on the management process. But these practices can aid or impede the effort of political leaders and municipal managers to properly employ resources to manage the business of a local government for performance. In many cases, the restrictions or impediments imposed by financial practices limit flexibility and complicate the process of allocating and spending resources to meet public needs.

States are primarily responsible for restrictions on the authority of local governments to generate revenue. For example, local governments have no taxing power except that granted by the state constitution or by state law. They must seek approval from the legislature for any new kind of tax they wish to levy, and in some states they must obtain legislative approval if they want to raise the level of an existing tax. These local-state dealings often frustrate municipal executives. Boston's Mayor Kevin White has pointed out, "The state must either fund us or free us to raise our revenue. It's like a father who says to a son: 'I'm not going to raise your allowance, but you can't go out and work for yourself.'" To the extent that Boston's revenue-generating powers are limited by state law, the city's performance can be affected.

Not only are local-government officials restricted in their ability to raise revenue, they are also restricted in their ability to use it. In a private business, revenue earned or obtained from whatever source can generally be used for any purpose consistent with corporate priorities. This is not the case in a public business, in which expenditures are usually restricted according to the source of revenue. Federal and state laws and regulations and local charters and ordinances may restrict the use of state highway taxes to streets and roads, federal grants to manpower training or land-use planning, and a specific percentage of local property taxes to the acquisition of new park land.

Such restrictions on the use of revenue may produce bizarre results that are as incomprehensible to local-government practitioners as they are to citizens. For example, it may be difficult to explain to citizens or to city employees why police sergeants and detectives are being laid off because of a shortage of revenue while at the same time untrained police paraprofessionals are being hired because of the availability of federal funds to counteract high unemployment in the area. It may be equally hard to explain that, because the city charter mandates that a certain percentage of property-tax revenue be spent for capital improvements, public-safety services are being severely curtailed at the same time that the city is constructing a new fire station.

Similar limitations apply to debt financing. Most state laws and city charters require a vote of the people prior to the issuance of bonds. Such a requirement can make the determination of the means of financing public projects subject to political considerations that may not be related at all to the merits of a specific project. Such restrictions, however, are not consistently applied; certain bond issues may not require a vote of the people because special state laws, court orders, or other circumstances exempt them from the requirement.

While it is clear that restrictions and constraints on the sources and uses of financial resources affect the performance of local government, it is less clear how such restrictions affect the quality of public decision making. Appropriately prepared and presented, financial information is essential to making informed, realistic, and financially prudent public decisions. If the practices followed in recording and reporting such information do not accurately represent what actually has happened or what will happen, or if such practices distort the information that is available, then the decisions made based on such information will be similarly inaccurate or distorted. As we shall see in the remainder of this chapter, current municipal financial practices permit, and in some cases, encourage, the recording and use of financial information that inaccurately reflects the costs of providing government services or the financial conditions of the local government at a particular time. These practices satisfy finance officers' or the accountants' requirements for a clear and precise audit trail that follows incoming funds to the point at which they are disbursed. However, this is not the kind of information needed by political leaders and managers in order to carry out decision-making responsibilities.

Criteria for Evaluation

The set of criteria in this section provides a starting point for assessing the impact of financial practices on the performance of a local government. Applying these criteria to conditions in Flint provides a basis for identifying improvement opportunities. Although there is some overlap, the ten criteria presented here fall logically into the following categories: (1) assessing financial health, (2) raising and spending financial resources, (3) providing financial information for decision making, and (4) meeting fiduciary responsibilities.

Assessing financial health

An individual who does not know his or her present financial condition and who cannot make reasonable projections of future financial conditions cannot make intelligent decisions about alternative ways to spend current income. Without this understanding, it is impossible to know whether it is economically prudent to buy a house instead of renting one or purchase a new automobile instead of continuing to use the old one. Similarly, a business—public or private—cannot make intelligent expenditure and investment decisions without some understanding of its current and projected financial health.

In simple terms, *financial health* refers to the capacity of a local government to meet its short-term and long-term financial obligations while providing stated levels of service. *Short-term* means a period of time, generally one year, in which tax rates, the mix of services, the costs of providing services, and the population being served are all fixed. *Long-term* refers to periods longer than one year in which the same factors are variable and thus must be projected or estimated. In both instances we are primarily concerned with what services will be provided, what they will cost, and how they will be paid for.

Unfortunately, no one has yet developed a generally accepted or widely applicable model for assessing and predicting the long-term financial health of a local government. Analysts usually can assess financial conditions at the end of the current fiscal year; auditors can determine whether revenues exceeded expenses for a past fiscal period; and politicians can confidently announce that the coming year's budget will be balanced. But the financial future, beyond the budget year, is uncharted territory for most local governments.

This difficulty is compounded by a number of factors. One such factor is the practice of making "transfer" payments from higher levels of government to a local government. In recent years such transfers have significantly affected both the amount of revenue received by local governments and the relationships between the ones who finance and the ones who receive government services.

Another factor is the manner in which financial information is accounted for and recorded by local government. Fund accounting and other municipal accounting practices often confuse rather than clarify information needed to determine a local government's financial health. For example, generally accepted municipal accounting practice discourages the preparation of a consolidated balance sheet or an income statement that reflects the overall financial condition or past record of performance of a complete unit of local government. Thus there is no consistent basis on which to compare one local government's financial health with that of another.

A third factor is that, unlike private corporations, local governments do not provide standard information to support bond financing. Each issuing government agency prepares its own "official statement" containing the information that it has available, that it deems appropriate, or, in some cases, that is required by state law. Bond ratings, one of the few common denominators for comparing the financial performance of local governments, are often based on fragmentary and less-consistent information than are corporate ratings.

A last factor is that projections of financial health present both political and analytical problems. A financial forecast can raise important political questions; for example, should a past policy be continued? Will a new initiative succeed or fail in the legislative process? Are the estimated costs of additional programs realistic? In short, a financial forecast may be limiting political options, thus making the forecaster unpopular. Analytical problems may be just as significant, in that analyses may reveal inadequate sources of information, the uncertainty of future funding, and the difficulty of anticipating the mix of future services.

The following criteria represent what we believe are the most important questions to ask about a local government's financial health:

Does a local government know the full costs of the services it provides? In order to assess the financial health of a local government, one must first determine accurately the actual cost of the mix of services being provided. Only if the true costs of services are known can one determine whether the local tax base or other sources of revenue will be sufficient to pay for them or whether sufficient value is received for the costs incurred. This question, attempts to determine whether the full costs of present and future services are calculated, understood, and communicated in financial reports. Have the costs of current services been paid by past taxpayers or deferred for payment by future taxpayers? To what extent do municipal financial practices help conceal, distort, or illuminate the true costs of government services?

Are the individual and corporate citizens of a local government capable of paying the full costs of current and future services? The demographic characteristics of a community, the strength and diversity of its industrial and commercial base, its physical characteristics, and many other variables create the local economic conditions that determine a community's ability to support a given level of local-government services. This question examines (1) whether these variables are properly weighed, analyzed, and understood in assessing future revenue-raising capabilities and (2) the sensitivity of a local government to economic conditions, both national and local.

Does a local government provide comparable and consistent information concerning its financial health? The current and project-ed financial condition of a local government is a relative concept; that is, we can understand its implications in one local government only if we can compare that government with others. Comparability is especially important to those who lend money to municipalities. In order to make appropriate comparisons, financial information must be provided in a uniform and comparable manner from one jurisdiction to another.

Raising and spending financial resources

The ways in which local governments are permitted to raise and spend financial resources may have a significant effect on performance. In this context we shall not address general taxation policy—the selection of what to tax and how much to tax, the regressiveness or progressiveness of a particular tax, or the economic implications of alternative tax policies. We recognize, of course, that tax policy has an impact on the community and its residents and that it may, in turn, affect the performance of a local government. For example, tax policies that encourage the relatively affluent to relocate in the suburbs can have a deleterious affect on the capacity of the central city to achieve desired levels of government performance. In Detroit, city residents pay a 2-percent income tax, while those who live outside the city and work within it pay only .5 percent. This economic incentive to live in the suburbs has encouraged middle-class families to flee Detroit, taking jobs and the tax base with them. Left behind are those whose needs are relatively greater and whose ability to pay for services is relatively less.

Our concern here is with the relationship between revenue received and services provided, the ability of a local government to obtain debt financing, and the restrictions placed on raising or using public monies.

Is revenue received related to services provided? In private business, the fact that revenue earned is related to each consumer's evaluation of the product produced serves as a major stimulus to improved performance. This is not the case in a public business such as local government. However, it is possible in some cases to relate a service directly to the price or fee the public pays for it, thereby creating performance incentives. Therefore, where possible, specific services should be paid for by fees rather than by general funds.

Does the local government have access to debt financing? Local government should borrow in a prudent manner in order to finance investments in long-term capital assets and, at times, to cover short-term cash needs. The capacity to issue bonds successfully at low interest rates requires a good standing in the bond market. Such credit ratings are based primarily on the wise use of debt in the past, the underlying financial health of the local government, the absolute amount of debt outstanding at any time, and the government's record of debt servicing and repayment.

Are there unnecessary restrictions on the raising and using of financial resources? Local governments not only must adhere to local ordinances in raising revenue, they must also abide by state and federal laws and regulations in order to qualify for so-called shared (transferred) revenue. This question examines whether the requirements that accompany funding are unnecessarily complicated and restrictive. Are efforts made to meet the restrictions of state and federal law and auditing guidelines? Are available resources employed at the same time to meet locally determined needs?

Providing financial information for decision making

We noted earlier that the need of public decision makers for management information is often considered less important than the need to account for and control funds in accordance with legal and administrative restrictions (the "custodianship" function). Nevertheless, political leaders and public managers must have appropriate and useful financial information in order to make prudent financial and public policy decisions. Meeting this requirement need not lessen the importance of the custodial function; public funds must be safeguarded diligently, and the accounting of these funds must be open to public scrutiny. However, an emphasis on acquiring the necessary financial information to support the decision-making responsibilities of local-government officials is essential when the performance of local government is the main concern. In this regard, two questions must be asked:

Is the finance and accounting system uniform, and is it integrated with other management systems? A uniform system of accounts applies the same accounting requirements to all government functions and thus is an important means of maintaining and reporting consistent financial information throughout the various departments and agencies of a local government. Unfortunately, all too often different departments and agencies within the same government unit use different accounting methods. At a minimum, such inconsistency leads to confusion and to a lack of adequate financial control. To be of most service to decision makers, a finance and accounting system must be integrated with other management reporting systems, specifically those which report budgetary and performance information.

Is finance and accounting information useful and usable? Finance and accounting information that can be understood by citizens as well as by elected and appointed public managers can provide a critical contribution to the political decision-making process. This question examines whether a city's finance and accounting system produces information that is tailored to the needs of a variety of users ranging from accounting clerks to members of the general public.

Meeting fiduciary responsibilities

City treasurers, controllers, and finance directors are charged with the fiduciary responsibility of ensuring that funds are collected, safeguarded, and used strictly in accordance with legislative and regulatory restrictions. The current literature and practice of municipal finance is almost exclusively oriented toward the performance of this function. If finance directors and other local-government officials strictly follow federal, state, and local laws, the pronouncements of the American Institute of Certified Public Accountants (AICPA), and the guidelines of the Municipal Finance Officers Association (MFOA), they will in all likelihood be able to trace every penny through the accounting system from receipt to expenditure.

Nevertheless, within the local-government finance community there is disagreement about which accounting and auditing principles and practices should be used in meeting this responsibility. In contrast to the practice in the private sector, annual independent audits in accordance with generally accepted accounting principles are seldom conducted for governments. Prior to the early 1970s, municipal accounting and auditing was the stepchild of the public-accounting profession. In 1972, the AICPA established its first committee on governmental accounting and auditing in order to develop an audit guide for state and local governments. This guide was published in 1974,[1] but it applied only to those cities that required independent audits—probably less than half of the nation's local governments.

The most significant efforts to regulate governmental accounting, auditing, and financial-reporting practices have been made by the MFOA. The MFOA's National Committee on Governmental Accounting periodically publishes guidelines for accounting, auditing, and financial reporting.[2] Local governments that voluntarily comply with these standards in their annual reports receive a certificate of compliance.

But there are no penalties for noncompliance, and less than 1 percent of the approximately 70,000 local governments and special districts actually comply. Moreover, the MFOA standards and the AICPA audit guide differ from each other and from an increasing number of state laws governing local accounting and auditing practices, thereby adding to the confusion in this field.

Local governments are entrusted with the custody of large balances of financial assets (cash and securities). While in the hands of a local government, these assets should be used as efficiently as possible while remaining subject to proper protection. To ensure that a local government is maintaining proper custody of the resources taxpayers entrust to it, the following questions should be asked:

Are financial assets professionally managed? Responding to the profit motive, private businesses attempt to maximize the profitability of all their assets. Because a public business receives revenue independent of its performance, it does not feel this incentive so acutely. This question examines whether government officials manage assets—idle cash, retirement funds, and the like—so as to obtain the maximum return feasible within prudent levels of risk.

Is an audit of financial statements and accounting records conducted annually? An independent audit of a local government's accounting records and financial statements is an important tool for those who depend on the financial information provided by a local government. An independent audit by a public-accounting firm provides an additional check on government at relatively low cost and is preferable to an audit by another government agency or by an elected or appointed government auditor.

Conditions in Flint

From 1960 to 1974, Flint, like many other cities and counties throughout the country, experienced minimal financial constraints. This was generally a period of financial abundance for governments. The most pressing financial issue of the period for local government was how to spend incremental revenue, most often obtained from state or federal programs or from income or sales taxes. Rarely was there a necessity to reduce expenditures in order to balance the annual budget. The future, however, promises to present local-government officials with a very different set of problems.

In this section we examine conditions in Flint with respect to each evaluation criterion. As a background to this analysis, the appendix to this chapter reviews the overall financial condition of Flint's city government in 1974.

Assessing financial health

In 1973 the City of Flint had neither the political desire nor the analytical capability to determine its long-term financial health. From 1964 to 1973 Flint had enjoyed a financial surplus. There was little incentive to address the difficult questions that might be raised by a projection of future financial conditions. In the post–Great Society environment it was politically imprudent to publicize the facts that Flint's operating costs were increasing at an annual rate of approximately 9 percent, that revenues were increasing at only about 3 percent per year, and that federal and state governments had stepped in to fill the gap.

Even if political leaders had had the will to face the facts, staff support and the information required to analyze the situation would not have been available. The full costs of providing city services were nearly impossible to calculate. Projecting long-term costs required a determination of when capital infrastructure would be replaced and how it would be financed; an estimate of future wage, salary, and fringe benefits; and an analysis of when deferred costs might catch up with the city, requiring increased expenditures to make up for insufficient past payments.

These analytical problems were compounded by the fact that since the mid-1960s the mix of services provided by Flint's city government had changed considerably. In part this change reflected the impact of legislation that required Flint to assume responsibility for new services in such areas as housing, manpower training, health, and environmental protection. Would these become permanent services? Would more be added and some dropped? Without answers to these questions, accurate projections would be difficult.

On the revenue side, the picture was just as confusing. The city had become increasingly dependent on state and federal sources of revenue. Would this trend continue at past rates of growth? Would the next grant program be categorical, or would it provide unrestricted revenue? Had local tax rates reached their maximum limit, or could one forecast a tax increase? As unsophisticated as the analysis presented in this chapter's appendix may appear, it was the first of its kind prepared and made public in the city of Flint.

Some unique circumstances in Flint contributed to the lack of interest in understanding the financial condition of the city. Until 1973 the city's finance director, who had brought the city through a number of recessions without a single defaulted payment on its bonds, had resisted this type of analysis. He had a deserved reputation for fiscal conservatism. Many people believed that he had maneuvered the city's accounts in such a way that the city had ample reserves ("cookie jars," some called them) to weather any future financial storms, but no one knew for sure. Exhibit 34 shows what happened when this philosophy was challenged.

EXHIBIT 34

How Much Money Should Be Kept in the City's Cookie Jars?

In August 1972 the city manager proposed a $2.2 million capital-improvement budget to the City Council. In this budget, he proposed spending $937,000 which had previously been contained in an account called "Reserve for Future Debt Service" in the Public Improvement Fund. The manager's proposal to spend these "reserves" was vehemently opposed by the finance director.

Appointed by the City Council and independent of the city manager, the finance director had served in his position for almost twenty-five years. He stated that he had supervised the buildup of this reserve to be used only in case of emergency when tax collections were insufficient to meet the city's annual bond payments. He felt that the reserve was needed so that the city would not have to borrow in an emergency.

In February 1973, the City Council appointed a new finance director who had different views on the subject of reserves. He expressed the view that the city should not function as a bank. In his view, the city taxed citizens to provide vital services; if the city did not have an immediate use for the tax funds it collected, it should return them to the taxpayers or lower the tax rate.

The new finance director further pointed out that, under the law, annual debt service had first claim on property-tax collections. It was highly unlikely that the city would not be able to collect enough revenue from property-tax collections to cover debt service, which represented less than 10 percent of annual revenue from property taxes. Therefore, the city did not need a large "Reserve for Future Debt Service."

The new finance director recommended that the reserve be spent for the proposed capital-improvement projects, and that other such reserve accounts, often referred to in Flint as "cookie jars," be reduced to minimum levels sufficient to meet safely the financial obligations created by current operations.

Determining the full costs of providing services

The need to determine the actual costs of city services rests on the simple propositions that (1) taxpayers should pay, or at least know, the full costs of the services they are provided, so that they can compare these costs with the costs of other goods and services they purchase in the marketplace, and (2) only if elected and appointed government officials know and understand the full costs of public goods and services can they make financially prudent decisions.

In determining the full costs of services, four major problem areas are encountered. These are related to the calculation, recording, and reporting of (1) capital costs, (2) financing costs, (3) indirect costs, and (4) deferred costs.

The recording and reporting of capital costs in local government are affected by one of the basic principles of government accounting—*depreciation shall not be considered an expense.** In private enterprise, depreciation charges provide a means of allocating capital costs to the goods and services produced. For a corporation to calculate its profits, it must know what proportion of "long-lived" assets (a truck that lasts five years or a building that lasts thirty years) should be allocated to each product that is produced and sold. Local governments use exactly the same kind of "long-lived" assets to provide public services, but, in accordance with standard municipal financial practice, the annual costs of using them are seldom recorded or reported. The following is an excerpt from the basic guidebook to accounting, auditing, and financial reporting in local government published by the MFOA.

The committee recommends that depreciation of general fixed assets *not* be recorded as an expense in governmental accounting because no constructive purpose would be achieved in doing so. . . . in commercial accounting depreciation charges must be recorded as an expense because they must be related to revenue produced by the fixed assets in determining accurately the net profit or loss. . . . with the exception of self-supporting enterprise funds, governmental units are not faced with the same requirements for profit and loss

* Capital costs may be divided into two types: infrastructure capital and capital to support operations. *Infrastructure capital* is represented by the community's investment in streets, roads, park equipment, swimming pools, and the like. *Capital to support operations* represents the plant and equipment used by public officials and public employees to provide public goods and services.

determination. . . . governments exist to provide government service and regulatory activities on a continuing basis, and the general expenses incurred therefore have no positive relationship with and do not generate any general revenue.[3]

It is not difficult to conclude that this principle discourages the calculation of annual capital costs, thereby discouraging the reporting of the full costs of providing local-government services. Granted, local governments are not in business to earn a profit, and depreciation is a cost element used in calculating profit. Nevertheless, *breaking even* on the full cost of providing public services would appear to be a reasonable goal for a government in order to ensure its long-term financial health. The calculation and recording of depreciation as an annual cost or as a cost per unit of service is a necessary step in achieving this goal.

Flint's financial practices closely adhered to those recommended by the municipal finance profession. This meant that depreciation allowances were not recorded as part of the annual costs of providing most city services. The confusion that the prevailing practices created is best illustrated by examining the way Flint accounted for two types of city sewers. Sanitary sewers appeared on the city's books as an asset in the city's Water-Sewer Fund—an enterprise fund. (In municipal finance, an *enterprise fund* is a means of accounting for a city-owned utility that charges a fee for each unit of service it provides. Because this type of fund charges a fee instead of collecting general taxation, municipal accounting rules treat it like a private corporation rather than like other governmental entities.) The capital costs of constructing and installing sanitary sewers were depreciated as a basis for determining the rates to be charged to water users. Storm sewers, on the other hand, appeared in the "general fixed assets group of accounts." According to the municipal accounting rules, these assets were not depreciated. The costs of using them showed up only in the year they were installed.

The reason advanced to explain the existence of the two different approaches was that the use of sanitary sewers by a customer could be determined to be roughly proportionate to the water consumed by that customer, and water bills provided a means of proportioning the cost to each user. It was, therefore, important to communicate to the customer the actual costs of using sanitary sewers. But because there was no immediately obvious way to prorate the expense of storm sewers to individual residents, the logic of municipal accounting held that it was not important to know and report the actual cost of this service.

Municipal financial practices relating to depreciation can create even more complicated situations. As Exhibit 35 illustrates, the city of Flint accounted for the costs of its equipment in at least three different ways. All of these approaches were permitted by MFOA and AICPA accounting rules. The one practice which came closest to the objective of indicating the full costs of providing city services was the *motor and equipment pool approach*. During 1973 and 1974, attempts were made to convert all city departments to this approach and to phase out the use of the others.

The way capital items are financed also affects the way city-government costs are recorded and reported. If an infrastructure item—say, a bridge—is constructed with the proceeds of a bond issue, the citizens who use that bridge pay a portion of the annual cost of its use by paying off the bonds over time. On the other hand, if a bridge is financed on a pay-as-you-go basis (constructed with funds previously accumulated in a reserve), the cost of the bridge will not appear as a cost to the local government at any time during its useful life. Earlier taxpayers paid for the bridge used by today's citizens.

In the early 1970s, Flint had many examples of both types of financing. Many capital items then in use had been financed by bond issues, while others had been paid for by lump-sum cash expenditures. In recent years, because of the difficulty of obtaining public support for bond issues, most capital expenditures had been made out of the accumulated reserves of the Public Improvement Fund. Thus, city sewers, buildings, streets, park equipment, and the like might or might not show up as annual costs of providing city services, depending solely on the means used to finance them.

The practices of federal and state governments exacerbated these problems. An example of this occurred in 1974, when the city was in the process of upgrading its sewage-treatment plant. Eighty percent of the funds for this capital improvement had been provided by a federal Environmental Protection Agency grant. Under the terms of the grant, the federal costs of the capital improvement could not be passed on to residential users in the form of depreciation. On the other hand, the grant required that the depreciation cost of the federal share be charged to corporate users. Calculating the cost of providing this service thus became very complicated indeed.

The way in which a local government records and reports indirect costs can also affect its ability to calculate the full cost of governmental services. Indirect costs are those costs incurred by a government which are not related directly to the provision of a specific service. There are different degrees of indirect costs. At one extreme are such costs as salaries, office space, and staff support for a city council or a chief executive. These are the costs of providing "general government," and it is not clear whether they should be allocated to the provision of services. At the other extreme are such costs as fringe benefits for city employees. These are much closer to direct costs and should be associated with the costs of providing services.

The process of allocating indirect costs to the provision of specific services in any business is called *cost accounting*. Techniques of cost accounting have become very sophisticated as it has become an indispensable tool for the control and management of private

EXHIBIT 35

There Are Many Ways To Finance and Record the Cost of an Asset

The city of Flint employed three different methods to account for the costs of equipment used to provide city services. Each method was tied to the way the city paid for the asset, and each resulted in a different cost calculation for providing the same service.

The first approach was to record the original cost of the equipment, not as an asset, but rather as an expense at the time of purchase. Such items were usually purchased under direct appropriation. Under the *direct appropriation approach,* city departments requested the purchase of equipment in their annual budgets in the full amount of that equipment's purchase price. If funds were available, the equipment was purchased; if they were not, a department made do with what it had. Once purchased, the equipment was used until it was no longer serviceable, at which time a request would be made for funds to replace it. Under this method, the annual budget of a department and the costs of the services it provided could fluctuate on the basis of whatever equipment was purchased in any given year. The disadvantage of this approach was that it often led to the use of outdated or obsolete equipment when the climate was not conducive to obtaining an appropriation for replacement. During the budget season, when cuts had to be made it was easier to postpone the purchase of a piece of equipment than to displace an employee.

The second approach also did not record the cost of the equipment as an asset which was then depreciated. However, this means of financing spread the cost

(continued)

businesses. Unfortunately, cost-accounting techniques are very new to local government. Most local governments have no capability to do cost accounting, and thus do not properly allocate indirect costs to the costs of city services.

Flint in 1973 had minimal cost-accounting capabilities. For instance, the city did not even allocate the cost of fringe benefits to the departments in which employees worked. All fringe benefits—and, of course, all other indirect costs—were budgeted and expended centrally through catch-all accounts called General Government Fringe Benefits. In 1974 all the different health-insurance programs, life-insurance programs, social security payments, and the retirement contributions of the many city employee groups were included in this $5.5 million account.

At that time, an effort was launched to allocate the most obvious indirect costs to the departments which incurred them. The results were achieved by 1975, at which time

EXHIBIT 35 (cont'd)

over the years prior to the purchase. This *trust fund approach* was used primarily by the fire division. Under this method, the fire division would annually request a budget appropriation for the Fire Equipment Trust Fund in order to accumulate funds over a period of years sufficient to pay the large cost of replacing a fire truck or similar item when the time came to make such a purchase. With this approach, the annual appropriation was supposed to approximate the annual utilization costs of fire equipment. The approach may have been a reasonable one; however, it suffered from the disadvantage that an appropriation to a trust fund is an easy budget item to cut. Hence the trust fund seldom accumulated sufficient funds to meet equipment replacement needs as they occurred.

The third approach, used primarily by the police division and Public Works Department, was the *motor and equipment pool approach.* With this procedure, the motor and equipment pool purchased vehicles and equipment and then, in turn, rented them to city divisions and departments. The equipment purchased was recorded as an asset in the Motor and Equipment Pool Fund. Annually, the departments included the rental costs of the equipment in their budgets. During the course of the year, the divisions and departments paid the motor and equipment pool the costs of operating the equipment. The price paid by each department was the sum of operating costs, administrative costs, and depreciation.

Under this last system, the motor and equipment pool was able to accumulate funds that permitted the replacement of equipment when it deteriorated or became obsolete. At the actual time of replacement, a vote of the City Council was necessary to approve the purchase, but an appropriation was not required since money was already available in the fund. The annual budget of each department showed only the rental or annual cost of usage. This approach encouraged the timely replacement of vehicles and equipment, since the funds for purchasing the replacements could not be diverted to other purposes.

the $5.5 million spent for fringe benefits in 1974 was suddenly reduced to $1.1 million. In 1975 most of these costs were included as part of the costs of services provided by the employees who received the benefits. The effect on the apparent costs of providing certain services was significant. For example, the costs of providing public-safety services, which had increased $3.6 million from 1971 to 1974, suddenly jumped by $4.6 million in one year. To the layman, it would appear that the cost of public-safety services had gone up significantly. In reality, the apparent rise was simply a paper adjustment made in order to more accurately reflect the true costs of providing this service.

Deferred costs is the last factor that can distort the calculation of the full costs of providing city services. The major item of deferred costs that one is likely to confront in the financial records of a local government is employee retirement benefits. During the 1960s, public employees obtained substantial increases in retirement benefits. One reason

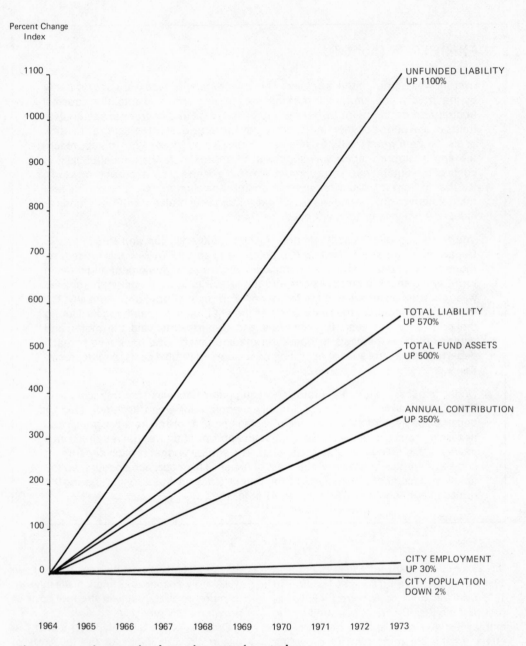

Figure 5. A retirement fund growing out of control.

for this was that mayors, city councils, county boards of supervisors, and others found it politically easier to grant a future retirement benefit than to pay a higher current salary.

This was certainly the case in Flint. As Figure 5 shows, there was a sixfold growth in the total future liabilities of Flint's employee retirement system over the ten-year period 1964–

1973, while the number of employees increased only slightly.

In order to fund such liabilities, local governments should make annual contributions, determined by actuarial methods, which ensure that total contributions over the years of employment will provide enough funds at the time of an employee's retirement to pay the retirement benefits during the employee's remaining life. If a city does not contribute the appropriate amount under this equation, the cost of the retirement benefits are deferred. Eventually, the city is going to have to pay the costs of negotiated benefits, either before or after the employee retires. Paying the costs over the years of employment more accurately relates the costs to the services being provided by the employee receiving the benefits. Deferring such costs entails the risk that sufficient money will not be available, thus forcing future taxpayers to pay benefits to employees who had provided services to a previous generation of citizens.

The problems inherent in the practice of annually deferring pension contributions first show up in the form of large and growing "unfunded liability" in the pension fund. Technically, this liability reflects the amount owed by the local government to the pension fund for benefits *already earned* by employees. It is, in effect, a debt payable to employees (but never recorded as such on the city's financial statements). Annual city contributions should be sufficient to amortize this unfunded liability over a reasonable period of time (usually twenty to thirty years).

Flint did not have major problems with its pension fund. The fund was administered jointly by employees and management independent of other city operations. The actuary retained by the retirement system annually determined the contribution rate necessary for each class of employee. The city then paid this amount to the fund as employees received their paychecks. Nevertheless, even with such actuarily sound practices, the rapid growth of benefits caused the un-

funded liability in Flint's system to grow by a factor of eleven (from $2.4 million to $25 million) between 1964 and 1974.

Paying the cost of government services

Before federal and state revenue-sharing and other transfer payments became a large component of local-government budgets, one could look at the economic conditions within a community and calculate whether local tax revenue would be sufficient to pay the cost of providing services. This is no longer the case. The growing importance of federal and state revenue presents new and particularly difficult analytical problems for those evaluating the financial health of a local government. For example, should analysts disregard federal and state revenues, consider them a perpetual source of funding, or something in between? Should such revenues be related to federal and state economic conditions, or should they be estimated on the basis of political rather than economic criteria? Multiyear appropriations have mitigated some of these problems; nevertheless, estimating the amount of federal and state revenues a local government will receive continues to be the most difficult analytical problem facing municipal financial analysts.

Recognizing this problem and concluding that little can be done about it at the local level, let us turn to the easier task of examining local economic conditions and demographic characteristics in order to determine a community's ability to support a given level of municipal services. Although this process will not reveal the entire financial picture, at minimum it will provide a basis for determining which services a local community could support in the absence of federal and state aid.

The analysis presented in the appendix to this chapter points out that Flint's local economy has traditionally been strong, providing sufficient revenue to finance the needs of

EXHIBIT 36

"When the Economy Sneezes, Flint Catches a Cold"

In November 1973, the local economy of Flint and Genesee County appeared very healthy. Automobile factories were producing at record levels and unemployment was a respectable 4 percent. However, within a period of four short months the Arab oil boycott and the resulting energy crisis had put more than 20,000 employees out of work indefinitely. At 15 percent, unemployment hit depression levels.

If Michigan was the state most affected by the energy crisis, Flint may have been the city most affected. The home of General Motors' Buick Division and the largest manufacturer of Chevrolet trucks, Flint was dependent upon the production of large automobiles and their parts. A reduction in the gasoline supply and the commensurate increase in prices combined to reduce the demand for large new automobiles to practically zero. General Motors reacted by drastically reducing production and laying off workers at its Flint facilities.

The city of Flint was affected by these circumstances in two ways. First, there was a dramatic impact on city revenues, since Flint depended on its city income tax for

(continued)

city government. By 1974, however, Flint had become a mature and partially decaying city. The costs of providing the existing mix of services were rising at a rate in excess of 9 percent per year. On the other hand, property taxes were increasing at an annual rate of only about 3 percent. It was becoming clear that the local economy, which was almost entirely dependent upon the automobile industry, could not match the inflated costs of local government with corresponding increases in property values and personal income.

Contributing to the problem of increasing costs was the city's changing population mix. Like most other industrial cities in the Northeast, Flint was experiencing an emigration of white middle-class residents, who were moving to the suburbs and being replaced by black residents. Census data showed that more than 20,000 white residents (10 percent of the population) had been replaced by an

equal number of black residents in the period between 1960 and 1970, and the trend continued into the 1970s. Flint's new population had lower relative incomes and required more public services. The increased demand for services occurred at a time when the city's infrastructure was growing older, creating higher annual maintenance costs and eventually requiring costly replacement. Assuming that the automobile industry remained relatively healthy, the long-range economic outlook for Flint in 1974 was not totally negative. What was clear, however, was that Flint would become increasingly dependent on outside sources of revenue as its expenditures outdistanced the capacity of the local economy to pay for them.

In addition to these long-range problems, Flint was subjected periodically to severe short-term economic swings. Cities that are heavily dependent on property taxes and utility fees for local revenue, and which have

---

EXHIBIT 36 (cont'd)

one-fifth of its income. Revenue collection from this source fell by 20 percent. In addition, state sales, income, and gas tax revenues, which were distributed to the city, also decreased.

The second impact did not occur in real dollars but was just as significant. For a period of six months, little except the energy crisis received the serious attention of the City Council and the community.

The city government itself would not have faced great financial hardship even if the crisis had become worse; despite the reduction in city revenue, most basic services could have been adequately provided. However, at such a time of community crisis there appeared to be a need for the City Council to reflect the community's concern with economic hardship by cutting budgets, reducing programs, and taking other steps to give the impression that the city was suffering in the same degree as its corporate and individual citizens. An attitude of financial distress and crisis pervaded city government. It was not the time to propose any bold new spending measures.

Flint weathered this storm, as it had weathered previous short-term economic setbacks. The lesson, however, was clear: Flint's city government had to be prepared financially and politically for short-term economic swings.

---

a fairly diversified local economy, need not be too concerned about short-term economic health. Flint's near-total dependence on General Motors, however, combined with the automobile industry's sensitivity to changes in national economic conditions, made Flint's economy extremely vulnerable to a short-term economic downturn. The case described in Exhibit 36 supports the often repeated observation that when the economy sneezed, Flint caught a cold.

Providing comparable financial information

One would think that it would be in the best interests of each local government to provide consistent and comparable financial information to the public and to the investment community. However, for a variety of legal, historical, and political reasons, this is not the case.

In this area, the public sector might do well to follow the lead of the private sector. The accounting profession has developed and promulgated a system of accounting principles and practices that have been generally accepted as standards for financial reporting in the private sector. When these principles are followed, an audited financial statement of any given corporation is, in most respects, comparable to the statements of all other corporations. These reports are comparable because they follow the same principles, not because the companies' accounting systems are identical or their businesses similar. To achieve comparability in evaluating the financial performance of local governments, uniform reporting principles and practices must eventually be developed and implemented. However, this does not mean that detailed accounting procedures must also be developed and put into force—a fact that seems to have escaped many people who have advocated state or federally prescribed accounting systems for local governments.

There are four major problems related to the accounting principles and practices promulgated by the AICPA and the MFOA, the two organizations who have assumed responsibility in this area. These are as follows:

The accounting principles and practices advanced by these organizations reinforce the custodianship responsibility and the auditing function. Private-sector accounting principles, on the other hand, are oriented toward reflecting financial performance for investors, stockholders, and lenders. Custodianship practices are inadequate to meet performance-reporting needs.

There are inconsistencies in the principles promulgated by these two organizations. In some cases, the principles supported by the MFOA are significantly different from those of the AICPA. For example, the MFOA requires that reports be consistent with state and local statutes. The AICPA, on the other hand, requires that reports be consistent only with its generally accepted accounting principles, footnoting discrepancies between these and applicable laws.

Legal restrictions that control the financial activities of a local government often violate fundamental principles of accounting and financial reporting. This poses a difficult problem: how can government accountants obey the law while at the same time ensuring the provision of useful and comparable financial information? Private corporations have resolved similar problems by producing separate financial reports for the Internal Revenue Service and other regulatory bodies. Local governments might follow their lead and prepare two annual financial reports: one that meets legal requirements and another that meets generally accepted accounting principles oriented toward the description and evaluation of financial performance.

Compliance with AICPA or MFOA accounting and reporting principles is voluntary. Because local governments are con-

sidered quasi-sovereign entities, they have not been subject to requirements established either by the accounting profession or by the federal government. Only those local governments in states that require independent annual audits have had to adhere to the principles and practices of the AICPA (less than half of the cities in the United States are estimated to fall in this category). Only those cities that voluntarily comply with MFOA principles and practices are subject to them.

In accordance with Michigan state law, the city of Flint was audited annually by an independent public accounting firm. Beginning in 1972, attempts were made to adhere to both the AICPA and MFOA principles and practices. After two years of effort, the city received a certificate of compliance from the MFOA for its 1974 financial report. The city's financial information was therefore comparable to that of other local governments which had qualified for the certificate. Yet, the information contained in this report still suffered from a number of deficiencies that will be explained later in this chapter.

Raising and spending financial resources

Neither taxes, nor fees, nor revenue from other levels of government in Flint were related in a systematic way to either operating expenditures or investment decisions. General revenue, for the most part, was raised independent of the service provided. Debt financing was limited solely to selected capital projects. Moreover, Flint was subject to a variety of unnecessary and complicated restrictions that interfered with the development of a coherent revenue and financing policy.

Relating revenue to services provided

The free-enterprise system provides ample evidence to support the proposition that performance will improve if revenue is related to goods or services offered for sale. Because a private business obtains revenue solely on the basis of consumer acceptance of products sold or services provided, it has a mandatory concern for performance. In similar fashion, local governments have an opportunity to improve performance by asking those who consume specific municipal services to pay for them. A *fee-for-service approach* not only relates revenue to results but also relieves pressure on general tax revenue, thereby increasing the capacity either to finance public services for which fees cannot logically be charged or to reduce taxes. Four criteria are useful in determining those services that may be eligible for a fee-for-service approach:

- Is the output or service clearly identifiable?
- Is the service measurable in units so that prices can be determined and charged according to units consumed?
- Can the service be provided to individuals or individual property owners at different consumption rates?
- Is the service provided by an identifiable organizational unit under the responsibility of a single manager?

As Exhibit 37 points out, Flint did provide some services on a fee-for-service basis; however, as this exhibit further indicates, other services that met the above criteria were not offered on this basis.

The fee-for-service approach was not widely adopted in Flint for a number of reasons. The most important reason was inertia. As one councilman put it, "We've never done it, so why should we start now?" Another reason was political. Placing a service formally subsidized by all taxpayers into a category wherein only specific users pay for the service is likely to create an unhappy— and, in many cases, very vocal—interest group. In Flint, attempts to charge fire-inspection fees—to those commercial businesses that, by law, were inspected—created a howl of protest. Regardless of the facts that inspection fees could be considered a legitimate cost of doing business and were offset by lowered insurance rates, owners of commercial property were outraged by the city's plan to charge them for required fire inspections. After considerable political pressure was applied, the council was persuaded to drop this plan.

There are, of course, limitations to the fee-for-service approach. Because a local government is essentially a monopoly, the fact that revenue collected is a function of services provided will not necessarily have the same impact on performance as it does for a competitive business. If citizens do not like the service they receive for a specific fee, they have nowhere else to turn. Moreover, in some cases where it is theoretically possible to charge a fee for a particular service, it may not be desirable to do so. For example, a local government could charge citizens a toll for using local streets, but the resultant inconvenience would make this action impractical.

Finally, many city- or county-run businesses, even though they are monopolies, could not survive solely on the revenue received from fees. These operations require a subsidy because the public is not willing to pay the full cost of each unit of service. Public transportation is a good example of this. In 1973, the city of Flint was faced with the problem of determining what to do with its bus system. Transportation analysts had concluded that a private bus franchise could not break even, let alone earn a profit, by operating a transit system in Flint. Politically, however, it was deemed desirable to maintain public transportation primarily to serve certain segments of the population—mainly, the very old, the very young, and the very poor. Consequently, the City Council decided to subsidize the bus system at an annual cost in fiscal year 1974 of approximately $300,000, or 75 cents a ride.

Maintaining access to debt financing

Some government officials declare with almost religious fervor that their jurisdictions

EXHIBIT 37

When Should the City Charge a Fee for Its Services?

The city of Flint provided a number of services on a fee-for-service basis. The most smoothly working example was the city's water division. The water division was established as a separate operating business (a public utility) within city government under the Department of Public Works. The fees charged for the amount of water residents used covered the total costs of operating the city's water and sanitary sewer systems, thereby ensuring a financially sound operation. Fees were established by the City Council, acting as a public-utility commission.

Other services provided by the city on a fee-for-service basis were not self-supporting. One example was the golf division of the Parks and Recreation Department. The golf division was recorded on the city's books as an enterprise fund; however, greens fees collected from golfers were set at a level that covered only the annual operating expenses of the golf courses. Neither the depreciation of the buildings nor the capital equipment used to maintain the golf courses was considered in calculating the fee. Therefore, the fees covered only part of the true costs, and the general public, through property and income taxes, unwittingly subsidized the remaining cost of each round of golf. The subsidy was hidden in the form of a budget appropriation to the park department as a whole; it was never clear how much the public was actually paying to subsidize each round of golf or each golfer.

Flint provided other services that met the criteria for placement on a fee-for-service basis. An excellent example can be found in the waste-collection and disposal division of the Department of Public Works. The service provided by this division was clearly identifiable; it could be measured in units; it was provided to individual property owners; and it was provided by a distinct and recognizable organizational unit. The city had ample statistical information to calculate the costs of this service for each customer on almost any use basis. Traditionally, however, waste collection and disposal was financed by a budget allocation from the city's General Fund. Administratively and organizationally, it would have been relatively easy to put this service on a fee-for-service basis, but politically it was not an acceptable idea.

have never borrowed and will never borrow to meet either capital or operating needs. These officials point with pride to the fact that they have paid for schools, sewage systems, and other municipal facilities directly from previously collected revenue.

Nevertheless, most municipal finance experts agree that debt financing is an appropriate financial tool that, if used wisely, can have a significant impact on government performance. There is some disagreement, however, about the appropriate level of debt and debt service for a particular local government. Some believe that debt service should not exceed 20 percent of current revenue. Others contend that, as with any other expenditure, allowable debt-service requirements depend upon the extent to which government officials properly budget for them. Philip Dearborn, former director of the Advisory Commission on Intergovernmental Relationships, argues in a study entitled *City Financial Emergencies* that the percentage of debt service is not as important as the rate at which it is increasing. He believes that a stable rate of debt service is most easily managed and accommodated by local-government budgets.

Despite these disagreements, there is a reasonable consensus that borrowing is appropriate when it is used to (1) finance fixed assets that have a long-term life or (2) provide for short-term cash to meet operating expenses in anticipation of taxes to be collected or bonds to be sold by a specific date.

A more important question concerns the relationship between a local government and the bond market—a relationship that may dramatically affect the extent to which a local government can meet its borrowing needs in a timely and economic manner. A fundamental problem that counties and cities face is that they do not go to the bond market very often; one bond issue a year is a significant number for a medium-sized county or city. Nevertheless, a good relationship with the bond market is essential, so that when a local government does borrow it can do so without spending an inordinate amount of time and money creating a receptive market.

To maintain a positive relationship with the bond market, a local government should meet at least the following four criteria:

- Maintain a flawless record of meeting all payments and obligations on existing bond issues.
- Make available information to investors and bond-rating agencies concerning the financial health of the local governmental unit.
- Borrow only at appropriate times.

- Demonstrate public support for proposed bond issues.

In 1974 Flint met the first two of these criteria. The city had maintained a flawless record of repaying past debts: it had never defaulted on a payment. By conventional, historical measures, the city's financial condition was good: the General Fund had always been balanced, and the Public Improvement Fund always produced ample revenue to cover debt service. Moreover, for twenty years the city's bonds had maintained the second-highest possible rating: "AA." In other words, those who held the city's debt had never had to worry that the city would default.

The timing of bond issues was a different story. Prior to 1973, the city had last issued general obligation bonds in 1961 and revenue bonds in 1966. The only other form of bonding during this period was for very small special assessments. Consequently, the city's total bonded indebtedness had steadily decreased, while its tax base and ability to pay interest and principal increased. During this period Flint did not maintain a presence in the bond market commensurate with its size or eventual needs. Ironically, over this same period the need for capital investment to improve and maintain the city's infrastructure may have increased at a greater rate than at any other period in the city's history.

The major reason for the reduced use of debt as a means of financing capital expenditures in Flint was lack of public support. The city charter required a 60 percent affirmative vote of the electorate to issue a general obligation bond. The fact that the city's finance director was reluctant to use debt as a means of financing and that citizens in several other Michigan cities had recently defeated proposed bond issues convinced Flint's City Council that public support could not be assured for general obligation bonds.

In 1973, however, the City Council wanted to complete a series of projects which could not be financed from current revenue. One such project involved the upgrading of the city's sewage-treatment plant; another was a river-beautification and flood-control project; and another the development of the downtown campus for the University of Michigan—Flint. In these instances, state law permitted the city to issue bonds to finance part of the costs of these projects without a vote of the electorate. As a result, in 1974 the city issued over $10 million in bonds for these purposes.

To obtain the best price (pay the lowest interest rate) for these bonds, the city needed the most favorable bond rating it could obtain. As Exhibit 38 explains, the city was able to maintain its favorable rating despite growing economic problems. If the city had dropped one level in its bond rating, it would have incurred about $20,000 per year in additional interest cost on the $10 million it borrowed.

Coping with restrictions on the use of revenue

In private business, revenue obtained from any source (the sale of a product, the liquidation of an asset, a bank loan) goes into the same pot and can usually be used for any purpose consistent with the priorities of the business. In short, the source of money does not dictate the way in which it will be used. This is not the case with a public business. Local-government officials are restricted with respect to the use of revenue by federal and state laws and regulations as well as by charter provisions and local ordinances. In many instances, these restrictions make it impossible for government officials to use available revenue to meet what they have determined to be the highest-priority needs of the community.

Restrictions on the use of revenue are usually implemented in local government through the unique practice of *fund accounting*. Fund accounting is based on the concept that, in order to ensure proper control over the way in which revenue is used, discrete funds must be established. A *fund* is formally defined as a self-balancing set of accounts. In effect, it is a separate and distinct financial entity within the financial accounts of a local government. Within each fund, a different set of legal restrictions and regulations is established to govern the way in which money received into the fund can be spent.

The Federal Highway Trust is a well-known example of a fund. It receives revenue from federal taxes on gasoline purchases. The revenue is accumulated separately from all other tax revenue of the federal government and under law can be used only for the purpose of constructing new highways or improving existing ones. By law, it cannot be used to buy buses for mass transit, to meet military payrolls, or to reduce the national debt. The central question related to fund accounting is this: could the same degree of expenditure control be achieved through appropriations and budgets specifying a level of expenditure, rather than tying that expenditure directly to a source of revenue?

The concept of fund accounting dates back to the earliest days of municipal finance. Historically, a fund was a way to control the use of a revenue source by setting up a separate bank account for it, depositing money in it as received, and spending that money only on authorized expenditures until the account was depleted. Before budgeting techniques were developed, this approach provided a crude but effective financial control; if there was not money in the fund, it didn't get spent.

During the past half-century, local governments have at times carried the practice of fund accounting to extremes, setting up a fund for almost every expenditure purpose. As Exhibit 39 illustrates, overreliance on fund accounting makes it almost impossible for political leaders, municipal managers, or the public to understand how a city's financial structure is related to the services it provides.

EXHIBIT 38

Can the City Hold Its "AA" Rating?

In 1974 the city of Flint faced some serious problems in attempting to hold its "AA" rating on two bond issues. Because the city had not issued a significant bond for more than ten years, the rating agencies required a complete reevaluation. Conditions in Flint had changed dramatically since the last bond issue in 1961. The city's population had declined by 2 percent. This decline was accompanied by a significant population shift toward lower-income minority residents. In general, the city was experiencing very slow growth in new construction and investment. Moreover, the city in early 1974 was just beginning to suffer from the impact of the energy crisis. Unemployment was rising and automobile production was falling. The near-term future did not look good.

There were, however, a number of positive indicators. The city had begun major renewal efforts in the central commercial district. It was attempting to relocate the University of Michigan–Flint campus downtown, beautify its riverfront, and implement a flood-control program. Some businesses in the central city area were in the process of expanding. And, city charter revision was under way.

Anticipating potential problems in selling the two bond issues, the director of finance sought and obtained the assistance of a municipal finance consultant. This was a first. The previous director had for twenty-five years personally prepared the city's "official statement" (prospectus) and obtained the bond ratings.

The consultant advised the director of finance that a personal presentation to a representative of a rating agency would give the city the best chance of maintaining its rating. Heeding this advice, the director and the consultant traveled to New York to make their presentation. The consultant was correct. Based on their presentation, the city maintained its "AA" rating for the two bond issues.

It was indeed fortunate that the city was able to maintain its favorable rating at that time. The full impact of the energy crisis hit in the summer of 1974 and unemployment rose from its November 1973 low of just under 4 percent to over 15 percent. These factors eventually caught up with the city. Its bond rating was subsequently reduced from "AA" to "A." In the future, the average annual interest rate that Flint will have to pay on bond issues will be about .2 percent higher. On a $5-million bond issue, interest would cost the city an extra $10,000 per year for the life of the bonds.

EXHIBIT 39

You Can't Find the Department of Public Works in the City's Financial Records

Flint's financial report for 1974—the year in which the city obtained a certificate of compliance from the Municipal Finance Officer's Association—contained 212 pages of data; to the city manager, the council, and the public, however, much of the data was not very useful. The report showed all the city's revenues and expenditures and the status of all major accounts of the city's thirty-six different funds. Yet it was difficult to read because, in accordance with standard accounting practice, financial information was not summarized by department or for the city as a whole. General funds, enterprise funds, trust funds, intragovernmental service funds, debt service funds, and other funds were each reported separately as if they had no relationship to each other.

The annual financial report was based on the financial structure of the city, which did not correspond to the city's organizational structure. If one wanted to know what was spent by the Department of Public Works, he would have to do a considerable amount of digging. (In fact, he would need more information than was contained in the annual financial report.) The result of this analysis would show that in terms of financial structure, the Department of Public Works showed up in six different city funds. Its $20-million annual expenditure would break down as follows:

Fund	FY 1974 Expenditures (in $ millions)
General Fund	4.0
Gas and Weight Tax Fund	2.7
Public Improvement Fund	.7
Water and Sewer Fund	8.5
DPW Fund	1.6
Intragovernmental Service Funds	2.5
TOTAL	20.0

One would have found a little bit of the department in six different places. To complicate matters, each different fund was controlled by a different set of accounting and reporting rules. For example, the Water and Sewer Fund was an enterprise fund which presented information on a business-type income statement and balance sheet using full accrual accounting. The Gas and Weight Tax and General funds presented information on a revenue/expenditure basis, employing modified accrual accounting. The others were in between. If you looked only at the annual financial report or took information from the city's accounting system, you would not realize that the city of Flint was one governmental entity reporting to one city council or that its services were provided by departments, divisions, and agencies managed by managers within one organizational structure.

In Flint's case, we find that the city's largest operating department, the Department of Public Works, was financed from six different funds; because of a total reliance on fund accounting, it was difficult to obtain financial information about the total operating budget of this department.

Fund accounting and managerial accounting are not incompatible. Reports showing the financial performance of the entire Department of Public Works need not violate the principle of fund accounting. As long as fund-accounting data can be prepared from the same accounting system, legislative and auditing requirements can be met. The problem arises when government officials permit fund-accounting requirements to dominate the content of financial information. This was the case in Flint prior to 1974. To comply with fund-accounting requirements, the production of managerial information was sacrificed and the director of public works, along with other department heads, was not provided with the appropriate financial information he needed to control the expenditures of the department he managed. The city's financial structure was complex, to say the least. Exhibit 40 describes the initiation of one effort by the new finance director in 1973 to make more sense out of the city's financial information.

As a result of the study described in the exhibit, many of the city's unnecessary accounts and funds were eliminated or consolidated. For example, the city's Income Tax Fund was eliminated. Although there was no legal requirement for it, this fund had been created administratively as a vehicle for collecting city income-tax revenues. The use of the Income Tax Fund permitted the General Fund to appear financially very restricted; any large reserves were maintained in the Income Tax Fund. The director of finance could then transfer funds from the Income Tax Fund to the General Fund as needed to keep the General Fund in tight balance. As a result of this process, some members of the City Council referred to the Income Tax Fund, as well as other such funds, as the

finance director's "cookie jars."

The city's auditors and the new director of finance concluded that this practice was unnecessary and, in fact, confusing to council members, managers, and the general public. The Income Tax Fund was therefore eliminated and the income-tax revenue entered directly into the General Fund.

Another example of an unnecessary fund was the Tax Map Revenue Rund. This fund had been set up to accumulate revenues from the sale of tax maps by the city assessor's office. Over a period of four or five years, the proceeds from these sales would build up to about $5,000. When they reached this level, the city assessor would use the money to hire an aerial photographer who would fly over the city to produce the large-scale photographs on which the city tax maps were superimposed.

This fund kept tax-map revenue out of the General Fund and therefore out of the city's budgeting process. In this manner, the city assessor was assured that funds would be available to take aerial photographs of the city without having to compete for a General Fund appropriation. The Tax Map Revenue Fund was also eliminated.

These efforts and others to reduce the number of funds and simplify the city's financial structure were not totally successful. However, as Chapter 18 relates in full, the city was successful in developing a comprehensive budgeting and performance-measurement system. As a result, the old system, in which finance and accounting technicians determined what information would be kept, how it would be reported, and in what form, was altered significantly.

Another major restriction on the use of revenue in Flint was the city charter provision that property-tax revenue equivalent to $2.50 for each $1,000 of assessed value be used for capital improvements. During deliberations about a new city charter, special-interest groups throughout the city appeared before the Charter Revision Commission asking that in the new charter a certain percentage of tax revenue be allocat-

EXHIBIT 40

How Many Funds Are Too Many Funds?

In March 1972 Flint's new finance director, in office less than two months, felt frustrated because he could not totally understand the rationale for the city's accounting records. He requested and received approval from the council to conduct a special audit to determine if the city's accounts were unnecessarily complicated and if the city had an unnecessarily large number of funds. He wanted to determine which accounts and funds could be eliminated or revised to make the city's financial information more understandable. One may be able to sympathize with this request by simply scanning the list of the forty-two different funds used by the city of Flint in the fiscal year 1973:

General funds
- General Fund
- Income Tax Fund
- Recreation and Park Board Fund

Special revenue funds
- Gas and Weight Tax Funds
    Major Street Fund
    Local Street Fund
- Urban-Renewal Fund
- Public-Housing Fund
- Doyle Project Fund

Enterprise funds
- Bishop Airport Fund
- Hurley Hospital Fund
- Mid-City Parking System Fund
- Water Supply System Fund
- Sewage Disposal System Fund

Intragovernmental service funds
- Central Garage Fund
- Data Processing Fund
- Duplicating Fund
- Motor Pool Fund
- Central Stores Fund
- DPW Fund
- Asphalt Plant Fund

Trust and agency funds
- Firemen's Pension Fund
- Workmen's Compensation Fund

- Unemployment Compensation Fund
- Hardship Cases Fund
- Fire Department Equipment Fund
- Equipment Replacement Fund
- Off-Street Parking Fund
- Voting Devices Fund
- Federal and State Grants Fund
- Improvement and Restoration of Parking Facilities Fund
- Tax Map Revenue Fund
- District Courts Fund
- Retirement Fund

Debt service funds
- General Debt Service Fund
- Act 175 Bond Debt Retirement Fund

Capital projects funds
- Public Improvement Fund
- Bond Issue Funds
    Flood Control Fund
    Saginaw Street Bypass Fund
    Expressway Extension Fund

Special assessment fund
- Special Assessment Fund

Other accounts
- General Fixed Assets Group of Accounts
- Statement of General and Special Revenue Long-Term Debt

ed permanently to support their respective programs. Such a provision would free certain municipal activities from the necessity of competing with other departments for annual budget allocations. In other words, a department with a guaranteed revenue through a specified tax allocation would have less incentive to continually demonstrate the value of its services in the competition created by the budgeting process.

In addition to the special tax allocation related to public improvements, the charter also placed financial restrictions on bonding, general taxation, and special assessments. Some requirements went so far as to specify the format of financial reports the city would prepare annually. The overly complex set of requirements established by a combination of city charter and state law led to such embarrassing problems as the one presented in Exhibit 41. In this case, excessively conservative financial-management practices and the system of fund accounting combined to create an enormous fund balance which the city was at a loss to explain and with which it legally could do nothing.

Restrictions on the use of revenue are also imposed by federal and state legislation and administrative regulations. Prior to 1972, the year in which federal revenue sharing was approved, all federal programs were categorical; that is, monies could be used only for a specified activity stated in the terms of the grant (e.g., land-use planning, purchasing buses, traffic-control devices on urban streets, and the like). Categorical grants were awarded only to cities that complied with an arduous application process. Grant approval was presumably based on national priorities as well as on local needs. Yet, as Chapter 11 discusses in detail, the categorical grant programs resulted in federal bureaucrats' becoming excessively involved in the day-to-day operations of these programs. This bureaucratic involvement, combined with endless red tape, served to limit severely the effectiveness of these grants and a city's ability to accomplish their intended purposes.

Federal revenue-sharing and bloc-grant programs have resolved many of these problems for the small proportion of money affected by them. Both general and special revenue-sharing funds can be spent with relatively few restrictions. Funds are allocated according to a formula that, in theory, is related to overall needs at the local level. The application process has been simplified or eliminated. The role of the federal bureaucrat has been minimized, and emphasis has shifted toward post-audit review of accomplishments rather than detailed pre-screening of grant applications.

From a management standpoint, Flint benefited from general and special revenue sharing in that it acquired greater flexibility over the way in which federal resources were used. The city did not, however, benefit in terms of the total financial resources provided by the federal government. An analysis completed in late 1973 showed that Flint actually experienced a net loss of about $6 million in federal funds as a result of conversion to revenue sharing.

Providing financial information for decision making

Prior to 1973, Flint's finance and accounting systems were characterized by the same bias found in similar systems in most other local governments: they were oriented more toward custodianship than toward decision making. These systems did not provide the kinds of information that political leaders and municipal managers needed to make financially prudent public decisions, nor did they provide information that citizens need in order to understand and evaluate public decisions.

The absence of timely and accurate financial information in Flint often resulted in bad decisions. Perhaps the most dramatic example involved the city's urban-renewal program. By 1971 Flint had entered into agreements with the federal government to implement seven urban-renewal projects covering almost one-seventh of the city. Each project was designed initially to be

EXHIBIT 41

What Should the City Do with a $1.7-Million Surplus in the Special Assessment Fund?

In February 1973, the press reported that Flint city officials were concerned about an excessively high surplus in the city's Special Assessment Fund. The Special Assessment Fund was used to construct public improvements (sidewalks, streets, gutters) that theoretically benefited individual property owners and therefore were charged directly to them. It was reported that a surplus fund balance had accumulated over two decades because of possible overcharges for the work done by the city and interest earned on the balances.

In April 1973, a special audit requested by the finance director disclosed that this surplus amounted to $1.7 million, and that because of inadequate records it would be extremely difficult, if not impossible, to trace the specific sources of the surplus so that the money could be returned to those who had paid it.

The city manager suggested that the surplus funds be used for a citywide capital-improvement project that would benefit all property owners. The city attorney cautioned that if the city did this, it could be liable if a citizen sued and could prove he had been overcharged. The director of finance said he would seek the assistance of the state in resolving the issue. The city charter provided no guidance.

(continued)

completed in five years. In 1972 Flint's new community development director estimated that, at current funding levels, it would actually take almost thirty years to implement the agreements. Unbelievably, the city at that time was considering an eighth project, which, if approved, would lengthen the implementation period to almost fifty years. This case (discussed in greater detail in Chapter 11) illustrates what happens when political ambitions are unconstrained by financial realities.

The city's flood-control program offers another example. In this case, a multi-million-dollar project was initiated without a detailed budget and without a financial control system to ensure that costs were kept in line and funds were adequate to complete each phase of the project (see Exhibit 32).

In summary, Flint's City Council was accustomed to making decisions without complete knowledge of their financial implications, and it was Flint's citizens who suffered. The residents of urban-renewal areas saw the city's promises to improve their neighborhoods or relocate them to better housing broken year after year. Flint citizens suffered from delays in the flood-control project and ultimately had to help finance the additional costs of its completion.

Why was there no adequate financial information? The answer is twofold. First, municipal accounting practices did not encourage the provision of financial information for

EXHIBIT 41 (cont'd)

The state treasurer's office was of little help; therefore, the city requested that its outside auditor examine in more depth the history of the fund so that some decision could be made on the basis of full knowledge of the condition of the fund and its records. While this effort was under way, the state treasurer's office requested an accounting of the Special Assessment Fund under the state Escheats Law. This law permitted the state to claim funds that had accumulated in individual accounts but had not been claimed in a seven-year period. The law was intended primarily for unclaimed bank accounts. The state assumes future liability if claims are eventually made and proved, and if no claims are forthcoming the funds go into the state's general fund.

City officials felt that this law did not directly apply to the Flint situation, and that the excess funds from the community should be spent within the community on projects similar to those for which property owners may have been overcharged. The city at that time was considering a number of neighborhood improvement programs and bond issues in an attempt to upgrade the physical character of the city. Funds for such programs were scarce, and $1.7 million would have helped immeasurably.

The state agreed to postpone its confiscation of the funds until the city had completed its study to determine the sources of the excess and recommended a disposition scheme to the state and the courts. Unfortunately little attention was paid to understanding and correcting the financial practices that had led to this excessively large fund balance.

---

use in the decision-making process. The emphasis, as we have said, was on custodianship. Second, and more important, the city charter provided for the separation of the finance and management functions. The director of finance and the city manager were appointed separately by the City Council.

According to the charter, the finance director had the responsibility to maintain a check on city government financial operations. But he also had a responsibility to provide information to the council and to managers which would enable them to make sound financial decisions. In Flint, the latter responsibility took a back seat to the former.

Exhibit 37 in Chapter 10 provides an example of the kind of difficulty the city manager encountered in dealing with an independent director of finance. Another example occurred annually when, after the annual financial audit, the city received a "management letter" from its auditing firm recommending improvements in the way the city did business. Prior to 1973 the finance director had refused to share these recommendations with the city manager.

Achieving an integrated and uniform finance and accounting system

A finance and accounting system should be internally consistent and fully integrated with other managerial decision-making systems. By *internally consistent* we mean simply that a local government should use the same accounting system for all funds, activities, departments, and grants for which it is responsible. By *fully integrated* we mean that the finance and accounting system should be integrated with planning, budgeting, performance-reporting, personnel, and other decision-making systems.

The city of Flint used three different accounting systems for internal operations. The first, and by far the most extensive, was the uniform accounting system required by the state of Michigan for use by all local governments. The city kept most accounting records using an account coding system devised and prescribed by the state treasurer's office. The state permitted additions and minor modifications to these codes, but the local accounting system had to be capable of producing information within the state's coding structure.

Although this system worked fairly well, it had two deficiencies. First, the code structure was oriented toward monitoring and recording financial transactions, not toward providing financial information for decision making. For example, the code did not provide for an organizational designation for financial transactions. Second, the code applied only to traditional municipal activities. It permitted the city to use separate accounting systems for the utilities and for federal grant programs.

The city maintained a separate accounting system for water and sanitary-sewer services. Because this department was operated like a public utility, financial information was accounted for in accordance with procedures prescribed by the state Public Utility Commission. It was never clear whether the water division was a public utility or a basic municipal service. In 1975, after several years of effort to obtain an answer to this question, the state permitted the city to place its water division on the accounting system used for other municipal operations. The city maintained a third accounting system for housing

and community-development programs. Public-housing and urban-renewal programs required that the city maintain separate accounts using codes prescribed by regulations of the federal Department of Housing and Urban Development.

Confusion and lack of comparability of financial information were the major consequences of multiple accounting systems. In many cases, municipal managers were responsible for major programs that were accounted for by more than one system. This made it difficult to obtain and use comparable information. Moreover, multiple accounting systems led to piecemeal budgeting. It was extremely difficult for the public, the City Council, or even the city manager to see how different city operations fitted together in a cohesive mix of services.

The major cause of this confusing situation was incremental legislation. Viewed separately, each accounting system had merit and could be justified at the time it was approved. But, taken together, they produced inconsistency and duplication. Federal and state legislative bodies did not adequately consider existing systems when they prescribed new ones as part of new legislation. Moreover, so as to ensure "proper control" over federal and state monies, bureaucrats have reasoned that the more detailed the requirements, the more control that can be exercised. Such good intentions have produced a confusing and complex system of financial accounting requirements which often impedes rather than aids the achievement, not only of program results, but also of real financial control.

Prior to 1972 there was a minimum of integration among the city's finance and accounting systems and other management-information systems. As described in Chapter 8, prior to 1972 the city's budgeting system had been integrated with its finance and accounting systems because, in essence, they were the same. The budgeting system was not a management system but a modified finance and accounting system. Other than this, there was little or no integration.

The city's payroll system was completely separate from the city's personnel system. Performance and activity reporting (what little there was) was totally separate from financial reporting. In short, finance and accounting systems were designed and operated to satisfy the needs of the city's Finance Department in carrying out such functions as payroll, accounts receivable, and accounts payable. There was little or no emphasis on the development of information that would satisfy the needs of the city manager, department heads, division heads, or line supervisors.

Two results were produced by this situation: either managers made decisions without adequate financial information or they were forced to develop their own unofficial methods of estimating and controlling costs. The fire chief, for example, maintained his own financial information system on fire division projects. In budget hearings, it was not unusual for his estimates to conflict with those in the city's formal financial reports. In most cases, the information system he maintained was more useful.

Providing useful and usable financial information

Flint's finance and accounting systems prior to 1973 produced a vast amount of information that was generally unintelligible and often confusing. The city's annual financial report was written by accountants for accountants, and as a result it was rarely, if ever, used in the decision-making process.

In 1972 the city's budget was a 1,000-page document that was difficult for the average person to carry, much less read. Many municipal managers found it incomprehensible. Apparently, the only people to whom this document made complete sense were the Finance Department personnel who prepared it. In 1972 the city used this one document for all budgeting and financial purposes. The budget was used by the City Council to record budget decisions and

revisions, by accountants to make entries into the city's financial records, and by the city clerk to provide public information to Flint citizens.

The city's annual financial report was a very different type of document. It was prepared by the Finance Department as a financial statement, and it presented information by fund and by account. However, the annual report was also difficult to use because it was poorly organized and far too detailed. It was a document that an accountant would understand but which made little sense to a member of the City Council or to the public.

In 1973 and 1974 the city tried to produce more useful reports. A new budgeting and financial-management system permitted new possibilities in the presentation of financial information. Thus, the city prepared a "Budget in Brief," a thirty-page document for the general public. Using charts and graphs, it explained the annual budget adopted by the City Council and the city's financial condition. Copies were available at city hall and were also mailed to interested citizen groups. It was used by the media and by community leaders as a basis for better understanding the city's budget and financial condition.

The city also made revisions to the annual financial report. For the first time in thirteen years, the report received a certificate of compliance for meeting the requirements set forth by the Municipal Finance Officers Association.

Meeting fiduciary responsibilities

The city of Flint exercised fiduciary responsibility in three ways. The first and traditionally most important way ensured that monies received by the city were collected and spent in accordance with law and accepted accounting practices. The second way was related to the management of financial resources while they were in the possession of the city. The third way was related to the management of financial resources that were not the city's alone. The Retirement Fund is a good example of the last category. That fund belongs to both employees and the city, but the latter holds funds in trust in order to pay employees benefits upon their retirement. The city participates in the management of the fund both for its own benefit and for the benefit of its employees. The city benefits, of course, through the return realized on the investment of funds: the higher the rate of return, the lower the contribution that the city must make to the fund.

Managing financial assets

Seeking to maximize profit, private businesses are always looking for ways to improve the productivity of their assets. If a company has excess computer capacity it has an incentive to advertise for users, thereby generating revenue from an underutilized asset. Similarly, businesses continually try to find ways to get an extra day's interest on cash deposits. Accordingly, they have set up sophisticated cash management systems and developed elaborate relationships with banks to ensure the maximum return possible on every available dollar.

A local government has two types of financial assets: liquid assets, usually cash on hand or in the bank; and securities, usually in a retirement or trust fund. The benefit from more wisely managing the investment of idle cash is obvious: more revenue, in the form of interest, is produced. The benefit from more wisely managing a city's retirement fund is not so evident. A retirement fund only indirectly affects the financial position of a county or a city. A fund that earns a high return on its investment will not produce immediate returns. Eventually, however, it will require less in contributions to meet future obligations.

Cities have been slow to apply the aggressive asset-management practices used in businesses. Cities are not profit maximizers and usually are not motivated to squeeze every last penny out of every financial asset. As municipal leaders realize the difficulty of raising property taxes, however, and discover that better management of financial assets can be a nonpolitical way of increasing revenue, this condition may change.

In 1973 Flint did not manage its financial assets well. Earlier in this chapter we explained how the city's Retirement Fund obligations and contributions had increased rapidly. During this period, the management responsibility for the Retirement Fund increased correspondingly. In the ten-year period from 1964 to 1973, the city's Retirement Fund assets grew fivefold; yet the ways in which the fund was managed and its assets were invested did not change.

In 1964 the Retirement Fund was only $10 million; in 1974 it was well over $50 million. City contributions to the fund in 1964 were only $600,000, while in 1974 the city contributed $5 million. The increasing unionization of city employees, the growing value of retirement benefits, the increasing complexity of benefit plans, and the rapidly growing retiree population all contributed to one indisputable conclusion: managing the retirement fund required substantially different skills in 1974 than that process had required ten years previously. Nevertheless, the fund was still being managed personally by the director of finance, who bought securities only when money had accumulated in the retirement account and sold them when the securities matured. To assist him, the city retained an investment adviser, a member of a small local firm for which the city's account was by far the largest. The city still kept its securities locked up in a safe-deposit box in the bank across the street. This finance director retired in 1973 and Exhibit 42 explains some of the attempts to improve management of this fund during the following two years.

Flint's cash-management practices in 1972 were equally unsophisticated. The city had a crude system for investing idle cash. The treasurer's office would identify any large receipt of funds and notify the deputy director of finance, who would immediately invest them in a local bank. To complement this process, an assistant to the deputy daily monitored the city's cash balances, and when they had accumulated to a given level (about $100,000) he would inform the deputy. Together they would estimate how long they felt the money could be invested and then would purchase a security from a local bank.

This system worked fairly well, but it had a number of deficiencies. The city did not have a cash budget to guide the amount and length of time of its short-term investments. (Cash budgeting is the estimation of cash receipts and disbursements on at least a monthly basis. A cash budget is affected by, but is substantially different from, a revenue-expenditure budget. The latter recognizes both revenues and expenses when they are due, which can occur well in advance of the corresponding cash receipt or disbursement.) For example, Flint collected property taxes in three installments. This meant that three times a year the city would receive very large amounts of cash from taxpayers. These receipts were processed rapidly and placed in a local bank to earn maximum interest until the funds were needed. The city's ability to invest these funds for the maximum period of time, however, was hampered by the fact that it did not have a cash budget to show when these funds would actually be needed.

The most expensive problem with the city of Flint's approach to cash management was the self-imposed limitation on the banks in which the city would invest. As the story in Exhibit 43 relates, attempts by the finance director to increase the competition for the city's cash, and thereby generate an estimat-ed $100,000 a year in additional interest, were unsuccessful.

Conducting an annual audit

The Advisory Commission on Intergovernmental Relations, in a special report entitled "City Financial Emergencies," indicated that the majority of local governments do not obtain outside audits. An independent audit shows the extent to which a local government's financial and accounting statements have been compiled in accordance with accepted municipal accounting and reporting practices on a consistent basis. It is not surprising to learn that the city of New York did not have independent audits prior to 1973. It is surprising, however, that such cities as Los Angeles, Cleveland, and San Francisco are in the same category.

Michigan, unlike most states, required that all cities have an annual audit. The law required that independent auditors conduct these audits even if a local jurisdiction had an appointed or elected city auditor. Any wrongdoing on the part of local officials was reported to the state treasurer's office, which was charged with the responsibility of enforcing this part of the law. An audit report was presented to the chief executive and to the legislative body, and was made part of the public record.

An important side benefit of an outside audit is that the auditor, in fulfilling this responsibility, makes recommendations about improvements in the accounting and financial-reporting systems used by the city. Auditors may also point out useful management improvements within local-government operations.

The independent audit conducted in Flint assured members of the council, as well as the citizens they represented, that the city's financial information was reported in a manner consistent with the state accounting

EXHIBIT 42

A $50-Million Retirement Fund Is Not a "Mom-and-Pop" Operation

"The Retirement Board must complete its evaluation and select a new investment adviser. . . . define the investment objectives of the Retirement Fund. . . . retain a new medical adviser. . . . make a complete and independent analysis of the future financial health of the fund. . . . take action to further separate the board from city financial administration. . . . separate the administration of hospital retirement benefits from those of other city employees."

These were some of the recommendations made by the director of finance to the city's Retirement Board in August 1974. The Retirement Board was made up of three elected representatives from city employee unions, three representatives of management (the director of finance, the city manager, and the hospital administrator), and a representative of the City Council. The director of finance completed his presentation by telling the board that the Retirement Fund in recent years had grown into a large and complex business with more than $50 million in assets but still was being run as if it were a "Mom-and-Pop" operation.

In making these comments, the director of finance acknowledged that some improvements had been made during the past year. For example, the fund had retained a local bank to be the custodian of its securities; to keep accurate records on their status, value, yield, and maturity dates; and to provide periodic reports to the board for use in managing the fund.

The director of finance, however, expressed his disappointment that during the past year he had not made any progress in replacing the city's investment adviser. The Retirement Board had retained the same investment adviser for more than twenty years, since the days when the Retirement Fund was very small—less than $2 or $3 million in value. The director of finance concluded that the city's needs had expanded beyond the capability of this firm, and proposed to the board that a new adviser be sought. Unenthusiastically, the board agreed to consider the idea.

With this reluctant support the finance director prepared a questionnaire and sent it to a variety of potential investment advisers. Seven major investment-advisory and management firms, including two local bank trust departments, responded. Each answered all of the questions and provided information about the number of accounts it managed, its past performance in managing them, its past performance in managing accounts similar to that of Flint's Retirement Fund, and the names and backgrounds of its fund managers.

To provide a comparison, the city's current investment adviser was also invited to answer the questionnaire. This firm responded in a letter, saying:

(continued)

EXHIBIT 42 (cont'd)

We have been thinking about the questionnaire you sent out . . . but for a number
of reasons we do not believe we should spend the time and effort that would be
necessary for us to answer it in detail. After twenty years of association, you
certainly know a great deal about us. . . . We simply do not maintain a compilation
of figures that could be translated into answers for very many of your questions.

Comparing this response to those of others led the director of finance to
recommend that the board select a new adviser as soon as possible. The
recommendation was tabled by the board after long and heated debate. The
majority of the board members, most of whom had no experience in managing
such a fund, were hesitant to change the status quo. The current investment
adviser provided a continuity with past policies that apparently made them feel
secure in carrying out their significant responsibilities.

---

system, the laws of the city, and state and
federal regulations, as well as the accounting
principles promulgated by the accounting
profession and adopted by the city of Flint.

As Exhibit 44 illustrates, an added benefit of
an independent audit was that it made it
difficult to play politics with the city's financial information.

Opportunities for Improvement

The analysis of financial practices within
Flint's city government highlights two improvement opportunities that are beyond
the control of city-government officials: (1)
the development and implementation of
standard accounting and auditing principles
and (2) the elimination of restrictive financial
requirements imposed by the state of Michigan and the federal government.

Potential investors can look at the financial
reports of different private companies and
find information that allows comparison
based on past, current, and projected financial conditions. This cannot be done for local
governments. To ensure that council members, managers, and citizens can look at
financial reports and determine quickly, accurately, and comparitively the nature of a
city's financial performance, a standard set of
accounting and auditing principles, comparable to those which are employed in the

private sector, must be developed and used.
In the reexamination of financial principles
and practices, particular emphasis should be
given to the increased use of accrual accounting; the greater consolidation of financial reports, balance sheet, and income-
statement accounting; the use of depreciation of fixed assets; and, most important, the development of new, more
flexible concepts concerning fund accounting. The object of these efforts should be the
development of financial reports that will (1)
provide external users with information that
is comparable across cities and meaningful to
citizens, bondholders, and financial analysts
and (2) improve the capacity of internal users
to make day-to-day management decisions.

The MFOA representing municipal finance officers, and the AICPA, representing
the independent auditing profession, are the
two most logical organizations to undertake

EXHIBIT 43

The City Provides a $120,000 Subsidy to Local Banks

In 1974 the Flint City Council held a meeting with representatives of Flint's three banks. Reviewing the results, a councilman said, "I'll bet the people who attended this meeting laughed all the way to the bank." Since most of the attendees were bankers, this observation had a double meaning.

The bankers had successfully argued against an ordinance proposed by the director of finance which would have allowed the city to invest and deposit funds with any member of the Federal Deposit Insurance Corporation (FDIC). The city currently was limited by ordinance to using the Flint banks, with one New York bank and one Chicago bank for backup. The finance director had pointed out that the city seldom used the New York and Chicago banks. He argued that the city should maintain contact with a wider variety of banks in order to get the best return on its invested cash. He based his argument on a study which determined that the city would have earned $120,000 more in the past year had it invested in certificates of deposit offered by New York or Chicago banks instead of Flint banks. The finance director had asked for the authority to go to outside banks when there was a significant difference in the interest rates offered.

In response to the presentation, the bank representatives told the City Council that investments should not be made simply on the basis of high interest yield. The bankers claimed that their money did not go to New York, but stayed in the city and was loaned to local citizens and businesses. They claimed further that they performed many other public services: they made loans to Flint area college students who could not get loans outside the city, they restrained their mortgage-foreclosure activities during periods of high unemployment in the community, and more.

Most council members agreed with the bankers. Two councilmen equated the situation with that of General Motors, saying that because Flint is a GM town the city should buy GM cars, regardless of their cost.* "I just wouldn't vote to see money sent out of town," another said. He added, "The people in my ward just wouldn't stand for putting money in New York banks."

Only two council members supported the ordinance; it was defeated by a vote of 7–2. The city of Flint would continue to invest only in local banks.

---

* The city's purchasing ordinance required the city to purchase Buick automobiles only.

EXHIBIT 44

Petty Politics Thwarted by City's Auditing Procedure

In May 1974, the city of Flint was preparing for a change of administration. The director of finance had submitted his resignation to the City Council and was scheduled to leave office on August 1. The outgoing director was to be replaced by the deputy director, who for the past seven years had been responsible for all finance and accounting activities in the Department of Finance.

The current director was leaving office because he believed he had received inadequate support from the City Council in attempting to achieve improvements in the finance and management practices of the city. He had had a particularly poor relationship with some councilmen.

At a City Council meeting in late May, one of these councilmen, without prior warning, called for a state audit of the city's books. This was a serious matter. His request implied that there had been some wrongdoing in the handling of the city's finances, but he refused to be specific.

The City Council voted not to request the audit immediately. Rather, it asked the deputy director of finance to recommend at the next council meeting whether such an audit was necessary. It was pointed out to the City Council that the deputy director of finance, whom it had just designated the future director of finance, had been directly responsible for the city's finance and accounting functions. An audit would be an audit of his performance more than that of the outgoing director.

At the next week's council meeting, the deputy director advised that a state audit would not be necessary, since within a few weeks the city's annual audit would be conducted by a certified public accounting firm. He pointed out that these auditors would be hired by the City Council, and that, if the council had specific concerns for which it wanted special attention, it should point these out to the auditors at the time the contract came before the council. On the basis of this information, the City Council voted 7–1 not to request a state audit.

One month later, the proposed contract for the annual audit went before the council. None of the council members asked that any specific problems be examined during the audit.

these efforts. In fact, both organizations have slowly begun to do so. The severity of the financial problems facing many local governments and the enormity of the challenge to be met, however, do not afford the luxury of delay. If these traditional institutions cannot or will not move more quickly, the federal government will (and possibly should) assume responsibility for the development of basic financial reporting standards that would be applicable to all local governments.

The second opportunity is related to the elimination of the complex web of overlapping, redundant, and detailed requirements that local governments must meet in accounting for funds provided by national and state governments. The detailed financial restrictions imposed by higher levels of government reflect federal and state officials' lack of confidence in the accounting practices used by local governments. Unfortunately, in trying to fill a recognized void, federal and state governments have not been uniform. Rules and regulations have been developed on a piecemeal, program-by-program, legislation-by-legislation basis. As Chapter 11 points out, the federal government as well as state governments should seize the opportunity to eliminate restrictive financial practices.

As the finance and accounting profession and state and federal governments debate how best to take advantage of these two opportunities there is much that can be done by officials in cities such as Flint. These opportunities can be summarized as follows:

Recognize the full cost of providing municipal services. The opportunity here is twofold: (1) identifying the specific services that the city of Flint provides to its residents and users and (2) calculating and communicating the full unit cost of providing each service. For example, the city maintains a number of public swimming pools for its residents. The city, therefore, should be able to calculate the complete unit cost (operating costs as well as depreciation of fixed assets) of providing swimming-pool services

to individual users. This information could be used by public officials to (a) determine whether the private sector or another level of government could provide this service at less cost, (b) serve as a base line against which to measure cost-reduction efforts, (c) inform taxpayers about the true costs of providing this type of recreation service, and (d) ensure that municipal managers have the necessary information to make operating and capital-investment decisions.

Improve the management of financial assets. Flint's Retirement Fund is fast becoming the city's biggest financial problem. This is occurring because the rapidly growing level of contributions—already exceeding 12 percent of the city's General Fund revenue—is increasing the drain on city resources. In addition, the prudent management of over $50 million in investments is no small task. Improving the rate of return on these investments by only 1 percent annually would mean a $.5-million increase in the value of the fund and a proportionately smaller need for future contributions on the part of the city. At minimum, the Retirement Fund expansion must be brought under control and its assets put under full-time professional management.

The city could also benefit in the form of increased revenue from more wisely managing its idle cash. Establishing and using a cash budget, improving relationships with local banks, increasing competition for the city's cash accounts, improving the flow of internal information about the sources and uses of cash—these and other alternatives are available to the city. These techniques are not new; they have been proven successful and are being used in many other cities in Michigan and across the country. The opportunity is there for Flint to adopt them.

Provide services on a fee-for-service basis. The city of Flint has the opportunity to adopt a policy that would make a fee-for-service alternative the first option considered when providing a new service. If a service can be supported by a fee, it should not be financed by general tax revenue. The first candidate for a fee-for-service arrangement should be the city's garbage-collection and waste-disposal operation. Next, activities already charging fees should be examined to ensure that their fees cover the full cost of services. Last, new areas should be explored in which to apply this policy.

Calculate city subsidies on a unit-of-service basis. Providing a subsidy in an annual lump sum offers no incentive to increase the consumption of a particular service or to increase the efficiency with which it is delivered. For example, the city's annual subsidy to the Flint Transit Authority provides no incentive for the authority to increase ridership. If the transit authority's subsidy were placed on a per-unit-of-service basis (i.e., 75 cents per ride), a positive incentive would be created to make this service available to the maximum number of Flint citizens.

Prepare and annually update a five-year financial forecast. In 1973 the finance director prepared the first long-range financial forecast in the city's history. This analysis of the current and projected financial health of the city should be refined and updated annually. If widely disseminated, such a report would provide useful information to a wide variety of users, from ordinary citizens to underwriters of the city's bonds.

Improve the content and readability of financial information. The Finance Department should provide a short version of the annual financial report which could be distributed to every resident of the city. This report should be easy to read and should provide citizens a clear picture of the financial condition within their city.

Simplify the city's finance and accounting systems. The necessity of maintaining particular funds and accounts within these systems should be reviewed periodically, and those accounts that are unnecessary should be eliminated. In this regard, a balance must be struck between the need for information that will enable the city to perform its fiduciary role and the need to generate financial information that will allow public officials to exercise their management responsibilities intelligently.

Financial Conditions in Flint Did Not Augur Well for the Future

The city of Flint in 1974 had a "unified" budget in excess of $57 million. Included in this budget were all city agencies and programs under the direct control of the City Council. Excluded were local-government agencies that were managerially or politically independent of the council—notably the city hospital and the Board of Education, with annual budgets of $25 million and $55 million, respectively.

The unified budget incorporated all city revenues and expenditures and all city funds. For the purpose of analyzing the city's financial condition, however, it is useful to subdivide this budget. The city's water-and-sewer utility, which in 1974 accounted for approximately $8.6 million of expenditures, may be logically separated from all other operations. For the sake of brevity, the remainder of this analysis is concentrated on nonutility revenues and expenditures.

Two major events in the period 1964–1973 dramatically increased the city's financial resources and kept the city in a financially sound condition. The first was the adoption of a city income tax in 1965; the second was a major inflow of revenue from other levels of government, primarily federal. The passage of the Federal Revenue-Sharing Act in 1972 provided the most significant new source of funds.

The impact of these events is illustrated by comparing the fiscal years 1964 and 1973. In 1964, local revenue, primarily from the property tax, accounted for $10.7 million of the $14.5 million in city revenue; $3.8 million came from state and federal sources. Thus, excluding public-utility revenue, the city was financed approximately 75 percent by local funds and 25 percent by state and federal funds.

Data for fiscal year 1973 reflect a very different situation. By that year property-tax receipts had increased only $2.1 million, to $12.8 million. The city's new income tax, however, provided another $12 million, so that locally collected revenue had reached $25 million, two-and-a-half times that of ten years earlier. Incredibly, federal and state transfers to the city had been multiplied almost six times over this period, to $22.6 million: $5.4 million from revenue sharing and $17.2 million from a variety of other programs. In short, these events added more than $33 million in new revenue to the city's coffers, accounting for almost 63 percent of the city's $48-million nonutility revenue in 1973.

The next question obviously is: Where did all of this money go? Stimulated by the availability of federal funds, the city undertook, during this decade, such new programs as urban renewal, public housing, and manpower training. Inflation took its toll. Most of the traditional municipal services, such as police and fire protection, street maintenance, garbage collection, and the like, were expanded. The following statistics help to relate the $33 million increase over the 1964–1973 period to other factors:

Indicator	1964	1973	Change
City population	196,000	193,000	−2%
City employment	1,532	1,962	+28%
Consumer price index	—	—	+38%
Average employee compensation	$7,300	$16,400	+124%
City nonutility budget	$14,500,000	$47,500,000	+228%

These statistics point out that the growth of the city's budget was not caused by the need to serve a larger population with basic municipal services; population actually decreased over the period. They also point out that inflation was not the only cause.

Why the large increase? One reason was that employee compensation grew at three times the rate of inflation, so that in 1974 it cost the city $32 million to pay the same number of employees and to provide the same level of service that had cost $14.5 million ten years earlier.

Another reason was the institution of "new" or "improved" services. Approximately $16 million cannot be explained by employee compensation increases. Of this amount, approximately $10 million was for the salaries and wages of new employees and $6 million was for new program costs (such as urban-renewal land acquisition). About half of the increase in new employees over this period was in the police division and Public Works Department, for presumably "improved" traditional services. The remainder occurred in such "new" functions as community development and manpower training.

From 1964 to 1973 the city incurred some other major costs that did not show up in annual budgets during this period and which are nearly impossible to estimate without extensive analysis. These were the annual capital costs of the equipment and buildings used by city employees in providing city services and the streets, roads, bridges, and park facilities available for public use. Such capital costs are not recognized in municipal financial statements, the source of the financial information used here. Sooner or later Flint will have to pay the costs of replacing its aging and deteriorating infrastructure. At that time, the city may need to levy substantial tax increases, resort to heavy borrowing, or both.

In 1974 Flint's tax rates were higher than those of surrounding suburban areas, though they compared favorably with comparable cities in the state. Flint was the only incorporated city in Genesee County which had an income tax. This tax was 1 percent of income earned in the city by city residents and .5 percent of income earned in the city by nonresidents. The tax differential was one of the factors contributing to an emigration of the city's population to the surrounding suburbs.

Even though revenues for 1974 were less dependent on local tax sources than they had been at any time in the past, the city was still sufficiently dependent on local sources that its financial condition was largely determined by local economic conditions. In 1974 the city's property-tax base presented a serious problem. Property value per capita was high in relation to other Michigan cities, but property values were increasing at a relatively low annual rate (only 2 to 3 percent annually over the past ten years). This rate of increase had not kept pace with increases in the costs of city services or with general inflation. The property tax dividend that accrues to growing communities was not available to Flint. The city was almost completely developed in single-family residential housing, retail stores, and strip commercial and industrial development. Local new construction was decreasing. Existing housing was deteriorating faster than it was being improved, and the decreasing population of the city reinforced these conditions.

It was primarily through the city's income tax that local economic conditions affected local revenue. Flint's local economy was almost totally dependent on General Motors and the production of automobiles. When car sales slumped, as they did in the 1974 recession, the local economy was severely affected. In this instance, unemployment shot up from 4 percent to over 15 percent, and city income tax revenues fell correspondingly. Increasing costs of oil and gasoline, developing environmental concerns, and the unknown future plans of General Motors in Flint all contributed to uncertainties in the outlook for Flint's economic future.

Flint's tax base and local economy were also affected by a combination of less-significant yet important events and decisions. By 1974 a number of shopping centers surrounded the city limits of Flint, all trying to capitalize on city as well as suburban markets. Two large discount stores were established immediately outside the city limits. Such private investment could very well have taken place within the city. Apparently, however, tax rates, the demographic character of Flint, and other criteria that influence business decisions dictated a suburban site.

Countering these decisions were hopeful signs of revitalization in the downtown area. The University of Michigan–Flint had made the decision to move its campus to a forty-acre downtown site. Urban renewal had begun to remove some of the downtown blight. A major river-beautification and flood-control project was about to commence, and the exodus of downtown businesses appeared to have temporarily abated.

The net impact of all these factors on the long-run financial health of Flint was not positive. The table below shows what would happen to the city's nonutility budget by extrapolating recent revenue and expenditure trends, assuming inaction on the part of the city to reduce costs or to generate new sources of revenue (i.e., increased local taxes or new state and federal funds).

Fiscal year	Nonutility budget deficit	Federal revenue-sharing	Net deficit
1974	$ 3.8 million	$ 4.0 million	$ (.2) million
1975	6.1 million	4.1 million	2.0 million
1976	7.7 million	4.3 million	3.4 million
1977	9.4 million	2.0 million	7.4 million
1978	11.1 million	————	11.1 million

Some of the net deficits in earlier years could be covered by the $4-million revenue-sharing reserve that was available at the time these projections were made. However, the message was clear: (1) the city would be in severe trouble if revenue sharing were to cease at the end of 1976 and (2) some action to reduce expenditures or to find new sources of revenue would be required even with revenue sharing.

In summary, Flint's financial health in 1974 and the immediate future seemed secure. The future beyond 1976 or 1977, however, was very uncertain. The pressure of cost increases was not abating, and it was unlikely that another major source of revenue would soon be found. How the city could overcome major deficits, even with revenue sharing, might be the single most important challenge to face city administrations in the late 1970s.

CHAPTER 10

Internal Government Structure

Organization is a means to an end, rather than an end itself. Sound structure is a prerequisite to organizational health, but it is not health itself. The test of a healthy business is not the beauty, clarity, or perfection of its organization structure. It is the performance of people.

Peter Drucker
Management

The structure of local government, like the organization of a private business, is a means to an end, not an end in itself. Government structure does not determine what a local government will do to satisfy citizen or community needs. People—political leaders, municipal managers, and municipal employees—working within a structure of government make the decisions and carry out the actions that determine the quality of governmental performance. A sound local-government structure will not guarantee that public officials will improve performance, but an unsound government structure can certainly impede their ability to improve it.

The importance of the structure of local government has increased dramatically in the past two decades as counties and cities have assumed greater responsibility within the federal system. As local-government officials have taken on greater responsibility for achieving improved economic, social, and environmental conditions, the business of local government has become more complex. This increased complexity has correspondingly increased the importance of gov-

ernment structure as a factor affecting the capacity of public officials to get things done.

The subject of this chapter is internal governmental structure. By *internal governmental structure* we refer to the relationships among and between the powers assigned to the executive, legislative, and judicial branches of government at the local level. Usually, these relationships are defined by city charters and state laws.

We distinguish internal governmental structure from the organization of government in this way: governmental organization represents the way in which government functions, usually within the executive branch, are assembled and arranged to carry out the activities of government. In this sense, organization is a management tool. The line between structure and organization is not always easy to draw; nevertheless, we believe this distinction is important.

In theory, a *charter* is a legislative enactment that delegates the governing power of a state to local government. Practically, a charter is a document that defines the powers, rights, and obligations of a local government and describes the manner in which these rights are to be exercised. Typically, the purposes of a charter are to:

- create and define the boundaries of a local government and establish the basis for residency therein;
- establish the powers and obligations that will be exercised by a local government;
- allocate these broad powers and responsibilities to each branch of government;
- identify major positions within each branch of government, stating the manner in which they will be filled and their respective terms of office;

- prescribe the qualifications and powers of the electorate; and
- define the procedures for amending or changing the charter.

In achieving these purposes, a charter must strike a balance between too much structure and too little. A structure marked by excessive detail, fragmented authority, and an elaborate system of checks and balances can make it impossible for any public official to amass enough authority to properly carry out management responsibilities. Too little structure, on the other hand, may well open the door to the abuse of power.

Impact on Process and Performance

The structure of a local government does not determine how taxpayers' dollars will be spent, nor can citizens hold structure accountable for performance. Structure can, however, significantly affect the way in which public officials decide what to do and their ability to get it done. Moreover, structure can affect the ability of citizens, citizen groups, and other private interests to influence and interact with a local government. In this sense, structure has an important indirect impact on the management process in that it (1) determines the extent to which political leaders and municipal managers can be held accountable for their performance, (2) determines the degree to which policies and procedures impede or enhance productivity, and (3) defines the limits of government activity.

Public accountability—the process of relating the efforts of public officials to specific governmental results—is affected by the structure of local government. If a charter so fragments responsibility and authority that the legislative body or the chief executive (the elected mayor, the county executive, or the city manager) is not given managerial responsibility over those organizational entities that are essential to the achievement of

community objectives, the public has no basis for holding these officials accountable for their performance. For example, citizens cannot hold a county board of supervisors accountable for the quality of health-care services if the board is not directly responsible for the delivery (both planning and implementation) of public-health services. Nor would it be fair to hold an elected mayor accountable for the performance of a police department if an independent civil service told the mayor whom he had to hire as police chief and made it impossible for him to reward or remove that person based on his or her demonstrated performance. A city council cannot hold a city manager accountable for the quality of the city's physical planning if a totally independent planning commission is responsible for making all major zoning and land-use decisions. Similarly, a city manager cannot hold his department heads accountable for their performance if they do not have adequate control over the line and staff functions required to produce desired results.

The policies, procedures, and other mandated rules contained within a local-government charter, state laws, or local ordinances can have a major impact on performance.

For example, a requirement that all members of a legislative body must run for election every two years, producing rapid political turnover, can impede government performance by affecting the ability to maintain an ongoing level of experience and expertise. Such a requirement can put a board of supervisors or a city council at a considerable disadvantage in dealing with major interest groups within the city (municipal unions) and outside the city (private businesses) which have long-term vested interests.

Detailed policies and procedures that require members of a legislative body to play a role in the day-to-day administration of government operations force legislators to become so involved with administrative detail that they have no time to address the most important policy questions. On the other hand, some policies and procedures spelled out in a charter may have a positive impact on the management process. A requirement that political candidates and officeholders disclose all personal financial holdings and potential conflicts of interest may significantly improve the way council members vote and behave. Moreover, rules allowing citizens access to all public material used in the making of public decisions may well enhance the quality of analysis and the criteria

used in making those decisions.

Local-government structure, as established within a charter, may also affect the management process by defining the limits of what a local government can do. For example, a charter may allow a local government to operate its own utilities, using surplus revenues for general purposes, or it may prevent a city government from doing the very same thing. A charter may mandate that a certain percentage of property-tax funds be used for capital expenditures or it may leave such a decision to the discretion of public officials. A charter may encourage the development of public/private partnerships in the provision of municipal services or it may strictly prohibit contracting with the private sector for any activity that could be performed by local-government employees. A charter may limit the number of people who run for a municipal council by setting age restrictions or it may determine the nature of the electorate by setting rules concerning voter eligibility. In short, a charter affects the process of managing a local government through the limits and constraints it imposes on what can be done and the rules it establishes concerning how things will be done.

Criteria for Evaluation

The United States Constitution has served as the framework for our federal system of government for two centuries. Because the Constitution achieved a practical balance between too much structure and too little, it has not required major changes. The following six criteria draw heavily on the principles embodied in the Constitution. These criteria should facilitate an assessment of how government structure affects the management process within a given local government and establish a basis for identifying improvement opportunities.

Are the branches of government clearly

separated, with appropriate powers and responsibilities assigned and adequate checks and balances assured? A clear separation of powers among the distinct branches of government, combined with a system of checks and balances preventing the concentration and abuse of power by any one branch, is a deeply rooted part of American political tradition. This question examines the extent to which legislative and executive powers are clearly defined and appropriately allocated within the charter. What checks and balances affect the exercise of these powers? Do citizens know whom to hold accountable for the achievements or lack thereof of their local government?

Are the lines of authority within the executive branch of government clearly established? The chief executive is responsible for carrying out the policies and programs of a local government. If executive authority and responsibility are fragmented among a number of independent departments, boards, and commissions, neither the legislative body nor the public will be able to hold the chief executive accountable for performance. To do his or her job properly, an elected mayor, county executive, or city manager must have control over the functions and activities necessary to implement policies approved by the legislative body.

Are the interests of the entire city as well as of the discrete geographical areas adequately represented? A balance should exist to ensure adequate representation of separate geographic interests within the community as well as representation of the interests of the entire community. To answer this question, we must determine whether the interests of the entire jurisdiction are prejudiced by a system which ensures representation of separate areas, or vice versa.

Is the structure of government clearly defined and understandable to all citizens? The Constitution has served us well in large part because citizens can read it and understand it. A local-government charter should also be written in a concise, straightforward manner.

Can the structure of a local government be adjusted easily to meet changing needs and requirements? A charter should be flexible and adaptable to new problems and new demands on the business of local government. This criterion is closely related to the requirement that a charter be straightforward, simple, and easily understood. If a charter tries to anticipate every potential problem with a rule and every potential need with an organizational requirement, the result will be a complicated and voluminous document and a rigid governmental structure that will be difficult to adapt to inevitable changes.

Conditions in Flint

In 1974, Flint's government structure was determined by a city charter that had been drafted in 1928 and adopted in 1929. The most recent printing of this document contained 121 single-spaced pages. In November 1975, however, the old city charter was replaced by a new charter, which was approved by more than 60 percent of the electorate and which capitalized on a number of opportunities identified in the balance of this chapter. In the analysis that follows, we examine the old city charter, bringing into focus the problems that the new charter in large part corrected.

Separation of powers

Flint's 1929 charter did not provide for a separation of executive and legislative powers. Rather, it created a hybrid council-manager form of government as illustrated in Figure 6. This figure shows that the City Council supervised a few appointed officials (city manager, director of finance, city clerk, city attorney) and a number of boards and commissions (Hospital Board, Recreation and Parks Board). In addition, the charter called for some functions, such as civil service, to be carried out by boards or commissions that were independent of the council's appointive powers.

Adoption of the council-manager plan was a major objective of the "good government" reform movement in the 1920s. In this form of government, the city council is both the executive and the legislative body. Drawing heavily on the private-business analog of a board of directors that sets broad corporate policies and a chief executive who carries

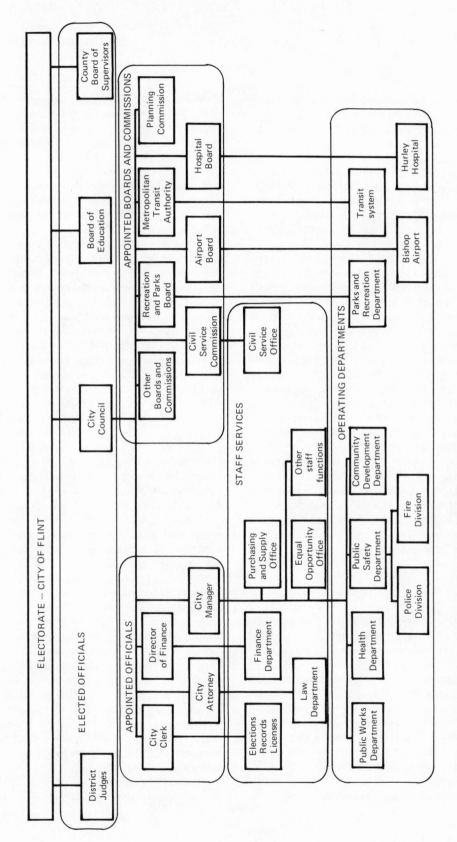

Figure 6. Flint's hybrid council/manager form of government.

them out, the council-manager form of government prescribes a policymaking council that will hire a professional city manager to administer government operations. The council, however, retains all formal executive power. If the council chooses not to delegate its authority, it becomes responsible for the exercise of both executive and legislative powers, thus removing an important internal check on the exercise of governmental power.

Flint's City Council delegated few executive powers to appointed officials. The city manager worked on a week-to-week basis for a council that made all major legislative and executive decisions. Because there was no separation of executive and legislative powers, there were few, if any, structural checks on the exercise of the council's powers. The only effective brake on this power was the fact that certain governmental units—such as the Civil Service Commission, the Recreation and Parks Board, the Planning Commission, and, of course, the courts—were not responsible to it. Exhibit 11 in Chapter 5 points out the kind of management problems that can arise under a system of shared executive and legislative power. In that case, the City Council adopted the policy of directly contacting and obtaining information from department heads who reported to the city manager.

Lines of executive authority

Executive responsibility within Flint's city government was highly fragmented. The city manager in Flint was not responsible for such basic administrative functions as finance, law, and personnel. The finance and legal functions were the responsibility of the director of finance and the city attorney, positions that were appointed separately by the City Council and considered equal in importance to that of the city manager. Personnel functions were administered by an autonomous three-person Civil Service Commission, which in turn appointed a city civil-

service director. As the city's chief executive officer, the city manager did not have responsibility for such important functions as recreation, transportation, the city's hospital and airport, and the educational system. As Exhibit 45 illustrates, this fragmentation, which some people referred to as a system of checks and balances, often served to retard management performance rather than to prevent the abuse of power.

Excessive fragmentation of executive responsibility in Flint significantly hampered the ability of the city manager to achieve the objectives established by the council. Equally important, citizens often found it difficult to know whom they should hold accountable when they didn't like the quality or quantity of services they received. Flint's structure of government allowed elected political leaders, appointed officials, and numerous independent boards and commissions to continually pass the buck, each saying that someone else was responsible for getting the job done. The result was often citizen outrage, or at best a sense of alienation that often led to apathy. Flint was full of citizen "dropouts" who refused to vote or participate in public affairs because in the past they had found city government unresponsive.

No one experienced this problem of executive buck-passing more acutely than the tenants of public housing. To them, city hall was a maze of confusion and ambiguity, where responsibility was passed from bureaucrat to bureaucrat as though they were seals playing catch with a rubber ball. Exhibit 46 provides some insight into the frustration produced by a government structure that did not clearly pinpoint responsibility.

Fragmentation of executive authority also resulted in uncoordinated public decisions. Citizens who dealt with different parts of Flint's city government generally discovered that the right hand did not know what the left was doing. Consider the hypothetical case of a developer in Flint who decided he would build a new commercial facility in the downtown area. To get started he had to go to the Department of Community Development to

---

EXHIBIT 45

"This City Has Two City Managers"

Shortly after his arrival in late 1971, Flint's new city manager began preparing his first budget. To perform this responsibility properly, he needed comparisons of planned versus actual revenue received during the current fiscal year as well as revenue forecasts for the next several fiscal years. He therefore sent a memorandum to the Finance Department requesting this information.

To the manager's surprise, the finance director responded by saying that no such information was available. Subsequently, he learned that crude revenue forecasts had in fact been prepared, and that monthly revenue data were available to the finance director on tally sheets which he kept in his desk.

The manager decided to visit the finance director personally to see if he could get the information he needed. Under the city charter, the finance director held a council-appointed position on a par with that of the city manager. In view of this, and of the fact that the finance director had been in his job for almost twenty-five years, the manager decided that the problem was merely one of protocol; a personal visit would solve it.

At their meeting, the manager asked if he could review the revenue-control sheets in order to better prepare the city's budget. The finance director admitted that some of the information had been compiled, but refused to part with it. "What you must realize," he told the manager, "is that in Flint the finance director is a second city manager. My job is to conserve city revenue and your job is to try to spend it."

---

ensure that the land was properly zoned; then, if there was a zoning problem (which often was the case), to the Zoning Board of Appeals for a zoning variance; then to the Planning Commission to get approval of a site plan; then to the Architectural Review Board to get approval of the architectural plan; and then to the Department of Public Works for a building permit. This was the routine process. If the property were in an urban-renewal or code-enforcement area, the steps and departments involved would be doubled.

The 1929 charter also fragmented executive responsibility below the level of city manager. For instance, it was not clear what authority the city manager had over the department heads he supervised. Because of civil-service rules and regulations, he did not have the power to hire, fire, or reward department heads for their performance, good or bad. The city manager was designated by the charter as director of the Department of Public Safety, which in turn was divided into two divisions: police and fire. The charter language thus blurred the definition between department and division heads. It was not clear whether the police and fire chiefs (division heads), who reported to the city manager, should be included in departmental staff meetings, or, more important, whether they should be paid on a par with

EXHIBIT 46

Passing the Buck on Public Housing

Public-housing tenants in Flint had a problem: they didn't know where to go to solve their problems. For months they had come to City Council meetings to express their unhappiness with the way public-housing projects were managed. Each week, they complained of broken television antennas, inadequate garbage collection, poor maintenance, and inadequate safety.

Each week, the same thing would happen. The council would instruct the city manager to resolve the problems. The manager would, in turn, ask the city's housing director to do something about the problems. At times, the housing director would respond that funds were not available in the budget, which had to be approved by the Department of Housing and Urban Development (HUD). If the City Council wanted to resolve these problems, it would have to come up with the money from another source, such as local property taxes. At other times, the housing director would respond that the Flint Housing Commission had heard those complaints before and that its policies were in conflict with the recommended actions of the City Council.

In short, nobody seemed to have final responsibility for the public-housing program, and the public housing director was caught in the middle. He reported to the director of community development, who in turn reported to the city manager. Yet, as far as public-housing policy was concerned, he was supposed to

(continued)

department heads who reported to the manager. In view of his charter-mandated responsibility, it was also not clear whether the manager, as a department head himself, should allocate a disproportionate amount of time to police and fire problems, thereby taking time away from his executive responsibilities.

A major consequence of fragmented executive authority was further fragmentation. For example, black residents in Flint, as well as black council members, had for years claimed that the city manager did not take appropriate action to terminate police abuse in black neighborhoods. Yet, the council knew that for all practical purposes the city manager had no control over the police

chief, who was protected by both his civil-service tenure and his alliance with police unions. Consequently, following the shooting of a black youth in Flint's north end, the City Council voted to create an independent civilian complaint review board with full investigative powers. The purpose of this board was to investigate and recommend appropriate action to the City Council in cases where citizens felt that city employees had been guilty of misconduct and that the city had failed to do anything about it. The need for yet another independent board was primarily the result of the fact that, under Flint's 1929 charter, the city manager did not have the authority to deal properly with such situations. Exhibit 47 recounts this case.

EXHIBIT 46 (cont'd)

take direction from the five-member Housing Commission. When asked his opinion of these problems, he would throw up his hands and explain, "It is absolutely impossible to work for two masters!"

The tendency to pass the buck was highlighted in early 1974 when HUD told the city that $887,000 of federal funds, badly needed for public-housing modernization, would be held up until the City Council transferred total responsibility for managing public housing to the Housing Commission.

In response to this federal pressure and to its own strong desire to escape the political heat generated by disgruntled public-housing tenants, the City Council voted to give the Housing Commission total authority for managing the more than 1,100 public-housing units. At the next council meeting, public-housing tenants who had come to complain were instructed to attend the monthly Housing Commission meetings. The City Council no longer had responsibility for public-housing conditions.

The council action did not totally eliminate potential confusion over who was responsible for public housing. As one housing commissioner noted, in order to do its job the commission was still dependent on the council. The housing commissioners were appointed by the city manager, usually with council approval, and the council had to appropriate necessary funds to augment federal funds and rent collections which were not adequate to provide decent public housing. To this objection, a council member replied that he did not think that in the future the council would appropriate funds for a program which had been taken out of its control.

Another important consequence of excessive fragmentation was that the process of allocating public resources did not take into consideration the total extent of the city's needs. The political competition among independent boards and commissions responsible for such major government functions as mass transportation, parks and recreation, health, public housing, and the city's hospital and airport made it difficult to allocate resources to the areas where the impact on community conditions would be greatest. Twelve major independent boards and commissions and twenty minor ones annually used whatever political influence they could muster to increase their shares of the city's scarce resources. The opportunity to focus the expenditure of resources where it would do the most good for the most people was significantly reduced. There is no better example of this than the maneuverings of the Flint Airport Commission.

The five-person Airport Commission was established in 1966 to operate the city's airport. The airport, located within the city limits some ten minutes from the heart of downtown, served nearly 100,000 passengers in 1974. Although it provided daily flights to Chicago, Detroit, and Cleveland, it primarily served private pilots by providing storage and training facilities.

Given the normal temptations of empire building in government, it is not surprising that the Airport Commission wanted to ex-

EXHIBIT 47

Civilian Complaint Review Board Adds to the Lack of Accountability at City Hall

A black youth, aged twenty-two, was killed by Flint police on August 11, 1973, following what the police described as a high-speed automobile chase that ended on the front lawn of the young man's home. The police claimed that the victim was shot as he attempted to run over an officer who was approaching his car.

Following this incident, a coalition of civic, social, and religious organizations demanded the creation of a civilian complaint review board to investigate this and other complaints of police brutality and misconduct. Leaders of this coalition were told that the city already had procedures to investigate such allegations: the police division had an office of internal affairs to investigate charges of police brutality, and the city had an ombudsman in the office of citizen service to investigate charges of employee misconduct. Coalition leaders replied that these procedures had been tried in the past and found wanting; no one, they said, had the power to deal with the police—not the manager, not the council, not anyone.

The formation of a civilian review board was hotly debated by the council. Some members felt the city administration should be responsible for dealing with employee misconduct. Others felt that, given the power of civil service and city unions, the city manager had no control over police conduct, and that therefore an independent, external check on police power was necessary.

The mayor stated, "Until we rid the city of bureaucratic red tape so that employees know for whom they are working, we need a civilian review board." The city's unions referred to such a board as a "kangaroo court." The city manager stated that the excessive fragmentation within the city and his lack of control over city employees combined to make him agree reluctantly that such a board should be established.

In November 1973 the Civilian Complaint Review Board (CCRB) was created, and a former judge, two blacks, and two whites were appointed to be its first members. By 1975 the CCRB had heard only one case, involving a woman who claimed she had been mistreated and falsely arrested by the police. Lawyers for the police officers quickly filed suit, claiming that the CCRB was unconstitutional and that the officers had been denied due process of law. The future of the CCRB was not clear.

What was clear, however, was that the creation of still another independent entity had merely added to confusion and bureaucratic buck passing. Politically sensitive complaints about police conduct were passed from the police chief to the city's ombudsman in the office of citizen service, who referred them to the CCRB, which could not decide any of these cases until the court decided whether or not its existence was constitutional.

Confusion and lack of accountability—the elements that necessitated the formation of the CCRB in the first place—were its main products.

EXHIBIT 48

Airport Commission Wants a $30-Million Expansion of Its Empire

In July 1973, the Airport Commission voted 3–2 to revise its master plan and in the process double the size of Flint's airport. The new plan required the purchase of more than 1,400 acres of land and the construction of new runways, a passenger terminal, and freight facilities. The projected cost exceeded $30 million. The federal government presumably would pay 75 percent of the cost, although this could not be determined until a formal application was made.

This action by the Airport Commission ignored an earlier recommendation made by a nationally known airport planning firm that the commission had hired to update its old master plan. The planning firm had recommended an expansion requiring the purchase of only 390 acres at a cost of less than $15 million.

The desire to revise the plan was based on the premise that the airport had a capacity of roughly 195,000 "operations" (takeoffs and landings), and that current use, nearing 185,000 operations, was expected to reach full capacity within a few years. The city's recently appointed finance director, however, pointed out to the City Council that FAA reports showed that only 6 percent, or 9,500, of the airport's operations in 1973 were the result of commercial flights. More than 80 percent of current operations were recorded by small private planes, many of which were practicing touchdowns on the runway (one touchdown involves both a takeoff and a landing, and thus accounts for two operations).

Additional questions were raised. Some asked why Flint taxpayers should be asked to build an airport twice the size of the current facility if a 10-percent reduction in private flights would permit a doubling of the capacity for commercial flights. Others wanted to know why there was no indication from any of the airlines serving Flint that they felt commercial flights would increase significantly in the future. The Airport Commission responded that if a bigger airport were built, it would be used.

pand the size and scope of its domain. It seemed natural, for instance, to develop an air-cargo capability in Flint to serve the large number of automotive manufacturing facilities in the area. Many observers, however, felt that the existing airport was large enough to handle passenger and cargo demand and still provide private flying services for years to come. After hiring an experienced airport consulting firm to prepare a master plan for the airport which would specifically resolve this issue, a majority of the commission rejected the firm's recommendations for limited expansion. Exhibit 48 describes how the Airport Commission voted to approve its own expansion plan, which called for doubling the size of the airport at a cost to the taxpayers in excess of $30 million.

The fragmentation of executive power in Flint can probably be attributed in large part to the mood of the time during which the city charter was drafted. Looking back at the excesses and abuses of power during the first part of the twentieth century, the drafters of Flint's charter seem to have had one purpose in mind: to fragment authority and thereby eliminate all potential abuse of power. Ironically, the accomplishment of this goal made it impossible for future political leaders to amass enough power to satisfy legitimate community needs. By protecting the city against the negative consequences of poor political leadership, its charter denied Flint the opportunity to benefit from positive political leadership.

Representational balance

Under the 1929 charter, nine council members were elected every two years from nine separate wards. Council members thus found it politically difficult to balance the demands of their constituents with the demands of the city as a whole. Of course, council members were expected to address citywide problems; but when solutions to overall city problems conflicted with parochial ward interests, ward politics, as Exhibit 49 illustrates, usually dominated. Under Flint's old city charter, no one represented the entire city.

Simplicity

Flint's forty-five-year-old charter was not easily understood by citizens or, for that matter, by the professionals who labored under its provisions. The document contained an excessive amount of procedural and administrative detail and was written in often-convoluted legal jargon. For example, the charter presented the purposes of city government in one 1,300-word sentence that listed every possible power the drafters could think of, ranging from the "planning

and setting of trees, shrubs, or plants, and the care thereof; the maintenance and regulation of fountains and public drinking places, including water troughs," to requirements that "railroad companies keep flagmen or watchmen at all railroad crossings." It is interesting to note in comparison that the United States Constitution is roughly one-fifteenth the length of the Flint City Charter.

Flexibility

The drafters of Flint's 1929 charter, reflecting the reformist spirit of ths 1920s, tried to anticipate every problem that Flint's city government might ever face. They seemed to assume that future political leaders and their appointees would be incompetent or corrupt and that, therefore, their actions would have to be circumscribed by charter-detailed organizational, financial, and operating policies and procedures.

Amendments to the city charter adopted in reaction to specific problems aggravated the initial organizational and structural inadequacies. Once the specific problems had been solved, the added organizational and procedural grafts remained on the charter, thereby creating the next round of charter problems. For example, the civil-service system was an amendment to the charter in 1935 that resulted from reaction to the Depression and the desire to protect the jobs of city employees from the perceived excesses of the political spoils system. The detailed rules and regulations that were written into the charter to insulate the personnel system from political interference adequately protected the existing city employees—but at what future cost? In 1974, the problem within city government was not how to protect city employees from political interference, but how to increase their productivity in the interests of Flint's taxpaying citizens. Performance, not protection, was the critical issue, and the inflexibility of the civil-service system had become a major impediment to improving performance.

EXHIBIT 49

No Elected Official Represented the Interests of the Entire City

In January 1974 a Houston planning firm was preparing a physical plan for the development of the central part of the city. The area under study covered parts of three different council wards. The purpose of the plan was to determine realistic objectives for the area and to interest developers in undertaking projects that would help achieve these objectives. The planning firm requested a meeting in Houston with appropriate city officials to discuss progress in preparing the plan. The mayor and the city manager attended, as did officials of the Mott Foundation, which had paid most of the costs of the study.

The mayor of Flint was not then elected on a citywide basis. Rather, he was elected as a council member and then selected to serve as mayor by a majority of the council at its first meeting. The position was largely parliamentary and ceremonial. The mayor had only one vote on the council, although he presided over the business of the council. In addition, he represented the city at functions that required the presence of a top elected official. If anyone spoke for the city as a whole, it was usually the mayor.

After their return from Houston, the mayor and the city manager were publicly attacked by members of the City Council for exceeding their authority. A councilman from one of the three wards affected by the development plan said that he did not want the mayor, the manager, or anyone else to go anywhere to discuss projects that affected his ward unless he went along. Councilmen from the other two wards were also unhappy about the trip.

Frustrated, the mayor responded, "If the mayor and the city manager do not represent the whole city, who does?"

Charter revision

If Flint's old city charter was so detrimental to performance, it is reasonable to ask why it had not been changed. Cynical observers claimed that the charter was not changed because political leaders were milking the public and had a vested interest in not rocking the boat. A more reasonable explanation is that citizens, private-interest groups, and (especially) the press lacked an adequate understanding of the degree to which the structure of Flint's city government impeded its performance. Attempts in the 1960s to change Flint's city charter did not receive the necessary support of key interest groups within the city, and for this reason they failed. In large part, the lack of support from the most influential interest groups (the UAW and General Motors) was due to the fact that these groups had learned to operate within the existing structure and hence were able to obtain what they wanted from city hall without changing things.

When the media, the UAW, the Mott Foundation, and others began to see that the 1929 charter not only was a major barrier to achieving sustained community improvement but also was inflating the cost of government and increasing the taxes they had to pay, they began to respond to calls to change the old charter. Exhibit 50 describes the new city charter that was adopted in 1974 and how it corrected the deficiencies of the old charter.

Charter revision was not a new topic in Flint. Attempts to revise the charter had been advanced before, but had always failed. In 1966, a proposed new charter was soundly defeated by a 2–1 vote. In 1969, the question of charter revision was again put to the electorate. This time, the electorate voted not to even consider charter revision. The citizens appeared to be content with what they had.

Given this historical inability to change the charter, why was the 1974 attempt successful? There are three principal reasons: support of the City Council and the city manager, support of the media, and support of the United Auto Workers Union (UAW).

All previous attempts to revise the city charter had been resisted strenuously by members of the council and by the city manager. In the early 1970s, a majority of the council and the city manager had begun to realize that the structure of Flint city government was a significant impediment to improving their performance, and that therefore it should be changed.

Even more important to the success of charter revision was the support of the media. The *Flint Journal* (the city's only newspaper), Channel 12 (the most respected local TV station), and Flint's major radio stations supported charter revision. Their support was based on both a close working knowledge of how the current system functioned (or did not function) and a genuine desire to achieve better government in Flint.

The UAW support materialized for very different reasons. Union leadership had long been concerned with achieving better government. Many UAW leaders had had personal experiences in dealing with an unresponsive city hall, and therefore wanted constructive changes made. The UAW, however, was first and foremost a union. As such, it had close alliances with the unions at city hall. The city employees represented by the latter unions had the most to lose from the adoption of a new charter.

In 1974, municipal employee unions were clearly the most powerful force in city government. They had attained this power partly because civil service had kept them immune from management control. Moreover, the fragmented executive and political structure of the government had given organized unions a disproportionate influence over ward elections, and thus over the City Council. Charter revision was aimed directly at these problems.

In the past, city unions, with UAW help, had successfully opposed attempts to revise the charter. Two different circumstances in 1974–1975 made it possible to separate the interests of these two groups. First, the city employees' wage and fringe-benefit package had surpassed that of comparable UAW members; and UAW leaders realized that their membership was paying the cost of the higher salary and fringe benefits received by municipal employees. Second, while UAW leaders traditionally had dealt with Flint's city government through elected political leaders, they began to realize that if the power of the City Council were severely constrained by the increasing power of city unions, it would be more difficult for UAW to get what it wanted from city hall. After much discussion and dialogue, UAW leaders in 1974 endorsed and at times spearheaded charter revision efforts. In the words of one UAW leader, "Charter revision was the only way to make Flint's city government responsible to the people who pay for it."

EXHIBIT 50

City of Flint Adopts a New Form of Government

On November 5, 1974, more than 62 percent of those voting decided that Flint should have a new city charter and a strong-mayor form of government. The *Flint Journal* noted, "The new charter resembles the 1929 model about like the 1974 automobile represents its 1929 predecessor." The city manager observed that, while the new charter would not solve all of Flint's problems, it would make it considerably easier for public officials operating within this new structure of government to do their jobs in the interests of the citizens they served.

The major characteristic of the new charter was the separation of executive and legislative powers. In the new charter, the council-manager form of government (in which the council assumed both legislative and executive powers) was replaced by a strong-mayor form of government in which these powers were separated. The mayor, elected citywide for a four-year term, would exercise all executive powers and hire a city administrator to operate government on a day-to-day basis. Applying the principles found in the U.S. Constitution, the drafters of Flint's new charter concluded that separation would ensure better checks on the exercise of both executive and legislative powers.

In the new charter, the potential abuse of executive power is constrained by giving the council full investigative power over executive operations, by giving an ombudsman the right to investigate executive actions (at the request of any citizen), and by requiring that all rules (policies and procedures) be recorded and made accessible to Flint citizens, thereby preventing arbitrary action by the mayor. The mayor, on the other hand, can veto City Council actions; and his veto, in turn, can be reversed by a two-thirds vote of the council.

Under the new charter, the mayor is responsible for all major line and staff functions and for the personnel executing those functions. The thirty-five separate boards and commissions that had formerly existed were reduced to eight. Further, the new charter specifies that the mayor must appoint a chief administrator with extensive training and experience in city management to manage line departments.

The new charter is much more flexible than the old one. Much of the procedural and organizational detail that characterized the old charter has been eliminated or converted to ordinance form.

Last, and most important, the new charter is roughly 75 percent shorter than the one it replaced. It is clearly written, logically organized, and readable. Thus, it will enable citizens to better understand the structure and responsibilities of their city government.

Opportunities for Improvement

Applying the evaluation criteria presented in this chapter to the new city charter, we still find several deficiencies and thus additional opportunities for improvement which deserve mention.

Eliminate past personnel practices. A major shortcoming of the new charter is that it includes all past personnel policies. The charter states that "policymaking officials must be bound by collective bargaining agreements and by the rights, benefits, and conditions of employment existing pursuant to and/or by virtue of the previous Charter." These past rights are to remain in effect unless changed by mutual agreement between the city and the affected employees' bargaining unit. This means that the "rule of one," "rule of three," and all other restrictive personnel policies that made Flint's old charter inadequate are to be a part of the new charter unless removed through collective bargaining—an almost impossible requirement to meet. This concession to municipal unions by the Charter Revision Commission was calculated to gain their support or at least to neutralize their opposition. As most people expected, city unions accepted this compromise but opposed the new charter anyway. Nothing was gained, but a significant opportunity to affect the performance of Flint's city government was lost by including this provision.

Eliminate unnecessary procedural detail. Although the new charter represents a vast improvement over its predecessor, it still contains procedural details that will impede rather than help public officials get things done. For example, the charter requires that the budget be submitted by April 1, three months before the start of the fiscal year. This reflects a lack of understanding of the budget preparation and review process. This kind of procedural detail should be determined by the mayor and the council.

Remove organizational requirements. The new charter does not prescribe how city departments should be organized, but it does arbitrarily limit the number of operating departments to ten and obligates city government to perform certain functions (planning, purchasing, assessing) but not others (citizen service, equal opportunity, data processing). The determination of how best to organize and what to call divisions of the executive branch should be left to the mayor, who, with the approval of the City Council, is fully accountable to the public for the results of city operations.

Stagger the election of council members and lengthen their terms of office. A major drawback of the new charter is that it continues the practice of requiring all nine members of the council to run for election every two years. This continues the likelihood of high political turnover on the council and deprives it of needed accumulation of experience. In view of the fact that the mayor's term is four years, it seems even more necessary to have an experienced council, elected to four-year terms, as an adequate check on executive power.

CHAPTER 11

Intergovernmental Relationships

With a federal system we have diversity; without diversity, there is no choice; without choice, there is no freedom . . . the great glory of the federal system is that some damn fool at the top can't ruin it.

Frank Bane
Chairman, Advisory Commission on Intergovernmental Relations

The mosaic of local authorities in a single metropolitan area . . . results in increasingly wasteful duplications of local services, conflict and confusion in their execution, inequities in taxation, and, in many instances, complete paralysis in the solution of more and more urgent areawide needs.

Mitchell Gordon
Sick Cities

The federal system of government instituted in 1789 has become increasingly complex and confusing. Today, instead of a simple three-level structure, we find an intricate web of interdependent government entities that extends from the federal government (with more than 1,900 independent departments and agencies) through states, regions, counties, and special districts to the lowest level of general-purpose government: cities, towns, and villages. In 1975, there were in the United States 3,000 counties, 7,000 towns and townships, 18,000 municipalities, 21,000 school districts, and 21,000 nonschool special districts.

At the center of this complicated governmental web is the citizen whose quality of life is affected by each of these entities. Federal and state governments levy taxes and manage programs which provide direct services to local citizens. County and city governments do the same. In addition, citizens are dependent on services provided by an increasing number of regional bodies and special districts. It is not uncommon to find transportation services provided by a regional transit district; electric power, water, and sewer services provided by a special utility district; public-health services and job-training programs provided by a comprehensive countywide agency; air and water quality monitored and inspected by a special regional environmental agency; and educational systems managed by independent boards of education. The result, for the citizen, is often complete confusion. Increasingly, citizens do not know which level of government they should hold accountable for the quality of life they experience.

In early 1975, the Advisory Commission on

205

Intergovernmental Relations (ACIR) held its first national conference on American federalism. Echoing the sentiments of government practitioners at all levels, this conference identified two major issues: (1) the appropriate allocation of responsibility and authority to levels of government within our federal system and (2) the increasing fragmentation of units of government at the local level.[1]

There is no easy resolution of the first issue, and it is not our purpose to provide one. With its origins in the 1770s, the centralization/decentralization controversy will still be debated in the 2070s. As Allan Campbell, dean of the Maxwell School, observed, "Ever since man began designing governmental systems or thinking about such systems, he has been troubled by the question of what part of the system should do what." Campbell added, "There is no internally consistent theory which can be used to guide either the placement of functions or the design of a system in which to place these functions."[2] Our concern here is with improving local government as it exists and probably will exist for some time. The pertinent question in the short and medium term is not how to change the federal system of government but how to cope within that system as successfully as possible.

In the mid-1970s, the federal system remains highly centralized. To be sure, many existing programs—from revenue sharing to community-development bloc grants—indicate a trend toward decentralization of responsibility and greater devolution of power to state and local governments. Yet, on balance, power still resides in Washington. Paternalism, rather than partnership, continues to dominate the relationship between the federal government and state and local governments and between state governments and local governments.

The primary mode for the delivery of federal assistance in the mid-1970s is the categorical grant. Despite the attention revenue sharing has received, in 1974 it amounted to only 11 percent of the total federal assistance going to state and local governments.[3] The 1974 *Catalog of Domestic Assistance* enumerated some 1,100 programs that provided federal funds to local governments for conducting prescribed activities required to achieve centrally determined objectives. Despite political rhetoric about the virtues of decentralization, the reality is that Congress still acts as if it wants to be the nation's city council, determining which local problems are important and deciding how they should be solved.

It is ironic to note that the federal government provides almost no assistance to improve the management capacity of state and local governments to back up its alleged decentralist policies. A presidential task force examining the nature of federal assistance to state and local governments concluded in 1975 that less than 1 percent of all federal assistance to state and local governments was directed toward improving their managerial capacity to spend the other 99 percent.[4] It is true that revenue sharing could be used for general management purposes. But the practical politics of funding management improvements from unrestricted funds is, and will probably remain, unpopular. As one local-government official put it, "If it is a question of hiring another policeman or another management analyst, the policeman wins 99 percent of the time."

The second problem identified by the 1975 ACIR conference was that of the fragmentation of local units of government. In explaining this problem, Richard Luger, mayor of Indianapolis, noted: "The municipal official that was elected must now confront not only the federal guidelines and officials, the state governmental apparatus, and elected county and township officials, but also nonelected regional officials who comprise a growing tier of government spawned by federal legislation and the states' attempts to comply with guidelines."[5] In a similar vein, the 1975 presidential task force on federal/local relationships concluded that in 1975 there were more than 4,000 special districts in the United States which had been created by twenty-four separate federal programs. These districts included 481 law-enforcement planning regions, 957 community-action agencies, 419 cooperative area manpower councils, 195 comprehensive areawide health-planning agencies, 115 economic-development districts, 56 local-development districts, 165 resource conservation and development districts, and 147 air-quality regions.[6] As Mitchell Gordon pointed out in *Sick Cities*, this mosaic of local authority in any given metropolitan area is a major impediment to improving local-government performance.[7]

Some people find value, however, in the diversity represented by the increasing number of local governments. Frank Bane, for example, views structural fragmentation as a way of preventing both the concentration of power and its potential abuse.[8] Others see the proliferation of local-government agencies as the best guarantee that public officials will be responsive to individual citizens' preferences for public services.

Still others argue that multiple levels of government stimulate competition analogous to that in the private sector, resulting in the more efficient and effective delivery of public services. Robert B. Hawkins, chairman of Governor Ronald Reagan's 1974 Task Force on Local Government Reform, asserted that the existence of 5,800 units of local government in California is a positive factor, and that "the existence of numerous special districts does not create serious problems for the delivery of economical and high-quality public services."[9]

Given these various opinions, we are still left with the "What do I do Monday morning?" question that practitioners must face. How can local-government officials deal with fragmented units of local government as they find them, not as they would like them to be? What is the impact of structural fragmentation and federal centralization of power on the performance of local governments?

Impact on Process and Performance

The nature of a local government's relationships with federal and state governments and with other units of local government can have a dramatic impact on the ability of public officials to respond to local needs. Federal and state programs that work at cross purposes provide good examples of this generalization.

Much has been written about the paradoxical situation wherein federal highway programs have provided local governments with funds to destroy old, established neighborhoods, while at the same time other federal programs have provided monies to preserve the same neighborhoods. A recent example of this paradox was the decision by the Occupational Safety and Health Administration (OSHA) that certain vehicles at construction sites must use backup beepers in order to enhance worker safety. This order was immediately challenged by the Environ-

mental Protection Agency (EPA), which contended that the beepers exceeded EPA's allowable noise levels.[10] The inability of the federal government to develop consistent policies and programs has resulted in wasted time and money. More important, it has prevented many federal programs from achieving their intended objectives.

When the federal government mandates that a local government develop an affirmative-action program that must be written in a specified manner, or when a state government orders a local government to change the way in which it handles juvenile offenders, the performance of that local government may be directly affected. A federal order to develop and implement affirmative-action plans may require organizational changes, divert the attention of scarce analytical resources, require the unbudgeted expenditures of funds, put new demands on management tools that are already overburdened, and consume the valuable time of elected and appointed officials. When states mandate new rules and regulations for prosecuting juveniles accused of breaking the law, without providing a basis for financing the implementation of these rules and regulations, they are placing a claim on local resources, thereby reducing the capacity of local officials to allocate available funds in accordance with locally determined priorities.

The availability of federal and state grants that include local matching-fund requirements also directly affects performance. These grants are often used as "carrots" to entice and persuade local governments to take specific actions, thus distorting the establishment of local priorities and affecting the allocation of local resources. A board of supervisors or a city council could, of course, refuse to accept federal or state grants, but doing so is likely to be difficult: council members realize the political consequences of the charge that they "let all that federal or state money go to someone else."

When the federal government assumes the role of banker it also assumes the role of regulator—imposing rules, regulations, and red tape as conditions for the provision of federal funds. The administrative costs of learning, let alone complying with, such rules and regulations are considerable. Worse, these rules are constantly changing. The direct impact of this unpredictable situation on performance has been succinctly stated by Dan Evans, former governor of the state of Washington:

Dealing with the federal government is a "Catch 22" proposition where you are told to conform to certain rules and regulations, you write programs to conform, [only] to be told that rules and regulations have been changed, and you didn't live up to the new rules which weren't written when you started out. [11]

In short, it is difficult to comply with federal requirements when they represent a moving target.

Dependence on federal funds has another direct impact on performance in that it creates the potential for discontinuity in the implementation of programs. A local government that accepts a three-year federal grant to implement a highway-safety program, knowing that the intended results cannot be achieved for at least five years, builds into the program the prospect of failure if the federal grant is not renewed or if the local government is not willing to finance completion of the program. On the other hand, Congress often refuses to adequately finance federal programs, either because sufficient funds are not available or because it hopes that the constituency created through the program will be sufficient to ensure the political pressure necessary to increase the required level of local resources at a later date. In either case, the resultant uncertainty about a program's future and about the inadequate level of funding may significantly affect the capacity of local-government officials to administer it successfully.

The federal government and, to some extent, state governments have influenced the performance of local governments through their funding and special recognition of independent planning agencies. The federal government indirectly has encouraged the separation of responsibility for planning (deciding what to do and how to do it) from the responsibility for implementation (getting it done). This violation of the integrity of the management process has produced a duplication of planning efforts and has contributed to the inability of government officials to relate the day-to-day operations of government to objectives contained in independently developed plans.

Intergovernmental relationships also indirectly affect performance through their impact on other factors. Political leaders, for example, are affected by federal programs that provide resources to nongovernmental groups, thereby encouraging the development of potential political rivals. (It would be interesting to know how many elected public officials in the 1970s got their start in community-action programs in the 1960s, and, of these, how many now argue that all federal money should be channeled through general-purpose governments instead of through community groups.)

Another indirect impact of overreliance on federal and state programs is the reinforcement of the natural bureaucratic tendency to pass the buck. Community-development managers throughout the country respond to questions about the performance of the housing and urban-renewal programs they administer by saying that they are hamstrung by federal requirements and regulations that make successful implementation impossible. Dependence on federal and state bureaucrats increases the incentive for local-government officials to blame somebody else for a program's failure.

Another problem is that federal and state programs often reward failures instead of successes. Bill Donaldson, city manager of Cincinnati, observed: "If you have a federal demonstration program and you do well, the money gets cut off. But if you screw it up, you get another grant, and it seems to me there are a lot of programs that the feds have been running where the penalties are for success and the prizes are for failures."[12]

An important and somewhat ironic impact of federal programs on the performance of local government is related to citizen involvement. Many federal programs require the involvement of citizens in the administration of federally funded and regulated programs. This is a laudable goal that, in some cases, has had an unintended result: when citizens learn how impotent their elected representatives are to resolve local problems and how dependent they are on federal dollars and federal rules and regulations, the incentive to become involved is reduced. Citizen apathy can be traced, to some degree, to the simple fact that local-government officials often do not have the authority or the responsibility to deal adequately with problems that affect local citizens.

Criteria for Evaluation

Attempts to improve intergovernmental relationships, thereby enabling local-government officials to improve performance, must begin with an understanding of the problems and opportunities posed by existing intergovernmental relationships, both vertical and horizontal. There are a number of important questions that legislative officials, mayors, city managers, and concerned citizens should ask about the existing intergovernmental system and its impact on the performance of their local governments. In so doing, they could understand more precisely what ought to be done to help localities develop more productive relationships with federal, state, and other governmental agencies.

Is a local government responsible for an appropriate mix of government functions and activities? To say that a local government should be responsible only for "appropriate" functions and activities begs a most difficult question: what is "appropriate"? There is considerable debate over which criteria should be used in making this judgment; yet, despite the difficulty involved, local-government officials and concerned citizens in any given locality must develop some basis for an answer. Four primary criteria provide a starting point:

- Equity: Do the residents of a local government who benefit from specific government services pay for them? If not, who else benefits? Who else pays?
- Efficiency: Is each service area large enough to allow the realization of economies of scale, yet small enough to avoid diseconomies of scale? In short, could a service provided by a local government be provided by another at less cost; and, if so, which level is most appropriate?
- Accountability: Can responsible public officials (elected legislators or an elected

mayor) be held accountable for the quality and quantity of services being delivered? That is, are there factors beyond the control of responsible local government officials which affect their ability to provide a service in the most economic and effective manner? If, so, what are these factors?

• Responsiveness: Is the quality of service delivery responsive to the desires of individual citizens?

These criteria are interrelated and are not mutually exclusive; they must be considered simultaneously in reaching judgments about which levels of government should be responsible for conducting specific government functions or activities. Other criteria— such as administrative practicality, geographic realities, and the necessity for coherent planning—must also be considered, but these are less important.

Do government officials have the authority and the responsibility required to manage assigned functions and activities? Devolution of responsibility for certain government activities without the authority to manage them responsibly is a prescription for failure. Therefore, this question examines whether local-government officials are granted the fiscal capacity, legislative authority, and political power to manage a mix of functions and activities for performance. Is the intergovernmental assignment of responsibility and authority clear in regard to the delivery of a specific service? Do citizens know whom to hold accountable for the quality and quantity of services they receive?

Do regulations and red tape imposed by other levels of government restrict the ability of local-government officials to do their jobs? Externally imposed rules and regulations can have a significant impact on the conduct of the management process. Therefore, this question examines the extent to which federal and state rules, regulations, and reporting requirements make it difficult, if not impossible, for local-government officials to achieve desired results on which improved performance depends.

Do separate units of local government cooperate in the achievement of common community objectives? The first three standards focus primarily on the vertical relationship between a local government and the state and federal government. This question is concerned with the horizontal relationships among units of government at the local level. It examines the degree of cooperation in the establishment of common objectives at the local level and the extent to which there is cooperation in their achievement.

Conditions in Flint

Intergovernmental relationships presented particularly difficult and frustrating problems for Flint's city government. Its relationships with both the federal government and the state of Michigan were marked by a growing ambivalence. On the one hand, the city depended on federal and state funds to finance almost half of its operating budget. On the other hand, the "strings" that accompanied these funds were often so counterproductive that many Flint officials questioned whether the benefits justified the added expense, confusion, and complexity. Relationships with other units of local government were strained and often nonproductive.

Ensuring appropriate responsibility for government functions and activities

In Flint, neither the City Council, the city manager, nor major civic leaders ever really addressed the question of whether Flint's city government was responsible for an appropriate mix of government functions and activities. Few asked whether Flint was the appropriate level of government to operate a public bus company that also served other parts of the county. Few questioned the advisability of the city's operating a hospital, constructing low-income housing, or managing public utilities.

If Flint's government officials in 1973 had related each activity for which they were responsible to the criteria of equity, efficiency, accountability, and responsiveness, they might have concluded that city government was not the appropriate level of government to manage several important activities. As the preliminary analysis presented in Exhibit 51 suggests, the city of Flint was not the appropriate level of government to assume responsibility for public health, hospital services, detention and correction, bus and air transportation, water supply and distribution, public housing, air-pollution control, and storm water/flood control. In some cases, such as criminal apprehension, licensing, and highway/street maintenance, the analysis suggests opportunities for the county and the city to share responsibility.*

The difficulty of analysis involved in the application of these criteria should not be underestimated.† Such analysis is essentially a subjective exercise that depends on the relative importance assigned to each criterion. For example, economic efficiency may dictate that a transportation system

should be constructed and operated on a regional basis in order to achieve appropriate economies of scale. The same conclusion could be reached concerning the problem of controlling air pollution, which unfortunately does not stop at a city government's boundaries. Yet there may be no general-purpose government at the regional level capable of managing these functions and ensuring that appropriate tradeoffs are made between them. Because of the lack of political accountability, there is serious doubt whether these functions can or should be performed at the regional level. An independent regional transit district or air-pollution control district managed by nonelected officials would meet the economic efficiency and the equity criteria but would not meet the criterion of accountability. At this point, the analysis depends on the relative weight given to each separate criterion.

As the cases presented in Exhibits 52 and 53 make clear, once a desired change in the allocation of government responsibility is identified, making it happen can be thwarted by political inertia, union pressure, and public apathy. In the case of the airport, as Exhibit 52 shows, neither county nor city officials could cut through the political ambivalence that surrounded the issue of appropriate airport ownership and operation. Unfortunately, no higher level of government, either regional or state, had the power to recognize and resolve this issue. Similarly, inaction and delay in developing a single county health department, as Exhibit 53 illustrates, were caused by political pressures and union resistance. Again, there was no place to go to resolve this issue. The result was a continuation of an inequitable and uneconomic allocation of government responsibility.

---

* Distinguishing between functions and activities poses a definitional problem. For example, public transportation may be considered a government function; but its components, ranging from fixed-rail, mass transit to automobile control, are also defined as functions. In our nomenclature, transportation is a function and traffic control is an activity necessary to the exercise of that function. Activities, in turn, may be broken down in different ways. For example, traffic control might be conducted by a city government on certain streets and roads and by the state and federal government on major streets and highways.

† Exhibit 51 should be used for illustrative purposes only. Simply listing functions, activities, and criteria is not sufficient to derive the allocations we have shown here. A longer, more detailed analysis would be required to justify each entry properly.

Equating authority with responsibility

A city government may be responsible for the right activities but lack the money or the authority to manage them for performance. A government must have the appropriate

EXHIBIT 51

The City of Flint May Not Have Been the Appropriate Level of Government To Provide Major Public Services

Function	Criteria				Appropriate Level of Government
	Equity	Efficiency	Accountability	Responsiveness	
PUBLIC SAFETY					
Crime prevention	City	City	City	City	City
Criminal apprehension	County/State	City/County	City/County (1)	City	City/County (2)
Fire suppression and rescue	City	County	City	City	City
Fire inspections	City	City	City	City	City
Health inspections	County	County	County	City	County
Housing/building inspections	City	City	City	City	City
Licensing	City/County	County	City	City	City/County (2)
JUSTICE					
Detention and correction	County/State	County	County	City	County
Adjudication (district courts)	City	State	State	City	State

TRANSPORTATION					
Construction and maintenance of highways, streets	(1)	(1)	(1)	City	City/County
Traffic control and safety	(1)	(1)	(1)	City	City/County (2)
Bus transportation	County	County	County	City	County
Air transportation	County	County	County	City	County
ENVIRONMENTAL PROTECTION					
Solid-waste management	City	County	City	City	City
Air-pollution control	County	County	County	City	County
Storm water and flood control	County	County	County	City	County
PUBLIC SERVICES					
Water supply and distribution	City	County	City	City	County
Sanitary-sewer collection	City	County	City	City	City
PHYSICAL DEVELOPMENT					
Urban renewal	City	City	City	City	City
Physical planning	City	County	City	City	City
Zoning	City	City	City	City	City

(continued)

EXHIBIT 51 (cont'd)

HOUSING					
Public housing	County	County	County	City	County/City
Housing-related services	City	County	City	City	City
HEALTH					
Public health	County	County	County	City	County
Hospital and emergency medical care	County	County	City	City	County
RECREATION					
Provision of facilities	City	City	City	City	City
Recreation programs	County	County	City	City	County
ECONOMIC DEVELOPMENT					
Manpower planning	County	County	County	City	County

(1) These activities should be carried out at city, county, or state levels depending upon the street systems to which they apply. State highways through the city should be constructed and maintained by the state.

(2) One must go below this level of activity to determine the appropriate level of government responsibility.

legal authority, political power, and financial resources to manage those functions and activities for which it has responsibility. If this is not the case, citizens cannot hold their local officials accountable. When authority is separated from responsibility, the result is often governmental drift and inaction. Applying this standard to Flint produces two conclusions: first, that the city was responsible for important functions but lacked the financial base to manage them properly; and second, that the City Council was responsible for the implementation of major programs but did not have the authority to carry them out.

The case involving Flint's airport provides a clear illustration of an important function that was assigned to a level of government that did not have an adequate financial base to perform it efficiently or effectively. The performance of the airport suffered from the lack of adequate financing. Needed improvements in airport facilities were continually delayed because the city could not afford them and the county would not accept responsibility.

Flint's urban-renewal and public-housing programs suffered because the City Council—in this case the appropriate level of government to exercise responsibility—lacked concomitant authority. The city of Flint participated with the federal government in a large number of community-development programs. In 1973, the city had eight separate urban-renewal projects under way, covering almost 15 percent of the city. In addition, the city was responsible for the management of more than 1,100 units of public housing for both elderly and low-income families. In both cases, the City Council was held accountable by the public for producing results. However, the City Council, as Exhibit 54 clearly indicates, did not have the authority required to carry out these responsibilities. As a consequence, the city continually failed to live up to the promises it made to public-housing tenants as well as to urban-renewal-area residents.

The inability to pinpoint responsibility for

these programs resulted in a seemingly endless game in which the city of Flint and the federal government exchanged the familiar bureaucratic charge, "It's not our fault—it's theirs!" The citizens were the losers, and their frustration and anger often turned into alienation and finally into apathy. As one public-housing tenant remarked in a speech before the City Council, "I simply don't give a damn anymore."

It takes little insight to realize that the federal government's unwillingness to give local governments the authority required to manage federally funded programs stems from a basic lack of trust. Federal lawmakers and the bureaucrats who implement most of the laws have, for a variety of reasons, regarded county and city government officials with a skepticism that often borders on disdain. Yet few federal bureaucrats have ever ventured beyond the banks of the Potomac to find out how competent local-government officials really are. This climate of distrust and skepticism has produced unfortunate consequences: it has made many local governments dependent on federal aid; it has discouraged other local governments from taking the initiative to solve their own problems before they are recognized as "national priorities"; and it has discouraged many able people from working at the local level.

Perhaps the most important consequence of the separation of authority and responsibility is that many important things do not get done. Because of an endless chain of partial responsibilities, the implementation of important public programs often requires more money and consumes greater amounts of energy and time than was originally estimated. The case presented in Exhibit 55 is a classic illustration of this generalization. This exhibit recounts Flint's experiences in trying to get the final section of a freeway completed through the central part of the city. The process of preparing, reviewing, and processing an environmental impact statement (EIS) resulted in almost ten years of delay and a significant increase in cost as a result of

EXHIBIT 52

Everybody Wants To Fly—But Nobody Wants To Pay for the Airport

Who should pay the operating subsidy for a city airport that is used mostly by non-city residents? This question faced city and county officials in Flint in the early 1970s.

Bishop Airport was owned by the city of Flint. It had been constructed on land donated to the city by a wealthy Flint family. The airport never produced sufficient revenue to cover the costs of operation, much less the costs of capital replacement or expansion. Therefore, it required a city subsidy.

The subsidy was not a problem when the vast majority of the population served by the airport lived within the city of Flint. In those days, the taxpayers who were subsidizing the airport benefited from its services. By the 1970s, however, this was no longer the case. A significant population shift in the metropolitan area had created a situation in which a majority of the people who used the airport were residents not of the city of Flint but of the metropolitan area surrounding it. Hence, those who paid for the airport were not the ones who used it.

The logical remedy for this situation would have been to transfer control of the airport from the city to Genesee County, which totally surrounded Flint and contained 95 percent of the metropolitan-area population. Transferring the airport to county control would also transfer the operating subsidy to all county residents—who, of course, included city residents.

(continued)

inflation. Perhaps this delay could have been justified if the EIS had been aimed at correcting design or engineering problems or even at dealing with social conditions affected by the freeway location. But in this case more than 90 percent of the freeway had already been completed, at a cost in excess of $30 million. The final six-mile link, for which land had been purchased and cleared, was all that remained to complete a project that had been initiated almost a decade earlier. The EIS requirements served in this case to waste

time, energy, and money; they accomplished very little else.

Cutting through red tape

In addressing a group of students in 1976, Floyd Hyde, former under secretary of the Department of Housing and Urban Development, explained that, on the basis of his years of experience in the federal government, he could personally attest to the fact that federal

EXHIBIT 52 (cont'd)

Despite the equity principle embodied in this proposal, it was not implemented. County government officials were ambivalent about a transfer of airport owner- ship. On the one hand, they wanted jurisdiction over the airport because they recognized its broad user base. On the other hand, they did not want to assume the subsidy. The county budget, like the city's, was becoming tighter each year, and elected county politicians had little incentive to add a new cost—especially when more than half of the people they represented could enjoy the airport without paying that cost. Moreover, the Airport Commission had recently indicat- ed that a major expansion program was necessary if the airport was to serve the entire metropolitan area adequately. Understandably, the county was reluctant to assume financial responsibility for this expansion.

The City Council was also undecided. Council members wanted to shed respon- sibility for the airport, thereby reducing the annual operating costs and future capital requirements from the city's budget. The airport, however, was located on city property, and there were indications that future industrial and commercial expansion (a new source of city tax revenue) might occur in the airport area. The City Council was reluctant to give up this potential tax base.

Finally, a number of legal problems were involved in the transfer. These were related to the intent of the donors of the land on which the airport was located, the transfer of revenue-bond obligations from city to county, and the status of city employees who would work for the county if the transfer occurred.

From 1971 to 1974 this issue consumed an inordinate amount of the time of both city and county officials. County commissioners, airport commissioners, City Council members, and their respective staffs presented numerous plans to implement what nearly all recognized to be a sensible proposal. Nothing hap- pened. Forces on both sides of the question were too evenly balanced; the result was a continuation of the status quo.

bureaucrats were dedicated to cutting red tape—lengthwise.

For local-government practitioners, this observation is especially poignant. Every county executive, city manager, and mayor has his own favorite horror story about trying to guide a program through the intricate maze of conflicting federal guidelines, baf- fling regulations, and mountainous paper- work. Many such stories were told about Flint's battles with federal bureaucrats and their requirements. The best one is present- ed in Exhibit 56.

Two general conclusions emerge from an analysis of the federally funded programs administered in Flint. First, every separate federal program had its own set of rules, regulations, and administrative require- ments, many of which extended to incredi- ble depths of detail. Second, and perhaps more important, these rules and regulations were constantly changing, thereby making it difficult, if not impossible, for city officials to understand what the "feds" really wanted.

EXHIBIT 53

The City Is Part of the County—
Except When It Comes to Public Health

Flint's mayor put it this way: "It just doesn't make any sense. Flint city residents pay 40 percent of the costs of the County Health Department, but this department serves only noncity residents." Pausing a moment, the mayor added, "City residents are also county residents, aren't they?"

Under Michigan law, counties were responsible for public health, including inspecting commercial establishments, controlling infectious and communicable diseases, and reporting vital health statistics. Flint's 1929 charter, which preceded the state law, provided that the city maintain its own health department. Thus there were two health departments in Genesee County—one operated by the city for city residents and one operated by the county for noncity residents. For more than twenty years there had been discussions concerning the advisability of merging these two departments. These discussions were stimulated by the fact that four other city/county health departments in Michigan had been merged during the previous decade.

By the early 1970s, some progress had been made toward a merger. The county and city health departments had a common director whose salary was paid by both the county and city. However, the city and the county continued to maintain separate departments under one director. This resulted in dual budgets, dual organization structures, dual inventories of equipment, dual personnel policies, and dual employee union membership.

(continued)

(In some cases, as Exhibit 57 suggests, it appeared that the "feds" themselves didn't know what they wanted.)

Given the legislative process followed by Congress and the fragmentation of the federal bureaucracy, it is perhaps understandable why federal departments do not issue uniform grant-application, reporting, and evaluation requirements. It is less understandable why a single federal department, such as the Department of Housing and Urban Development, does not have a common set of administrative rules and regulations governing all its programs. Yet, this

was the case. In Flint, HUD was responsible for administering programs that ranged from public housing and urban renewal to water and sewer projects. Each of these programs had a different operations manual; each had a different accounting system; each had a different set of reporting forms and requirements; and each had a separate administrative bureaucracy within HUD to interpret the rules and regulations. To be sure, different programs may require different rules to reflect different purposes and constraints. This does not explain, however, why the coding for public-housing accounting reports

---

EXHIBIT 53 (cont'd)

In 1972 Flint's City Council, responding to increasing budgetary pressures, decided that it should transfer responsibility for public-health services to the county; this, it concluded, would save the city about $1 million per year. The argument was based on equity. City residents paid taxes to the county but did not receive the benefits of county health services. In effect, 40 percent of the cost of health services received by non-Flint residents were paid by the taxpayers in the city of Flint. The council approved a plan whereby the county would take over health services, providing a minimum level of service to all county residents. In addition, the city would be permitted to contract with the county if it desired additional services that were not being provided throughout the county.

The county Board of Supervisors did not respond to this proposal. The supervisors believed they had a good deal under the current arrangement. If they did not have to assume responsibility for providing public-health services and pay the attendant costs, why should they change the status quo?

After two years of fruitless debate and discussion, the city of Flint unilaterally proposed a plan to dismantle the city's health department over a three-year period. Under state law, the county would be forced to provide a minimum level of public-health services to all areas of the county. The greatest resistance to this plan came from city unions that represented Health Department employees. Union leaders demanded that the city guarantee that the county would hire all the city employees at their current salary rates with current benefits, both of which were substantially higher than those received by county employees.

Union resistance, combined with the political disincentives for the county to assume this responsibility, prevented a successful merger. By early 1976, little progress had been made.

---

should be different from the coding for the urban-renewal program, nor does it explain why the reporting frequency for Model City grants should be different from that for public-housing subsidies. The failure to standardize administrative procedures, as Exhibit 58 indicates, had a dramatic impact on the capacity of local-government officials to manage HUD-funded programs.

A number of factors explain the amount of red tape involved in federal programs. First, agencies like HUD were put together in the early 1960s from a number of independent agencies, each with its own bureaucratic baggage. In addition, despite the fact that certain federal programs may be administered by a single agency, they all must emerge from a legislative process in which compromise, not consistency, is the governing principle.

Second, the federal government understandably does not want to give up control over the federal dollar. A legitimate desire to ensure that national policies are not subverted, combined with a deeply embedded distrust of the ability of local-government officials to implement programs successfully, often leads to a greater rather than a lesser

EXHIBIT 54

Too Many Cooks in the Public-Housing Kitchen

At a meeting of the Flint Housing Commission the summer of 1974, one of the commissioners threw up his hands in despair. Directing his anger at the Department of Housing and Urban Development (HUD), he said: "We've got all of the responsibility for the problems and have to take all of the heat from tenants, but we have no authority to do anything about them. If we can't do a thing without first getting HUD approval, then let them come up here and run the damn program."

Public housing was not originally a complicated program. On the basis of legislation passed by Congress in 1937, Flint's City Council approved a public-housing program in 1964. Under this program, the federal government would agree to pay the debt service on bonds to construct low-income housing, while annual operating expenses would be covered by tenants' rents. The city, through a public-housing agency, would then sell the bonds and construct and manage the housing.

The catch in the program was that HUD, because of the guarantees, had to approve each step in the development process. During the 1960s this became extremely complex, as new options and new controls multiplied rapidly into a stack of almost incomprehensible rules and regulations.

By 1973, Flint operated, or was in the process of developing, 1,535 public-housing units—644 for the elderly and 881 for low-income families. This represented an investment of almost $20 million and required an operating budget in excess of $1 million per year.

Who was responsible for managing the public-housing program? Depending upon the respondent, there were at least four answers to this question—the city manager, the City Council, the Housing Commission, or HUD. Under city ordinance, the Department of Community Development was responsible for administering the program. This department reported to the city manager, who was also responsible for appointing the five members of the Housing Commission. The five commissioners, in turn, were responsible for formulating and monitoring public-housing policy. The city manager reported to the City Council. In reality, he had to obtain council approval prior to making all Housing Commission appointments.

(continued)

EXHIBIT 54 (cont'd)

Indirectly then the City Council was responsible for the public-housing program. But did the council have the authority to exercise this responsibility? The answer was clearly no. In March 1973, HUD told the city of Flint that $887,000 for modernizing public-housing units would be withheld pending a "comprehensive management review" of Flint's program. On the basis of this review, HUD proposed that the city make a number of changes to its public-housing program before the money would be released. A few of the recommendations were:

- Revise the functions and salaries of the administrative staff.
- Change rent-collection policies and practices.
- Improve work order and maintenance control.
- Change day-to-day operations of facilities.
- Change leasing and occupancy policies and procedures.
- Increase the involvement of tenants in operations.
- Improve community services provided to tenants.
- Change the city's employment policies.

As if these weren't enough, a last recommendation was that the City Council divest itself of the housing program and place it under the independent control of the Housing Commission.

In order to obtain the badly needed funds, the City Council, after protracted debate, passed an ordinance to create an independent housing commission. The city hoped that through this action the commission would be given the authority to manage the public-housing program in a way that would satisfy the council as well as the public-housing tenants.

Unfortunately, HUD didn't trust the new Housing Commission any more than it trusted the City Council. In August 1974, again as a condition for releasing the modernization funds, HUD demanded that the Housing Commission answer such detailed day-to-day management questions as: How will accountants spend time with community-development staff? How and when will decisions be made concerning the staffing levels for the commission? What actual reductions in grade levels of office staff are being proposed? What further reductions are planned in maintenance staffing? What steps will be taken to develop policies and procedures for city government involvement and assistance in managing housing projects?

The housing commissioner quoted at the beginning of this account concluded his statement this way: "I think we ought to sue HUD to either get them out of our hair or force them to take over the program."

EXHIBIT·55

Completion of Downtown Freeway Delayed More Than Ten Years

The public and private leaders who gathered in Flint's city hall in March 1974 were not happy. Their purpose, in the words of one citizen, was simple: "All we're asking—and we don't have to be engineers to do that—is for those boobs to link up two ends that have already been completed." A prominent Flint businessman added, "What we need is a little table-pounding in front of television cameras at the state Highway Commission meeting to help this project along." The chairman of the county Board of Commissioners agreed, noting that "the groups should get a little belligerent . . . it's apparently the only language those birds will understand." In summing up, a Flint councilman observed, "Sometimes the only thing a politician will respond to is pressure."

These civic leaders were angry about the Michigan Highway Department's announcement that the completion of a 6.3-mile freeway through the heart of downtown Flint (for which land had already been acquired and cleared) would be delayed from 1977 to 1979 because of the need to process an environmental impact statement (EIS). Originally, this freeway section had been scheduled for completion in 1968. Delays in land acquisition moved this target to 1972. When the city requested the state to prepare an EIS for the final section, the scheduled completion date was delayed to 1976. Further delays encountered by the state had set back the schedule first to 1977 and now to 1979. What seemed to anger Flint civic leaders most was that this final freeway section was intended to link two freeway segments that had already been completed. Both sections would be of no value until the final link was completed.

This freeway project, financed primarily by the federal government, was of critical importance to the development of the central city. Completion of the freeway affected completion of five urban-renewal projects, construction of the $60-million University of Michigan—Flint campus, and completion of $5 million in

(continued)

role for the federal government. Federal politicians believe, possibly incorrectly, that a program carried out by federal civil servants will adhere more closely to their wishes than one carried out by local officials. The result is more red tape to control local actions.

The third factor is related to a phenomenon that might be termed the "freight-train effect." This describes the evolution of many federal programs which were initially created with limited objectives and minimum constraints on the process of achieving them. In the early years, many such programs were successful. Over time, however, these programs have accumulated more and more "freight" as special interests attempted to expand them, control them, or achieve other

EXHIBIT 55 (cont'd)

planned street and transportation improvements. Moreover, each year's delay resulted in an 8–10 percent increase in construction costs.

Responding to pressure from Flint's civic leaders, as well as from Flint's congressman, the governor promised to expedite the processing of the EIS, in the hope of cutting as much as two years off the 1979 completion date. The governor, however, did not have the authority to approve an EIS. It had to go to Washington, where it would be reviewed first by the federal Highway Department and then by the office of the secretary of transportation and then would be sent to the Council on Environmental Quality, where, assuming all problems had been resolved, it would be filed. In short, *no one* approved an environmental impact statement.

Despite the fact that this final freeway link had undergone intensive planning, was in compliance with local land-use plans, and had been the basis for major public and private development decisions, new problems were identified. The citizens' district council representing residents in an urban-renewal area affected by the freeway development reiterated an old but legitimate complaint that the freeway would isolate a neighborhood of more than 200 residents. The U.S. Department of the Interior challenged the necessity of taking small pieces of five city parks, preferring an alternative route that would require the further acquisition of 1, 191 residences, 71 commercial properties, 16 churches, a hospital, a fire station, two private clubs, and 133 vacant parcels. The additional property acquisition costs for this route were estimated to be $26.5 million. Finally, the Office of Environmental Affairs within the Department of Transportation worried about the level of noise from the freeway and its effect on several hundred nearby homes. After reviewing the proposed freeway site, DOT officials stated categorically that the EIS would not be processed until the noise question was resolved. In almost complete exasperation, Flint's director of community development responded, "The noise levels they object to aren't predicted until the year 2000."

By 1975, these issues still had not been resolved. In fact, the State Department of Highways indicated that the final section of freeway might not be completed until well into the 1980s.

---

objectives through them. After a number of years, the result of such a process is a program so overburdened with conflicting purposes that it becomes extremely difficult, if not impossible, for it to arrive at its intended destination. The public-housing program is a classic example.

Perhaps the most important consequence of overregulation is excessive administrative cost. If the man hours required to understand and cope with the labyrinth of federal reporting requirements and accounting procedures could be devoted to simply running the program, the performance of most local governments could be improved immeasurably. It is unfortunate that the general public is unaware of the extent of these administrative requirements, for in many

EXHIBIT 56

HUD and City Play Ping-Pong with Urban-Renewal Project

In June 1970 Flint civic leaders traveled to Washington to seek special HUD funding for an urban-renewal project that would redevelop 38 acres in the center of Flint. This area, known as Doyle, was the most blighted area of the city. More than 85 percent of its residents were black, possessing the lowest per-capita income in the city. At least half of the existing housing units were deteriorated or dilapidated, and most were owned by absentee landlords. The Doyle area contained the greatest population density in the city and experienced the highest incidence of crime.

Secretary George Romney himself assured his Flint visitors that $5 million of urban-renewal funds would be reserved for the development of the Doyle area. The civic leaders returned home, satisfied that they had obtained a federal commitment to accomplish a much-needed, and widely supported, community project. Little did they know that the secretary's approval was only to initiate a seemingly unending series of bureaucratic delays, in which the fate of the Doyle project was batted back and forth between the city and the HUD area office.

A month after the secretary's decision, the city of Flint submitted a planning application. HUD quickly responded, announcing in August that $5 million had been reserved for this project, with only one contingency—the city's submittal of a final application and HUD's approval.

The community development staff, working closely with the citizens' district council representing the area, immediately began to prepare a development plan for Doyle that would be the basis for a final application. After preparing the plan, holding requisite public hearings, following all appropriate procedures, and making final revisions, the city submitted its final application to HUD in June 1971. The process was conducted by the city in a period of less than ten months— near-record time for a project of this magnitude.

Apparently, HUD was not impressed. The plan, it said, did not meet recently developed criteria. HUD made a series of demands: first, more data on the relocation housing opportunities for displaced residents: the city complied. Then, more information about the city's affirmative action program. The city provided this information. Finally, HUD required a formal commitment from the Board of Education to build a new school in the Doyle area. After considerable debate between the city, the board, and the HUD area office, a document was prepared that everyone felt comfortable signing. By this time, it was early 1972, and most concerned individuals in the city felt confident the project would soon be approved—but not so.

(continued)

EXHIBIT 56 (cont'd)

Without warning, the HUD Detroit area office announced that there were problems. Instead of approving the rebuilding of homes in which existing residents could relocate, thereby maintaining the existing racial pattern—a premise on which the original Doyle plan was based—HUD now wanted to reduce racial impaction. To do so required a new plan which would ensure a different racial and income mix in the new housing proposed for the area.

So, in early 1972, the city went back to the drawing board. In less than six months the city was prepared to submit a new plan according to the latest HUD requirements. Accordingly, the director of community development and his staff put the requisite ten copies of the final application in a box and personally delivered them to the HUD area office in Detroit. Expecting immediate approval, they were shocked and angered when HUD officials told them they could not accept the box of plans because they did not comply with the most recently passed legislation covering the payment of relocation benefits to displaced residents. The city was told that it would now have to amend the project budget to ensure that the city would pay the relocation benefits which the federal government would have paid under the old regulations.

Back in Flint, the City Council, after long debate, finally agreed to appropriate $250,000 from the city's Public Improvement Fund to meet the new financial requirement. With this authorization, the city in June 1972 resubmitted its third "final" application.

This time, HUD accepted the application. Then, because HUD was beginning a new fiscal year, it did nothing. For nearly four months it did not react to the application. When the agency finally responded, it was bad news again. This time, HUD officials announced that during the period they had been reviewing the Doyle application Flint's "workable program" had expired, and that no new programs could be approved until a new workable program had been submitted and approved.

Three months of work by the city staff produced a new workable program in January 1973. The document was submitted and subsequently approved by HUD. Now, certainly, the Doyle project would be approved, the money would be forthcoming, and the city could get on with this major public improvement. No such luck! In late January, HUD in Washington announced that it was placing a moratorium on all federal subsidies for the construction of low and moderate income housing. This was a serious blow to the Doyle project, because a major objective of the project was the construction of 150 units of low and moderate income housing using federal subsidies. Without these subsidies the housing could not be built and the project, despite almost thirty months' planning, was effectively dead.

(continued)

EXHIBIT 56 (cont'd)

Community leaders were not prepared to give up on this project after so much time and energy had gone into it. They decided again to go directly to the top, and arranged a meeting with a representative of the new secretary of housing and urban development, James Lynn. In April 1973 a contingent of civic leaders met with the under secretary of HUD to examine alternative ways to get the Doyle project under way. The results of the meeting boiled down to this: HUD would approve the project if the city could demonstrate an ability to relocate residents displaced by the project and guarantee that 50 percent of the newly constructed units would be available to low and moderate income residents.

Back in Flint, civic leaders met with the City Council to determine if these requirements could be met. It was clear, given the city's budget situation, that the city itself would not be able to subsidize the low and moderate income housing. After much agonizing, the Mott Foundation agreed to replace the federal government as the provider of subsidies under a locally run program. This major commitment, combined with a relocation plan, allowed the city to make its fifth "final" application to HUD.

At last, all the existing, past, and future regulations appeared to have been met. The Doyle project was finally approved in June 1973, three years after its inception. Ironically, this program was the last, or one of the last, urban-renewal programs ever approved by HUD. As of July 1, 1973, the federal urban-renewal program was terminated by the Nixon administration. The Community Development Act of 1974 placed future urban-renewal programs within community-development bloc grants administered by a whole new set of rules and regulations.

cases they are responsible for an inability to produce promised results. Citizens in Flint often complained that city officials lied to or misled them. This was often true, simply because city officials did not fully understand federal rules and regulations and, as a result, promised results that they did not have the power to produce. Those citizens who actually became involved in making federally funded programs work often became disillusioned, as Exhibit 59 indicates.

Moreover, federal rules and administrative requirements are constantly in a state of flux. Trying to hit a "moving target" results in wasteful expenditures of time, energy, and financial resources. The three-year effort to institute an urban-renewal program in the oldest and poorest section of Flint, described in Exhibit 56, is an excellent illustration.

Coping with local-government fragmentation

Because of the fragmentation of government entities at the local level, intergovernmental cooperation is imperative. Yet every day metropolitan newspapers are full of stories showing that the record of cooperation is not good. It is not uncommon, for example, to read of conflicts between a regional transit district and the local governments within the district it serves, of disputes between county boards of supervisors and

EXHIBIT 57

Sometimes the "Feds" Don't Understand the Politics of Their Own Programs

In the spring of 1974 Flint's manpower staff, which was in the process of preparing an annual manpower plan, faced a major dilemma. A few months earlier, federal legislation had combined a number of categorical manpower programs, including the summer youth-employment program, into a single "special revenue-sharing" bloc grant. The new guidelines stated clearly that there would be no separate federal appropriation for the summer youth-employment program in 1975. Any city that wanted this program would have to indicate this in its plan and use bloc-grant funds for financing.

In the past, the U.S. Department of Labor had made similar statements to the effect that there would be no summer youth-employment program; yet, each time, Congress ended up appropriating additional money for this popular program. The dilemma, therefore, was this: should the City Council trust the new written federal guidelines and the emphatic statements of the under secretary of labor for manpower or should they trust their own political judgment, which told them that funds would be made available despite the guidelines? They decided to trust their own judgment. As a result, the city's manpower plan allocated only a small reserve for the summer youth-employment program. In making such a decision, the city staff took a considerable risk. If Congress did not appropriate additional funds, this program would not be implemented in Flint, and the political consequences could be devastating.

At first it appeared as if the staff had made the wrong decision. In the fall of 1974 the under secretary for manpower requested that certain recipients of manpower revenue-sharing funds submit to the department an explanation of why they had not funded the summer youth program. Armed with these letters, the under secretary went before Congress to demonstrate that, although each local government had had the opportunity to fund a summer youth-employment program, some had chosen not to do so. He argued effectively that Congress should *not* make a special appropriation for this program.

Many of the largest cities in the country had taken an even greater gamble than Flint. They had reserved *no* funds for summer youth employment, and, therefore, in January they began to lobby Congress and the president for a special appropriation. Some hinted at the prospects of a "long, hot summer" if funds were not available; others pointed out the record of success this program had enjoyed. Their lobbying was effective. In the spring President Ford announced that he would request a special appropriation for a summer youth-employment program, and in June the appropriation was approved.

Flint and other cities that had not followed the guidelines were rewarded: they received sufficient funds to operate manageable youth-employment programs that summer. The lesson they drew from this experience was that sometimes even the "feds" do not understand the politics of their own programs.

EXHIBIT 58

Public Housing—A Program Entangled by Red Tape

The four decades following the passage of public-housing legislation in 1937 witnessed the accumulation of so much federal red tape that a housing director in 1974 needed at least a foot and a half of shelf space to contain the volumes of public-housing rules and regulations.

There was a regulation to cover almost every aspect of public housing. There were regulations that prescribed the account codes that a city should use. There were regulations that prescribed personnel policies a housing commission should adopt and the bylaws the commission should follow. There were rules that governed where public housing would be located, how it would be built, how tenants would be chosen, how tenant grievances would be handled, how rent would be collected, and much, much more.

In 1974, shortly after the Flint Housing Commission had gained its independence from the City Council and therefore, in theory, was supposedly in a position to manage its own program, the commission decided to hire a new executive director. Based on the belief that the public-housing program needed the infusion of new leadership, the Housing Commission decided to conduct a search throughout the Midwest. By definition, this meant that applicants for the position would have to travel to Flint for interviews. At this apoint, the HUD area office told the housing commissioners that HUD rules and regulations required them to obtain *prior* approval for each recruiting trip. This requirement was levied in spite

(continued)

local city councils, of differences between the objectives of a city-run public-housing agency and a county-run welfare department, or of jurisdictional disputes between a city-run police department and a county-run sheriff's office. As resources become scarce and difficulties in balancing budgets become greater, the costs of intergovernmental fragmentation rise to the surface and citizens may demand government consolidation or, at minimum, more intergovernmental cooperation.

In Flint, the record was mixed. Flint's governmental counterparts included a county (which surrounded the city), unincorporated townships and other cities located within the county, a board of education, a community college, the University of Michigan–Flint, and many special districts and quasi-independent governmental bodies. There were many examples of successful cooperation between the city and these other local-government entities. Despite decades of conflict over Flint's attempt to annex areas within the county, an effort that had fostered considerable distrust and suspicion, the city had a generally positive working relationship with the county. City and county officials worked together in exploring ways to develop a county airport and establish a unified county health department. Positive cooperation also marked city/county efforts to resolve flood-

EXHIBIT 58 (cont'd)

of the fact that HUD had endorsed the idea of finding the most qualified executive director and had approved Flint's public-housing budget prior to the recruiting effort.

The intrusion of HUD officials into the day-to-day management of the public-housing program in Flint was not confined to personnel policies. In 1973 HUD requested the Housing Commission to obtain an independent audit of its financial condition. Responding to this request, the city's finance director recommended that the Housing Commission employ the city's auditor to also audit the Housing Commission's books at the same time that he conducted the entire city audit. This would save the time required to select another auditor and it would be less expensive to the Housing Commission. HUD's response, in a memorandum, was as follows:

> HUD's circular 7476.1 states that the Housing Commission is required to solicit proposals from independent public accountants after furnishing interested firms with a HUD Audit Guide for low-rent public-housing programs. . . . We question the "independence" of the selected independent public accountant. The ongoing relationship between the city and the selected auditing firm may offer several advantages when conducting a citywide audit. However, HUD requirements concerning the selection of an "independent" public accountant might exclude this firm from consideration.

In other words, an independent public accountant, as defined by the profession, would not be independent in HUD's eyes if it had previously conducted an audit of the city. After reading HUD's memorandum, the city's finance director responded, "This not only violates established auditing principles, it violates common sense!"

control and drainage problems that originated in the county but made their greatest impact within the city limits. The county's Economic Development Commission played a pivotal role in obtaining the financing for an industrial park in Flint's north end. The city, in turn, participated in the development of a countywide police communication center and encouraged a dialog concerning the development of a common city/county jail. Despite threats by the city Recreation and Parks Board that non-Flint residents would be forbidden from participating in the city's recreation leagues and counterthreats by the county that Flint residents would be charged for admission to all county facilities, the problem was amicably resolved when the county agreed to let the city's recreational program use its recreational facilities, and the city agreed to admit noncity participants.

A spirit of cooperation also marked the relationship between the Model Cities program (administered by the county) and the Urban-Renewal program (administered by the city). The Department of Community Development worked closely with county personnel in developing the plan for the urban-renewal area that extended into the Model Cities program's jurisdiction. The county, in turn, contracted with the city for property acquisition, relocation, and demolition services.

EXHIBIT 59

Federal Programs Can Create Rather Than Reduce Citizen Alienation and Apathy

The newest federal guidelines for manpower programs required that a manpower area planning council (MAPC) be created to make recommendations concerning the delivery of manpower programs. Therefore, Flint's newly hired manpower planning coordinator began the process of involving citizens in an effort to make this program work for those it was intended to serve. A number of citizens enthusiastically agreed to serve on the council, sensing an opportunity to become involved in an important program of their local government. These citizens included labor leaders and business executives as well as a number of ordinary citizens who otherwise were not involved in local government affairs. All of them participated on a volunteer basis.

Prior to the latest regulations, manpower programs had been funded directly from Washington to a number of individual agencies in Flint. The Urban League, the Opportunities Industrialization Center, Goodwill Industries, and many other agencies had pieces of the federal action. The new guidelines were intended to ensure local control over expenditure of these funds.

A manpower plan was completed within a month, but it was downhill from then on. The first jolt for the members of MAPC came when they learned that federal guidelines prohibited them from making recommendations that substantially changed the existing manpower programs; the roles of the existing delivery agencies could not be altered. A second jolt came when the committee was informed that their recommendations could not change the existing funding levels for manpower agencies by more than 5 percent.

At this point, several citizens indicated that they had been "had" by the federal government or by the city; they weren't sure which. They had been appointed to help allocate and control manpower dollars but weren't being permitted to do so. A final jolt came when, after several months, committee members inquired about the Department of Labor's response to Flint's plan. They were informed that the city had not even received an official notice that the department had reviewed the plan, let alone accepted or rejected it. In fact, the plan was never officially accepted or rejected. Most members of the MAPC doubted that it had ever been read.

The MAPC continued to meet monthly, but more and more frequently the meetings degenerated into frustrating discussions about issues members now knew they had no power to alter. As a result, fewer people came to the meetings. It was often difficult to get a quorum.

Eighteen months later, new federal legislation was passed that provided a much more specific role for a manpower advisory council. But citizens who in the past had enthusiastically volunteered their services were now reluctant. It was evident that their experience with this federal program, instead of increasing their desire to become involved in the decision-making process, had created the opposite effect.

As might be expected, there were problems. Lack of coordinated planning, if not distrust, had led to simultaneous but independent decisions by the city to build a $50-million tertiary sewage-treatment plant and by the county to build a secondary treatment facility at a cost of over $30 million. The lack of adequate analysis made it difficult to determine whether one metropolian county needed two separate multimillion-dollar sewage-treatment plants. The absence of any attempt to work out a joint project was troubling and costly.

In another area, the county refused to participate in efforts to develop a county-wide housing program for low- and moderate-income families. A proposed plan to allocate 15,000 subsidized housing units through a fair-share formula to all units of government within the county was flatly rejected by all other cities.

Perhaps the best illustration of lack of coordination at the local level was within the area of planning. As Exhibit 60 suggests, responsibility for local planning in the Flint area was fragmented and isolated from the real problems facing government decision makers, whether in the county, the city, or another governmental unit. The existence of separate planning entities, financed by higher levels of government as well as by the private sector, each trying to guard the sanctity of its own turf, made coordination an impossible goal to achieve. It also reduced the impact of planning activities. In reviewing the state of planning in the Flint area, a consultant hired to review one particular planning agency noted in his final report, "My guess is that if all this planning stopped tomorrow nobody would know the difference."

The relationship between Flint's City Council and the Board of Education was not marked by cooperation. Both the city and the board were elected to serve the same constituents. Each was responsible for services that were central to the quality of life of Flint citizens. Cooperation was necessary to ensure that educational factors were considered in planning and carrying out city programs in such areas as health, housing, and income maintenance, yet personality differences, parochialism, and bureaucratic inertia made cooperation difficult to achieve. The consequences, as Exhibit 61 indicates, were felt most by the citizens. In this case institutional parochialism was at the heart of the Board of Education's unwillingness to consider a program that represented significant opportunities for Flint citizens to participate more actively in their local government as well as in educational affairs.

Cooperation between the city of Flint and the University of Michigan was excellent. (A joint city/university project to develop an urban campus in the heart of downtown Flint is described in detail in Chapter 19.) The problem with respect to both the university and the community college was not the absence of cooperation with the city but the absence of means within the city for taking greater advantage of the problem-solving and analytical resources of these two institutions.

Opportunities for Improvement

On July 4, 1976, Americans celebrated the 200th anniversary of an unparalleled declaration of individual independence and responsibility. In 1987 Americans will celebrate another bicentennial anniversary—the creation of a federal system of government founded on the principle of individual sovereignty and dedicated to the proposition that the federal government should share the exercise of power with individual states (and ultimately with local governments). This organizational response to the Declaration of Independence launched the American democratic experiment.

During the past two decades our federal structure of government has become ex-

EXHIBIT 60

Planning Agencies in Flint Created Confusion Instead of Results

A common cry of local-government reformers in the 1960s was "We need better planning at the local level." Heeding this cry, federal and state governments as well as many local jurisdictions went to work to do more planning—which, of course, meant creating more planning agencies. Let's take a look at the planning agencies that were responsible for understanding the needs of Flint's citizens and translating them into action programs.

The city of Flint was served directly by a traditional Planning Commission that, pursuant to state law, was responsible for preparing a land-use plan and enforcing it through zoning ordinances. In addition, the city manager had a planning and evaluation office that served as the staff to the Planning Commission and also provided planning, budgeting, and evaluation assistance to the manager and the council. Finally, separate departments within the city had their own planning functions. The Department of Community Development, for example, had a planning staff responsible solely for urban-renewal planning.

Genesee County, which included the city of Flint, had its own planning agency. The Genesee County Metropolitan Planning Commission (GCMPC) was responsible for transportation and land-use planning for the entire county. GCMPC was independent of the county Board of Supervisors and was responsible for land-use planning in unincorporated areas of the county as well as for coordinating the plans of the incorporated jurisdictions. GCMPC had "A-95" review power, which meant that it reviewed and commented on all applications for federal funds by all jurisdictions within the county.

(continued)

ceedingly complex as layers and subdivisions of local government have been created. In this chapter we have examined conditions in one local government so as to better understand how intergovernmental relationships within our federal structure affect the ability of government officials to get things done. Armed with this understanding, we are better able to identify opportunities to improve these relationships.

The place to start is with the federal gov-

ernment. Common sense demands that the federal government continue the policy of decentralization, both of resources and of the authority for their use. People live and work in towns, cities, and counties. Because local-government officials are closest to these people and to their problems, it stands to reason that they will be most responsive to them. If the purpose of government flows from a collective desire to allow individuals an opportunity to fulfill their potential, it

EXHIBIT 60 (cont'd)

While GCMPC was presumably responsible for "comprehensive planning," it did not have planning responsibility for many basic functions that affected the quality of life of county residents. It had no responsibility for health—a three-county health-planning council was responsible for planning health services. It was not responsible for manpower—a separate Comprehensive Area Manpower Planning System (CAMPS) was responsible for manpower planning. It was not responsible for public safety—a special regional crime commission had been established to coordinate planning in the area of criminal justice.

After surveying the quality of planning (certainly not the quantity of planning agencies), the private sector in Flint decided that yet another planning agency was needed. Therefore, in 1970, the Human Services Planning Council (HSPC) was established as an independently funded agency to coordinate the planning for the delivery of a variety of "human services" throughout the county. It was a planning agency for the planning agencies.

Apparently, state officials were not happy with the quality of planning being done in Flint, Genesee County, or throughout the state of Michigan. In 1974 the state designated thirteen planning regions. A new regional planning commission was conceived for each region to be responsible for "comprehensive regional planning." It was unclear how this new regional planning body would be coordinated with existing planning agencies, none of which would be replaced by the new planning body.

How were all these planning agencies related to each other? Why was responsibility for planning fragmented along functional lines? Why were planning agencies separated from general-purpose governments responsible for delivering the public goods and services for which the agencies planned?

seems reasonable to assume that local officials can best understand and remove the barriers that prevent the achievement of this purpose. The proposition that Congress should attempt to be the nation's city council—viewing human needs in Flint, Michigan; Plains, Georgia; Palo Alto, California; and some 39,000 other units of local government equally—is preposterous!

This does not mean that the federal government should abdicate all responsibility for what local governments do. To the contrary, the federal government should be responsible for setting national policies and standards and making sure that local governments adhere to them in administrating federally funded programs. In this way, the federal government will have a greater impact on the quality of life all Americans experience.

There are, however, acceptable and unacceptable ways to achieve this end. For exam-

EXHIBIT 61

Board of Education Rejects Citizen-Participation Program

In May 1973 Flint's city manager proposed to the City Council that the city and the Board of Education jointly sponsor a citizen-participation program that would increase the involvement of citizens in the process of making public decisions that affected their neighborhoods. This proposal suggested that the community school councils already established and operating in elementary-school districts throughout the city be utilized as the building blocks of the proposed citywide citizen-participation program.

This program was intended to create communication between neighborhood councils and the Board of Education and City Council, respectively. The city would provide information to community school councils concerning projects and services that might affect their neighborhoods. Community council input would then be obtained prior to final decisions on city policy or program implementation. In addition, the community school councils would bring to the attention of the city manager and the City Council neighborhood issues and problems that city government ought to address. Presumably, the Board of Education would take advantage of the same two-way process.

The independently elected Board of Education flatly rejected the citizen-participation proposal, despite the fact that it had the backing of the superintendent of education. One board member blasted the city manager for making the proposal, stating, "He doesn't run the school system" and that his proposal was "out of line." Other members of the board noted that they were in the process of changing the roles of the community school councils and that this proposal would create an undue burden on scarce staff resources. They suggested that the proposal made sense but that the timing of its implementation was inappropriate.

The most important opposition, however, came from those who felt that educational problems should not be intermixed with general governmental problems that were the responsibility of Flint's city government. As one board member put it, "We do not want to complicate educational matters by involving the city."

ple, the principle of "management by exception" has long proven its value in private corporations. This principle places primary responsibility for setting directions on higher levels of management, and delegates to lower levels the responsibility for getting things done. Once a direction is set, a manager does not interfere until a problem arises, and then he tries to help solve it. Emphasis is placed on developing objectives and evaluating progress toward their achievement, not controlling each step in the process. If the federal government is more concerned with the results of its programs than with the paperwork it generates, there is no reason why this principle should be any less useful in managing national efforts to satisfy human and environmental needs than in managing a private corporation.

Along with an emphasis on management by exception must come a simplification and standardization of the rules, regulations, and red tape that enmesh federally funded programs.* Efforts now under way to eliminate excessive administrative requirements must be accelerated. Moreover, federal departments and agencies must be monitored more carefully to ensure that they comply with the policies and procedures that have already been promulgated by the U.S. Office of Management and Budget. Progress toward greater simplification and standardization could be enhanced if local-government officials participated more in the development of the rules and regulations which govern the development and administration of federal programs. This would not only ensure that Washington-based bureaucrats have a better understanding of the reality of local-government conditions, it would also serve to educate local-government officials about the difficulties federal officials face in managing large federal programs.

In its attempts to meet national needs, the federal government could choose *not* to channel nationally collected revenue through general-purpose units of government (e.g., as in the case of comprehensive health-planning agencies). Conditions in Flint argue strongly against this course of action. Recognizing that the purpose of government is to serve individual citizens, it makes little sense to fund a vast array of specialized government entities concerned with only one or a limited number of desired conditions (health, housing, manpower, education) that in combination determine the quality of life citizens experience. In particular, the federal government should termi-

nate the funding of independent planning agencies, a practice that has served to widen the gap between those responsible for planning and those responsible for getting things done—two functions that cannot be separated.

Continuing decentralization of resources and responsibility, reducing red tape, and channeling federal funds through general-purpose units of local government—all represent opportunities that are based on a common assumption: the federal government cannot tell 39,000 units of local government what they should do to solve local problems or how they should do it. Local governments, aided by federally collected revenue and unencumbered by excessive regulation, must assume this responsibility themselves. Without violating this assumption, additional opportunities exist for the federal government to help rather than hinder local-government officials' efforts to improve performance:

Support management improvements through existing general and categorical grants. Without telling local governments what to do, the federal government could use its grant-making power to help local officials improve and modernize their management processes. This could be done in several ways: (1) by requiring that a fixed percentage of federal grants (e.g., revenue sharing) be expended for management improvements, (2) by requiring that local governments which accept federal grants adhere to agreed-upon management standards or criteria, (3) by making additional federal funds available to local governments that develop and implement management-improvement programs,[13] and (4) by placing primary emphasis in the administration of categorical grants on the achievement of objectives and the production of results.†

Increase financial assistance for general management. In Flint, the ability of the City

---

* These efforts include reducing the complexity of grant applications, reducing the time between grant submittal and approval, consolidating grant application in related areas, and giving federal regional offices greater authority in grant administration.

---

† A special report prepared by the U.S. Office of Management and Budget in 1975 indicated that less than 1 percent of all federal assistance in 1974 was directed toward general management improvements.

Council to significantly modernize management tools was totally dependent on funds provided by the Department of Housing and Urban Development's "701" planning and management assistance program. Without these funds, improvements would not have been made. (Chapter 18 provides a complete case study of these improvements.) By 1974 this source of general management assistance had dried up. Developing new programs (or funding old ones) that would provide financial assistance for general management improvements would correct this problem. It is true that many functional programs in such areas as health, education, housing, and environment provide money that could be used to strengthen program management. But the emphasis on discrete functions has often served to weaken, not strengthen, overall management capabilities.

Increase the relevancy of federal research and development. Efforts in Flint to obtain the results of research and development projects conducted in other local governments throughout the country proved futile—in part because of the absence of organizational responsibility within the city for receiving and properly disseminating this type of information. Moreover, most research and development projects did not appear to address practical needs. In large part, this could be corrected by including more local-government officials in the design and dissemination of federal research projects.

Assign organizational responsibility for intergovernmental relationships. It was impossible for local officials in Flint to understand how federal programs could best be used to improve performance. Some local governments have solved this problem by hiring a "broker" to extract from Washington the maximum amount of financial assistance possible. Such a step, however, seems unnecessary and unwarranted for a city of Flint's size. The federal government should seize the initiative and assign specific organizational responsibility for providing local governments with information about federal programs and available funding sources so that each local government has an equal opportunity to share in the largesse. Further, one agency should be responsible for both transmitting knowledge about what other local governments have done to improve performance and passing on the results of research and demonstration projects in various localities. In a similar vein, there is an opportunity for regional and area offices of respective federal departments to improve their capacity to serve as consultants, helping local governments within their jurisdictions better understand how to deal with the federal government.

States, too, can play a role in helping local-government officials improve the performance of their local governments. Because the city of Flint could exercise only those powers formally delegated to it by the state of Michigan, performance-improvement efforts were considerably affected by what the state did or did not do. For example, by limiting the level of income tax the city of Flint could levy, the state affected the ability of public officials to solve local problems in a manner that local citizens were willing to finance. Similarly, the state Public Employee Labor Relations Act, which did not include criteria for defining what was a bargainable issue, had a significant impact on management/labor relations. In Michigan there is a major opportunity to identify and remove structural, financial, and administrative impediments to improved performance at the local level.

A first step for the state should be to assign organizational responsibility—perhaps establish an office of local-government relations—responsible directly to the governor which, among other things, would:

- Identify state-imposed barriers to improved local-government performance,
- Work with local-government officials to determine how the state could provide more and better financial and technical assistance.
- Develop performance measures, collect

data, and publish comparative results about local governments in the state of Michigan; this would produce healthy intercity and intercounty competition in improving community conditions.

- Publish information about local government "successes" in achieving productivity and performance improvements.
- Identify and disseminate information concerning new initiatives that local governments might take to improve performance (e.g., development of multijurisdictional collective-bargaining and management-training programs, development of city/county cooperation in contracting for services, development of intergovernmental contracting and purchasing programs).

The state provides considerable resources to local governments, and therefore may exert considerable leverage over the way in which these resources are spent. The principles of decentralization and management by exception are as appropriate for the relationship between Flint and the state of Michigan as they are for the relationship between Flint and the federal government. So, too, is the need to simplify and standardize the rules and regulations governing the administration of state-funded programs. Like the federal government, states should establish consistent policies and procedures that local governments, such as Flint, must follow in utilizing state funds.

One positive action the state could take is to require annual "performance audits." In Michigan all cities must have an annual financial audit, the purpose of which is to ensure that the taxpayers' funds have been accounted for according to generally accepted accounting principles. A *performance audit* would concentrate not on how tax dollars have been spent but on what they have produced. This audit would answer such questions as: were service objectives set? Were they realistic? Have annual performance targets been set? Have annual targets been met? Each local government would have the responsibility for conducting this audit in the manner it felt most appropriate within state guidelines. The state of Michigan would merely require that it be performed and that the results be made public.

The most direct and important action Michigan and other states could take to improve local-government performance is to recognize and pay for the costs of actions they impose on local governments. For example, if the Michigan legislature believes that minimum-security prisoners should be located within the Flint community and enacts legislation to implement this belief, it should provide funds for the program.

Cities like Flint can do little to improve the impact of federal and state actions on their own performance. In simple terms, the city of Flint must play according to rules established by the state of Michigan and the federal government. Recognizing the considerable constraints under which the latter operate, the most significant opportunity for public officials in Flint to improve intergovernmental relationships exists at the local level. Although the relationship between the city and its municipal neighbors has improved somewhat during the past decade, it is fair to say that there is potential for considerably greater improvement.

One major opportunity is to strengthen existing metropolitan institutions in an attempt to identify and pursue opportunities to strengthen the relationships between the city of Flint and other local units of government in Genesee County. Efforts to develop a county airport and health department should be accelerated. More important, systematic efforts should be undertaken to (1) identify criteria for determining the most appropriate level of local government to perform specific government functions and activities and (2) negotiate appropriate reallocation of responsibility.

In a similar vein, the city of Flint should establish specific staff responsibility for intergovernmental relationships. In this manner, the City Council would know whom to hold accountable for progress in strengthening intergovernmental relationships.

The Board of Education represents a unique opportunity. Serving the same constituency as the council, the Board of Education had always enjoyed a more positive public image than that of the City Council. Given the importance of community schools and the potential role of community school councils as the infrastructure for the integrated delivery of public services, the city of Flint should pursue every opportunity to improve its relationship with the Board of Education.

A final opportunity concerns the simple but often difficult process of educating citizens about the impact of intergovernmental relationships on performance. For example, few Flint citizens realized that 40 cents of each tax dollar they paid went to the county, yet Flint citizens received far less than 40 cents' worth of services from the county. County government services were directed primarily to those who lived outside the city but paid the same basic tax rate. Broad understanding of this fact might have significantly increased public support for City Council attempts to unify the city and county health departments and transfer airport responsibility to the county.

Ultimately, local governments such as the city of Flint must assume direct responsibility for improving their own performance. In the process, they must recognize that no local government functions independently; each interacts within a federal system that, in many respects, can improve or impede its performance.

CHAPTER 12

Citizen Involvement

Governments are instituted among Men, deriving their just powers from the consent of the governed.

Declaration of Independence

The problem . . . is to devise ways of giving the individual the opportunity to play a more meaningful part in shaping the governmental policies and programs which affect his physical, esthetic, occupational, recreational, and human environment.

Elliot Richardson

In July of 1776, delegates to the Continental Congress adopted a declaration of profound significance. Declaring that the "United Colonies" were free and independent states absolved of all allegiance to the British Crown, these delegates proclaimed their intent to create a new government. This government was to be founded on a revolutionary principle—the right of governors to govern (make public decisions) would be based solely on the consent of the governed (the citizens affected by those decisions).

Implicit in the word *consent* was a new set of responsibilities for each citizen. To ensure an informed basis for giving their consent, citizens must do more than merely exercise their right to vote; they must become actively involved in the process of governing. Only in this way can they communicate their needs and aspirations to their elected leaders and evaluate the extent to which their expectations are satisfied. In short, making a representative democracy work depends on the willingness and the ability of each citizen to become involved in the process of government.

Involving citizens in the decisions of their local government was a difficult task when America was a small, rural society. Today, two centuries later, the difficulty is compounded. In the years since 1776, America has become a large, complex urban nation. No longer can all the citizens of a local government sit together in one room, as they did in New England town meetings, and collectively resolve their common problems. Some citizens, of course, write to their congressmen or attend public hearings. Most people, however, interact with their government only every two or four years, when they go to the polls to cast their ballots. Alarmingly, many citizens fail to exercise even this fundamental democratic responsibility.

As the volume and complexity of public

issues have increased and direct citizen involvement in the decision-making process within government has decreased, public officials have been forced to assume greater responsibility for defining and acting in behalf of what they perceive to be the public interest. Understanding what citizens really want is not an easy task. Public officials may gain some sense of what citizens want and are willing to pay for through personal contacts, public meetings, or citizen opinion surveys. Yet such tactics often prove inadequate in capturing a comprehensive sense of the public will. Therefore, public officials and citizens together face the critical challenge posed by Elliot Richardson: how can we devise ways to give individual citizens an opportunity to play a more meaningful role in shaping the governmental policies and programs that affect their physical, esthetic, occupational, recreational, and human environment?[1] Meeting this challenge will not be easy, but it may well constitute the most important item on the nation's agenda as we begin our third century.

What Is Citizen Involvement?

To bring the definition of *citizen involvement* clearly into focus, it may be useful to understand what this term does *not* mean. Citizen involvement is not limited to the simple act of voting every two or four years for a mayor, county executive, member of the board of supervisors, or city councilperson. Nor is it limited to attendance at public hearings or participation on advisory committees, special boards and commissions, and public authorities, although all of these are part of effective citizen involvement.

Citizen involvement does not mean responsibility for, or control of, public programs. Political leaders are elected to determine government policies and objectives and to develop and implement programs that will achieve these objectives. Citizens cannot manage these programs; they can only hold those who do manage them accountable for performance. Underlying this interpretation is a fundamental principle: representative self-government must be based on trust between citizens and the public officials to whom they have delegated responsibility. If this trust is violated, citizens cannot substitute themselves in place of their representatives. They can, however, elect new ones.

Finally, citizen involvement is not limited to *citizen participation,* as the term was defined and used in the 1960s. That term is generally associated with federally mandated participation by poverty area or minority-group citizens in the conduct of federally funded programs. Given this narrow connotation, a new term is needed to suggest a broader need: that of involving *all* citizens in the *full range* of government decisions, not just those decisions related to federal funding.

Citizen involvement, then, refers to the process of providing all residents of a local government a full and equal opportunity to influence those government decisions that affect the quality of their lives. By *residents* we mean ordinary citizens who are not generally represented by established interest groups or private institutions. By *decisions* we mean the final policies and programs adopted by political leaders which determine what a local government does with scarce tax dollars. By *full and equal opportunity* we mean that all residents should have the same opportunity to influence government decisions regardless of their social, economic, or corporate status.

Under this definition, citizens identify what they want government officials to do, communicate their desires, participate actively in the process of making public decisions, and evaluate the actions of their elected representatives. Only by being so involved can citizens really be sure that their government and its leaders deserve their continuing consent.

Impact on Process and Performance

Citizens, individually or in groups, affect performance indirectly through their ability to influence decisions made by public officials. This influence takes several forms. In a democratic system of government, a majority of those voting determines which political leaders will assume responsibility for the management of local government. Thus citizens are directly responsible for the public officials who are elected and indirectly responsible for the quality of the decisions these officials subsequently make. This responsibility extends beyond election day. Threatening the withdrawal of support or promising more enthusiastic support in subsequent elections can influence significantly the decisions of incumbent political leaders. In an extreme situation—one in which political leaders blatantly disregard the views of those they serve—citizens may, in some states, initiate the process of recall and remove public officials from office.

Citizen involvement may also affect the quality of public decisions by ensuring that such decisions are based on complete and accurate information. Obtaining citizen views before decisions are made increases the likelihood that all potential alternatives have been identified. Citizens, motivated by their opposition to proposed decisions, may identify more realistic alternatives than those already under consideration. At a minimum, citizen involvement in the decision-making process increases the probability that the costs of proposed alternatives, especially the nonmonetary costs, will be fully considered.

Citizen involvement can provide information to public officials which will alert them to potential problems and pitfalls that could inhibit program implementation. This input should enable public officials to fine-tune programs so as to take into account the unique conditions and characteristics of neighborhoods or sectors of the population affected by these programs. Furthermore, if public employees (police officers, housing inspectors, sanitation workers) know that

citizens are monitoring the quality and quantity of services, their motivation to improve service delivery should increase.

Citizen involvement may also affect the management of a local government through an indirect effect on the community's financial base. To the extent that greater involvement in the making of government decisions creates a positive incentive for citizens to remain in a community and work for its betterment, the community's tax base will be maintained and may even be strengthened. Greater involvement in the process of deciding what needs to be done within the community may also increase citizens' willingness to pay for the programs and projects that will satisfy economic, social, and physical needs.

Increased citizen involvement in the resolution of neighborhood problems may also create incentives for local citizens to solve their own problems. If, for example, citizens become involved in the development and operation of programs designed to meet community housing needs, they may, in the process, identify additional ways of solving housing problems which do not require government involvement. This has important implications, because, in the long run, neighborhood development depends primarily on the willingness and ability of citizens to develop solutions to their own problems.

In 1974 a Harris poll indicated that 63 percent of all adults agreed with this statement: "The people running the country don't really care what happens to you." Only 26 percent had agreed with this statement in 1966.[2] The sentiment expressed in the 1974 poll reflects the fact that citizens increasingly feel unable to communicate with government officials and believe that these officials "don't really give a damn' about their needs. When such feelings create the perception that opportunities to become involved are closed, the result is often alienation, anger, and frustration. These feelings can be changed by including citizens in the decision-making process of a local government.

Permitting greater citizen involvement can make government officials more accessible to the citizens they serve and educate the public about the challenges officials confront in attempting to manage a local government.

Clearly, government officials cannot consult with every citizen on every issue or conduct a poll before every vote, and they should not attempt to do so. Nevertheless, providing an opportunity for citizens to express their views on critical issues before decisions have been "locked in concrete" should create greater incentives for citizens to become actively involved in civic affairs and restore citizens' trust in their government.

It should be clearly understood that expanding the role of citizens in the process of governmental decision making imposes certain costs. Greater citizen involvement may increase the time required to reach public decisions and thereby increase the overall cost of programs and projects. For example, if citizens affected by the development of a proposed highway are fully included in the decision-making process, the time needed to plan and construct the highway may be lengthened at a considerable increase in cost.

There are also political costs to citizen involvement. Involvement mechanisms may produce rival political leaders who may threaten established leadership. In addition, there may be a cost associated with greater citizen frustration and anger if political leaders do not accept their requests and suggestions or are not capable of satisfying the needs they have encouraged citizens to articulate. Finally, the development of adequate mechanisms to ensure appropriate and meaningful citizen involvement costs money and requires competent staff and adequate management controls—resources that are in short supply in most counties and cities.

On balance, the advantages of greater citizen involvement far outweigh the potential costs or disadvantages. Therefore, it is important to evaluate the extent to which citizens of a local community are involved in the process of making government decisions. To the extent that they are not, it is important to examine how this condition may be improved.

Criteria for Evaluation

There are many ways to ensure that residents of a local community have a continuous opportunity to influence the decisions of their local government. The following criteria may be used to evaluate the quality of citizen involvement and the nature of its impact on governmental performance:

Do citizens actively participate in the election process? The primary way in which citizens affect the performance of their government is through the ballot box, not only in the election of representatives but also in deciding measures related to millage, bond issues, charter amendments, referenda, initiatives, and other questions requiring a vote of the people. This question examines whether those who are eligible to vote exercise this right. Is there wide citizen involvement in the financing and conduct of election campaigns?

Do citizens want to be involved in the decision-making process of their elected officials? If citizens are to have a role in shaping governmental decisions, they must do more than just vote and participate in political campaigns. This question examines whether citizens are knowledgeable about the activities of their city government. Do citizens make use of existing citizen-involvement mechanisms to present their views on particular issues?

Are public officials committed to a partici-patory process? Public officials must dem-onstrate a willingness to hear citizens' views on public issues and to incorporate them into the decision-making process. They must be willing to provide citizens with accurate information on pending decisions, allowing enough time to obtain citizen views before decisions are made. They must also be will-ing to inform citizens of the extent to which their views were considered or rejected and why. Accordingly, this question examines whether this is the case. Do public officials take the time to identify all points of view? Do they keep an open mind until all the evidence is presented? Are citizens informed of pending decisions? Do public officials provide feedback to citizens concerning how their views were treated in the deci-sion-making process?

Is the role and responsibility of private citizens clearly defined? In our system of representative democracy, political leaders are accountable for final public decisions. Citizen involvement is the process of advis-ing or helping these decision makers arrive at informed decisions; it is not an attempt to divert responsibility for these decisions. This question explores the extent to which citi-zens and public officials understand each other's complementary roles. Is it clear where the "buck" stops? Are decisions dele-gated to individuals or groups who are not accountable to the public for the results of their decisions? Are public officials willing to assume responsibility for their decisions?

Is there a formal mechanism for involving citizens in the decision-making process? A process for involving citizens should be in-cluded within the formal procedures of gov-ernment. This question is aimed at determin-ing whether such a formal mechanism exists and evaluating how well it works. Do citi-zen-involvement mechanisms provide an equal opportunity for all to participate? Is the process credible to all segments of the citi-zenry? Does the process produce reliable information about government initiatives and citizen reactions?

Does the city have the administrative cap-acity to respond to citizen requests? If citi-zens expect local-government officials to take action in response to their requests for better service, and if government depart-ments do not respond, citizen frustration and anger may well create a more serious problem. Do citizens' points of view get wide circulation within the bureaucracy? Do com-plaints get resolved? Is there follow-through to ensure that complaints will not recur?

Conditions in Flint

Most Flint residents were indifferent to the affairs of their city government. A poll con-ducted by a local organization in May 1974 found that 76 percent of those interviewed (all above voting age) could not name their City Council representative and that 69 per-cent were not aware of the existence of the Charter Revision Commission, even though more than 80 percent said they desired a change in the way the mayor was elected.[3] The Charter Revision Commission had been in existence for more than five months and was moving rapidly toward drafting a revised charter to be put before the public at the following November election.

Citizen participation in the electoral process

Most Flint citizens did not exercise their democratic right and responsibility to vote. In the City Council election of November 1973, only 25 percent of those registered exercised this right. As low as this turnout may seem, it compared favorably with voter participation in other local elections, as the following table attests.

Purpose of Election	Type	Date	Percent of Registered Voters Who Voted
Local, state, congressional	Primary	August 1970	30
	General	November 1970	63
Local (Board of Education)	General	June 1971	17
National, presidential, state, congressional	General	November 1972	74
Local (City Council and Charter Revision Commission)	Primary	August 1973	15
	General	November 1973	25
State, congressional, and local (new charter)	General	November 1974	37

In a special election held in August 1974 to approve funds to finance special education in Genesee County, only 13,000 of more than 200,000 registered voters went to the polls. In several precincts, not a single voter appeared. The unwillingness of Flint's citizens to participate in the electoral process occasioned the following editorial from Flint's major television station.

It is said that in a democracy we get what we deserve. If we get bad management in our local government, it is because we, the voters, have failed to tell our legislators and administrators that we have even the smallest interest in how our government is run. Why is it that we turn out 60 to 65 percent of the vote to elect a congressman to a two- or six-year term, but we can only turn out 8 to 10 percent of the vote when we are electing the school board, who can set the educational standards for our children for the next twenty years? Granted, congressmen make monumental decisions, but the decisions by school boards, city councils, and mayors also have a personal impact on our lives. Through a simple majority vote, a city council or board of education can decide on what kind of police and fire protection we are going to have, they can decide on the quality of education, on the standards of streets and roads, and on

whether we will have a beautiful, growing city or a sprawling, deteriorating slum. . . .

In recent primaries, voters indicated to our political and educational leaders that we simply don't care. In the Flint primary for City Council, less than 10 percent of the available vote went to the top votegetter. In Bay City, where the adult population is about 31,000, the winning mayor polled less than 6 percent of that. If we feel our leaders are unresponsive, we must first realize that in such cases the elected officials feel the need to listen only to those who voted for them, while the rest of us sit by, helplessly complaining.

If you care for better government, you can get it by voting for those candidates who are best suited to run our cities. It is your democracy and your future, and the only way you can affect it is to vote![4]

The "Why should I vote? It won't matter anyway" attitude was commonplace in Flint, and in large measure it explains why most citizens did not register or vote. In addition, Flint residents—many of whom worked in the auto plants during the week and took their campers and snowmobiles to northern campsites and cottages on weekends—did not participate in local elections because they did not feel they had a stake in their city. A survey of citizen attitudes toward Flint conducted in November 1973 revealed that two of every three people in the city had a negative view of Flint's city government. Only two people in ten had ever contributed money to a political candidate or worked in a political campaign of any kind.[5] Of course, there were exceptions to these statistics. In 1975, 44 percent of registered voters actually voted on the question of a new city charter. This dramatic increase in participation reflected the fact that this election gave citizens the opportunity to determine the form of local government in which their elected representatives would serve.

The scheduling of elections also contributed to low voter turnout. It was not uncommon in Flint to have four or five separate elections in a given year, all for different purposes. In 1975, for example, there was a presidential primary election in May, a special education millage vote in June, a senate primary vote in August, and a general election in November. It would not have been surprising if the Genesee County Intermediate School District or the Genesee County Recreation and Park District had also held special millage elections. This fragmentation reflected the practical reality that if the Board of Education or other public body wanted to increase the tax rate for a specific purpose, it had a greater opportunity of doing so if this was the only issue on the ballot. In this way, positive supporters would have a relatively greater impact. It was not uncommon to have less than 10 percent of the electorate actually vote in such elections.

The major consequence of low voter turnout and the low level of participation in the election process was the expanded power awarded by default to organized special-interest groups—primarily municipal employee unions, the UAW, and downtown business interests. In the mid-1960s, after they were permitted by law to organize, municipal employees moved quickly to fill the vacuum created by citizen disinterest in

city government. The result was a situation in which public officials were generally more responsive to city unions and special-interest groups than they were to the citizens they were elected to serve.

Citizens' willingness to become involved

The record of citizens' involvement in the decision-making process at city hall was roughly equivalent to their record as voters. Participation by individual citizens or citizens' groups in government activities was rare. It was difficult to find private citizens who were not aligned with a special-interest group to serve on the city's many boards and commissions. As a result, many of the same people were reappointed term after term. Attendance at public hearings and other public meetings was generally low, even when important issues were discussed. From 1971 to 1974, few citizens addressed the council even to ask a question about the city's most important document—the annual budget.

Of course, there were exceptions, and these usually occurred as a result of a major community crisis. For example, many citizens were anxious to be appointed to the Citizens' Complaint Review Board (CCRB). This board was established to review citizen complaints concerning the conduct of city personnel and to recommend appropriate action to the city manager and to the City Council. The creation of this board grew out of the black community's charges of police brutality and racism following the killing of a black youth by Flint police. There was considerable citizen involvement in council meetings and hearings related to this incident. A few weeks after the CCRB was established, however, things were back to normal—that is, low public attendance at important meetings and a process of public decision making marked by a minimum of citizen involvement and interest.

Citizens' unwillingness to become involved can be partly explained by the nature of Flint's population. A majority of its citizens, both black and white, had migrated from the South to take jobs in Flint's automobile plants. The typical Flint citizen was a blue-collar worker in a General Motors factory who had received less education but was better paid than the average United States citizen. The drudgery of work in the automotive assembly plants (about a third of Flint's work force was employed in automotive plants) created a desire to escape the city whenever possible rather than to improve it. Disregard for the city may also be explained by its physical decay and blight. Many residents felt that Flint had a terminal illness and consequently was not worth the effort of trying to save. To many it was better to spend time improving a cottage in northern Michigan than to waste time trying to improve the quality of life in Flint.

Another important reason why Flint citizens did not become involved in the affairs of their city government was that they lacked both resources (dollars and time) and understanding. Many of the citizens who most acutely needed representation in the decision-making process were simply too poor or too ignorant of the process to become involved. Many citizens had little confidence that their personal efforts stood a chance of penetrating the powerful fortress they imagined city hall to be. As a result, they placed greater importance on individual concerns, leaving to "others" the responsibility for getting involved and improving the quality of their government and their community.

Perhaps the most important reason for the lack of citizen involvement in Flint was the simple fact that it didn't work—or, at least, people did not think it worked. The following sentiment expressed by a Flint citizen was probably typical of views throughout the city: "I don't get involved because nothing will happen if I do. It's just not worth the sweat and bother." As Exhibit 62 suggests, however, there were important exceptions to this feeling and to the conditions which produced it.

Public officials' commitment to a participatory process

Prior to 1971, public officials in Flint had done little to develop mechanisms that would allow citizens a continuing opportunity to influence city government decisions. In fact, past councils and managers had resisted efforts to involve citizens even in federal programs in which "citizen participation" was mandated. This began to change in the early 1970s. Between 1971 and 1974, the City Council and its appointed managers encouraged a greater degree of citizen involvement than had previously been the case. Yet the higher level of involvement that was achieved was not evidence of a total commitment by public officials to a full participatory process.

Citizen involvement was encouraged after 1971 in a number of areas. Citizens were invited to participate in the process of deciding how the City Council should spend its first-year revenue-sharing funds. In this case, citizen groups throughout the city were asked to develop program requests and to present them to a budget review committee chaired by the city manager.

As Exhibit 63 indicates, a number of community projects were identified, submitted, and recommended to the City Council as a result of this process. Ultimately, the council appropriated $260,000 (13 percent of the total) to seven community programs including a work adjustment and placement program for the vocationally handicapped (administered by Goodwill Industries), a convention bureau (administered by the Chamber of Commerce), an employment development program (administered by the Community Action Agency), and a mortgage default counseling program (administered by the Urban League).

In 1973, the City Council created an additional opportunity for citizen involvement by establishing the Citizen Complaint Review Board. As we noted earlier, this board was the product of intense citizen involvement; however, during the two years after its

EXHIBIT 62

Citizens Block City Street-Widening Project

In June 1973, the residents of a Flint neighborhood noticed that stakes with little yellow ribbons tied to them had been hammered into their front lawns. After getting what someone called "the normal city hall runaround," they learned that the city was embarking upon a project to widen their street at a nearby intersection. The project called for the city to remove parts of the front lawns of a number of residences as well as eight large trees that bordered the street.

The residents claimed that they had never been notified of this project and that the plan was a complete surprise to them. Officials of the Department of Public Works produced records to show that the city had followed strict legal procedures in proposing, approving, and funding the project; that all of the required hearings had been held and procedural steps completed; and that there had been no recorded opposition to the project.

When citizens realized that they were not going to get any action from the department, they quickly organized into a neighborhood committee, hired an attorney, and sued the city and the construction company that was doing the work. A court order stopped the project on the first day of excavation. The contractor was extremely upset and was quoted as saying, "It's a sad day when a bunch of housewives think they can design streets." Within a few days, the contractor countersued the citizens for damages resulting from his inability to complete the project. This was no small project. The total cost was more than $750,000, shared among the city, state, and federal governments.

After a week of negotiations among the city's Department of Public Works, the state and federal Departments of Transportation, the contractor, the citizens, and the judge, a compromise was reached. The final compromise called for a reduction in the size of the proposed lanes, the elimination of a left-turn lane, a reduction in the number of trees to be removed, and a commitment by the city to plant additional trees to replace those that would be removed.

Surprisingly, everyone was very satisfied with this ultimate resolution. The question in many people's minds, however, was why the same resolution could not have been arrived at by involving neighborhood residents in the planning and design of the project from the outset. Had this happened, the citizens, the contractor, and the city would have saved valuable time and money—only the lawyers would have lost.

EXHIBIT 63

Citizens Are Cut In on Revenue-Sharing Decisions

How does a city spend $4.3 million it didn't know it would have? This was the problem that faced the city of Flint in early 1973 as it prepared for an annual budgeting process that for the first time would involve revenue-sharing funds.

Every city department head had ideas about how the money ought to be spent. The fire chief wanted to construct a new fire station in a part of town that was least accessible from existing stations. The police chief wanted to repair the police garage and remodel some of the police division offices. The director of public works wanted to catch up on a long list of postponed capital-improvement projects. The city had no trouble finding worthwhile projects on which to spend revenue-sharing funds.

However, the Flint City Council had its own ideas on how these monies should be spent. After allocating $2.7 million to balance the city's General Fund, the council determined that $2 million would be considered "discretionary funds" to be used for new projects. The council members further decided that the process of allocating discretionary funds should involve the entire community, not just city departments. They therefore instructed the city manager to develop a process whereby citizens' ideas could be captured and used in the decisions to spend these funds.

The city manager returned to the City Council with a recommendation for a citizens' survey. He recommended that the city spend $20,000 to determine how citizens wanted the city to spend this money. The City Council rejected the idea, stating that the council was elected to determine community needs. The council said it wanted a process involving not citizens in general but organizations which represented groups of citizens.

The manager's next proposal was accepted by the council. Through this process, any citizens' organization could request an application for discretionary funds from the city. Applicants received information that prescribed a format in which to submit an application and described the process that would be used in making selections. They were given a deadline by which to submit their proposals, and each was guaranteed a hearing before the budget review committee to make the best case for its proposal. All applicants were well aware that their proposals would have to compete for funding against those made by other external groups and by city departments.

Approximately 177 requests for discretionary funding were received (exclusive of capital projects, which were handled separately). A total of $9 million was requested for the first fiscal year and $34 million for the five subsequent years. Twenty-one of these requests, amounting to $2.5 million for first-year funding, were made by community organizations. Of the $2 million in discretionary funds ultimately appropriated by the City Council, $260,000, representing seven projects, was provided to these groups.

creation it heard less than four cases and was the subject of litigation. Citizen interest quickly waned, and public officials made no attempt to make effective use of the board. The council also created a number of citizen advisory committees for major community projects. The most significant of these were organized to advise the city on river beautification and flood control, the development of a land-use and transportation plan for the central city, and a review of the necessity of charter revision.

The most important citizen involvement program launched by Flint's City Council during this period was the Citizen Action Center (CAC) described in Exhibit 64. The purpose of the CAC was to handle citizen complaints and service requests. This effort was advanced as a means of evaluating the impact of city operations on the people being served by them. The council supported the program but with little enthusiasm. This attitude could be attributed to the political value council members attached to personally receiving and satisfying citizen requests to fill potholes, remove trees, replace lights, and the like. Instead of viewing themselves as problem solvers of *last* resort, they wanted all citizen requests channeled through them so that they could extract the maximum political value from their efforts to solve them.

Managers of city departments were also cool to the idea of the Citizen Action Center. Understandably, department heads wanted complaints to come directly to them. In this way, the complaint could be addressed, and hopefully resolved, without coming to the attention of the manager, the City Council, or the public. City departments were accustomed to providing their own estimates of the quality of service they provided and to not being challenged on their evaluations. They did not want an external agency monitoring their performance, following up on complaints within departments to ensure that action was taken, and making the results available to the city manager, the council, and the public.

The City Council opposed greater citizen involvement as often as it supported it. As Exhibit 63 indicates, efforts to persuade the City Council to authorize funds for a survey that would ask citizens how they evaluated current city services, what additional services they wanted, and how much they were willing to pay for these services were consistently defeated.

Several factors explain the City Council's resistance to this program in particular and to greater citizen involvement in general. Council members felt that citizens already had had an opportunity to participate when they voted for members of the council. In a representative democracy, the council pointed out, political leaders are elected and charged with making decisions which they believe serve the public interest. If they fail to do this, they will not be reelected. Others feared that a continuous citizen-involvement process might provide a fertile training ground for emerging political leaders who one day could challenge their own positions of leadership. This was a lesson they had learned from the Model Cities and poverty programs in the Flint area. Perhaps the most important reason for the council's lack of support for greater citizen involvement, however, was that citizens themselves did not seem to demand it. Public officials already had to extinguish many fires; if no one seemed interested, it did not make much sense to create additional ones.

The council almost always responded, however, to one form of citizen involvement—individual appearances at council meetings. According to a custom that one council member called "oiling the squeaky wheel," many personal requests for governmental action made by citizens speaking at the public microphone were satisfied. (Council meetings were broadcast live over the radio every Monday evening.) Moreover, as Exhibit 65 indicates, political leaders made sure that the public knew who was responsible for the successful resolution of these citizen complaints.

Municipal managers were also resistant to

EXHIBIT 64

City Develops Citizen Action Center

Effective citizen involvement doesn't "just happen." It needs to be encouraged and, above all, given a permanent place within the structure of a local government.

After his first few weeks in office, the city manager recognized that this was not the case in Flint. There was no effective followup to citizen complaints or requests for service, no permanent organization available to serve the customers of the city's services.

During City Council meetings, citizens who came to the microphone to complain about the quality of a city service or to request service would usually be directed to see the city clerk. During the following week the clerk would send out short memoranda to the city manager and department heads informing them of the council referral. If the city manager or a department head did not take a personal interest in the particular request, no matter how small, it was likely that nothing would be done. There was no followup to determine whether the referral had been acted upon—unless, of course, the individual who had made the request or filed the complaint showed up at another council meeting to report that nothing had been done.

If a council member were particularly interested in a complaint or request, he would make a direct request to the city manager for specific action. This usually produced action and an eventual report back to council.

This "system" was not only hit or miss, it also required considerable personal attention and time from the city's top executives, making it extremely costly. In the hope of overcoming these deficiencies and providing better service to citizens, the city manager recommended to the City Council that a citizen action center (CAC) be established. Its purpose was to make the city government more responsive to citizen requests and to provide citizens with information about city government. This was to be accomplished by providing a service desk at a central location within city hall and a central telephone number through which the CAC could receive and process all complaints and requests for service. Because the staff and the budget of this office was to be quite small, citizens were requested to first attempt to satisfy their service needs by directly contacting city departments. The CAC's staff, which reported to the city manager, would be responsible for following up complaints and requests that were not resolved by departments. To complete the process, information on the nature of citizen complaints was to be compiled and reported so as to indicate to the City Council, the city's management, and the public how well city departments were responding to citizens' requests.

Though supported by most council members, citizens, and citizen groups, the CAC was slow to achieve its intended purpose. Delays occurred in funding and staffing the program and in remodeling the area in city hall where it was to be located. Eventually, by 1974—two-and-a-half years after it was proposed—the CAC was operating nearly as planned; it had gained a permanent place within the city-government structure and was performing an important service for both citizens and government officials.

EXHIBIT 65

Squeaky Wheel Gets the Skates Rolling

At times the political process responds to citizens' problems in a way that makes one optimistic that the system works after all. Such a situation occurred in Flint in midwinter of 1973.

At a regular Monday night council meeting, during the period when individual citizens were permitted five minutes during which to address the City Council, a elderly black man approached the microphone. He asked the council to assist him in repairing or replacing the radiators in the roller rink that he owned and operated in one of Flint's most-depressed neighborhoods. He said that his radiators had stopped functioning a few weeks before and that he did not have the money to repair them. He was turning to the City Council because he had nowhere else to turn and because he felt that the city was responsible indirectly for his problem.

The old man painted a convincing picture. He noted that almost ten years before, the city had approved an urban-renewal project for the area in which he lived. The original plan had called for total acquisition and clearance, starting near his roller rink. In fact, his property was one of the earliest to be acquired. Under urban-renewal regulations, after the approval of the project, a property owner whose property is to be acquired is forbidden to make improvements to his property. As a result, his requests to the city for building permits had been denied, and he could not improve or properly maintain his building.

Subsequently, as a result of a major shift in priorities within that urban-renewal project, his property had been rescheduled to the bottom of the acqustion list. However, because he was scheduled for eventual acquisition he was still not permitted to make improvements.

From the time his neighborhood was declared an urban-renewal area, the business at his roller rink had steadily declined. Presently, he said, he had very few customers, but he pointed out that the rink was one of the few recreational activities left for young people in that part of town. He continued to operate the rink—not to make a lot of money, but to provide this service and to keep the property until the city eventually bought it.

Without raising his voice, he asked the council for its help. The council was moved. It unanimously referred the issue to the Department of Community Development for immediate attention. The council wanted a report back the following week indicating that the roller rink was operating.

The Department of Community Development was almost totally funded by federal urban-renewal money. The program budget approved by the federal government did not have money in it to repair or replace radiators in dilapidated buildings. However, the department's rehabilitation staff, bending the rules and regulations a bit, found some old radiators in a building that had been purchased by the city which was soon to be demolished. They removed the radiators and installed them in the roller rink. The next week, the City Council received its report: the rink was again in operation.

the establishment of a stronger voice for citizens in determining what city government departments did and how they did it. The absence of a service ethic permeated nearly all city departments and affected the way in which services were delivered. Rudeness to citizens calling city hall for help or information was a common complaint.

Some managers feared that citizen involvement would result in a loss of control over departmental operations. This, in part, had happened in the urban-renewal program, where citizen demands had led to increased involvement by the City Council in the daily affairs of the Department of Community Development. This political involvement significantly reduced the control and responsibility of the department head. Even the best managers pointed out that if citizens were involved in the decision-making process at the department level it would be more difficult to hold managers accountable for the activities and functions they managed.

Clarification of the role of citizens

The success of a citizen-involvement program depends on acceptance of the fact that under our system of government public officials alone are accountable for getting things done. The "buck" must stop at the desks of elected political leaders and nowhere else. Responsibility cannot and should not be delegated to citizens or to citizen groups who are not accountable at the ballot box. The essential purpose of a citizen-involvement process is to provide elected political leaders and appointed managers with accurate information about citizens' views. This, in turn, will enable them to make well-informed decisions. Its purpose is not to shift the responsibility for making decisions.

In Flint, it was often unclear who had responsibility for important public decisions in areas where there was significant citizen involvement. As Exhibit 66 suggests, there is no better example of this than the confusion surrounding the function and responsibilities of the citizen district councils (CDCs) which represented the city's urban-renewal areas. Each participant in the urban-renewal decision-making process had a different interpretation of the citizen's role. This confusion enabled council members, urban-renewal area residents, and federal government representatives to duck responsibility for the poor performance of Flint's urban-renewal programs.

Several facts explain the lack of clarity in relationships between citizen groups and public officials in Flint. First, public officials did not seek clarity. By failing to define the responsibilities of citizen groups, council members could use them as a means of avoiding accountability. Although a majority of the council resisted attempts to establish citizen-involvement mechanisms (or to broaden the ones that existed), once such groups had been established council members often found it expedient to escape responsibility for program performance by blaming citizen groups. This was especially true of the city's urban-renewal program.

Second, citizens did not seek clarity. In many cases, the last thing citizen groups and their leaders wanted was a clear definition of their responsibilities. The head of the Citizen District Council Coordinating Committee (which consisted of representatives from all urban-renewal citizen district councils) explained this reluctance: "If we pushed for a clear definition of our power, we might find out that we didn't have any." Furthermore, a number of community leaders used citizen-participation programs as a means of building their own power bases. They wanted the illusion of authority (to advance personal ends) but they did not want the reality of decision-making responsibility. Making specific program decisions (e.g., which part of an urban-renewal area would receive funds in a particular year) could either bring these leaders into conflict with the City Council or could jeopardize their bases of support within the community; either was unacceptable.

Finally, the federal government, which was

EXHIBIT 66

What Role Do Citizens Have in the Urban-Renewal Program?

Federal legislation establishing the urban-renewal program called for a high level of involvement by project area residents in planning and implementing urban-renewal projects. Unfortunately, neither the legislation nor its implementing regulations was ever clear about what "involvement" meant. As a result, each participant in the urban-renewal process defined involvement differently, and most—except the people charged with day-to-day administration of the program—seemed satisfied with that situation.

Project area residents, working through a project area committee called a citizen district council, liked to believe that when they reviewed the urban-renewal plan or an annual program budget they were giving it final approval. In fact, they often were, if what they approved created no political problems for the City Council. "If that's what the residents want, then that's what we should give them—it's their neighborhood," council members were fond of saying. However, if project area residents wanted something that did not have the political support of the council, its position was often very different.

The area office representatives of the Department of Housing and Urban Development (HUD) also seemed to benefit from the ambiguity surrounding the meaning of citizen involvement. Depending on the specific issue, participation could be made mandatory (usually if the residents sided with HUD against the wishes of the City Council) or only optional (if the residents wanted something HUD could not provide). Other participants in the process, such as private developers and administrators of the program, could play similar games with the involvement of project area residents.

An example of how these roles were played occurred in November 1972. At that time, the city's new director of community development had completed an analysis showing that the city was considerably overcommitted in urban renewal. Over the ten previous years, the city and HUD had approved urban-renewal projects covering 2,000 acres of the city, requiring a total expenditure of more than $166 million. At the 1972 urban-renewal program funding rate of $5 million a year, it would have taken twenty-eight additional years to finish these projects. There were no indications that annual funding from HUD would increase; nevertheless, the city had approved and HUD was about to approve an additional 1,000-acre project requiring an additional $46 million of public funds.

The community development director made what was to him the most obvious of recommendations: that the city drop its request for HUD approval of the newest

(continued on page 254)

EXHIBIT 66 (cont'd)

project and reduce its existing commitment to smaller projects that could be completed within a five-year period.

Citizen district councils, especially the one representing the area which had not yet been completely approved, vigorously opposed this recommendation. They took their opposition to the City Council, to the press, and to HUD.

City Council members privately agreed with the recommendation not to pursue approval. They had not been on the council when these projects were approved, and they felt that reducing the scope of the programs would be financially prudent. However, politically, they could not take such a public stand. For a long time the council had given the project area residents decision-making power over urban-renewal–related issues. They could not now reverse their view and completely oppose the desires of the residents. They looked to HUD to impose a decision.

HUD area office personnel faced the same problem as the City Council. Privately, HUD representatives realized that the city was significantly overcommitted and endorsed the idea of scaling back to a realistic program. However, they, too, did not want to oppose the residents because they were very unclear about their own role in relation to that of the residents and the city.

As it turned out, no decision became a decision. Over the following months, the City Council did not act on the specific recommendation. Instead, it provided a forum so as to hear everyone's point of view. The Community Development Department developed an approach that would focus urban-renewal activity in the highest-priority target areas for the next five years. HUD continued to postpone approval of the project, listening to the citizens on the one hand and complimenting the administration's efforts to lower expectations on the other. In the end, the final decision seems to have been made at the time the following year's urban-renewal budget was submitted. This budget greatly scaled down and concentrated urban-renewal efforts in the city to only two project areas.

Project area residents still complained that the role of citizens in the urban-renewal program was unclear.

responsible for writing the legislation and for the rules that governed many of Flint's citizen-participation programs, did not seek clarity. Repeatedly, Flint's city manager and director of community development asked the Detroit area office of the Department of Housing and Urban Development to clarify precisely what responsibilities and authority the district councils had. To each inquiry came the same reply: the matter should be worked out between the city and the citizen councils. The "feds" wanted it both ways: when the issue was affirmative action or public housing, the area office wanted to dot every "i" and cross every "t" in telling Flint officials what they could and could not do; but when the issue was a politically sensitive one like that involving citizen district council responsibilities, the area office said the problem was not its concern.

Formal citizen-involvement mechanisms

In Flint there were a number of informal, ad hoc techniques for encouraging citizen involvement in the decision-making process. In addition to participating in elections and public hearings (hearings that were seldom well attended and that rarely if ever altered predetermined outcomes), citizens could affect the decision-making process through the formation of single-issue citizen coalitions and committees. Historically, citizen committees had been formed to resist pending government decisions—a change in the city charter, a bond issue, or a new highway through a residential neighborhood. In these instances, citizen involvement with city government was intense, brief, and related to a specific issue of personal concern.

As a rule, these ad hoc attempts to influence governmental decision making were not successful. Because of their transitory nature and the inability of their leaders to fully understand the decision-making process, these groups were easily sidetracked before they could realize their objectives. Usually they started too late to be effective. In many cases, such as the one presented in Exhibit 67, councils would give the impression of agreeing to citizen demands, primarily because there was a large number of citizens in the audience. Then, at a later meeting when citizens were not in attendance, the decision would be reversed or modified. As citizens find it increasingly easy to take their cases to the courts, however, exceptions to this rule may well increase.

In Flint there were two formal types of citizen-involvement groups: (1) geographic groups, consisting of citizen councils that represented geographic areas of the city, and (2) program or functional groups, consisting of individual citizens who had organized in an attempt to change conditions in such specific, substantive areas as housing, transportation, and environmental protection.

Geographically based groups generally emerged as a result of federal legislation creating such programs as Model Cities, urban-renewal (later the neighborhood development program), and the economic opportunity (antipoverty) program. Citizens affected by these programs were required to participate in the planning, evaluation, and, at times, implementation of these federally funded programs. Other citizen-involvement groups representing geographic areas included the community school councils (one for every elementary-school district), which advised the Board of Education on school-related issues, and block clubs formed by citizens for mutual protection and assistance.

Citizen involvement in functional areas took the form of either participation in an existing governmental entity (Civilian Complaint Review Board, Planning Commission, Human Relations Commission) or serving on an advisory committee to a governmental entity (Riverfront Beautification Committee, Comprehensive Area Manpower Planning Council).

Neither of these forms of participation corresponds to the definition of citizen involvement presented in this chapter. Both forms were exclusive, limiting involvement to a select few; both were limited to involvement in a small range of government decisions; and, because of their extreme reliance on city government, both suffered from a lack of credibility within the community. In short, Flint's city government did not have a continuous, formal process for involving citizens in governmental decision making. The major reason for this was that neither city-government officials nor individual citizens had taken the necessary action or provided the necessary support to create such a mechanism.

Administrative capacity to support citizen involvement

The city government of Flint was ill equipped to support anything more than the

EXHIBIT 67

The Public Decision-Making Process Can Be Fickle

In 1974 a group of Flint environmentalists learned that, once made, a public decision is not always final.

Environmentalists became concerned when a billboard advertising company requested the city to rescind a three-year-old ordinance prohibiting billboards from being placed within 600 feet of freeways. This request came about because the makeup of the Planning Commission had recently changed. The new commission was more disposed toward commercial interests than its predecessor had been. In June 1974, after a series of hectic Planning Commission meetings, the replacement of two experienced planning commissioners by the City Council, and the resignation of a third, the Planning Commission approved the company's request and recommended a revision of the ordinance to the City Council.

On the evening that the City Council received the recommendation, the council chamber was packed with representatives of environmental groups who opposed the ordinance change. A long string of opponents made impassioned speeches attacking the City Council for its lack of concern for the environment and the beauty of the city. Two members of the City Council, whose views on the billboard issue were not yet known, were absent from the meeting. Of the remaining seven, four clearly opposed a change in the ordinance and three seemed to support it. Sensing the mood of the crowd, the three council members who favored the change were granted a brief adjournment to discuss the issue. At the appointed time to reconvene, they refused to return, thereby forcing the meeting to end for lack of a quorum. The audience was understandably upset and disappointed.

(continued)

most elementary level of citizen involvement. Prior to 1972, a minimum of support was provided by the city clerk, who recorded the complaints citizens made at the weekly council meetings and notified departments of these during the week. It was assumed that departments would be responsible for taking action. There was no followup to ensure that anything in fact was done.

In 1972, the city manager proposed the establishment of a citizen action center to provide a minimum level of support for citizen involvement. The Citizen Action Center was only partially successful in encouraging widespread citizen involvement. However, as Exhibit 64 explains, it did a reasonable job of resolving specific complaints and reducing the complaint work load of the City Council and the city manager. As Exhibit 61 points out, a proposal for achieving broader citizen involvement by relating the Citizen Action Center's activities to the existing community school councils of the Board of Education was flatly rejected by the board.

The reason for the lack of administrative

EXHIBIT 67 (cont'd)

The following week one of the absent council members returned. Again crowds showed up in large numbers to oppose the change in the ordinance. To almost everyone's surprise the council voted 8-0 to retain the ordinance. Environmentalists left the meeting satisfied that political process had indeed responded to their involvement.

The next City Council meeting, like most, was very poorly attended. The ten or fifteen regulars who attended every council meeting were in attendance. The crowds that had been at the City Council meeting the previous week were not there. During the course of the meeting, one member pointed out that the councilman who had been absent from the previous meeting had a strong opinion on the billboard issue and had not had a chance to express it. He moved that the City Council reconsider its action and refer the issue to legislative committee. This action received a favorable 5–4 vote.

A newspaper editorial reflected the public confusion about what had happened and why: "If the present council is nothing else, it is unpredictable. Last Monday night five council members voted to reconsider the billboard matter—leaving open the question of what happened between the two meetings." The editorial concluded by questioning the City Council's apparent disregard for the views of citizens and its susceptibility to high-powered lobbying by special interests. The message was clear: if citizens were to achieve what they desired, they had to be as diligent and effective as the special interests. Attendance at one or two meetings was not enough involvement.

Representatives of both sides attended the legislative committee meeting held the following week. After a long and heated debate, the committee voted 6–2 to drop the matter from its agenda. The issue was finally resolved—or was it?

---

support required to implement an effective citizen-action program in Flint was twofold: citizens did not demand it, and the City Council and many municipal managers did not want it.

Opportunities for Improvement

The Declaration of Independence and the Constitution provide American citizens with a unique role in the allocation and use of governmental power. By making government institutions at all levels the responsibility of the people, the founding fathers made citizen involvement a practical and a political imperative. Consequently, when citizens feel impotent and unable to influence government decisions, and as a result become cynical, angry, alienated, and finally apathetic, the essential foundation of our representative democracy is eroded.

Barbara Jordan, congresswoman from Texas, eloquently summarized the value of citizen involvement in her keynote address to the 1976 Democratic Convention:

We believe that the people are the source of all governmental power; that the authority of the people is to be extended, not restricted. This can be accomplished only by providing each citizen with every opportunity to participate in the management of the government. They must have that. [6]

Our analysis of conditions in Flint reveals a number of opportunities to increase citizen involvement and thereby strengthen the process on which improved performance depends. A primary opportunity is to improve voter registration and increase the number of registered voters who vote. There are a number of ways in which this might be accomplished. Efforts could be made to make voter registration easier—by mail, for instance. In addition, the city could aggressively advertise elections rather than depending entirely on the media. The city could ask the cooperation of local employers to permit time off for voting. Finally, elections could be consolidated so that they would generate greater interest and hence greater involvement.

A second opportunity involves the nature of information available to citizens and citizen groups. Better information concerning how Flint's city government operates and the issues that will be resolved by the City Council should be provided. For example:

- The City Council agenda and the meeting times of major boards and commissions could be published in the newspaper.
- Detailed minutes of all council meetings could be mailed to any citizen or citizen group requesting them.
- A basic manual on how the city govern-

ment works, organized by problem areas (e.g., how to determine when trees on your street will be trimmed), could be available to all citizens.
- An annual "budget in brief" and city government performance report, written in layman's language, could be provided to citizens as a reference for determining how their tax dollars are being spent and what they are buying.
- Detailed analyses of specific council and managerial decisions could be available for the asking.

A mechanism for continuous and structured citizen involvement should be developed. The most logical base for a continuous citizen-involvement program is the system of community school councils. Located throughout the entire Flint community, these councils provide a decentralized network that could be used to identify citizen needs and desires as well as to communicate pending council actions and decisions. In addition, community schools could be bases from which neighborhood service directors could develop block clubs, survey neighborhood needs, and serve as a conduit for citizen complaints to local-government agencies and the City Council. The Board of Education, therefore, should be encouraged to utilize existing community school councils as the framework within which to develop an effective citizen-involvement program in Flint.*

---

* In 1975, a neighborhood service program was implemented in Flint. This program places neighborhood service representatives in schools throughout the city to handle complaints and requests for service. Under the leadership of Flint's director of the office of citizen service, this program, utilizing CETA funds, is developing block clubs, surveying neighborhood needs, and serving as a conduit of citizen complaints to the council.

Finally, if citizens are to believe that citizen involvement is in their best interests, an administrative support structure must be developed that will follow up and be responsive to citizen requests for improved service. The Citizen Action Center in Flint should be expanded, drawing to the extent possible on the help of volunteers. Helping city government respond to complaints is just one opportunity to take advantage of those within the community who desire to serve but do not have a vehicle to do so. To the extent that citizen involvement is best achieved through active participation, developing a citizen volunteer program may be the most important opportunity to reignite citizens' interest, enthusiasm, and involvement in their city government.

CHAPTER 13

The News Media

. . . a people who mean to be their own Governors, must arm themselves with the power which knowledge gives.

James Madison

Today newspapers are big-business enterprises operated for private profit, yet the First Amendment shields them almost absolutely from official interference or regulation.

Alan Barth

The exercise of citizenship depends upon access to reliable information. As citizens, if we do not have accurate information about what government officials intend to do and what they have done, we have no basis for holding them accountable for their performance. Citizens, as James Madison suggested, cannot be their own governors unless they are armed with "the power which knowledge gives." But who will provide this knowledge—politicians, public managers, government employees? Not necessarily. In a self-governing society it is the ultimate responsibility of the news media (newspapers, television and radio stations, and magazines and other periodicals) to provide citizens with the information they need to meet their civic responsibilities.

From the time of Madison to the era of Watergate, government officials and citizens alike have recognized the political importance of newspapers and, more recently, of the electronic media. In fact, independence of the press from government control has

long served as the test of a democratic system of government. Unlike authoritarian societies, which use the press as a tool of government, self-governing societies leave the media free to report their own interpretations of public events and decisions. The news media's independent checks on the exercise of government power have caused many to label them "the fourth branch of government." Supreme Court Justice Potter Stewart underlined this point in a 1974 address to the Yale Law School: "The primary purpose of the constitutional guarantee of the free press was . . . to create a fourth institution outside the government as an additional check on the three official branches."[1] By providing citizens with reliable information about government decisions and activities, the media may prevent the abuse of power by the executive, legislative, or judicial branch.

Freedom, however, is enjoyed only at the risk that it may be abused. What if the news media abuse their independent power? In a commentary on the political role of the press, James Madison answered the question in this manner:

Some degree of abuse is inseparable from the proper use of everything, and in no instance is this more true than in that of the press. It has accordingly been decided by the practice of the states that it is better to leave a few of its noxious branches to their luxuriant growth than, by pruning them away, to injure the vigor of those yielding proper fruits. [2]

Despite the potential for abuse, maintaining the freedom of the press to interpret the decisions and actions of a representative government was, for Madison, a political imperative.

Although there are no formal checks on the independent exercise of the media's political power, there is an important self-imposed constraint. Members of the electronic and print media know full well that, in order to maximize their influence and serve as the primary source of public information, they must maintain their credibility with the public. Like the Supreme Court, the press depends on public confidence in order to exercise its full potential within the political process.

But the news media do not constitute a branch of government. Their survival, unlike that of governmental institutions, depends on their performance in the marketplace. Newspapers and broadcasting stations are, as Alan Barth suggests, businesses that are operated for a profit. If sufficient revenue cannot be generated to cover its costs, a radio or television station goes out of business. Unlike a government agency, a newspaper cannot bail itself out of economic difficulty by increasing taxes.

The potential interaction between the news media's economic constraints and their political role raises several important questions: what happens when their political and economic imperatives become incompatible? How should a democratic society resolve a situation in which a newspaper, in order to stay in business, does not provide the information people require to exercise their responsibilities as citizens? What should citizens do if a broadcasting station decides to satisfy the popular appetite for violence and sex at the expense of the public's need to know about civic events and government decisions? In short, how can citizens ensure that the news media do not abdicate their responsibility to inform in satisfying their need to make a profit?

There are no simple answers to these questions. However, attempts to control the press or orchestrate its activities must be resisted. In the last analysis, each of us has the power to ensure that the news media's economic and political objectives do not become mutually exclusive through our decisions about which paper to read, which station to listen to, or which periodical to purchase.

Impact on Process and Performance

In the wake of Watergate, public awareness of the media's impact on the performance of the federal government reached an unprecedented level. *Fortune* magazine, in its Bicentennial issue, observed, "These are the glory days of the American press," and went on to note that "never before has [the press] exercised so much power so independently or found itself vested with such prestige and glamour."[3] The fact that two *Washington Post* reporters could earn more than $1 million apiece for telling the story behind their story supports this view.

Despite the highly publicized role of the press in the Watergate scandal, the impact of the news media on local-government performance is even more profound. In many counties and cities, newspapers enjoy monopolistic positions. (In 1975 only 215 cities in the United States had more than one newspaper, and of these, all but 60 had a single owner.[4]) In these cities and counties, the power of the press to interpret what government officials have done (or to influence what they do) is relatively unchallenged. This power, as the following excerpt from a *Los Angeles Times* report suggests, can be formidable:

Top executives of Long Beach's only daily newspaper played active roles in key governmental decisions while the newspaper shielded much of the city's business from public view.... The *Independent Press-Telegram* became so powerful that for more than a decade few major decisions were made at city hall unless the newspaper approved.[5]

In recent years, however, the power of newspapers has declined somewhat as television and radio stations have presented alternative channels of public information, thereby providing competition in the shaping of local opinion.

A second explanation for the profound impact of the local press is that its reporters and editors are close to the events and people they cover; the issues on which they report are related directly to the communities in which they live. Proximity to government decisions creates an incentive to take personal or institutional positions on issues. Finally, the press in many parts of the country has traditionally viewed local governments with some distrust. This kind of skepticism increases the media's diligence and often intensifies their ultimate impact on the abili-

ty of government officials to get things done.

Despite the importance and the power of the news media, they are not directly responsible for the performance of local government. Newspaper reports do not make government decisions, radio broadcasters do not determine community objectives, and television commentators do not deliver municipal services. Yet, through its power to inform and educate the public and challenge the actions of public officials, each medium may have a significant influence on the way in which its community is governed.

In sum, the news media affect government performance indirectly through their ability to influence other factors. Such influence may take the form of supporting political leaders or attempting to persuade voters to approve changes in a city charter. The media may be influential in urging municipal unions to accept reasonable settlements of labor disputes or they may contribute to improved performance by encouraging private-interest groups, community leaders, and citizens to become more involved in the government decision-making process. To the extent that other internal and external factors have a positive impact on government performance, the role of the local press declines in importance. Conversely, to the extent that other factors have a negative impact on performance, the role of the press is expanded. Indeed, the news media's ability to focus the attention of the public on negative aspects of a situation constitutes their most important contribution.

Criteria for Evaluation

The relationship of the news media to local government is complex and often ambiguous. Each medium is a profit-making enterprise, but we do not judge it here primarily by its commercial success. Although the news media perform a critical public function, they are neither regulated nor, in the case of newspapers, licensed. Reporters have an almost unlimited ability to help or hurt

public officials, but there are few, if any, standards of performance against which the actions of reporters can be measured. All that many citizens know about their local government is what they read in the newspaper, see on television, or hear on the radio.

Given this complexity and potential ambiguity, it is important to have a set of criteria with which to evaluate the nature of the news media's impact on performance. The following list provides a starting point:

Is reporting accurate and fair? News reporters generally have access to all stages of the decision-making process. In many cases, they have exclusive power to report on public events. It is imperative, therefore, that the reported information be accurate and fair. Are facts reported accurately, and are the conclusions drawn from these facts valid? Equally important, are mistakes corrected as quickly as possible, thereby preventing the public from reaching judgments on the basis of erroneous information?

Are both sides of controversial issues presented in media reports? If citizens are to be well informed, they must understand different points of view about how to resolve major public issues. Given the complete dependence of most citizens on the news media for information, it is imperative that the press report opposing views on controversial issues. This question examines the extent to which the press has made an active effort to present fair and balanced reports of critical issues.

Do reporters explain why things happen as well as what happened? Through its guarantee that the press will remain independent of government, the First Amendment implies that the news media have a responsibility to educate as well as inform the public. Accordingly, this question examines whether reporters explain the causes as well as the consequences of public events and decisions. Does media coverage enable listeners, viewers, and readers to place events and decisions in the proper historical and chronological context?

Do editors take public positions on important community issues, and is editorial opinion clearly identified as such? The news media have a unique vantage point from which to gain insight into the nature of public issues; therefore, it is proper and desirable that newspapers and broadcasting stations take editorial positions on issues of interest to the community. It is imperative, however, that editorial opinions be clearly identified as such. This question examines whether viewers or readers know when the media are speaking for themselves in editorials and when they are simply reporting the facts. It also examines whether the placement of a story in a newspaper or newscast reflects an editorial point of view.

Do the news media attempt to provide a forum for public information? The unique position and function of the press allows it to serve as a neutral forum in which people on both sides of controversial issues can state their respective cases as persuasively as possible. The monopoly that many print and electronic media enjoy in controlling the flow of information to the public means that they can determine, to a large extent, what the public is told about government-sponsored activities and projects as well as community events. This question, therefore, examines whether the press attempts to serve as a marketplace for ideas and viewpoints. Does a newspaper or broadcasting station provide space and time for the independent expression of different points of view on issues of interest to a majority of community residents? Do the news media present information about public events?

Conditions in Flint

Events at city hall in Flint were covered by one newspaper, an afternoon paper serving the entire metropolitan area. In addition, several limited-circulation weekly newspapers were directed to special audiences—primarily the black community and subur- ban townships. There were three accessible television stations (one located in Flint) and four major radio stations. Of the media serving Flint, the daily newspaper had the greatest impact on local government. Accordingly, the following analysis of conditions in

Flint is disproportionately weighted toward the printed press, although the roles of both television and radio stations were also important.

Accuracy and fairness

The *New York Times* has emblazoned on its front page, "All the news that's fit to print." Walter Cronkite signs off his television commentaries with " . . . and that's the way it is." But what if that is *not* all the news? What if that is *not* the way it is—or was? What if the news considered "fit to print" was inaccurately presented?

Citizens are becoming increasingly concerned that reporting is often inaccurate or that it provides a false impression of what has actually happened. A Gallup survey conducted in January 1974 showed that 60 percent of those interviewed said they "definitely agreed" or "partly agreed" that newspapers were not careful about getting their facts straight.[6] The editor of the *Atlanta Constitution*, reflecting on what he perceived to be a growing public cynicism about the media, commented in 1975, "I am not sure the First Amendment would pass if you had a referendum on it today."[7]

One solution, of course, is for the news media to not make mistakes. But as long as news is reported by people, it will contain errors—some major and some minor. Therefore, what is most important is not the elimination of error at all cost but rather the development of procedures whereby the press can admit and correct errors in a timely and uniform manner so that its audience has the opportunity to correct false conclusions or impressions.

The news media in Flint provided full coverage of public events and the decision-making process within city hall. Often as many as three newspaper reporters, three radio-station newscasters, and three television reporters attended weekly council meetings. One radio station broadcast the City Council meetings live. The television

stations often shot considerable footage of council debates and key meetings. Although the selection of footage to be shown provided some room for editorializing, live coverage of public events was generally accurate. Commenting on the impact of television coverage, Flint's mayor noted, "If the city manager or a councilman makes an ass of himself on the council floor, he can hardly blame the news media for his condition." Most radio and television news stories were short and sharply focused; they were, on the whole, accurate and rarely misleading or confusing.

Newspaper coverage of Flint's city government was extensive. In addition to the regular city hall beat, one reporter covered community-development programs and additional reporters covered such special areas as health, transportation, and intergovernmental relations. The newspaper's reporting of public events and government decisions generally was accurate and fair. The extent and scope of coverage and the quality of reporting, especially editorial reporting, was excellent. Of course, there were exceptions. In some instances, as Exhibit 68 illustrates, these exceptions could have a major effect on public decisions.

An important and often unappreciated reason for inaccuracy in news reporting is related to the complexity of the issues facing the city hall reporter. In Flint, one person had to understand subjects ranging from program budgeting, bond financing, and data processing to transportation and environmental protection. Complex federal programs in such areas as urban renewal and public housing had to be mastered and intelligently reported by one person. In addition, the city hall reporter had to cover the political activities of nine separate council members. Thus it is perhaps surprising that city hall reporters functioned as well as they did and that news reports were as accurate as they were.

Inaccurate news reports are also in part the fault of the organizational structure of most metropolitan daily newspapers, including

EXHIBIT 68

Newspaper Inaccuracies Threaten Reorganization Plan

"City Manager Wants More Administrators"—this headline was troubling. The lead paragraph in the accompanying story seemed to confirm the suspicion: "Once again the city manager will have to convince the City Council to add more administrators to his staff, this time as part of the reorganization plan he has recommended for city operations." The message seemed clear: the city manager was trying to increase his personal staff at a time when city taxes and costs were rising.

The balance of the article reinforced the initial image of a top bureaucrat building his own empire. The key statements in the article were:

- "When the city manager came to Flint seventeen months ago, he had two staff administrators under him . . .
- "now, because of additions in his first year as manager, there are nine administrators holding staff positions under him . . .
- "and, under his proposed reorganization, there would be four more by the end of the next fiscal year.
- "Last year, the city manager convinced the council to add two of his present staff administrators. . . . Four other staff administrators were added with the help of federal funds.
- "Besides the addition of four new administrators to his staff, the city manager's reorganization plan would add nine other administrators. . . ."

By the time even the most objective of readers had finished this article, an image of the city manager's office as being crowded with new assistants had been deeply implanted.

(continued)

Flint's. Typically, four separate individuals are involved in reporting one public event or decision. First, a reporter is responsible for writing an article about the decision or event. Second, a copy editor is responsible for reading and correcting the article and selecting a headline that summarizes its content. The rapidity with which the latter function is usually performed creates the possibility that the headline, which often has the greatest impact on readers, will not accurately reflect the content of the article. Third, a news editor is responsible for selecting the proper location of the article in the newspaper. He has the power to bury articles he considers unimportant. Finally, an editorial writer is responsible for commenting on a particular event or issue. In many cases, the editorial writer is dependent on the facts used in the initial article. Given the tight writing and printing schedule, there is rarely time to follow up on a report or an article to ensure that it is accurate and that it fairly represents all sides of an issue. Often the only checks on the system of reporting public events are the objections of public offi-

EXHIBIT 68 (cont'd)

But was this accurate reporting? The city manager did not think so. He offered the following corrections:

- There were five staff positions, not two, reporting to the city manager when he assumed his position.
- After seventeen months there were seven staff positions, not nine, reporting to the city manager.
- Under the proposed reorganization plan, only five positions (four staff offices and a deputy city manager for operations) would report to the city manager—not thirteen, as reported.
- The council in 1972 had created an office of planning, budgeting, and evaluation and the federal government helped finance an office of equal opportunity and a manpower development office. The directors of these staff functions reported to the city manager—the employees who worked in these offices were not on the city manager's staff, as reported.
- The new reorganization plan would add two or three new city administrators—not nine, as reported.

Some of the differences between these accounts may be explained by semantics. The newspaper reporter and the city manager may have defined a "staff administrator" differently. The newspaper reporter may have believed that any new management employee, because he ultimately reported to the city manager, should be considered a "staff administrator reporting to him." But, this did not explain why the reporter made no attempt to clarify these semantic differences or to verify the accuracy of the facts used in this article. When asked by the city manager why he had not checked the facts the reporter replied: "You did not return my phone call on time, so I had to submit the story as written."

Although the reorganization plan didn't depend entirely on the reception it received in the press, the impression created by this article, in the words of Flint's mayor, "made it harder to sell to the public."

cials or private citizens who are adversely affected by what they consider to be inaccurate and unfair reporting.

In Flint, inaccurate reporting had to do with the attitudes and capabilities of the reporters who covered events at city hall. As most reporters readily admit, there is no such thing as totally objective reporting. Events must be interpreted, facts must be arranged, and judgments about the statements of public officials must be made. Hence the personal views of a reporter can play an important role in what is reported and how accurately it

is presented.

Recognizing the power of the newspaper, city managers in Flint had always paid deferential attention to the city hall reporter. In 1971, when Flint's new city manager arrived, he was advised by the acting manager to "keep the city hall reporter advised of what you are doing or he'll screw you." Yet, in paying special attention to the press, past city managers had often found themselves at odds with the City Council. The city manager who resigned under pressure in 1971, a former newspaper reporter himself, had been told by members of the council prior to his departure that they were tired of reading about his recommendations in the paper before they heard them directly from him. They accused the manager of trying to build a constituency for his views by leaking one-sided stories to the press before the council had an opportunity to hear the facts and to establish its position. The council's ire over this issue was a major factor in the manager's departure.

Reacting to the intense council feelings on this issue, the new manager attempted to postpone discussion of major policy and program recommendations with media reporters until the council had had an opportunity to discuss them. This did not appear unreasonable, in view of the fact that the manager worked for the City Council. The newspaper reporter covering city hall, however, was unhappy with this policy, as the following excerpt from a report entitled "Fighting the City Hall Shell Game" indicates:

Top administrators, who are bossed by the council, are blatantly managing the news by withholding and timing the release of information. And officials under these administrators are following the example. In so doing the administrators are catering to the wishes of councilmen. [8]

Accustomed to being given information ahead of other media reporters as well as the council, this reporter was upset by the prospect of having to wait for news items. As his words suggest, he felt that the city manager should cater to the press and not to the City Council for which he worked. His unhappiness was increased by the manager's decision to coordinate through his office all announcements of major policy changes. This procedure, reviewed in Exhibit 69, ended a long-standing tradition whereby each department or division head had made independent announcements of major policy changes directly to the press.

If the news media's reaction to the manager's plan to coordinate the announcement of

policy decisions seemed harsh and unreasonable, it was calm compared to the reaction that followed the council's decision in early 1972 to hold executive sessions from which the press and other media representatives were barred. These sessions, quickly labeled "secret sessions" by the newspaper, were viewed by the press as a threat to its very existence. The reasons behind the council's decision to hold executive sessions are presented in Exhibit 70.

The major short-run consequence for city government of the newspaper's unhappiness with the council and the city manager on such issues was the loss of an important ally on other, less controversial issues. Unfortunately, honest disagreement over one issue of importance to the press resulted in disagreement with the council on issues where common ground could have been found.

The importance of having a competent city hall reporter was underlined in the fall of 1973 when the newspaper decided to make a change. Unburdened by preconceptions about the nature of the job or the people with whom he would be dealing, the new city hall reporter brought enthusiasm and a sense of professionalism to his job. He was as interested in understanding why things happened as he was in what had happened. During the next year and a half, not a single complaint was registered about the accuracy of city hall reporting. Despite this change, images, impressions, and misconceptions stimulated by earlier stories remained in the minds of many Flint citizens. In a dramatic farewell speech, the outgoing mayor had stated in 1973 that in reviewing the results of his administration he felt that "the council's major failure in selling its programs to the public could be attributed to the negative, often inaccurate reception these programs received in the columns written by one city hall reporter."

Elected and appointed officials, of course, could attempt to correct such inaccurate and misleading stories as the one presented in Exhibit 68. The mayor—or the manager, in

EXHIBIT 69

Is the City Manager Trying To Gag the Press?

In early 1972, Flint's new city manager announced a policy whereby all department heads would coordinate the announcement of major policy decisions
through the manager's office. This policy reflected the fact that in the past Flint's
city government had resembled a loose confederation of separate departments
whose heads had been allowed considerable freedom in announcing major policy
initiatives and changes in program direction. The new policy was initiated in
response to City Council criticism that council members were not informed about
major changes and as a result had to read about them in the newspaper. In view of
the fact that council representatives were accountable to Flint citizens, they felt
that they should know in advance about such announcements.

The response to the manager's new policy was swift. Television, radio, and newspaper reporters were in the manager's office within an hour of the issuance of his
directive at a morning staff meeting. Reacting with a vehemence that startled the
manager, reporters demanded to know why a "gag" rule had been imposed on
their major sources of information. They argued that if every answer to every
question had to be cleared through the manager's office, their jobs would become
impossible to perform and the public's right to know would be adversely affected.
News stories, they protested, would be delayed and decisions would be made
without adequate "citizen input" (a phrase that meant "media input").

The manager explained that this new policy was not intended to reduce the
access of the news media to department heads. He pointed out that the policy
would affect only 2 percent, not 100 percent, of the information that department
heads would normally provide. For example, the police chief would not have to
seek managerial approval to announce the adoption of more-advanced radar
equipment, but he would be asked to coordinate the announcement of a new
narcotics control program. Only in this way, the manager pointed out, could the
council be informed and the public be given a clear understanding about the city's
position on major policy questions.

Reporters were not persuaded.

this case—could have called a press conference to explain his view of the facts or waited
until the next council meeting to make a
formal speech outlining his views. In an
extreme situation, he could have prepared a
special news release. These, however, are
dramatic steps. Most government officials
know that they can exercise these options
only in unusual circumstances. In most cases,
they have little opportunity to correct mistakes and inaccuracies in news reports. They
must rely on the willingness of the press itself
to acknowledge errors.

In Flint, neither the newspaper nor the

EXHIBIT 70

Press Attacks Council Decision To Hold "Executive Sessions"

In early 1972 the City Council voted 8-1 to hold executive sessions. Flint's newspaper responded immediately, demanding that the council terminate a practice that, in the words of an editorial, was "an insult to the public." Characterizing its role as that of a mirror in which the public can accurately see all that happens at city hall, the newspaper argued that its function was "to transmit reports of what transpires in city government directly to those most affected by city government—the citizens of the city of Flint. . . . Executive sessions," the newspaper argued, "would make it impossible to perform a function that [is] basic to the conduct of a representative democracy."

The council's case for executive sessions had several bases. In the first place, it was common knowledge throughout the city that for years city councils had met in bars, hotels, and council members' basements to discuss city business. The newspaper had occasionally called for the termination of this practice but had never made it a major issue. Further, the elected Board of Education held scheduled executive sessions twice a month from which the media were barred. The council argued that if it was to meet to discuss issues affecting the future of the city it should do so openly, explaining to the public what was being done and why. Executive sessions, therefore, would be scheduled and held in city hall.

A second reason for the council's decision was the difficulty of discussing critical issues in a political forum. Given the fact that most members of the council tended

(continued)

major television stations were willing to acknowledge factual errors in a timely and consistent manner. This, in large part, reflected their lack of an economic incentive to do so. In the absence of competition, there was no incentive for the newspaper to be accurate or to correct inaccuracies. Moreover, there seemed to be a feeling on the part of many reporters and editors that correcting errors on the basis of third-party objections somehow reduced their independence and violated their First Amendment powers. As a result, citizens were not always correctly informed about the facts related to critical issues facing Flint's city government.

Presenting both sides of controversial issues

Because many people form their opinions on the basis of what they read in the newspaper or see on television, it is imperative that reporters make every effort to present the best case for each side of a controversial issue. Television and radio stations in Flint generally tried to do this. One radio station developed a popular program on which representatives of opposite viewpoints on critical issues answered questions submitted over the telephone. Flint's major television station had a program, "Tell It Like It Is," on

EXHIBIT 70 (cont'd)

to address their constituents, not the issues, during public meetings, the council felt that private meetings would create an environment in which a free and frank discussion of critical issues could be conducted. The council pointed out that its intent was not to make backroom deals that would be ratified at official council meetings every Monday night. Rather, its purpose was to ensure that important issues affecting the city of Flint would receive adequate discussion by elected political leaders. Finally, members of the council pointed out that public discussion of such issues as the purchase or sale of property, the nature of labor contracts, personnel decisions (hiring, firing, and discipline), appointments to or removal of people from boards and commissions, and potentially inflammatory racial problems was not in the public interest.

The newspaper was not persuaded by the council's argument. It filed a lawsuit seeking to enjoin the council from holding what the press termed "secret sessions." This suit was upheld in the local circuit court and was appealed by the City Council. In 1975 the Michigan Supreme Court returned the case to the Genesee County Circuit Court, saying, "We cannot apply the law to facts we do not have." Speaking for the high court, Justice Mary Coleman said that the justices wanted to know what specifically was discussed at private council meetings. Surprisingly, the lower courts had not asked this question.

While this issue was being argued within the judicial system, the City Council declared its intention to refrain from holding further "secret meetings," and the newspaper agreed to treat with "special consideration" public meetings that involved labor relations, personnel decisions, private property transactions, appointments or removal of people from boards and commissions, discussion of records not open to the public, and severe social or political unrest.

which key public figures were invited to present their positions on a range of public problems.

There were, of course, exceptions. One of the three television stations serving the Flint area (actually located in Saginaw, some thirty-five miles from Flint) failed consistently to report both sides of many important local-government issues. Because of distance and deadlines (film had to be sent from Flint by eleven each morning to be processed in time for the evening news), it was often difficult for the station to obtain the views of parties on both sides of a critical issue. Tight deadlines and distance also made

reporters vulnerable to city officials and employees who would call the reporters with their own versions of a news story. Often there was insufficient time or inclination to challenge the accuracy of these stories. In addition, the management of this station tended to slant its news reports of many public issues. Hence there was little incentive for reporters to provide equal time and attention to positions with which their station manager disagreed.

Despite what often appeared to be the negative personal views of its city hall reporters, Flint's major newspaper usually did present both sides of most important issues.

EXHIBIT 71

Two Public Officials Debate Future of Civil Service

"The top management structure of the city of Flint should be removed from civil service to give the manager more power in hiring the people he wants to fill critical jobs," argued the city manager.

"Flint is not mature enough politically to avoid abuse of such a change in the city's civil-service system," replied the civil service director.

And so the issue was joined. In separate interviews with the city manager and the civil service director, the newspaper's city hall reporter explored what changes, if any, these public officials felt should be made in Flint's civil-service rules as established in the city charter. The results of separately taped interviews were reported in a six-column, full-page presentation. Questions put to the city manager included these:

- In view of the power of city employee unions, do you feel that employees are protected enough so that the civil-service system could be abolished?
- Do you feel that city employees enjoy so much job security that the administration can't get rid of incompetents?
- Do you need more power to hire and fire employees?
- When you say that top management structure of the city ought to be outside of civil service and appointed by the manager, what positions do you mean?
- Would this result in a spoils system in top-level management positions?
- Do you think changes in civil service can be sold to the public over the opposition of city unions?
- Do you think the civil service director should be responsible to the city manager?

The civil service director was asked these questions:

- What changes do you think should be made in the civil-service system?
- Should impediments to the city's minority hiring program and restrictions on provisional appointments be removed from the charter?
- It's been said that civil service is too inflexible and slow to change. Do you think this is true? How could the current civil-service system be made more flexible?
- Do you feel that Flint's civil-service provisions are too detailed?
- If management positions were removed from the civil service, do you think the council would press the manager to appoint someone who was not qualified?
- How would you react if your job, which is now under civil service, were transferred under the control of the city manager?

Neither the city manager nor the civil service director objected to the presentation of his views. With some editing, their respective comments were directly transcribed from tapes. As a result of this extensive interview, the citizens of Flint could view both sides of a highly controversial issue.

Reform of Flint's civil-service system, for example, was a hotly contested issue in Flint. As Exhibit 71 recounts, the newspaper made a major effort to present both sides of this issue. As a result, citizens had adequate information with which to make a decision concerning the desirability of changing the city's civil-service system—a decision which would have required a charter amendment.

On some issues, however, the newspaper, like other private interests, used its power to influence the outcome. In these instances, little or no attempt was made to present the best case for each side of the issue. For example, on the questions of adopting a new city charter, relocating the University of Michigan–Flint campus, and terminating the holding of executive sessions, the newspaper took a firm position and used all of its resources to influence public opinion to support it. On these issues the newspaper was an advocate, not a reporter, of public events and issues. In many cases this advocacy extended beyond the editorial pages.

The newspaper's impact on the decision-making process was enhanced by the fact that council members tended to equate what they read in the paper with what their constituents believed. One council member commented, only partly in jest, "Don't ask me what I think until I read what the newspaper says." As Exhibit 72 illustrates, this attitude on the part of the council gave the media, especially the newspaper, significant power to help achieve (or conversely, to inhibit) change.

Investigative reporting

Most media reporting in Flint was descriptive and reactive. Flint's newspapers, television, and radio reports tended to focus citizens' attention primarily on what had happened during the previous twenty-four hours. Investigative reporting—defined here as in-depth analysis not only of what happened but also of why it happened—was the exception rather than the rule. As one news-paper reporter put it, "We only have time to write about the noises we hear, not about what produced them."

A young black reporter who worked for Flint's major television station had a different attitude. This reporter produced a number of filmed reports that examined in detail the causes and consequences of Flint's public-housing conditions. These were examples of investigative reporting at its best, because they educated the public not only about the nature of public-housing conditions but also about the factors that produced them. The result was a significant contribution to public understanding of a controversial and complex program. Unfortunately, the economic necessity of serving a large market area ultimately forced this television station to reorganize its personnel, reassigning this reporter solely to daily reporting.

The newspaper reporter covering the city's community-development programs also made a real effort to understand why the city's urban-renewal program was not producing promised results. As Exhibit 73 indicates, he was able to explain concisely and clearly the complex subject of relocation payments for urban-renewal residents. Did the time and effort it took to investigate this case really make a difference? Did such an investigation help sell more newspapers? Probably not. But it did allow Flint citizens to place this unique case in the perspective of the urban-renewal program. It did help avoid charges that urban-renewal residents were "ripping off" the program or that something dishonest had transpired. It removed potential suspicions that the program was poorly administered. In the case of most reporters, however, lack of time, complexity of subject matter, and absence of an investigative spirit produced articles or reports that did little more than describe the outcome of daily events.

The economics of operating a broadcasting station or newspaper in Flint made it difficult to afford assigning a reporter full time to the task of investigative reporting. In addition, the more cynical news editors

EXHIBIT 72

Newspaper Throws Full Weight behind University of Michigan Relocation

From the day the intention to relocate the University of Michigan–Flint campus from a seventeen-acre site shared with the community college to a forty-two-acre site in the heart of downtown Flint was announced, Flint's newspaper was an enthusiastic supporter and advocate. Editorials over the next year reflected this support. Major headlines read:

- "Riverside Campus Plan: Great Potential"
- "Flint Should Stretch for This Brass Ring"
- "Downtown Campus Offer Is Sufficient"
- "Long View Is Needed for Education Here"
- "Essential First Step"
- "Bright Challenge Given University of Michigan Regents"
- "Growing Pressures for River Campus"
- "Flint-Michigan Campus Plan Is 'Thinking Big'"

Support for this relocation project was not limited to the editorial pages. News reporting placed the case for relocation in its most favorable light. In view of the newspaper editor's active and enthusiastic support, reporters may have felt inhibited from reporting opposing views. One reporter, for example, explained, "There was a sort of unwritten communication to reporters on the paper: This newspaper supports the relocation project and your job is to sell it to the public."

Many in Flint felt that the editor's personal involvement in this project was a major reason for its eventual success. Focusing attention on the benefits the expanded campus would represent for the entire Flint community, the newspaper and its editor played a key role in building public support. This active involvement continued a tradition that had begun in the 1950s when the newspaper editor played a major role in the effort to develop and finance Flint's college and cultural center (a project which included a planetarium, music center, theater, and automotive museum).

Some people in Flint felt that the newspaper's open advocacy of the University of Michigan project made a mockery of the principle of "objective" reporting. The president of the NAACP, for example, issued a statement attacking the one-sided coverage of this issue by the newspaper. He concluded by asking, "Who will represent the other side?" A short time later, his question was answered by a small weekly newspaper, the *Flint Spokesman*. Directing its attention primarily to the black community, this newspaper presented a number of articles that asked city officials to reconsider their support for the downtown campus project on the grounds that it did not accurately reflect community needs or priorities.

EXHIBIT 73

When Will the City Pay $21,000 for a Home Worth Only $9,000?

"Woman's 'Profit' Is $7,000 in Residential Relocation"—the headline commanded the reader's attention. The newspaper reporter covering community-development programs in the city had discovered a quirk in the urban-renewal regulations. The opening paragraphs of his article explained what had happened.

Flint's urban-renewal program had paid an elderly woman almost $21,000 for a home that had a market value of $8,700. With the $21,000 payment, the woman purchased a home for $13,500, leaving a profit of over $7,000. The woman indicated that she would use this money to pay off old debts.

The reporter could have made this a sensational story, leaving the reader outraged at what appeared to be a major "ripoff." But he did not. Rather, he went on to describe the background of this particular case.

In the following paragraphs, the reporter briefly explained the purpose of the urban-renewal program. Then he explained that the objective of relocation payments was to help a person (or a family) relocate to a *comparable* home without undue financial hardship. For example, if the urban-renewal program purchased your home (valued at $10,000) and if it would cost $20,000 to buy a comparable home, the program would write you an additional check for $10,000. The largest relocation payment you could receive was $15,000.

The article then explained that if a portion of a residential home was used for business purposes (generally for rental), the relocation payment would be computed as follows: the percentage of the home used as a residence would be multiplied by the market value of the old home and then subtracted from the price of a new home. In this case, the elderly woman rented 90 percent of her home. Therefore, her relocation benefit was computed this way:

	$13,000	(price of new home)
less	870	(10 percent times $8,700 value of old home)
	$12,630	(partial relocation payment)

This $12,630 plus $7,830 (90 percent of $8,700) equaled the total amount ($20,500) that this woman was paid by the program. All of these calculations were made in accordance with program regulations and state and federal laws.

The article provided a basis upon which citizens could judge for themselves the merits of the urban-renewal program and the fairness of its specified relocation payments.

argued that well-researched investigative reports did not sell as many papers as less substantial but more interesting stories about automobile accidents, political corruption, personal scandal, and the like. In short, citizens did not demand better reporting of public events and decisions.

Finally, the absence of investigative reporting in certain areas in Flint may be attributed to the fact that the newspaper had an economic interest in avoiding careful investigation. For example, an investigation of almost any significant issue in Flint involved an examination of the role played by General Motors or the Mott Foundation, institutions with which the newspaper had a positive relationship. In other cases, there were certain institutions that the newspaper simply did not choose to investigate. One newspaper reporter on his own time prepared a detailed analysis of problems in the Board of Education. The newspaper, however, decided not to run these stories. The only explanation given to the reporter was that there was not enough public interest in the issue. Another example involves the newspaper's double standard concerning the right to hold executive sessions. In spite of the newspaper's emotional reaction to the City Council's decision to hold executive sessions and its subsequent lawsuit, the paper never felt inclined to challenge the actions of the Board of Education, which held "secret sessions" twice a month.

Taking an editorial position on critical issues

Flint's major television station, as Exhibit 74 describes, took active steps to influence such major public decisions as the adoption of a new city charter. The newspaper was equally active. Radio stations, on the other hand, were hesitant to take editorial positions. This seemed particularly unfortunate in view of the large number of people who listen to the radio and the need in the community for a wider variety of editorial views on important issues.

The active editorial support provided by the newspaper and Flint's television station may be attributed primarily to the fact that the managers of these institutions lived in the city and had a personal conviction that the media should support programs they judged to be in the community's interest. Both the editor of the newspaper and the manager of the television station were recognized community leaders who frequently reiterated their personal interest in finding ways to improve the quality of life in Flint.

Covering city hall week after week, media reporters had a firsthand understanding of the consequences of inept or improper political leadership, incompetent municipal managers, excessive union power, lack of active participation by private-interest groups, and inability of citizens to bring their case forcefully to the attention of the City Council. As a result of their personal exposure to the reality of life in city hall, these reporters were particularly well equipped to provide material for editorial positions encouraging change within city government. Editorial positions, as Exhibit 75 suggests, served as an important check on the political process. In view of the fact that the City Council combined both the executive and legislative functions, the press was often the only effective check on the exercise of governmental power in Flint.

Many community leaders, however, were not happy with the editorial positions taken by the newspaper and broadcasting stations. Blacks, in particular, felt that the newspaper took an elitist position on many issues. Discontent with such reporting led to the publication of a new weekly newspaper aimed specifically at black readers. The creation of this newspaper in 1972 was considered a positive development by most residents: the more alternatives for obtaining information, the better.

EXHIBIT 74

TV Editorials Emphasize Need To Change the City Charter

Convinced that a charter change was needed, the manager of Flint's major television stations asked the mayor and the city manager how he could help convince Flint citizens that the 1929 charter should be changed. Traditionally, his television station had not presented editorial opinions. He asked whether in this case editorials would help. Both the manager and the mayor answered affirmatively.

The following are excerpts from editorials presented by this station prior to the election to determine whether Flint voters wanted a charter revision commission formed to draft a new city charter:

> In 1929, General Motors was installing engines to meet the demands of the '29 cars, and now, forty-four years later, these engines have been almost completely redesigned because the demands have multiplied with air conditioning, power brakes, power steering, high speeds and almost limitless interstate roads to lure the traveler. If auto manufacturers had not improved the engines, we would have a 1970 car putting along on a 1929 power plant, which really doesn't work. Today, the city of Flint is faced with that problem. They have a 1929 charter which, at its writing, was capable of handling the problems that faced the city. . . . Since then the city has doubled in size, tripled in population, and become one of the most important manufacturing centers in the country, yet it still struggles through with a forty-four-year-old engine. In our opinion, this charter prevents the city from progressing forward. . . . Flint voters have the opportunity to review this charter in the coming election. We strongly urge them to vote yes on the charter revision proposal. . . .

> That was a play from the fourth quarter of the Wolverines' recent victory over Michigan State (ten seconds of film). It was a result of a well-coached, well-managed team, but you can imagine how it would have looked if Bo Schembechler did not have the authority to call the play, decide who was to be quarterback or tight end, or who was to be on the offense or defense. What would happen if Bo could not set up the blocking assignments or say which back goes where, or what would happen if the coach could not evaluate each player and determine whether or not he was doing the best job? In other words, what kind of team would there be if there was no clearly defined chain of command, no coordination between players, and where any individual could act on his own? I think the answer is easy. . . . It is hard to believe anything can run effectively without adequate authority, yet this has been happening in the city of Flint. The city's forty-four-year-old charter is designed to eliminate the head coach. . . . In short, the forty-four-year-old charter does not allow Flint leaders the opportunity to create a winning team. Flint voters have an opportunity to change that, and we urge them to vote for a charter revision, and so does the mayor, the council and the UAW.

More than 60 percent of those voting approved the decision to draft a new city charter.

EXHIBIT 75

"A Very Bad Week within City Hall"

With this headline, the newspaper was signaling to the public and the City Council that the citizens of Flint should receive more from their political leaders than they were getting. The first paragraph of the editorial from which this headline was taken read as follows:

> A few more weeks like this one in Flint city hall and there may be a groundswell to do away with municipal government altogether. Such is the state of affairs that in some eyes anarchy must be emerging as a practical alternative. If the public's tolerance of politicking and bickering isn't nearing its limit, it should be.

The editorial went on to describe the council's abortive attempt to fire the city attorney, the unsubstantiated charges that the outgoing city manager was "stealing" official papers, and the equally unsubstantiated charges that the current finance director was guilty of financial manipulation. The article concluded, "Damaging charges with no substantiation whatsoever, raised in a public forum, seemed to fit quite neatly into the present city government picture. It is a picture that is especially unattractive. . . ."

There was one area in which the city's major news media were not responsive to a significant community need: not nearly enough newspaper space or air time was given to announcements of community activities and other events of importance to citizens. The newspaper did publicize certain events in an ad hoc manner, but community information was not displayed consistently in the same part of the newspaper so that readers could find it easily. Efforts to encourage the newspaper to expand its coverage of community events were rejected, primarily on economic grounds. As Exhibit 76 shows, the newspaper argued that it could not afford to publish the City Council agenda, print summaries of the minutes of key council meetings, or summarize major public events in a consistent format. The editors felt that these services would neither increase readership nor attract more advertis-ing, and that therefore they were not justified on economic grounds.

Provision of a forum for debate of public issues

In general, both the electronic and print media in Flint did a good job of fairly presenting the views of those citizens and community leaders who took the initiative to prepare material for public consumption. Letters to the editor by civic and community leaders as well as private citizens were readily printed. Flint's television station and several radio stations also developed programs designed to draw attention to the differing points of view on major city hall issues. Exhibit 71 is a good example.

Media managers in Flint were strongly committed to the concept of personal in-

EXHIBIT 76

Newspaper Rejects Public-Service Section on Economic Grounds

Responding to an editorial arguing that a newspaper's function was to "transmit reports of what transpires in city government directly to those most affected by city government—the citizens of the city of Flint," the city manager proposed that the newspaper develop a public-service section. This section would be included in the same part of the paper each day and would include factual information about community events, city government services, and other items of public interest.

Examples of public-service information, organized by subject area, were recommended as follows:

General city information. Election dates, the dates absentee ballots are available, city license expiration dates, proposed ordinance changes and those citizens affected by them, dates of special public hearings, change in dates of regular City Council meetings.

Urban renewal. Announcements of citizen district council meetings, public hearings on urban-renewal plan changes, requests for proposals from contractors doing work in urban-renewal areas, special events.

Zoning. Planning Commission meeting dates and agenda items, public hearings on City Council or zoning ordinance changes, Zoning Board of Appeals meetings and agenda.

Public works. Notification of road repairs (their location and duration), listing of traffic detours, notification of new traffic-signal installations, announcement of special programs (weed cutting, paving, and the like), information on special waste-collection pickups, notification of landfill and sanitation collection procedures.

Public safety. Notification of fire-prevention week activities, announcement of spring cleanup procedures, announcement of the mobile city hall schedule, announcement of special neighborhood crime-prevention activities.

Public housing. Housing Commission meetings and agenda, tenant council meetings, project activity schedules.

Health. Announcements about immunization clinics, notification of procedures for reporting food poisoning, announcement of the schedule and location of insect and rodent-control program, procedure for reporting dog bites.

(continued on page 280)

EXHIBIT 76 (cont'd)

Mass transit. Announcement of changes in bus schedules, announcements of special services, communication of route changes, including maps.

Recreation. A weekly senior citizen calendar, information about special recreation programs (swimming, hockey), announcements of special events and dedications.

After fully considering this proposal, the editor of the newspaper indicated to the city manager that, although desirable, it would not be economic for the newspaper to provide such a service.

---

volvement in community affairs and thus to the idea of using the media as a public forum. Providing an arena for the debate of public issues may actually have had an economic value to the press, in that it encouraged greater involvement on the part of private-interest groups and community leaders with the newspapers and broadcasting stations. Such relationships might eventually be turned into advertising revenue.

Opportunities for Improvement

The press has a responsibility to ensure that citizens are informed about public events and decisions. Yet, given the latter's First Amendment protections, it is not government's role to make sure that the press exercises this responsibility. As Elliot Richardson noted in a speech to the American Society of Newspaper Editors in the spring of 1974, "One thing, in any event, is clear: there cannot be, there should not be, any external authority capable of reviewing the degree of responsibility with which you [the press] exercise your own obligations to the truth."[9] In short, the impact of the "fourth estate" on local-government performance depends on the ability of each news medium to establish and adhere to its own internally developed standards of responsibility. Accordingly, there are a number of opportunities for the press in Flint to improve its impact on the capacity of government officials to do their jobs well.

The media in Flint, especially the newspaper, could act more diligently to correct errors of fact or conclusion. The costs of allocating space and time to the systematic correction of errors may be significant, but the benefits in terms of more accurate reportage and enhanced public credibility should be sufficient to justify these costs.

Flowing from a willingness to correct errors should be a greater incentive to prevent them. In early 1974 Flint's newspaper created an internal organization responsible for reviewing news reports and special features to ensure that they met certain reporting standards. Strengthening and expanding this function will increase the likelihood that news reporting will be accurate, that all sides of important issues are examined, and that both the causes and the consequences of public decisions are fully presented. As television and radio expand their coverage of local-government affairs in Flint, the need to exercise quality control on their news reporting will also increase.

Competition in news reporting cannot help but improve the quality of coverage and provide citizens with a wider range of viewpoints on key issues. Accordingly, radio stations have a major opportunity to expand their coverage of events at city hall. Expanded news coverage should be accompanied by an increased willingness to take editorial positions. Several radio stations have already taken steps in this direction.

There is also a major opportunity for the press, particularly the newspaper, to serve as a forum for the communication of community and government information. If the economic realities of publishing or broadcasting argue successfully against providing this service, public officials should consider the feasibility of providing public financing for a weekly or periodic insert. There can be no better expenditure of taxpayers' funds than providing citizens with better information about the activities of their local government and the major events scheduled in their community.

Because of the cost and time involved, investigative reporting may not always make economic sense for each medium. Nevertheless, if the press is to serve effectively as a check on the abuse of government power, it is imperative that this type of reporting be continued and expanded. In a city such as Flint, where internal controls on the use of power by the legislative branch were often absent, investigative reporting proved to be a very important check on the potential abuse of this power.

Although local-government officials can do little directly to improve the impact of the media on government performance, they should consider the following ways of helping media reporters better exercise their responsibilities:

Bring errors of fact to the attention of media personnel. Given the complexity and volume of material a city hall reporter must cover, errors of fact and inaccurate conclusions are bound to occur. Therefore, political leaders and municipal managers must be willing to take the time to bring errors to the attention of media reporters and, in fairness, reporters should be willing to correct these errors. Government officials may not receive complete satisfaction; but if they are not willing to take the time to correct errors, they have only themselves to blame if citizens do not have accurate information.

Use all media to inform the public. Public officials must use the newspaper as well as television and radio stations to communicate information to the public. Using only one medium reduces the alternatives for reaching the public. Television and radio interviews provide political leaders and municipal managers with the opportunity to present their views directly to the public. In addition, the preparation of news releases will ensure that public officials are quoted accurately and that facts are presented as logically and as precisely as public officials can make them.

Allocate time for media briefings. If media representatives are going to report public events and decisions accurately, they must understand such complex issues as program budgeting, data processing, urban renewal, and public housing. In many cases, media reporters will have no background in these areas. Therefore, there is an opportunity for municipal managers, as well as political leaders, to take the time to inform the media. In some cases, this may involve two or three meetings per week to ensure that a proper basis of fact is established with respect to a given issue. Moreover, it may necessitate the inclusion of the media in all stages of the decision-making process. There are, of course, risks that premature disclosure of important information as well as inaccurate reporting may jeopardize the successful resolution of an issue. The potential benefits of having a better-informed reporter, however, will usually justify this risk.

Open all public meetings to the media. The deep-seated mistrust of city government officials in Flint and the traditional fear of dishonest backroom deals compel public officials to open all meetings to the media and to the public. Regardless of the positive and laudable intentions to create a forum wherein debate could be more easily directed to issues and not to political considerations, the necessity of satisfying the public that decisions are open and unbiased by secret deliberations must take precedence. There are, of course, some issues which, if reported, would damage the public interest. These involve personnel decisions, labor relations, property acquisition, and the like. In these instances, the media should be encouraged to accept the necessity of closed meetings or to exercise restraint in the public interest.

Public officials can take advantage of these opportunities and thereby help media reporters do a better job. But in the long run the burden rests solely with the media. Protected by the First Amendment and shielded from competition, the newspaper in particular must continually reaffirm its self-imposed decision to seek a balance between political responsibility and economic objectives, between the interests of citizens and the interests of its stockholders.

CHAPTER 14

Private-Interest Groups

Pluralism has a weakness.... The danger is that the many independent elements in the system find it almost impossible to work together in achieving any common purpose.... Unfortunately ... each person and each group guards with fanatic zeal the tent peg that holds his corner of the system in place—and taken altogether, the innumerable vested interests frustrate and subvert plans for the common good.

John Gardner

The role of private interests in our democratic system of government is a subject that has generated long and hot debate. Some, like Ralph Nader, chronicle the economic and political power of special-interest groups and argue that ours is not a government "of the people, for the people" but rather one "of special interests, for special interests." Critics such as Nader claim that labor unions, financial institutions, corporations, foundations, and other private interests have a disproportionate impact on the decision-making processes of government—to the detriment of individual citizens.

John Gardner, on the other hand, sees a different problem in the role of private interests. He sees private interests as consuming great energy in combatting one another instead of working together to achieve "plans for the common good." His view departs from the traditional belief that spe-

cial interests, acting on their own behalf, serve as a positive check and balance on each other as well as on the exercise of governmental power.

Regardless of how we view the role of private interests, the facts remain that they affect the way government carries out its business and that they are, in many cases, partners with government in the implementation of public policy. As such, they represent forces that must be recognized and considered in the formulation and implementation of government policies and programs. Our purpose, therefore, is to provide a basis for identifying opportunities to increase the positive impact of private interests on the performance of a local government. By private interests, we refer to such entities as local banks or branches of larger banks, civic associations, consumer and environmental organizations, foundations, universities, associations of local business executives, and private corporations. If a local issue has broad significance, a local government may be affected by private interests that operate on a statewide or national basis. Usually, however, local governments deal with local private interests in determining local issues.

Impact on Process and Performance

Private interests and institutions indirectly affect the performance of local government through their ability to influence the decisions of political leaders and municipal managers who directly affect the way in which a local government performs. They play a significant role in determining the capacity of elected political leaders and appointed managers to achieve community objectives with available resources. They can do this in a number of ways:

Private interests may exercise political power. Large private corporations, deriving influence and power from their economic role within the community, may attempt to influence governmental actions by determining who will and will not be elected or appointed to government positions. Labor unions, deriving political power from the fact that their constituents (and friends of their constituents) may represent a large percentage of the electorate, can influence government performance in a similar manner. In addition to supporting candidates for public office, private interests may exercise political power through their public support of issues or through their personal influence with incumbent public officials.

Private interests may affect performance through the provision of financial resources which enable local governments to achieve and maintain desired community conditions. For example, banks and other financial institutions are large purchasers of municipal bonds that finance city or county projects. In addition, nonprofit foundations and even profit-making corporations often provide direct funding for community projects. Even a small financial contribution by a private interest, especially if it has leverage on other sources of funds, may have a significant impact on the capacity of public officials to get something done.

Associations with private institutions may influence the decisions of public officials. This reflects the fact that people in positions of government leadership and management often come from employment with a corporation, labor union, foundation, university, or other private institution. When they enter government, they may find it difficult to shed their institutional biases and views. In fact, they are often selected precisely because of such views. For example, it is not unusual to find a representative of a local real-estate firm on a city planning commission. This ensures that a major private-interest group affected by a city's land-use policy is represented on the body responsible for recommending such policy to a city council.

Private interests can affect government performance by providing information required by public officials to make informed decisions. Many government policies and programs at the local level, especially those related to land use (zoning), housing, physical development, and transportation, depend for success upon information that accurately reflects the motivations and incentives of private interests. A local government will find it impossible to maintain a zoning classification if it does not understand the economic motivations of local property owners and developers. Therefore, private interests must provide information that will help public officials make intelligent decisions. There is, of course, the danger that a private interest will present only the information that best supports its position. Despite this danger, such information is a necessary and desirable ingredient in public decision making.

Private interests may also have an impact on performance because they are involved directly in the process of implementing government policies and programs. A developer under contract to a local government to build and manage a housing project represents a private interest charged with carrying out a public policy. The same is true for a highway construction company that builds a city's streets and roads, a private research and consulting firm that provides analyses and research to assist government officials, or a private sanitation company that contracts to pick up the garbage. Government, at any level, could not function without employing the private sector to carry out public programs and to assist in the conduct of the public's business.

Criteria for Evaluation

Some people argue that we should decrease or even eliminate the influence of private interests in the process of making and carrying out public policy. From a practical standpoint, this is not feasible. A more realistic approach recognizes that private interests exist, understands that their impact can be significant, and seeks to balance their role with that of other participants in policy formulation and implementation.

In evaluating the role of private interests and institutions, one must be careful to be objective—resisting the temptation to support the role of private interests whose views one favors and to oppose those whose views one does not favor. For example, we cannot support the lobbying and backroom politicking by the Sierra Club because we favor improving the environment and at the same time oppose the same methods employed by the National Rifle Association because we oppose the proliferation of handguns. From the standpoint of their impact on the management process, the role of private interests must be examined without concern for the issues they represent.

The following criteria should help focus efforts to assess the impact of private interests on the performance of a local government:

Are private interests willing to make sacrifices for a community purpose? Private institutions and special interests are in business to achieve their own narrow objectives. Yet, some circumstances necessitate putting the public interest above institutional self-interest. In fact, successful government performance largely depends on the extent to which private citizens and private institutions are willing to make sacrifices for the common good. Therefore, it is important to examine how private interests determine and pursue their self-interests. Do private interests and institutions appreciate the conflict and compromise inherent in the public decision-making process? Are they willing to take their bumps and bruises along with everyone else, and, at times, set self-interests aside in the process of achieving common community objectives?

Do public officials and private interests share information? If government officials and private interests understand and use the same information, the potential for conflict between them will be reduced and the potential for cooperation will be increased. This criterion examines the extent to which government officials and private interests communicate their goals and positions on major public issues.

Do private interests conduct public business publicly? Properly balancing the role of special-interest groups in the decision-making process depends on the public's knowledge and understanding of what special-interest groups want and why they want it. The efforts of private interests to affect public decisions is part of the public's business. Therefore, it is important to examine how private interests carry out their roles relative to the general public. Do citizens know the position of private-interest groups on public issues prior to final public decisions? Are lobbying efforts clearly identified as such?

Do private interests provide resources for projects that benefit the public? The financial contribution of private interests is often critical to the performance of local government. Meeting the development needs, rather than merely maintenance needs, of a community depends in many instances on the philanthropic role of private interests. Do private interests and institutions, without consideration of direct gain, provide resources (dollars, people, time) to ensure the development and implementation of important public projects?

Conditions in Flint

Flint contains a wide variety of private institutions and special-interest groups, each with an ability to affect public decisions. Because of this diversity, it is difficult to evaluate the degree to which they collectively meet the above standards. Therefore, we have applied these evaluation criteria separately to the four important private interests in the community: United Automobile Workers (UAW), Mott Foundation, General Motors Corporation (GM), and University of Michigan–Flint (UM–Flint).

We then examine the influence exerted by a number of other special interests. These include local banks; major civic associations, such as the Downtown Trade Association, the Chamber of Commerce, and the Urban League; local lobbying organizations, such as the Manufacturers Association, the Flint Environmental Action Team (FEAT), and the Flint Area Conference Incorporated (FACI); ministers; and, finally, influential private individuals.

The United Auto Workers

The UAW in 1974 was a powerful private-interest group in Flint that exercised its influence in areas considerably beyond the narrow confines of labor-management relations. The UAW began in Flint, and as a result the community has a strong tradition of unionism. In 1974, UAW membership in the Flint area exceeded 50,000. UAW members were organized into six local unions, including Chevrolet Local 659, the largest union local in the world. In the Flint area the UAW also had a district office, headed by an elected district representative. In addition, the union had an areawide community action program (CAP), administered by a council of elected representatives from each local. Union local presidents, district representatives, and the CAP Council were responsible for the political and community activities of the UAW in Flint.

As Exhibit 77 indicates, UAW leaders were actively concerned about finding solutions to local problems, often at what some considered a sacrifice of their own self-interests. In this case, the UAW was willing to take a controversial public stand in favor of a new city charter with the full realization that its position would be opposed by municipal unions with whom it had long tried to maintain a unified labor front. UAW support for charter revision was critical to the successful passage of the new charter.

Further evidence of the willingness of the UAW to transcend its narrow institutional interests in favor of broader community interests can be found in its support of political candidates. In local elections the UAW supported individuals it felt were the best qualified, even when this meant opposing candidates with labor affiliations. In the 1973 council elections, the UAW's CAP Council endorsed only one of six incumbent city councilmen, despite the fact that this council had not been antagonistic to the interests of the UAW and that three of the six incum-

EXHIBIT 77

UAW Breaks with City Unions—Supports New City Charter

Shortly after Flint voters overwhelmingly approved a new city charter, the chairman of the Charter Revision Commission indicated that without the support of the UAW, victory might well have been defeat. He was well aware of the fact that in 1966 UAW opposition to a proposed charter revision had been a primary cause of its defeat.

Perhaps the UAW supported the new charter because it gave the union new powers or because the Charter Revision Commission had been unduly influenced by UAW leadership. Not so! In fact, the UAW was not successful in persuading the Charter Revision Commission to accept its highest-priority change—the establishment of partisan local elections. The vice-president of the Greater Flint CAP Council had argued strenuously that partisan elections would result in better representation because candidates would be forced to take public positions on issues on the basis of political philosophy. He argued that nonpartisan office-holders could change their positions quickly after being elected, claiming that they had changed their minds and were doing the "honorable" thing. He added, "With partisan elections, an officeholder owes some allegiance to his political party which can exercise some discipline over him." For a variety of reasons, the Charter Revision Commission did not accept this position and maintained nonpartisan elections in the new charter.

Despite this decision, the UAW still endorsed the new city charter. Perhaps its support reflected a desire to maintain a consolidated union position. Not so! City unions strenuously opposed the new city charter despite concerted efforts by the Charter Revision Commission to meet their objections and gain their support. A coalition of city unions, including general employees, supervisors, firemen, and policemen, urged voters to defeat the new city charter because, in their view, it represented "a blank check for politicians." It also reduced the substantial power city unions were able to apply in the advancement of their self interests.

Why, then, did the UAW endorse the new city charter? The answer, in the words of the president of the CAP Council: "It will improve the quality of city government." He indicated that the charter was not without flaws but that, on balance, the new charter would "ensure that taxpayers get more for the taxes they are paying." The UAW's position reflected the fact that a substantial proportion of Flint city taxpayers were also members of UAW locals. UAW leaders recognized that UAW members were paying the increasing costs of Flint's city government and that adopting a new charter might provide government officials with a better opportunity to control or reduce these costs.

bents had a union background. One councilman whom the UAW did not endorse had
once been a UAW negotiator. In response to
a question concerning how the UAW could
afford to sacrifice its organizational interests,
the present of the CAP Council summarized
the UAW's position this way: "The candidates we endorsed are the ones we believe to
be the best qualified to represent the interests of the citizens in their respective wards.
This will ultimately be in the best interests of
the UAW."

UAW leaders generally conducted their
lobbying and political activities openly, taking public stands on both candidates and
issues. Candidate endorsements were based
on lengthy interviews and a vote of the
members of the CAP Council. In general
elections the CAP Council publicly endorsed
and supported a slate of candidates. In some
cases, candidates were endorsed in primary
elections as well.

The UAW was a generous provider of
financial and manpower support for political
campaigns. Moreover, union leaders participated in many local boards, commissions,
and community organizations. The UAW,
however, did not provide financial support
for city or other community projects except
through such programs as the annual United
Fund drive.

The overall impact of the UAW on local
government was judged by most people to
be positive—a judgment attributable to the
high quality of leadership in most locals and
in the regional office. Building on a long
tradition of social and community concern,
the UAW in Flint knew what it wanted, had
reasonable and realistic expectations of what
it could accomplish, and, above all, was
careful not to abuse its considerable power.

The Mott Foundation

In 1974, the Mott Foundation was one of
the ten largest foundations in the United
States. Its assets, primarily General Motors
stock, had a market value in excess of $400

million. The Mott Foundation was established in 1927 by Charles Stewart Mott, one
of the original stockholders of General Motors.

C. S. Mott first visited Flint in 1905. Two
years later he was persuaded by William C.
Durant to move his family's axle and wheel
manufacturing business from New York to
Flint in order to supply the newly organized
Buick Motor Car Company. General Motors
was formed around Buick three years later.
In 1913 C. S. Mott exchanged the stock of his
business for stock in General Motors, thereby creating the basis for a fortune that
eventually totaled hundreds of millions of
dollars. C. S. Mott died in 1973 at the age of
ninety-seven. At the time of his death, he was
the largest single stockholder of General
Motors and in his sixtieth year as a member
of the board of directors.

C. S. Mott was a classic example of the
pioneer industrial leader turned philanthropist. His efforts to make Flint a "model"
community were extensive, as Exhibit 78
indicates. Although both Mott's personal
efforts and those of the foundation were
focused almost exclusively on Flint, the Mott
Foundation has gained national recognition
for its contributions in the fields of education, health, and recreation. While he was
alive, C. S. Mott singlehandedly ran the Mott
Foundation. After his death, the foundation
was run less autocratically by his son, Harding, and a small staff under the guidance of a
family-dominated board of directors.

The Mott Foundation was in an ideal position to act in its own self-interest; on behalf
of individual board or staff members; or in
the interests of General Motors, whose stock
was the foundation's major asset. It did not
do so. The foundation was extremely careful
to avoid political intervention or any appearance of promoting publicly the interests it
represented. In fact, if anything, the foundation may have been too careful in this respect, thus creating the impression of a general unwillingness on the part of foundation
officials to take public stands on critical
public issues. As a result, the community was

EXHIBIT 78

Charles Stewart Mott—Flint's Godfather

"Come hell or high water, I'll be there!" said C. S. Mott. At ninety-six, C. S. Mott was determined to attend the General Motors stockholders' meeting to be held in May 1972. He did!

In fact, C. S. Mott accomplished most things he set out to do. As a businessman, he had built a small family enterprise, making bicycle wheels, into one of the largest personal fortunes in the United States. Working with such automotive pioneers as Billy Durant, Walter Chrysler, Charles Nash, Robert Olds, the Dodge brothers, David Buick, and Alfred P. Sloan, C. S. Mott helped establish General Motors as the largest manufacturing concern in the world. Mott served as a director of the General Motors Corporation from 1913 until his death in 1973. During those sixty years he seldom missed a board meeting.

In addition to building a private corporation, C. S. Mott helped build a city. In 1912, 1913, and 1918, Mott served as Flint's mayor. His plan to separate storm sewers from sanitary sewers in Flint was considered one of the most innovative public-improvement projects of its time.

It was as an industrialist-turned-philanthropist, however, that C. S. Mott made his greatest contribution to Flint. After 1927, he devoted a great part of his considerable energies to making Flint what he called a "model" city. His vehicle for accomplishing this goal was the Mott Foundation. The foundation's greatest achievement was developing and nurturing the community school system in Flint, a concept that has been exported to other parts of the country and the world. Mott Foundation grants were also responsible for developing a two-year community college, a University of Michigan–Flint campus, a children's health center, an extensive park system along the Flint River, a community cultural center, and many other projects that helped to improve the quality of life in Flint.

As important as the nature and scope of Mott's philanthropy was the philosophy that underlay it. In providing financial support for projects, C. S. Mott continuously emphasized the necessity of self-development. He did not want the Flint community to develop a dependence on his generosity at the expense of its own initiative. Therefore, he inisisted that the Mott Foundation never fund 100 percent of a project but, rather, make up the difference "after others had put up all they could." Mott's philosophy was to "grease the wheels," allowing established agencies and incumbent public officials to accomplish what they felt the Flint community needed. He emphasized the value of pilot projects. As a result, he was

(continued on page 290)

EXHIBIT 78 (cont'd)

willing to provide grants for a vast number of very small projects that had the potential for growing into larger, more significant programs if they proved successful.

It is impossible to accurately describe the impact of C. S. Mott on the city of Flint. Perhaps the spirit of this automotive pioneer, city mayor, and distinguished philanthropist can best be captured by his own words. In responding to an article in *Fortune* magazine describing him as one of the thirteen richest men in the country, C. S. Mott replied, "What I am worth is what I am doing for other people."

often deprived of knowledgeable and re-spected points of view.

An example of this deprivation occurred in 1974, when newly elected members of Flint's City Council began making a series of political attacks on the current administration and on the members of the council who support-ed it. The attacks were politically motivated and largely based on incorrect or distorted information, but they were successful in disrupting the council and the city's manage-ment team. Privately, foundation personnel expressed concern that this behavior would undermine a number of public-private pro-jects that were then under way with the city. They had worked closely with the people under attack, and therefore knew from first-hand experience that the attacks were un-justified; yet, they were unwilling to make their opinions known to the public.

Information exchange between the city and the Mott Foundation was imperfect. Because the foundation had a limited re-search staff, very little information was col-lected and disseminated in an orderly fashion about either city or foundation programs. The foundation was often in the dark as to the city's desires and intentions. It was not uncommon for the city to announce its desire for foundation funding or support of a project before the foundation had even been contacted. One major communication problem was determining who spoke for the

foundation. This problem became acute dur-ing the transitional period following C. S. Mott's death. Organizations and institutions that were dependent on foundation funding were often unsure about who could commit the foundation to a course of action and unclear about the process that would be followed in reaching a final decision.

Aside from these communication difficul-ties, the foundation, for the most part, car-ried out its business in public. Although the foundation held its board meetings privately, did not disclose the nature of debate over particular issues, and did not reveal votes on final decisions, it did make public the terms and conditions of all its grants. When working on a public project, such as the University of Michigan–Flint campus relocation, it kept its dealings in the open. The public knew where the foundation stood and why.

The foundation was willing and able, as Exhibit 79 indicates, to put financial resour-ces behind projects and initiatives it support-ed. In fact, without the financial support of the Mott Foundation, the city of Flint could not have persuaded the University of Michi-gan to develop a $60-million urban campus in the heart of downtown; it could not have persuaded the Department of Housing and Urban Development to finance a $30-mil-lion urban-renewal project in the most acute poverty area in Flint; and it could not have

EXHIBIT 79

The Mott Foundation—Flint's Rich Uncle

Without the Mott Foundation, the city of Flint would not have been able to capitalize on many development opportunities. Here are a few.

In February 1975 the Mott Foundation announced a grant to the city of Flint that totaled more than $1.8 million. This grant, which was $200,000 more than the city had asked for, was to be used to launch an economic-development program in the city. The bulk of the money was to provide the local share of a federal economic-development grant to begin development of an industrial park in Flint's oldest urban-renewal area.

This was not the only Mott Foundation gift that had helped launch a major community-development project. In 1973, the Mott Foundation persuaded the Department of Housing and Urban Development (HUD) to honor its commitment to provide Flint with $5 million for the development of residential housing in another urban-renewal project. This came about because the Nixon administration had placed a moratorium on all subsidized housing. Flint's urban-renewal project was dependent on subsidized housing to meet its contractual obligations with HUD. To salvage this project, the Mott Foundation pledged $102,000 per year for forty years, replacing the federal government as the guarantor and subsidizer of loans to support the construction of low-income housing. Subsequently, the HUD moratorium was partially lifted, and the foundation was relieved of its financial obligation. Without its intervention, however, this project would have been terminated.

In 1972 the Mott Foundation's $5-million contribution to persuade the Board of Regents to relocate the University of Michigan—Flint campus to a downtown location was a primary factor in the success of that project. The foundation subsequently provided funds to prepare a downtown development plan that would guide change in the central-city area over the next decade.

The list of Mott Foundation contributions to Flint community projects could fill many pages. Yet, there were those in Flint who felt the foundation's philanthropy did not reflect the right priorities, or accused it of having a paternalistic approach toward the community. Few, however, could argue with the fact that the quality of life enjoyed by Flint residents had been enhanced by its generosity. Flint may not have been the garden spot of the world, but it is difficult to imagine what it would have been like without the Mott Foundation.

been successful in initiating the development of a large industrial park adjacent to
Flint's Buick assembly plant.

The Mott Foundation, like any other organization, had its problems and its detractors. Many in Flint criticized the foundation
for exacerbating, not solving, community
problems. Critics claimed that the foundation had not done enough to meet the city's
needs and that it had participated in the
wrong programs for the wrong reasons. For
example, from the viewpoint of the city
administration, it appeared that the $5-
million annual funding of the Board of Edu-
cat'on's community education program violated the foundation's own grant-making
criteria, which emphasized its catalytic role.
In this case, support for the community
school program had continued for almost
thirty years. The foundation's support had
become an annual operating subsidy, not a
catalyst for innovative change. Because this
program had proven its value to the public,
many people felt that it was time for the
Board of Education or the community to
assume the funding of the program, freeing
foundation money for other community
purposes.

General Motors

By almost any measure, General Motors
dominated the city of Flint in 1974. Its name
and Flint's were almost synonymous. Without General Motors, Flint would not have
had the UAW, the Mott Foundation, or, for
that matter, a significant population to be
served by these institutions. On the other
hand, without General Motors, Flint would
not have had many of its physical, social, and
economic problems.

In 1974, General Motors operated nine
manufacturing plants in the Flint area, in
addition to three divisional headquarters, a
major parts-distribution center, and its own
university (General Motors Institute). In just
one complex, the Buick Motor Division, GM
employed more than 20,000 people. In fact,

in 1973, General Motors directly employed
more than 75,000 people—one-third of the
area's total work force. That year, GM's local
payroll exceeded $1 billion, providing its
Flint employees with one of the highest
weekly wage rates of any community in
Michigan.

The dominance of General Motors was
also reflected in the city's property records.
In 1974, General Motors was the recorded
owner of almost half of the taxable real and
personal property within the city. That the
next-largest institution represented only 2
percent of the total is a clear indication of
General Motors' significance in the city.

This dominance, however, has had negative effects. In 1974, as a result of the energy
crisis and reduced automobile production,
GM employment dropped to below 65,000
employees. More than 10,000 employees
were placed on permanent or indefinite
layoff, and many more were laid off for
shorter periods. The combination of the
direct impact of General Motors' layoffs and
the indirect impact on GM suppliers pushed
local unemployment from less than 6 percent in 1973 to more than 15 percent in 1974,
making Flint one of the areas most severely
affected by the energy crisis and the subsequent economic recession.

Given the impact of GM on Flint and the
surrounding metropolitan area, one would
expect that the corporation and its management would play a direct role in the public
affairs of the community. This was not the
case. General Motors' management personnel did not become involved in local government except when a major corporate interest
was at stake. For the most part, GM management was clannish; most lived in an upper-
middle-class suburb outside the city of Flint,
where they belonged to the same country
clubs and moved in the same social circles.
To reinforce this separation, the General
Motors real-estate arm, which assisted GM
executives in buying and selling their homes
when they relocated, concentrated its efforts
in only one or two suburban areas. Judging
by actual sales, it appeared that real-estate

personnel counseled GM executives against purchasing homes within Flint's city limits.

On balance, General Motors was not willing to suppress its corporate self-interest to accomplish public purposes. Its participation in community affairs was limited to such activities as the annual United Fund drive, which had few political ramifications, and participation in such community organizations as the Urban Coalition and the Human Service Planning Council. General Motors' top-management personnel scrupulously avoided overt political activities. As Exhibit 80 shows, GM made it difficult for young executives to become involved in civic affairs. In this case, GM officials appear to have taken direct action to block a young executive's attempt to become Flint's finance director. It is interesting to note that the GM employees who did particpate in local politics were usually not executives who could use their corporate skills to help solve public problems, but rather blue-collar employees who generally owed their allegiance more to the UAW than to GM.

There are many reasons why General Motors and its executives did not become involved in local politics or in efforts to improve local-government performance. When asked, GM officials would point out that they had an explicit corporate policy permitting involvement in government at the national or the local level. While this may have been true, it was clear that there were few incentives and little encouragement within the corporation for such participation.* As one General Motors executive put it, "I work a ten-hour day for General Motors, and to advance my career I have to devote a considerable portion of my free time to social and recreational activities with my corporate brethren. If I were to participate in outside activities, such as city government, I would have to do so at the expense of my career objectives." In short, as Exhibit 81 illustrates, it was very difficult for a young executive who wanted to advance within GM to also become involved in community affairs. In this case, a very able individual chose not to seek a seat on the City Council (which most felt he would win easily) primarily because he did not receive encouragement from GM.

GM's reluctance to become involved was not limited to political issues. In early 1972, General Motors officials refused to even consider a proposal to establish an executive interchange program in Flint. This program would have allowed GM personnel to work directly for the city of Flint or to participate on special task forces for specified periods of time. It was even contemplated that city government employees might spend a period of time working for General Motors, thereby improving their managerial skills and increasing their knowledge of Flint's most important corporate citizen. The reason given for GM's lack of interest was that it was not in the career-development interests of GM executives to participate in such a program.

Another cause of its lack of local involvement was that General Motors is a national, not a local, corporation. Its executives typically move many times in progressing up the corporate ladder. They are seldom in one community long enough to develop long-term interests and associations. This results in a situation similar to that found in the military or the foreign service, where personnel limit their relationships to others who live within the same circumstances. In fact, several managers did not even move their families to Flint, believing that their tenure in the city would be short.

Finally, General Motors did not take more interest in Flint because it did not need to do so in order to preserve or advance its corporate interests. GM was such a dominant force

---

* At the national level, General Motors was one of the few major corporations in the country that refused to participate in the president's executive interchange program, which was started in 1970. This program provided an opportunity for corporate executives to serve the federal government in top-management positions and for top federal executives to serve in the private sector.

EXHIBIT 80

General Motors Steers Executive Away from Top City-Government Post

Dejectedly, a young General Motors executive shook his head and commented, "I just don't believe it." He was referring to the fact that a special screening committee convened to recommend to the City Council qualified candidates for the position of finance director had just told him that he was not qualified. Looking at the facts, this decision seemed preposterous. This individual had degrees from the Harvard Graduate School of Business and the General Motors Institute. In addition to being a longtime resident of Flint, he had served with distinction in several management positions within GM. In his current position, he was responsible for financial control, budgeting, and financial planning in the Chevrolet Motor Division assembly plant.

The screening committee, which consisted of five members from the private sector with special expertise in several areas of finance, included the comptroller of the Buick Motor Division. Without explanation, this member of the screening committee asked that the GM executive's name be withdrawn from consideration on the ground that he did not have experience in municipal finance. The committee member's doubts about the applicant's management and financial ability seemed surprising in view of the fact that, in its efforts to prevent him from leaving Chevrolet, General Motors had offered him a number of management positions, including a position as a senior staff assistant to the General Motors corporate treasurer in New York City.

No official or unofficial explanation was ever offered for the committee's action. It was not completely clear whether General Motors had taken an official position against this candidate. Perhaps Buick's comptroller was acting solely on his own, although people involved in the selection process did not believe this was the case. The chairman of the selection committee stated later that he felt General Motors had vetoed this candidate because it did not want to create a potential conflict of interest wherein a former employee was responsible for recommending taxation and assessment policies that might affect GM. Regardless of the reason, the city of Flint lost an opportunity to hire a manager with substantial skill and ability.

that, regardless of its lack of support or involvement in government affairs, its positions on most issues were adopted. General Motors employees, even though they generally held blue-collar, nonsupervisory posts, had always served on Flint's City Council; there were three on the 1971–73 council and four on the council that followed. Even though most of these people had a stronger allegiance to the UAW, they provided General Motors with a direct line of communication to the decision-making process at city

EXHIBIT 81

Promising Local Politician Decides He Cannot Serve General Motors and the City of Flint at the Same Time

Many political and community leaders believed that the City Council elections in November 1973 were critical to the continued progress that had been made during the previous three years. A major effort was launched to persuade people with demonstrated leadership capabilities to run for vacant City Council seats.

One of the candidates asked to run from Flint's first ward offered a number of advantages. He was a new face on the political scene and carried with him none of the baggage that affected traditional political leaders. He was intelligent, with an exceptional amount of enthusiasm and energy. Moreover, he was black. This represented an important asset in a ward and in a city which was in transition from a white majority to a black majority.

Despite the facts that this individual was on the faculty at the General Motors Institute and was in the process of obtaining a Ph.D. from the University of Michigan, he agreed to run for the City Council. About a month later, when it was clear that he was the leading candidate for the seat, he dropped out of the race. Many claimed that he had received "the word" from General Motors that a term on the council would not be in his long-term career interests. This was true, but only indirectly. He decided that he could not perform all of the activities that he was pursuing equally well; something had to go, and it was the City Council race. He concluded that his career with General Motors would suffer if he did not do a good job in what he was doing. He had little choice but to put the city second.

---

hall. When absolutely necessary, these lines could be opened.

GM and the city of Flint did not exchange information readily or frequently. This was most evident during the economic recession that struck the city in 1974. When many citizens turned to city hall for action to alleviate the pain and uncertainty of layoffs, the city turned to GM. General Motors executives provided little information about the corporation's future plans, either because they were caught off-guard by the energy crisis and had no future plans or because the corporation believed such information to be proprietary.

General Motors was a private corporation which carried on its local business privately. Its executives arrived at corporate positions on specific local issues or made internal decisions that had local impact (such as the construction of a new building within the community) without involving the public or city government officials. What GM planned to do and how it intended to do it usually remained a well-guarded secret.

Direct contact with GM occurred primarily through the GM Plant-City Committee, a committee made up of the general managers

EXHIBIT 82

General Motors Cooperates with the City— Sometimes!

The local press hailed the 1973 agreement between the Buick Motor Division of General Motors and the city of Flint as ushering in "a new era of public-private cooperation" that would rebound to the "mutual benefit of the community and General Motors."

The newspaper was referring to an agreement that had just been signed under which Buick had agreed to purchase and redevelop seventy-nine acres of St. John's Street urban-renewal area land adjacent to its massive plant complex. Under the agreement, Buick would purchase the vacant parcels and the city would purchase all occupied parcels, relocating all affected residents. The city-purchased land would then be resold to Buick. This plan would permit Buick to expand its distribution, trucking, and waste-treatment activities and allow residents to relocate from this depressed area into decent housing elsewhere in the community.

This agreement allowed the urban-renewal program to proceed at an accelerated pace. The city could use its resources to purchase and relocate residents, what it could do best, while Buick used its resources to buy land that did not affect people. The agreement was also timely, for in 1973 the Nixon administration had placed a moratorium on all urban-renewal projects; only those for which there was a signed redevelopment contract would be funded. Because of General Motors' cooperation, the Flint urban-renewal project qualified for such funding.

To understand how unique this "new era of public-private cooperation" was, it is necessary to understand GM's historical role in the St. John's Street urban-renewal area. In January 1972, Flint's new community development director assessed conditions in the city's eight urban-renewal programs and found the St. John's Street project in total chaos. This project required the city to purchase approximately 1,500 parcels of land, approximately 700 of which were occupied, at a cost to Flint and to the federal government of more than $30 million.

Relationships between the residents of the area and Buick, its immediate neighbor, were, at best, terrible. The Buick complex, which was more than two miles

(continued)

of each of the plants in Flint. This committee supervised and coordinated GM's relationship with the local community. Any request by the community for GM participation in any activity would go first to this group.

Another channel of communication to and from GM was the Flint Manufacturers Association, a lobbyist group for Flint manufacturing concerns—which meant GM. A GM reaction to a proposed idea could generally be obtained indirectly through the director of this association.

EXHIBIT 82 (cont'd)

long and almost one-half mile wide, dominated the area. It housed more than ten major factories producing engine and transmission castings, sheet-metal stampings, and final assemblies. More than 20,000 people worked at this one site.

Regardless of what Buick's management did or did not do, it would have been difficult to maintain positive relationships with the residents who lived so close to "the Buick." Buick management, however, had made a bad situation worse. In 1970 the division decided that it needed to expand in order to construct a new steam-generating plant. This plant would provide more efficient energy and eliminate much of the air pollution that had been created by the older plant. Tired of waiting for the city to purchase the land through urban renewal and resell it to Buick as had been planned, Buick silently purchased the required parcels. To keep costs as low as possible, Buick purchased only those parcels on which the plant would be constructed. This resulted in the building of a massive seven-story plant immediately adjacent to a number of single-family homes and a church. The land was purchased and construction began.

Citizens of the area were outraged. They claimed that the Buick purchases violated the original urban-renewal plan. In June 1971, they sued the city and General Motors. Out of court, the city agreed to alter its acquisition strategy and to purchase during the next ten months 170 parcels immediately adjacent to the steam-generating plant. In January 1972, with only four months remaining in this agreement, the city had acquired only 27 properties. Not surprisingly, relationships between citizens in the area, city government officials, and Buick were strained.

Against this backdrop, the city-Buick agreement of 1973 was negotiated. After almost a full year of negotiation among city officials, residents, and Buick executives, an agreement acceptable to all parties was produced.

In part, the success of the Buick agreement caused Flint's civic and community leaders to be very disappointed by General Motors' rejection of a request that it participate in the relocation of the University of Michigan campus. In April 1972, General Motors had been asked to contribute to the campaign to relocate the University of Michigan campus site from an inadequate location to one in the heart of the city along the Flint River. The city had contributed $6 million to this effort; the Mott Foundation, $5 million; and other private interests, more than $3 million. General Motors was asked for a $2-million contribution. After six months of deliberation, General Motors officially stated that it could not contribute to the relocation project.

Requests by community and civic leaders for General Motors' financial support in carrying out community projects were usually rejected, except when GM's corporate interests were involved. Exhibit 82 describes two major GM decisions that had a dramatic impact on community development. The first decision was positive, reflecting the Buick Motor Division's desire to purchase urban-renewal land adjacent to its assembly plant. This decision clearly indicates that when corporate self-interest was involved,

GM could act decisively in the public inter-est. The second decision, a refusal to contrib-ute financially to the relocation of the Uni-versity of Michigan–Flint campus, stood out sharply in contrast to enthusiastic donations by almost every other major private institu-tion in Flint, including local banks, smaller corporations, and local businesses. One problem in obtaining GM financial contribu-tions for large projects was that they had to be approved by General Motors headquar-ters in Detroit. Local managers who were responsible for billions of dollars of local corporate expenditures did not have the latitude to make decisions about contribu-tions for local public projects.

University of Michigan–Flint

In 1974, the University of Michigan–Flint (UM–F) was a relatively new institution with-in the Flint community. It had been estab-lished in 1956 as a college of the University of Michigan—the first University of Michigan college to be located outside the main cam-pus at Ann Arbor. Initially, the college pro-vided upper-division courses in limited areas to augment Flint's two-year community col-lege, thereby permitting students to obtain a four-year college education in Flint. The junior college and the university were locat-ed on the same campus site. C. S. Mott had donated the land for this site as a means of inducing the University of Michigan's Board of Regents to place a college in Flint.

The University of Michigan–Flint grew considerably from this modest beginning. In 1971 the campus was given separate universi-ty status by the state legislature and the university of Michigan Board of Regents, and Flint's first chancellor took office. By 1974, UM–F offered 200 courses and a B.A. degree in twenty-six program areas. More than 3,000 students were enrolled on a full-time or part-time basis.

Even with this substantial growth, UM–F in 1974 was a small institution, by Flint's stand-

ards. It had a staff and faculty of 200 people and an annual budget of $8 million—one-half the size of the two-year community college and one-fourth the size of Flint's public-school system. The voice of UM–F within the community, however, was signifi-cantly greater than its size would suggest.

The university, like city government, was a public institution. Like all other state univer-sities in Michigan, UM–F had to be adept at statewide politics, which, in turn, required strong local political support. In Flint, indi-vidual faculty members and administrators took extremely active roles in the communi-ty. They were selected to serve on boards and commissions and participated in political campaigns. As an institution, the university was deeply involved with the city in the cooperative development of a new campus within one of the city's urban-renewal pro-ject areas. (See Chapter 19 for a detailed discussion of this project.) The university sponsored social-science research projects that benefited the community, and students were given class credit for internships in local public agencies. In addition, local public officials and professionals were encouraged to teach courses within the university.

Information exchange between the uni-versity and the city was excellent. During the period when the city and the university were working on the relocation of the campus, all plans and project data were shared thor-oughly. The city, in developing its new in-tegrated master plan, found university fac-ulty able and willing to provide a wealth of useful information. If anything, government officials failed to capitalize on all the valuable information resources provided by UM–F.

As one would expect, UM–F conducted its activities publicly. Understandably, the one criterion it did not meet was that of providing resources for community projects, except those directly related to campus or university development. Its source of public revenue was the same as that of other public institu-tions—the tax dollar.

Other major private interests, institutions, and individuals

The relationships of the UAW, the Mott Foundation, General Motors, and the University of Michigan to Flint's city government reflect some of the diversity of private institutions and interests in Flint. These four institutions were by no means the only private interests that had an impact on governmental performance. Financial institutions, downtown business interests, churches, and environmental and community groups, as well as individual community leaders, played a role in helping, and in some cases hindering, the performance of city government.

There were three major banking institutions in Flint, two of which had their headquarters there. Bank officers and employees actively participated in a wide range of community projects. In 1973, one Flint bank decided to expand its facilities and employment in the downtown area instead of moving to the suburbs, as many downtown commercial interests had done. Although this decision contained considerable short-term economic risk, bank executives felt that in the long run it would be in the best interests both of the bank and of the community of which they were citizens. This decision was not surprising. The executives of Flint's three major financial institutions had always played a major role in community activities, often placing corporate self-interest behind community interest. In fact, their willingness to pursue their own interests in an open and public manner, combined with their generous donations to a wide range of community-development projects, placed these institutions in an important leadership role in the community.

Lobbyists were also active in Flint. The Manufacturers Association of Flint (MAF) monitored public affairs closely for the industrial community—which primarily meant General Motors. When General Motors wanted to communicate with people at city hall or to affect a public decision, it often did so through the MAF. The MAF director was extremely close to all public issues and, more than anyone else, was aware of what was happening in city government. If a General Motors interest was not at stake, the director of the Manufacturers Association could be extremely cooperative in finding a solution to a problem or helping a government-sponsored program get off the ground. Prior to joining the Manufacturers Association, he had been a popular mayor of the city, and he had retained a high degree of respect from all segments of the community.

Another effective lobbying group was the Flint Environmental Action Team (FEAT). The purpose of this private volunteer organization, led by a group of young people in the community, was to improve the physical environment of Flint. Much of what they desired to do had to be done through government or with government help. Although FEAT was a new organization in 1974, it had quickly become an effective voice in the community on environmental issues, as Exhibit 83 illustrates. Its members were adept at collecting, analyzing, and presenting information to the public. Moreover, they made effective use of the media. It was common in Flint to hear or read that a FEAT survey showed that Flint citizens were squarely behind (or against) a particular issue. Survey results would be announced during the week in which that issue was before the City Council or some other public decision-making body, thereby maximizing their impact.

Although they could not be termed a lobbying group, black ministers were an extremely important force within the Flint community. In a number of instances, Flint's black ministers played a critical role in preventing the outbreak of violence within the black community. In 1973, for example, black ministers worked with the black members of the City Council to reduce the threat of violence following a police shooting of a black youth in Flint's north end. More important, black ministers were a positive force

EXHIBIT 83

Billboard Ban Survives Private-Interest Pressure—But Site Plan Review Does Not

In late 1973 and early 1974, private interests in Flint were concerned about two public-sector decisions: one related to the frequency and number of billboards permitted along Flint's freeways and the other related to the necessity of having a site-plan review ordinance.

Private interests were arrayed on both sides of the billboard issue. A local outdoor-advertising company wanted the Planning Commission and the City Council to reconsider an ordinance passed in 1971 banning the placement of billboards within 600 feet of a freeway. This request was bitterly opposed by the Flint Environmental Action Team (FEAT), which represented environmental and community beautification groups. FEAT was proud of the fact that in 1971 Flint was one of the few local governments that had followed the federal government's lead in banning billboards along major interstate highways. Its members did not want this ordinance repealed or modified.

Major governmental changes had occurred in Flint since 1971. The new City Council, elected in 1973, did not favor strong environmental or beautification legislation. Using its power of appointment, it had changed the character and makeup of the Planning Commission. Given its new makeup, few were surprised when the Planning Commission voted in June 1974 to lift the ban on billboards, permitting as many as five per mile in each direction along the interstate freeways. The chairman of the Planning Commission, who opposed the ordinance, noted that this would mean that citizens driving fifty-five miles per hour would encounter a billboard every seven seconds. Environmental and beautification groups launched a major lobbying campaign with the City Council.

Over the next weeks, the billboard issue was hotly debated before the City Council by private interests representing both sides of the question. FEAT presented the results of one of its surveys, which showed two-thirds of the citizens of Flint favoring strong control of billboards. The City Council was in the middle. At one meeting, the council defeated the recommended change 8–0, registering a win for the environmentalists. At the very next meeting, the council voted 5–4 to reconsider the ordinance. At the following meeting, however, the issue was again defeated. In the end, the environmentalist groups won, and the 1971 ordinance banning billboards within 600 feet of the freeway remained intact.

On the issue of site-plan review, environmentalist forces were not so successful. In this instance, the City Council acceded to the interests of the Chamber of

(continued)

EXHIBIT 83 (cont'd)

Commerce and the Manufacturers Association, representing commercial and industrial interests in Flint.

The purpose of site-plan review was to ensure that plans to develop and significantly remodel a structure, with the exception of a single-family home, would be submitted to the Planning Commission for review prior to the issuance of a building permit. Applicants were required to pay a large fee. This ordinance had been passed by the outgoing City Council at its last meeting, with a minimum of public debate.

The ordinance turned out to be extremely difficult to administer. Applicants complained about the arbitrary nature of the ordinance's enforcement. No criteria had been established with which to review site plans. The Chamber of Commerce and other organizations, therefore, requested that the ordinance be revised or repealed. FEAT, representing environmentalist groups, opposed this action.

Following a large number of meetings among the Department of Community Development, the Planning Commission, the Chamber of Commerce, the Manufacturers Association, and FEAT which did not result in an acceptable compromise on this issue, the City Council asked the Planning Commission to hold a public hearing to determine whether this ordinance should be rescinded. The Planning Commission refused. Instead, they reviewed the ordinance and proposed a number of changes that included the exemption of construction projects costing less than $15,000, a reduction in review time, and a lowering of fees. Commercial and industrial interest groups continued to demand outright repeal of the ordinance.

Differences between the City Council and the Planning Commission, whose members had been appointed by the previous council, deteriorated to the point that the chairman of the Planning Commission and one other member were not reappointed by the City Council when their appointments came up for review. Both were highly respected architects in the community. They were replaced by an auto-plant worker and a real-estate saleswoman. This action caused a third member of the Planning Commission to resign in protest.

The City Council's three new appointments significantly changed the complexion of the Planning Commission. During the next two months, public hearings were held on the question of repealing the site-plan review ordinance.

FEAT conducted a citizen survey during the course of the debate to demonstrate how Flint citizens felt about the issue. The survey showed that more than 60 percent of the public favored some form of site-plan review. However, these findings did not sway the new Planning Commission, which eventually recommended a modified ordinance to the council affecting about half of the projects included under the previous ordinance. The City Council, much to the dismay of FEAT and other environmental groups, approved this weakened ordinance.

EXHIBIT 84

In Flint the "Gray Eagles" Could Make Things Happen

In every community there are a few individuals who, although they represent private interests, are personally responsible for making things happen. Flint was no exception. A small group of individuals in Flint was behind efforts to implement nearly all community-development projects initiated before 1972.

The imprint of C. S. Mott was indelibly etched in the contours of Flint. In 1954, Michael Gorman, editor of the *Flint Journal,* was responsible for the development of a cultural center that was unique for a city the size of Flint. In 1972, Glen Boissenault (then editor of the *Journal*) and George Whyel (then president of a major Flint bank) were, in large part, responsible for the development of the University of Michigan campus.

Perhaps the most indefatigable of the "gray eagles" was Arthur Summerfield. Summerfield had developed one of the most successful Chevrolet dealerships in the country and was active in Republican politics. In the 1950s, he served as President Eisenhower's postmaster-general. Upon returning to Flint, Summerfield became a primary catalyst in many local improvement projects.

An illustration of the kind of role Summerfield often played occurred in 1970, when he decided that the city should redevelop the neighborhood in which he had been raised. This neighborhood,known as the Doyle area, now contained the worst poverty, crime, housing, and health conditions in Flint. His style was to go right to the top, so he went to Washington to talk to George Romney, secretary of housing and urban development. Primarily through personal friendship and what one person described as "unmitigated gall," Summerfield persuaded Romney to give Flint a $5-million urban-renewal grant to redevelop the Doyle area. The city would have to apply for the money and follow some rules, but the money was reserved for Flint.

(continued)

in Flint's city government. They accepted appointments to, and were effective members of, city boards and commissions; they were also active in political campaigns and spoke out from the pulpit on many public issues.

In Flint there were also many individuals who belonged to various interconnected civic, community, and private organizations but whose real influence was personal. These people, referred to by many as the "gray eagles," served as the catalysts who initiated the process of change in many important areas. Exhibit 84 discusses the accomplishments of two of the most prominent and effective of these individuals. As the exhibit

EXHIBIT 84 (cont'd)

After Summerfield's death in 1973, his son, Art Summerfield, Jr., continued his father's interest and involvement in the community. No one ever accused either Summerfield Jr. or Summerfield Sr. of being unaware of the family's self-interest. In 1971, when Flint's City Council hired a new city manager, they were the first community leaders to schedule a visit. Their purpose was to tell the new manager that they wanted the city's urban-renewal program to purchase their Chevrolet dealership. They presented their case openly, without deception. They made it clear that, regardless of the city's action, they would continue to support community projects. For a number of reasons, the city never purchased the Chevrolet dealership. The Summerfields, however, were true to their word. When something needed to be done, be it removing railroad tracks from the center of the city or persuading key members of the City Council to support a new budgeting system, the Summerfields could be counted on to help get the job done.

It was often repeated in Flint that no one had more energy than Ron Warner. According to one account, Warner, a former plant manager for Chevrolet, served on more than twenty different community organizations, ranging from the Urban League and the Urban Coalition to the Human Services Planning Council and the Hurley Hospital Board of Directors. In 1973, he became president of the Genesee County Development Corporation, a nonprofit sponsor of low-income housing. He also led the community drive to expand and upgrade the city's hospital, and he was the primary force behind the effort to develop a regional airport to be located in the Saginaw Valley area. There probably was not a single major development issue in Flint that had not attracted Ron Warner's attention and personal effort.

The only justifiable criticism of the tireless efforts of people like Ron Warner and Art Summerfield was that they did too much. A newspaper article in 1973 posed the question, "Who will be Flint's third generation of leaders?" Men like Mott, Warner, Gorman, Whyel, Boissenault, and Summerfield had so totally dominated the private sector's involvement in public projects that very few of the younger generation had had a chance to develop or demonstrate their leadership skills.

concludes, one consequence of the effectiveness of these and other older Flint leaders was that new leaders had not been groomed to take their places. In 1973 a program entitled "Leadership Flint," patterned after a similar program in Atlanta, was inaugurated by the Flint Junior League. Its purpose was to identify people with recognized leadership abilities and to involve them in the process of solving community problems, thereby helping to fill the growing leadership vacuum that had become so evident in Flint.

Responsibility for community improvement and development was fragmented among a number of private associations and community organizations. The most prominent of these were the Downtown Trade Association, the Chamber of Commerce, the Flint Area Conference, Inc., and the Flint Area Convention and Tourist Council. These organizations were marked by petty jurisdictional squabbles and bureaucratic infighting that significantly affected their ability to reach common development objectives. In part, the inability of these organizations to get things done reflected inadequate staff support; but mainly it reflected the fact that individual leaders were generally more concerned about who got the credit for a particular project than whether it produced desired results.

There was also in Flint a penchant for developing grand schemes for community development without considering how they would be carried out. As Exhibit 85 describes, there is a role within any community for dreams and dreamers, but only if there is an equal number of individuals with the capacity to convert dreams into reality. In Flint, this was not the case. As a result, community expectations were often unduly raised by ideas that could not be implemented regardless of the public fanfare and the pretty pictures. Moreover, such ideas diverted attention from other, more practical programs that, although less grandiose, could have been implemented.

Private interests and private leaders played an important role in the development and implementation of major community projects during the period from 1971 to 1974. Private interests were mainly responsible for the successful relocation of the University of Michigan campus to the heart of downtown Flint, the initiation of an industrial park in the area adjacent to the Buick Motor Division, the beginning of a residential housing development in one of Flint's most blighted neighborhoods, the inauguration of the Flint River Beautification and Flood Control Project, and the development of a commercial center in the downtown area. On the political side, private interests played a major role in the development and adoption of a new city charter.

The problem in Flint lay not in what was accomplished but in what could have been accomplished. Prior to his departure from the city of Flint in mid-1974, Flint's finance director told a gathering of the city's most prominent civic leaders what most of them inwardly knew: "This community has had a great ability to lie to itself." He was referring to the fact that many of the city's grandest schemes had remained on the drawing board and that community leaders in many cases had not pulled together a fragmented private sector to accomplish them. The newspaper, in reviewing these remarks in an editorial, commented: "It is doubtful that [the finance director] would have made his statements if he had not heard once again the great plans and rosy pictures and few solid, concrete and practical proposals on how to bring about a change in direction."[1] On balance, private interests exerted a positive impact on the performance of Flint's city government. This influence, however, could have been much greater.

Opportunities for Improvement

This chapter has advanced the proposition that the performance of a local government can be significantly improved if private interests assume a positive role in their relationships with city government. On the basis of conditions in Flint, we believe that a number of opportunities to strengthen the impact of private interests on the performance of Flint's city government should be considered.

First, private interests should consider consolidating the existing fragmented and often competing business-oriented civic associations (such as the Chamber of Com-

EXHIBIT 85

Flint's Dreams and Its Dreamers

Every city has its dreams and its dreamers. Flint was no exception. Perhaps its most exciting dream was of an automotive hall of fame; its dreamer was Saul Siegel.

The magnitude of this dream is perhaps best illustrated by quoting one of the financial feasibility studies that was prepared for this project. The preface of this study described the automotive hall of fame this way:

> The monumental impact which the automotive industry has had and will have upon civilization is a story which cannot adequately or dramatically be told by historians, by antique car museums, by occasional exhibits in corners of technology museums, or by lavish but short-lived displays at world fairs. . . .

> The story is an epoch—the hero of which, the industry itself, has neither official shrine or homeland nor a Homer to dramatize and humanize the breadth and scope of its trials and glories nor a Nostradamus to foretell its future. . . .

> The National Institute of Automotive Science and Industry is conceived as being the Homer and the Nostradamus of the automotive industry, dramatizing, humanizing, and foretelling the epic story of the industry's beneficial impact upon civilization, past, present and future. . . .

> Flint, where the industry can trace its earliest beginnings and from where it drew its nourishment, shall be its homeland, the site of its shrine, its showcase for all the world.

This was indeed a dream of great proportions. Its origin goes back to 1969, when Harding Mott, president of the Mott Foundation, proposed that a national automotive hall of fame be developed in Flint. In December of that year, a board of directors was organized and the name reserved. Saul Siegel, president of the newly created Flint Area Conference, Incorporated (FACI), became the primary spokesman for the project. Supported by an announcement by the Michigan Tourist Association that the proposed hall of fame would be one of the half-dozen top attractions in the Midwest, the eminent architect Minoru Yamasaki (the architect for the World Trade Center in New York) was hired to develop a plan.

Yamasaki selected a downtown site, literally in the middle of the Flint River. He proposed to dredge a new channel that would place the hall of fame on an island in the river. The plan required the relocation of water, sewer, telephone, gas, and electric lines as well as the demolition and replacement of a bridge, rerouting of traffic, and the replacement of parking areas. An engineering study estimated that the initial site work would cost $6 million; land acquisition would cost another $6 million. On top of this $12-million investment, development costs were projected at another $100 million.

(continued on page 306)

EXHIBIT 85 (cont'd)

This project initially received tremendous publicity and raised the expectations of many citizens and community leaders. There was however one problem with this plan. In retrospect it seemed almost unbelievable, but no one had stopped to consider how this dream would be financed or how it would be implemented. As the costs and implementation problems began to surface, the glamor surrounding this dream began to fade. In early 1972, the entire project was placed on the back burner while community leaders concentrated on a more feasible project— relocation of the University of Michigan-Flint campus to the same site along the Flint River where Yamasaki had proposed to place the hall of fame.

In late 1973 the climate appeared right to revive the concept of an automotive hall of fame; this time called an "autocade." It was estimated that this project would cost $23 million and would be financed in part by tax-free municipal bonds and would be operated by a redevelopment corporation formed by local citizens. It was estimated that nearly a million visitors would be lured off the freeways to visit this testament to the auto industry. This time, major questions about the feasibility of this project were overcome by the 1974 economic recession. It was hard to sell the dream of an "autocade" when more than 15 percent of the local work force was unemployed.

Throughout this period, Flint's principal dreamer was Saul Siegel. Siegel described himself as "a pseudo urban philosopher." He explained, "I wouldn't say I am a salesman, I am an organization technician. . . . I don't feel I'm a drum beater. I feel I am dealing with real things."

In Siegel's words, there was a need to "bring a renaissance of spirit to the Flint metropolitan area." Without a renaissance of spirit, he contended, there could be no renaissance of brick and mortar. Spirit in this case meant dreams, and Siegel was Flint's "dream-beater." In addition to the hall of fame, Siegel's limitless energies were directed at saving downtown hotels from being closed, urging private developers to construct new hotels, persuading owners of department stores not to leave downtown for the suburbs, and keeping all segments of the community up to date on downtown projects.

When events and the reality of implementation made one dream appear to be unfeasible, Siegel quickly moved on to another. The dream was not rejected; it was merely filed for reconsideration at a more favorable time. In looking back at the hall of fame idea, Siegel said, "The Yamasaki concept was tremendous, but we got racing our motor and got ahead of some of the other steps that come in a project like this. We're proceeding, retracing our position, but it still exists as a tremendous opportunity."

Many people in Flint derided Siegel's dreams. Some pointed to the "hall of shame" as a gross distortion of Flint's development priorities. When Flint's "urban philosopher" moved his family to a wealthy suburb ten miles from Flint because of the city's inadequate school system, many felt that the hypocrisy of downtown interests had reached its zenith. On the other hand, there were many others who defended the role of dreams and dreamers in the development of a city. As the director of the Manufacturers Association pointed out, "Without dreams, a city has no sense of what it could become."

merce, the Flint Area Conference, and the Downtown Merchants Association) into two groups. One group would be exclusively concerned with lobbying for the collective interests of its members. Thus, if this group felt that the adoption of a new ordinance by the City Council would be detrimental to private development, its collective point of view could be expressed openly and forcefully. The other group would work with city government and other public organizations to plan and implement development projects. In addition to raising revenue and preparing development plans in cooperation with local-government agencies, the latter group would be capable of "rolling up its sleeves" and making sure that the city's dreams were converted into reality.

Consolidating existing civic associations in Flint would also address a second area of opportunity: providing private organizations with the staff needed to maximize their influence within the decision-making process at city hall. Currently, civic organizations are inadequately staffed; in many cases staff members are not employed full time.

Development of a community improvement council represents a third area of opportunity. This council would consist of a broad spectrum of private interests, ranging from General Motors to the United Auto Workers, and would be funded by sources independent of government. It would be responsible for completing independent evaluations of county and city government performance as well as the performance of other public organizations. The development and application of criteria and standards of performance (such as the ones presented in this book) would enable this council to identify a full range of opportunities to improve the performance of Flint's government institutions. The council would be in an independent position to submit improvement proposals to government officials directly or through the news media. Most important, an independent, privately based council would have the power and position

to ensure that some of these improvements were implemented.

The development of a personnel interchange program between local government and private businesses in the Flint area represents a fourth area of opportunity. An interchange program that would allow private-sector managers to work temporarily for the city of Flint would increase private corporations' understanding of public issues while at the same time improving the performance of city government. In addition, government employees could provide private organizations with new perspectives on the way they conduct their businesses. In the absence of an exchange program, the city should continue to use task forces that, on a short-term basis, capitalize on the specific skills and expertise of private institutions and their personnel.

A fifth opportunity involves an expanded role for Flint's universities. Beyond the active involvement of individual professors and administrators at the University of Michigan–Flint, university involvement could be further expanded and improved. The General Motors Institute, in particular, represents an important, and as yet untapped, resource. City-government officials should identify ways in which the resources represented by all educational institutions in the Flint area could be applied more directly to the removal of barriers impeding improved performance.

Finally, city officials should develop an information-exchange program that would ensure that private interests, individuals, and government officials have a common understanding of the facts and trends affecting the Flint community. Representatives of private interests and government officials should develop a systematic means of exchanging information about community problems and opportunities to resolve them. Establishing a common base of information should reduce the potential for conflict and enhance the potential for cooperation.

CHAPTER 15

The Judiciary

The habit of bringing to The Court claims that belong in the political arena is not the less powerful because it is deeply illegitimate. . . . The Court should refer many of these issues to the political process even though that will anger groups that have been taught to hope for easier, more authoritarian solutions.

Robert Bork
Solicitor General of the United States

Our country has sustained far greater injury from judicial timidity in vindicating citizens' fundamental rights than from judicial courage in protecting them.

Arthur Goldberg
Justice of the United States Supreme Court

In 1921 Benjamin Cardozo, addressing a group of Yale University students, made what was then a startling admission: "I take judge-made law as one of the existing realities of life." By acknowledging that judges, through their decisions, exercise a legislative function, Cardozo formally recognized a reality that had been hotly debated for decades.

Today, more than half a century later, a new and equally intense debate surrounds the issue of appropriate judicial responsibility. Taking as a given Cardozo's view of judges as legislators, controversy now centers on the role of judges as administrators. The question at issue is the extent to which judges have assumed management prerogatives and responsibilities that in a representative democracy should be exercised by elected and appointed executives. Reacting to the advent of what Harvard sociologist Nathan

Glazer described as "the imperial judiciary,"[1] a growing number of people are wondering whether judges with limited time, staff, and, in many cases, experience should assume responsibility for making administrative decisions on complex social and technical issues.

Defenders of judicial intervention in the arena of public management point out that the court has been forced to fill a vacuum created by legislators and executives who have failed to correct inequities. If legislators or local-government executives refuse to act to resolve a social or environmental problem, defenders of judicial activism ask, why shouldn't the court step in as the "manager of last resort"?

The necessity of judicial intervention in the management of local government can be debated, but its existence can no longer be denied. Increasingly, judges are telling local governments not only what they should do but how they should do it.

In Mobile, Alabama's second-largest city, a U.S. district judge ordered the city to abolish its sixty-four-year-old commission form of government and replace it with a new form that would give black citizens a greater opportunity to be elected to the city council. Should a federal judge tell citizens and their elected government officials how to organize their local government? The mayor of Mobile did not think so. In explaining his position to the press, the mayor explained, "This is the first time that the federal government has told free people what kind of government they must have. If they can do that, they can tell you what time to go to bed and whether to have pork and beans for lunch."[2]

A similar example of judicial intervention in the management process occurred in Boston. In this case, a U.S. district judge, unhappy about South Boston High School's lack of compliance with a court-ordered desegregation plan, placed the high school in federal receivership. In effect, the judge became the principal of the school. In this capacity, he fired the principal, hired a new one, and required the Board of Education to pay the new appointee's moving costs. In addition, the judge mandated more than $100,000 in building renovations, ordered the purchase of a new piano, and directed the expansion of the school's library.[3] Reviewing this intrusion into basic management prerogatives, a cartoonist in the *Boston Herald-American* depicted a school blackboard on which was written "South Boston High School—now under new management." Below the caption was written

"There goes the judge."[4] The message was clear: a judge had decided that, in the absence of a compliant legislature and school administration, he was in the best position to administer South Boston High School.

Examples of judicial intervention in public management abound in other areas. In the field of hospital administration, a judge told Alabama's governor that for every 250 patients in the state's mental hospital there had to be 2 psychiatrists, 7 physicians, 18 nurses, 4 psychologists, and 7 social workers. In addition, the judge decreed that no more than 6 patients could be assigned to one room and that each patient had to have at least 80 square feet of space. The judge went on to establish specific procedures for patients' diets, mail privileges, and visitor rights.[5]

In the criminal justice area, a judge in St. Louis ordered city officials to improve prison conditions by meeting court-determined standards that included a designation of the proper number of inmates for the city's jail (a limit of 228), the number of staff required to supervise prisoners (at least 2 correctional officials per floor during every 24 hours), the natu.e and amount of required recreational facilities, and the quality of prisoners' diets.[6]

In short, whether one agrees with Robert Bork, who urges a less active judiciary, or with former Supreme Court Justice Arthur Goldberg, who advocates the opposite viewpoint, we must recognize that judges today are making decisions that political leaders and municipal managers were elected and hired to make. Proceeding from the assumption that judicial intervention in the management process is a reality, our purpose is to examine how this intervention affects the performance of a local government.

Impact on Process and Performance

In our constitutional system of government, one of the functions the judiciary performs is that of a referee. In a sporting event, the referee is responsible for ensuring

that the players and coaches play according to the rules. Referees are *not* players; players are constrained by rules as interpreted by referees. Similarly, in our system of government, appointed and elected officials (players) are constrained by laws as interpreted by judges (referees).

Obviously, the role of the judicial branch of government in our political and legal system is more complex than that of a referee in an athletic contest. Nevertheless, just as a referee affects how a sporting event is played and may in some cases determine its outcome, judges may determine how a local government is managed and ultimately its performance.

Accordingly, we are concerned in this chapter with the way in which judicial interpretations of federal and state laws as well as local charters and ordinances affect the capacity of local-government officials to get things done. We are also concerned with the role the judiciary plays in resolving differences between the executive and legislative branches of government and with its role as an arbitrator between the executive branch and the intended beneficiaries of government programs.

The judiciary has a direct impact on the management process when court decisions dictate or restrict executive actions. A judicial decision that establishes patient-care standards for a state hospital will have a significant impact on the management of that hospital. This intrusion into the management process is far different from a judicial decision that, because a hospital has been found to provide inadequate care, directs a legislative body, a hospital board of directors, or hospital administrators to find an appropriate remedy.

Similarly, judges have a direct impact on the ability of local-government officials to get things done when their decisions determine the type of people who may be recruited or hired for critical positions, establish who can be promoted, or dictate when an employee may be terminated. Judges may also impact performance by their unwillingness to apply existing laws. For example, judges in many states have been unwilling to apply state laws that prohibit public employee strikes, thereby significantly altering

the balance between the exercise of management responsibilities and the protection of union rights.

Judges have an even greater impact on the performance of local government when they assume direct responsibility for the management of specific government functions. This generally occurs when, in the judgment of the court, a local government has failed to carry out actions imposed by previous judicial decisions. In the Boston desegregation case cited earlier, the district court judge placed the school system under federal receivership on the assumption that local-government officials could not be induced by any other means to comply with court orders. In this instance, the judge assumed the role of manager because he felt that elected and appointed officials could not (or would not) accomplish the results required by the court.

The judiciary may also impact local-government performance by the manner in which it enforces civil and criminal laws. The judiciary is responsible for adjudicating civil and criminal cases in a fair and impartial manner. By ensuring that federal, state, and local laws are enforced, the judiciary works with local-government managers to secure the safety of persons and property. The way courts deal with those accused and convicted of violating the law may have a major impact on the quality of law enforcement and the level of public safety enjoyed by community residents.

Finally, the judiciary may have an indirect impact on performance through the power it gives minority groups. When a judicial decision allows a small group of citizens to halt the construction of a freeway that a majority within the community desires, that decision has a significant impact on the ability of government officials to implement programs for which a majority holds them accountable. The success of our representative democracy depends upon an adversary political process in which dissenting voices may be heard in advance of important political or administrative decisions. Its success also depends on the ability of government to make decisions and carry out the business of government in an expeditious manner. Therefore, balancing the need to hear all citizen viewpoints against the need to act is a major challenge facing government officials. It is often up to the courts to ensure that this balance is maintained. If the courts too often and too easily enfranchise dissident groups and, in effect, give them veto power over programs designed and administered for the benefit of the majority, the process of government will become cumbersome and ineffective and performance will be poor.

Criteria for Evaluation

The following questions should help citizens understand and evaluate the impact of the judicial system on the performance of a local government.

Do judges assume legislative and executive responsibilities? Judicial activism in legislative and executive spheres creates a fundamental challenge to the basic principle of separation of powers underlying our form of representative democracy. This question, therefore, examines the extent to which judicial decisions usurp legislative and executive responsibilities, thereby making it difficult for citizens to hold elected and appointed officials accountable.

Do judges accurately identify the costs and financial consequences of their decisions? In many cases judicial decisions carry a large price tag for a local government. This question explores whether judges identify the financial consequences of their decisions, determining how these costs will be financed and by whom.

Are judicial decisions influenced by political pressure? Independence from the political process is the cornerstone of an effective and equitable judiciary.

Is the judicial system free from undue dependence on legislative and executive decisions? If the referee of a sporting event were dependent on one of the contestants for his livelihood, one might question the degree to which the referee's decisions were totally impartial. Similarly, when the judiciary is totally dependent on a legislative body (a board of supervisors or a city council) for the resources it requires to conduct necessary judicial functions, its independence may be challenged.

Do judicial decisions support law-enforcement activities? Responsibility for law enforcement is shared among all three branches of government. The legislative branch is responsible for making laws, the executive branch for enforcing them, and the judiciary for interpreting them. The judicial branch, however, shares certain specific responsibilities with the executive branch. The judiciary interprets whether appropriate law-enforcement procedures have been followed, decides whether an accused person is guilty or innocent of breaking the law, and determines the nature of penalty to be imposed for a particular infraction. Therefore, this question examines the way in which the court enforces city statutes and ordinances. To what extent do court-imposed policies and procedures affect the ability of police and other local-government agencies to do their jobs?

Does the judicial system operate efficiently? If a citizen's interaction with the judicial system is time consuming, cumbersome and unpleasant, his experience may lead to apathy and alienation from government. Moreover, the failure of the judicial system to operate efficiently and expeditiously may impede the delivery of government services and generate unnecessary costs. Accordingly, this question examines the way in which the courts are administered. Are civil and criminal cases processed as rapidly as possible? Are citizens dealt with considerately and fairly?

Conditions in Flint

The judicial system in Flint consisted of three courts: district, circuit, and probate. Because of the specialized nature of the probate court, our attention will be focused on the district and circuit courts.

The district court in Flint was essentially a municipal court with jurisdiction limited to the city of Flint. Its responsibilities covered small claims, traffic violations, and minor criminal offenses. The circuit court had jurisdiction for all of Genesee County, which included the city of Flint. This court was responsible for more serious civil and criminal matters and for issues arising from the exercise of governmental power within the city.

District court operations were funded almost entirely by the city government, although a percentage of a district-court judge's salary was paid by the state. The circuit court was funded almost entirely by the county government, with a portion of each judge's salary paid by the state. Most of the time neither the district court nor the circuit court had any measurable impact on the performance of Flint's city government. But the impact of a few decisions was significant.

Judicial assumption of executive and legislative responsibilities

In April 1973, a circuit-court judge in Flint issued a decision which, in essence, mandated that every management position in Flint's city government must be filled by an *existing* city-government employee if, in the judgment of civil service, at least two existing employees met *minimum* qualifications. Practically, this judicial ruling prevented the City Council, elected by the citizens of Flint, and the city manager, appointed by the council, from recruiting and hiring the best-qualified people to manage a $60-million business. As the case in Exhibit 86 suggests, the judge's decision in this case was both

remedial and procedural. The judge had decided that the city charter had been violated and that action should be taken to remedy this condition. Going further, the judge developed and imposed personnel procedures which he ordered the city to follow in making all future hiring and promotional decisions. Instead of requiring responsible executive and legislative officials—the City Council, the city manager, and the Civil Service Commission—to develop procedures that would clarify vague charter language, and penalizing them if they did not, the judge chose to do this himself.

This decision eliminated the possibility that managerial personnel could be hired from outside the city's personnel system. As a result, a system already far too inbred and self-serving became more so. The introduction of new skills and fresh ideas into city government by the periodic infusion of new people was no longer possible.

This decision had two additional consequences. First, it significantly enhanced the power of city employee unions, intensifying their already-close relationship with the civil service staff and further unbalancing the relationship between city unions and the city's management. Second, it contributed to public support for a total revision of the city charter. Reacting to what one newspaper reporter described as "a blatant demonstration of city union power," many citizens began to ask who was running city hall. The result of this public concern, as Chapter 10 describes, was a new city charter.

Surprisingly, few in Flint seemed concerned with the role of the judge in this case. No one examined the judge's background to determine whether he had the ability or experience to establish personnel policies and procedures for the city. Only the City Council and the city manager seemed concerned about the political and managerial implications of this decision. The city manager reacted to the decision this way: "If the court is going to substitute itself for the city's

EXHIBIT 86

Judge Orders City To Vacate Top-Management Positions

In April 1973, as a result of a lawsuit initiated by city employee unions, a circuit-court judge of Genesee County ordered the city of Flint to remove from their jobs the deputy city manager, the executive director of the Department of Community Development, and the director of building and safety inspections, and to refill the positions with other city employees according to a process defined by the court.

The genesis of this decision was a September 1972 lawsuit brought against the city, the city manager, and the Civil Service Commission by a coalition of five city unions. The unions charged that the city manager had violated the city charter by filling these positions on a provisional basis and that the Civil Service Commission had acted improperly by authorizing the positions to be permanently filled on an open competitive basis.

All managerial positions in the city were covered by the civil service section of the city charter, except for the city manager, the director of finance, the city attorney, and the city clerk. According to the charter, a vacant civil service position could be filled on a provisional basis "whenever there [were] urgent reasons," and, further, that promotions to higher civil service positions would be made "so far as practicable" from the ranks of existing employees. It was up to the Civil Service Commission to determine the "practicability" of promoting from within.

The Civil Service Commission also had determined that the three positions in question would be filled on an open competitive basis, which meant that applicants would be accepted from outside the ranks of present employees as well as

(continued)

personnel department, then the citizens of Flint cannot hold their elected representatives accountable for the performance of city government. If the city manager cannot hire the best-qualified people to fill top management positions, the council cannot hold him accountable for getting the job done."

Reacting to the city manager's statement, many pointed out that judges in Flint were accountable to the public. In theory, the election of judges was intended to guarantee public accountability. Yet, in reality, most knew that incumbent judges seldom lost an election, and as a result Flint citizens had no practical basis for holding judges accountable for their decisions.

A number of factors explain why judges in Flint were willing to assume executive as well as legislative responsibilities. The threat of adverse public reaction created no disincentive to judicial intrusions in the management process. Furthermore, cases involving employee complaints or management issues could be brought easily into the judicial system; any employee group that was not successful in advancing its position within

EXHIBIT 86 (cont'd)

from present city employees. This process usually took from three to six months to complete. As a result, the city manager and the director of public works had made provisional appointments of noncity employees to fill the positions in the interim. To remain in his job, a provisional appointee would have to be one of the top three scorers among all competitors in the civil service examination eventually given for the position. In two of the three positions affected by the decision, the incumbents had received the highest scores on the civil service exam and had already been appointed permanently.

The five city unions which had brought suit were the general employees' union, a supervisors' association representing first-line supervisors, a regional council of public employee unions, another supervisors' association which represented middle managers, and a union of assistant city attorneys from the law department. In total, these unions represented all nonuniformed city employees except department heads and the four officials appointed by the City Council.

The unions requested the court to vacate the three positions and order the Civil Service Commission to fill them from the ranks of existing city employees. In addition, they requested the court to tell the Civil Service Commission how to determine the meaning of the charter phrase "so far as practicable" in deciding how positions would be filled in the future and to determine the criteria by which "urgency" was to be determined in making a provisional appointment.

The court decision granted all of the union requests. The judge declared that the positions were to be vacated and refilled by existing city employees; that, in the future, higher-level civil-service positions should be filled by present employees if two or more employees had *minimum* qualifications; that the Civil Service Commission should review employee records to determine employees' qualifications for promotion; and, that provisional appointments should not be made to noncity employees unless the Civil Service Commission had determined that no qualified applicant was on the city payroll.

the political process could quickly initiate a lawsuit at little cost. From 1971 to 1975, city employees and their unions initiated nineteen separate lawsuits against the city of Flint. Ten years earlier, such a suit had been an extreme rarity. A final reason, not unique to Flint, may be the peculiarly American tendency to seek the resolution of problems, both political and managerial, in court. Early in the nineteenth century, Alexis de Tocqueville, in his incisive commentary on American life, observed: "Americans have a strange custom of seeking to settle any politi-cal or social problem by a lawsuit instead of using the political process, as do people in most other countries."[7] This was certainly the case in Flint.

Recognizing the costs of judicial decisions

With few exceptions, judicial rulings that affected the management process in the city of Flint had significant financial consequences. These judicial decisions came at a time when Flint was experiencing operating deficits and taxpayers were increasingly concerned about rising tax rates. In no instance did a judicial decision indicate the magnitude of the costs it would impose on Flint's city government, the manner in which these costs would be financed, or who would pay them.

In most cases, as Exhibit 86 indicates, the costs associated with judicial decisions were not insignificant. In mandating new promotion and hiring procedures for the city of Flint, the judge was indirectly increasing the costs of administering the personnel system. To implement the judicial mandate in this case required adding people and support services and thus the expenditure of additional time and money. Nowhere in the judge's decision was there any acknowledgment that the mandated personnel procedures carried with them a significant price tag. If the judge in this case wanted to administer the city's personnel system, it seems reasonable that he should have been required to take these costs into account.

Other judicial decisions also had the effect of increasing the costs of administering Flint's city government. In one case a federal judge, acting on a lawsuit brought by minority police officers against the police division, determined the promotional examinations for sergeants were culturally biased and that they discriminated against blacks. The judge ordered the city to validate this examination before using it again. Validating such an examination is a very long and costly process, requiring a thorough analysis of each of the hundreds of questions on the test as well as a statistical verification that the questions are, in fact, answered in proportions that do not show a difference in response as a function of race. In addition to the direct costs of validating the sergeants' examination, an important indirect cost was imposed by the fact that the police division was not able to fill critical management positions as they became vacant. Nowhere in the judge's decision were such costs identified or taken into consideration. No matter how desirable the

particular end may have been in this case (the assurance that black police officers would have an equal opportunity for promotion), the fact remains that significant costs were associated with achieving it. The courts, local-government officials, and the public ought to be aware of such costs at the time they are imposed by the court.

Politicization of judicial decisions

A major constraint on judicial independence in Flint was imposed by basic electoral politics. Circuit- and district-court judges were elected for staggered six-year terms. Despite the fact that incumbent judges rarely were defeated, all judges recognized the realities of the electoral process. They recognized that a few special interests, city unions in particular, had a disproportionate impact on elections in which a small percentage of registered voters actually voted.

One of the most blatant examples of the politicization of judicial decisions occurred in 1973, when a circuit-court judge voided a section of the Flint city charter and ruled that city employee unions could campaign, raise funds, and otherwise participate in the election of City Council candidates. Exhibit 87 describes the circumstances that gave this decision its political overtones.

This decision surprised and alarmed those who believed that if individuals or special-interest groups did not favor particular charter language, the appropriate course of action was to change it by a vote of the people. Despite the significant impact of this decision, it was not surprising to those who realized that the judge issuing the decision was also running for reelection. Observers of city politics knew that it was not in the judge's political interest to render a decision that threatened the interests of the city employee unions, one of the most potent political forces in the community.

The consequences of this decision were far-reaching. Removing constraints on political activity encouraged the unions to launch

EXHIBIT 87

Judge Permits City Employees To Participate in Local Elections

In July 1973, two weeks before the primary election for City Council, the Flint newspaper announced that a local judge had overturned the section of the Flint city charter that prohibited city employees from participating in city elections. City employees and their unions could now participate actively in the current election for City Council.

The charter provision which the judge overturned was an amendment passed by the voters in 1935, along with other civil-service amendments, in part to protect employees from political exploitation. This section of the charter read, in part, ". . . nor shall any employee contribute in money or in active service to the promotion of any candidate or cause appearing on the city ticket or election." This wording had stood for almost forty years, even though, at times, it had been ignored by city employees at all levels. Now, however, even this restraint was eliminated.

The lawsuit that precipitated this decision was brought by the president of the city employees union. In the lawsuit, he requested that he be allowed to participate in the council election in his ward. He charged that city officials had told him that he and other employees would be disciplined and could face criminal prosecution if they violated the charter ban on political activity. In his decision, the judge declared that "a public employee has the same right to constitutional protection as any other citizen. Public employment does not make him a second-class citizen, denied of his First Amendment rights."

At the City Council meeting following the primary elections, the council voted 5–1 to appeal the ruling of the circuit court. On November 3, just a few days before the November general election, the Michigan court of appeals handed down a ruling that the case should be heard by that court and that prior to a decision city employees would be enjoined from political activity.

At this point, the president of the union local was not concerned. He said that his union had already completed most of its political activity for this election. The union had, for the first time ever, endorsed nine council candidates and helped finance their campaign expenses.

The city attorney was pleased with the appeals court decision and said that he felt that the city had a good case for getting the charter provision reinstated. Another city administrator commented that it might be an interesting legal question but politically it really didn't matter—the damage had already been done. Six council members endorsed by the city unions won the election.

an all-out election campaign. Free to raise money and provide personal services, city unions supported a majority of the candidates elected to the City Council that took office in November 1973.

The impact of this new labor-oriented council was immediate. One of the council's first actions was to reinstate four city employees who had been fired for using city equipment and material on city time for private purposes. Within eight months there was a major turnover in top-management personnel within the city: the city manager, the finance director, the planning director, the community-development director, and a number of other city managers terminated their employment with the city. In large part, their decisions reflected a belief that the new City Council was more concerned about preserving the interest and power of the city unions than about carrying out its management responsibilities. Many traced the composition of this new City Council to the judicial decision allowing city unions to participate directly in the council election.

Judicial dependence on the City Council

The judicial system in Flint was not totally independent of the executive and legislative branches of local government. The district court was dependent on city government for its budgetary appropriations, personnel allocations, salary and fringe-benefit determinations, office space, and other support services provided to the court. Annually, the judges would come before the City Council to justify, item by item, what they intended to do with their budgets. After an appropriation was made, however, they were not legally bound to these commitments. Politically, however, they could not stray too far from their promises or they would face more difficult problems in future years. In such situations, as Exhibit 88 suggests, a certain amount of political horse trading was a natural by-product.

Judicial support for law enforcement

Improving cooperation between the courts and the executive branch in the area of law enforcement is an important objective. Achievement of this objective should be based on a mutual desire to ensure that laws are enforced in the interests of all city residents, not on a wish to trade stricter law enforcement for larger judicial budgets. As Exhibit 87 suggests, the dependence of Flint's district court on the City Council worked to undermine the check-and-balance relationship between the judicial and legislative branches of government.

The district court judges' refusal to enforce housing-code and other related city ordinances demonstrated a lack of judicial support for an important law-enforcement activity endorsed by the City Council. There were other examples of negative judicial impact on the achievement of law-enforcement objectives.[8] A comprehensive planning study produced for the City Council in 1973 showed that the administration of justice in Flint was uneven and inconsistent. This conclusion was based on an analysis of three areas: (1) sentences given to those convicted of armed robbery for the first time, (2) the amount of bail required of an armed-robbery suspect, and (3) the conviction rate by race of those accused of armed robbery. This study indicated that, in each area examined, the enforcement of existing laws discriminated against blacks. In conclusion, this study pointed out that uneven enforcement of the law had an important impact on citizens' respect for the law as well as the ability of the police to enforce it.

The relationship between conviction rates or sentences and the level of crime in a community is complex and difficult to measure. Many attorneys and law-enforcement officials argue that the failure of the courts to enforce the law is a major factor contributing to the increase in the number of people who choose to break it. In Flint, plea bargaining, reduced sentences, and lenient probation policies produced a feeling within the com-

---

EXHIBIT 88

Horse Trading with the Judges

All employees of the district court in Flint, including judges, depended on the Flint City Council for establishing salary and fringe-benefit levels. In at least one instance, this led to a little horse trading, whereby the judges agreed to try harder to enforce local ordinances in exchange for an increase in fringe benefits.

During one annual budget review, the district court judges requested additional funds from the City Council to provide the local share of a federal grant for a court-administration program and for an increase in fringe benefits for the judges. During the discussion of this request, the council asked why the court was summarily dismissing defendants that had been issued citations under the city's housing-code ordinance. Under this ordinance, city inspectors could demand that property owners remedy dangerous structural conditions, remove junk cars, or take other actions on residential properties. If the violator did not comply within a ninety-day period, a citation would be issued requiring a court appearance, and if the property owner was found guilty, he was subject to a fine. In the past, judges had dismissed these cases because of their heavy work load of criminal and civil cases, which they determined to be more important. Moreover, it appeared that some of the judges personally did not endorse the idea of issuing citations for such violations.

After a series of private discussions with the judges, the City Council agreed to appropriate the necessary funds for the court-administration program and to grant the judges the "master medical" extension on their health insurance. The judges agreed that they would take a more active role in helping the city enforce its housing code.

---

munity that was perhaps best expressed by a young black community leader: "In Flint, black ghetto kids know that there will be no serious consequence to breaking a law until they have been convicted at least three and generally four times. This gives them three free tickets. . . ."

Efficiency of the judicial system

By its own admission, the district-court system in Flint was inefficiently administered, poorly organized, and understaffed.

By any reasonable measure, it was not able to adequately handle the work load before it. Priority was given to criminal cases, thereby creating a considerable backlog of civil cases, traffic violations, and appearance tickets for the violation of other city ordinances.

Some of the district-court judges were the first to recognize these problems and advocate solutions; however, other judges did not agree. Exhibit 89 relates the frustration experienced by the presiding district-court judge, who tried unsuccessfully to institute more efficient administration for the court.

The inefficiency of the court system con-

EXHIBIT 89

District Court Judges Resist Efforts To Make Court More Efficient

In July 1974, a judge of the district court resigned his position as presiding judge because of his inability to convince his five associates to institute a program to improve the efficiency of the court system.

The district court had six judges. The position of presiding judge rotated among them on an annual basis. The presiding judge had the responsibility to supervise the administrative activities of the court.

The most recent presiding judge had taken it upon himself to attack the problem of court inefficiency. To accomplish this, he had approached the state office of criminal justice programs for a federal grant to hire a court administrator, an assignment clerk, and a secretary on an experimental basis. The cost of this program would be $56,000 a year, of which 5 percent would be provided by the city and the state.

The purpose of the grant was to eliminate the bureaucratic tangles that had plagued the court. The administrator would handle all nonjudicial responsibilities, including budget preparation, liaison work with other government units, and planning of the court work load. Because the judges now performed all these functions, hiring a court administrator would free the judges' time to hear the large backlog of criminal and civil cases.

Early in 1974 the judges approved the program and applied for funding. On the basis of the application, the state, city, and federal government made financial commitments to the program. The funding was secured and the program was about to begin when suddenly the judges voted 4–1 (presiding judge abstaining) not to accept the money. Two reasons were given for this decision: (1) the district-court building did not have room for three more persons and (2) the program was oriented toward criminal cases, while most of the court's backlog consisted of civil matters.

The presiding judge explained that criminal cases were automatically given higher priority, and that relieving problems on the criminal calendar would inevitably improve the court's performance in regard to civil suits. In addition, relieving the judges of administrative tasks would permit them to spend more time on the bench, carrying out their judicial responsibilities.

These arguments were not persuasive for a majority of the judges, who apparently felt that they could carry on their administrative tasks while also performing their judicial tasks. In frustration, the presiding judge resigned his position.

tributed to the city's inability to enforce many of its ordinances and laws. To the extent that lack of enforcement fostered more crime, the courts directly and adversely affected city-government performance in achieving law-enforcement objectives. A further cost of the court's inefficiency was its negative effect on public attitudes toward the law, toward law-enforcement officials, and toward government in general.

There were many explanations for court inefficiency in Flint. One of the most im-portant was that judicial salaries did not create sufficient incentive for well-qualified people to seek these positions. Judges in Flint were significantly underpaid compared to attorneys in the private sector. This fact discouraged many of the best-qualified attorneys from seeking judgeships. Two of Flint's most competent judges resigned their positions in the early 1970s, explaining that they could no longer afford to serve the public in their current positions.

Opportunities for Improvement

Given the importance of an independent judiciary, opportunities for judges to help government officials get things done must ultimately be recognized by judges themselves. However, citizens of a community have access to several areas of opportunity which should be examined. Perhaps the most important of these involves intensifying public awareness of the impact of judicial decisions on the management and performance of local government.

Judges are aware of the power of public opinion and sensitive to its potential. If the public understands the consequences of judicial intervention in the management process and begins to demand that judges stop usurping the prerogatives of elected and appointed government officials, judges may think more carefully before intruding into these areas. At minimum, judges should be encouraged to provide sufficient time for elected and appointed officials to implement court-ordered remedies, so that these officials can be held accountable for the accomplishment of prescribed results. Moreover, citizens should demand that judges identify both the costs of court-imposed remedies and who will pay them.

A second area of opportunity concerns the independence of the judicial system from the executive and legislative branches of government. In 1974, Michigan's governor and the State Supreme Court advocated a major reform of the judicial system. The governor's proposal called for the creation of a totally independent court system funded entirely by the state. Such a system would eliminate the dependence of local courts on the resource-allocation decisions of city councils and local executives, thus allowing the judicial system to operate as a completely independent branch of local government. Overcoming the resistance to this badly needed reform represents a major opportunity to strengthen the role of the judicial system and its positive effect on the performance of local government.

The third major area concerns the need to develop incentives that would persuade able attorneys to seek positions as district- and circuit-court judges. Perhaps the most important incentive would be created by changing the manner in which judges are selected. In Michigan, the direct election of judges extends from district and circuit courts to the State Supreme Court. Consideration should be given to whether this method is the best way of choosing judges. In many states, judges are not chosen by popular election. Missouri, for example, uses a merit selection plan in which judges are selected from a list of qualified applicants nominated by the state bar association. Although the merit system has its detractors, the appointive process insulates judges from political pressures that may adversely affect how they do their jobs. This and other alternatives to the direct election of judges should be explored.

Changing the selection process, however, may not provide sufficient incentive to attract and retain the best-qualified individuals. Until judicial salaries are made relatively competitive with those in the private sector, the most able attorneys will not seek judicial positions. In Flint, the fact that private attorneys made from $15,000 to $20,000 more than local judges was advanced as the most important reason why the best attorneys did not seek judicial positions. Although raising judicial salaries would by no means guarantee that attorneys would want to leave their private law practices to serve in government, it could provide a significant incentive.

Few citizens understand how to determine whether their judges exercise a positive or a negative impact on their community. Without such knowledge, selecting a judge is an arbitrary process. This is true whether the judge is elected or appointed. Performance standards should be developed and used to measure the efficiency and effectiveness of the judicial system and to assess the relationship between court decisions, law enforce-

ment, and public safety.

Employing a professional court administrator would significantly improve the impact of the judicial system on government performance. In view of the growing administrative work load imposed on judges, the court administrator should have the skills required to manage an increasingly complex legal and judicial system.

Finally, elected and appointed local-government officials should make use of judicial decisions in supporting management initiatives. Using existing information services to examine how courts in other communities have resolved analogous issues may be of considerable help in accomplishing desired changes. For example, if a judge in a comparable jurisdiction decides that certain testing procedures are unlawful, local-government officials can apply this decision to conditions in their own community. This technique may be especially helpful in the area of labor relations, where judicial decisions concerning the relationship between management prerogatives and union rights can have a significant impact on government performance.

Part III
Getting from here to there

In Parts I and II, our purpose was to provide readers with a practical tool for identifying opportunities to improve the performance of a local government. As a tool, the analytical framework is both flexible and adaptable to the unique conditions of any local government. But it will accomplish nothing by itself. Its utility depends on the ability and motivation of its users.

Identifying opportunities without doing something about them is like considering various ways to spend a vacation and then staying at home. Given a list of specific opportunities, the critical question is: How do we get from here to there? Part III addresses this question.

Chapter 16 examines the steps involved in converting opportunities into realistic action plans. This chapter should provide legislators, managers, community leaders, and citizens with a better understanding of how to determine which opportunities are practical, given resource limitations, and how to convert these opportunities into strategies that will produce desired results.

Chapter 17 is based on the proposition that, regardless of the undertaking—raising children, playing football, managing a local government—there is no single recipe for getting the job done. Producing results depends on people, and there may be as many ways to achieve a desired result as there are people. However, we have found that certain principles and practical guidelines can be helpful to those who are trying to convert good intentions into actual results in local government. This chapter discusses these guidelines.

Chapter 18 is a case study of the efforts made between 1971 and 1974 to improve the internal management tools used by Flint's city government. The study is focused primarily on changes made in the city's budgeting and management-control systems. This chapter illustrates the guidelines presented in the previous chapter by describing what happened when they were (or were not) followed in an actual situation.

Chapter 19 is a case study of the implementation of a major community-improvement program in Flint—the development of an urban campus for the University of Michigan–Flint. This case is also used to demonstrate, in a different context, the guidelines described in Chapter 17.

CHAPTER 16

Deciding What To Do and How To Do It

The problem is where to take the first bite of the elephant.
Anonymous

To get anything done you must answer the "What should we do Monday morning?" question.
John Garrity
McKinsey & Co.

Deciding what to do to strengthen the management process in a local government is very much like deciding where to take the first bite of an elephant. The problem is so massive and the range of potential actions so vast that it is easy to become immobilized by the immensity of the decision. Yet, if we are to manage local governments for improved performance, paralysis must give way to action.

In considering ways to strengthen the management process and thereby improve performance, public officials, civic and community leaders, and interested citizens face a fundamental management problem: that of deciding how to convert opportunities into plans that can be implemented successfully with available resources. This chapter addresses that problem. It focuses on the specific steps that should be taken to convert the kind of improvement opportunities identified in Part II into action plans that can be carried out successfully with limited resources. This chapter provides an answer to the "What should we do Monday morning?" question.

Suppose that you have just been elected to serve a four-year term as the mayor of Flint, Michigan. You campaigned on a platform that stressed the need to reduce the level of crime, eliminate environmental pollution, develop adequate housing for low-income families, improve the quality of public transportation, and, above all, make city government more efficient and responsive—all without raising taxes. You must now deliver on these promises.

During your first week in office, you instruct your newly appointed staff to prepare a two-part plan that will guide your administration's actions and decisions during the next four years. The first part should identify specific programs and projects designed to meet identified needs in transportation, housing, health, environmental quality, public safety, and other community conditions. The second part should describe how these programs and projects can be implemented in ways that will achieve maximum benefits at the lowest cost to the taxpayer. (You refer to this part as "improvements in the management process.") You instruct your staff to pay particular attention to the changes that will be needed in the budgeting and management-information systems, the way in which municipal managers are promoted and compensated, and the balance between management prerogatives and employee union rights.

The bulk of this chapter is focused on the specific steps that you and your staff decide to take in developing the second part of your four-year plan: improving the management process.

Step 1: Identifying opportunities

During your campaign, you compiled a list of actions that you would take as mayor to improve the management process. Some of these actions were suggested by the people you encountered in your campaign and others by your staff. Despite this advance preparation, your first thought as you settle into the mayor's large leather chair is: "Help! There's so much to be done; how in heaven's name am I going to do it?" After considerable thought, you decide that the first step is to develop a comprehensive list of opportunities for improving the way the city conducts its business, organized in a way that will help you and the City Council decide what to do.

The following morning, you ask your staff to prepare such a list of opportunities. You want the analysis to be comprehensive; that is, you want all of the factors that affect the management process to be thoroughly examined. You also tell your staff to look at the causes behind the conditions they find and to estimate the consequences if present conditions are not changed. If you understand the causes of undesirable conditions, you will be able to develop precise and practical strategies for changing them and identify the benefits that can be derived from making changes. This knowledge can help you sell your program of change to the public, the press, and the City Council.

Three weeks later your staff returns with a completed analysis. *Note: The formality and length of such an analysis will depend on the purpose it is intended to serve and the time available to prepare it. Flint's mayor, in our example, will make this a formal process using both staff and outside consultants. After all, he is developing an action program that will affect his record of performance during his four years in office.*

Step 2: Determining responsibility

Having identified a number of ways to improve the management process, you are surprised to find that many of them are not in your power to implement. You discover that many individuals and interest groups can affect the performance of the local government you have been elected to serve. These range from federal and state government officials to civic and political organizations.

Reviewing the list of opportunities, you are most concerned about those that, as mayor, you can do something about, either directly or indirectly. By "indirectly" you recognize that successfully taking advantage of certain opportunities will depend on the cooperation of other individuals, institutions, and government bodies. Accordingly, you ask your staff to indicate the nature of the mayor's responsibility for each opportunity to strengthen the management process. Exhibit 90 shows how such an analysis might look. In this exhibit, the mayor's responsibility for doing something about each opportunity is rated as *direct, indirect,* or *none.* For example, the mayor would be directly responsible for implementing a management-training program, but would have to work with the city's retirement board, City Council, and city unions in order to develop a program to improve the retirement system. The mayor would have no responsibility for improving municipal accounting, auditing, and reporting standards; these are determined at state and national levels by finance and accounting professional organizations.

EXHIBIT 90

Determining Responsibility for Improvement Opportunities

OPPORTUNITIES	RESPONSIBILITY	OTHER PARTICIPANTS
INTERNAL FACTORS		
Municipal managers		
Institute a management-training program	Direct	
Institute an active recruiting program for management personnel	Direct	
Develop management-interchange program with private industry	Indirect	Private business leaders
Develop a "privatization" program for city services	Indirect	City Council, city unions, private business leaders
Implement a management-compensation program	Direct	
Municipal employees		
Establish a personnel department	Direct	
Extricate management employees from union membership	Indirect	City unions
Institute a career-ladder program	Direct	
Assign responsibility for labor relations to a professional administrator	Direct	
Develop a grievance-reporting system	Direct	
Financial practices		
Update and revise municipal accounting, auditing, and reporting standards	None	
Improve the management of the city's retirement system	Indirect	City retirement board, City Council, city unions
Complete an analysis of the city's current and projected financial condition	Direct	
Simplify and clarify financial-reporting information	Direct	

(continued on page 328)

EXHIBIT 90 (cont'd)

OPPORTUNITIES	RESPONSIBILITY	OTHER PARTICIPANTS
EXTERNAL FACTORS		
Intergovernmental relationships		
Expand revenue-sharing programs at state and federal level	None	
Simplify federal program rules, regulations, and procedures	None	
Reduce the number of special districts	Indirect	City Council, County Board of Commissioners, other local governments, state and federal legislative representatives
Judicial system		
Increase public awareness of the administrative implications of judicial decisions	Indirect	News media, City Council
Develop state financing of judicial system	None	
Eliminate election of judges	None	
Hire a manager to administer court system	Indirect	Judges, City Council
News media		
Make news media more aware of errors	Direct	
Ensure news media access to meetings and personnel	Direct	
Expand investigative reporting	None	
Establish a community-information section in newspaper	Indirect	Newspaper, City Council
Citizen involvement		
Increase voter registration and turnout	Indirect	City Clerk, other elected officials, news media
Improve the quality and quantity of information available about city services and decisions	Direct	
Strengthen administrative support for citizen involvement	Direct	

As mayor, you know that just because the press and other private-interest groups have been identified as key participants in taking advantage of a particular opportunity does not mean that they will accept this responsibility. From years of political experience, you know that the development of specific action plans must involve efforts to build coalitions. You know that successful implementation will depend on your ability to persuade other individuals and interest groups that they should participate in cooperative efforts to improve local-government performance.

Step 3: Ordering opportunities according to their impact on performance

Having identified opportunities for which the mayor is responsible, either directly or indirectly, you next ask your staff to place them in priority order on the basis of their potential impact on performance. In completing this step, they should answer the simple but important question "So what?" In other words, if the mayor, working with the City Council, is successful in doing something about an opportunity, what impact will that have on the management process? To keep this analysis as simple as possible, you instruct your staff to group opportunities into three priority categories according to their potential impact on performance. Exhibit 91 illustrates the final product.

Note: It is easier to group opportunities in categories than to place them in sequential order. The number and designation of categories are not important. A five-point scale ranging from significant to insignificant, or even a two-point scale (major and minor), could prove adequate for purposes of this analysis.

Step 4: Reordering priorities on the basis of available resources

Reviewing your staff's analysis, you cast your eye down the prioritized list of oppor-

tunities. You immediately recognize that, given limitations on available resources, many of the identified opportunities cannot be implemented. You know that time, energy, manpower, materials, personal capabilities, and, of course, money are limited, and that power and authority are constrained. As a longtime political combatant, you know that you cannot fight every battle in town. There is only so much ammunition in your political arsenal and there are only so many resources in your budget. Therefore, you must select your targets carefully. You must distinguish between what is *desirable* and what is *doable.*

In view of this necessity, you work with your staff to reorder the list of opportunities based on your administration's ability to implement them. Exhibit 92 presents the results of this reordering. In many cases, opportunities that received a high ranking on a scale of desirability (establishing a personnel department or implementing a program to contract with the private sector for the provision of municipal services) received a lower ranking on a scale of doability. Conversely, certain opportunities considered relatively less desirable (such as instituting a career-ladder program) receive a higher ranking when the primary consideration is your ability as mayor to implement them with available resources.

Step 5: Developing an action plan

Now that you have a final list of opportunities to improve the management process, you ask your staff to convert those in the first category (those designated "most significant" on the doable list) into specific action plans. Each action plan should answer the following questions. What objectives are to be achieved? When are they to be achieved? What results will be produced? What resources will be required to produce these results? Where will these resources be found? Who will be held accountable for converting resources into results?

The importance of this final step cannot be

EXHIBIT 91

Ordering Identified Opportunities According to Their Potential Impact on the Management Process

1. SIGNIFICANT IMPACT

Factor	*Opportunity*
Municipal managers	Institute a management-training program
Municipal managers	Institute a privatization of services program
Municipal managers	Develop a management-compensation program
Municipal employees	Establish a personnel department
Municipal employees	Extract managers from municipal employee unions
Financial practices	Improve the management of city's retirement system
Intergovernmental relationships	Simplify federal program rules, regulations, and procedures
News media	Ensure that the news media have access to meetings and personnel
Citizen involvement	Increase voter registration and turnout

2. MODERATE IMPACT

Factor	*Opportunity*
Municipal managers	Develop a management-interchange program
Municipal employees	Institute a career-ladder program
Financial practices	Improve understanding of city's current and projected financial condition

(continued)

overemphasized. The value of all the preceding steps depends on the quality of this last one. Identifying opportunities, determining responsibility, assessing limitations on resources, and developing priorities are little more than interesting exercises unless they add up to a plan that can translated into action. Exhibit 93 presents, as an illustration, an action plan for implementing one opportunity: the development of a management-training program.

The mayor in our scenario was correct in emphasizing the difficulty as well as the importance of distinguishing what is doable from what is desirable. There is an old Dutch proverb that says, "He who has choice, has trouble." As individuals, students, or parents, we continually face the reality of choice, whether it involves the right person to marry, the best job to take, or the appropriate life style to lead. Making choices is no less difficult for those attempting to improve

EXHIBIT 91 (cont'd)

2. MODERATE IMPACT (cont'd)

Factor	Opportunity
Financial practices	Simplify and clarify financial reporting
Intergovernmental relationships	Reduce number of special districts
Judicial system	Increase citizen awareness of the administrative implications of judicial decisions
News media	Establish community-information section in newspaper
Citizen involvement	Improve information available about city services
Citizen involvement	Strengthen administrative support for citizen-involvement activities

3. MINOR IMPACT

Factor	Opportunity
Municipal employees	Develop central grievance-reporting system
Financial practices	Update and revise municipal accounting, auditing, and reporting standards
Judiciary	Eliminate election of judges
Judiciary	Hire a manager to administer court system
News media	Make the news media aware of errors

the performance of a local government; in fact, it may be more difficult because of the environment in which local officials operate. Politicians, stimulated by constituent pressures and motivated by a desire to get something done in a hurry, are subject to a natural temptation to promise more than they can deliver. Like children surveying the merchandise in a candy store, political leaders often find it difficult to accept the fact that there simply isn't enough money to buy everything.

Recognizing the obligation to make difficult choices is not the same as actually making them in a responsible manner. As Elliot Richardson points out in his book *The Creative Balance,* "Realism in facing the necessity for choice must be matched by improvement in our method of exercising it."[1]

This chapter has addressed the methodology of making choices. One element of this methodology bears repeating: a decision

EXHIBIT 92

Reordering Opportunities on the Basis of Available Resources

1. SIGNIFICANT IMPACT

Desirability

Institute a management-training program

Institute a privatization program

Develop a management-compensation program

Establish a personnel department

Extract managers from municipal employee unions

Improve the management of city's retirement system

Simplify federal program rules, regulations, and procedures

Ensure that the press has access to meetings and personnel

Increase voter registration and turnout

Doability

Institute a management-training program

Ensure that the press has access to meetings and personnel

Develop a management-interchange program

Institute a career-ladder program

Increase citizen awareness of the administrative implications of judicial decisions

Improve information available about city services

Strengthen administrative support for citizen-involvement activities

Develop central grievance-reporting system

Make the press aware of errors

2. MODERATE IMPACT

Desirability

Develop a management-interchange program

Institute a career-ladder program

Improve understanding of city's current and projected financial condition

Simplify and clarify financial reporting

Reduce number of special districts

Increase citizen awareness of the administrative implications of judicial decisions

Doability

Develop a management-compensation program

Establish a personnel department

Improve the management of city's retirement system

Increase voter registration and turnout

Improve understanding of city's current and projected financial condition

Simplify and clarify financial reporting

(continued)

EXHIBIT 92 (cont'd)

2. MODERATE IMPACT (cont'd)

Desirability	*Doability*
Establish community-information section in newspaper	Establish community-information section in newspaper
Improve information available about city services	
Strengthen administrative support for citizen-involvement activities	

3. MINOR IMPACT

Desirability	*Doability*
Develop central grievance-reporting system	Institute a privatization program
Update and revise municipal accounting, auditing, and reporting standards	Extract managers from municipal employee unions
Improve public awareness of who spends local tax dollars	Simplify federal program rules, regulations, and procedures
Eliminate election of judges	Reduce number of special districts
Hire a manager to administer court system	Update and revise municipal accounting, auditing, and reporting standards
Make the press aware of errors	Eliminate election of judges
	Hire a manager to administer court system

about what to do cannot be divorced from considerations of how to do it. Deciding to vacation in Acapulco makes little sense if we do not consider how we are going to get there and who will pay for our trip. Similarly, a decision to develop a downtown mall or change the city's budget system will have little value if we do not consider the steps required to complete it, how much it will cost, who will be responsible, and when it will be finished.

The development of a plan that specifies how to get from here to there is valuable, however, only if the journey is completed successfully. Therefore, we now turn to the subject of how to implement an action plan.

EXHIBIT 93

Action Plan—Management-Training Program

Purpose
Institute a management-training program for middle- and upper-management personnel.

Objectives
By June 1, 1978, management personnel will be more aware of and better able to carry out their management (as opposed to technical) responsibilities.

Results
All middle- and upper-management personnel shall successfully complete six days of management training over the next twenty-four months.

Estimated cost
Total cost for 100 people: $60,000 (plus indirect cost of time away from job). Cost per person: $600.

Responsibility
Personnel director.

Implementation
Managers will participate in two three-day seminars approximately two months apart at the local graduate school of business. Seminars will be conducted by experienced personnel using the case method. Case material will be selected from city government as well as private business. Attendees will be mixed with private-management personnel and city personnel from other agencies and departments.

Potential problems
Scheduling of managers away from their jobs.

CHAPTER 17

Guidelines for Achieving Desired Results

The best plan is only a plan; that is, good intentions, unless it degenerates into work.
Peter Drucker

Good intentions aren't worth a damn unless they are converted to good results.
Bill Donaldson
City Manager of Cincinnati

The rhetoric of change is meaningless without the reality of change. As Bill Donaldson, the innovative city manager of Cincinnati, correctly suggests, the ability to convert rhetoric into results is the primary characteristic of an able manager. Some public as well as private managers can develop and present action plans with force and precision, but cannot implement them. Other managers find it difficult to decide what to do, but if given a desired destination have the capacity to get there. The best managers can do both; they are skilled in deciding what to do and adept at getting it done.

The critical question, then, is this: can you teach others how to get things done? Can you capture and communicate management skills? On the basis of examples of good management and observations of good managers, is it possible to instruct others how to produce results?

The answer, quite simply, is no. Whether the activity at hand is raising children, cultivating a garden, or managing a local government, it is impossible to prescribe a formula that, if followed, will in every instance guarantee desired results. In the last analysis, skill in doing is best learned by doing.

Despite this caveat, principles and guidelines extracted from practical experience can be extremely useful to those involved in the process of getting things done in and through local governments. The guidelines presented in this chapter represent a distillation of the authors' experiences as well as the experiences of a number of local-government practitioners throughout the country. Each guideline has a purpose and a primary audience. Certain guidelines, such as "achieving a spirit of due process" and "knowing when to compromise," are directed primarily at elected and appointed public officials—mayors, council members, county executives, city managers, and department heads. Other guidelines are as appropriate to private-interest groups who are trying to influence public decisions as they are to public officials who are responsible for making them. These guidelines include "understanding the status quo," "recognizing pow-

335

er where it exists," and "doing your homework." Other guidelines, such as "being a squeaky wheel," are intended primarily for private citizens who are engaged in efforts to influence public decisions. In total, these guidelines comprise a spectrum from which one may select those that are most useful and relevant to the specific conditions and circumstances of a particular local government.

Understanding the status quo

To achieve a desired change, it is important—indeed, imperative—to understand the reasons for and the beneficiaries of the conditions you are trying to change. Whether or not they are clear on the surface, there are sure to be compelling reasons why policies, procedures, and programs exist. Rarely is the status quo without justification or historical foundation. Failure to understand why current conditions exist may jeopardize the ability to change them.

There are important reasons why this guideline, as obvious as it may seem, is often neglected. One is the fact that government officials, private leaders, and other reformers become so convinced of the value of their proposed changes that they forget that the conditions they are trying to change, however absurd they may seem, are sure to have equally committed supporters. For example, when political reformers were advocating the installation of civil-service systems, they saw clear reasons why the political spoils system had to be eliminated in the interests of good government. Today, local-government officials are attempting to reform now-antiquated civil-service systems because they believe that the old political spoils system has been replaced by a bureaucratic spoils system in which government employees are insulated from public accountability. Despite mounting evidence in support of this conclusion, proponents of civil-service reform will be better prepared to deal with those who do not share their views

if they thoroughly understand the historical basis of civil service and the motives of those who benefit from its continuation.

Moreover, it takes time to understand why current conditions exist, and one of the scarcest resources available to elected and appointed officials is time. Government officials attempting to reform civil service might argue that there simply is not sufficient time to understand all the reasons behind the system; more important to them are the day-to-day management problems it creates. A sense of urgency creates an incentive to act immediately. Yet acting without taking into account the causes of existing conditions rarely conserves time in the long run. In fact, precipitous actions often result in wasteful expenditures of time and may actually impede the achievement of desired results.

Recognizing power where it exists

Getting a city or county to do something often requires the interaction and cooperation of many different individuals, institutions, and community groups. Simply stated, achieving a desired change may depend on the ability to put together the right coalition. Who has power (the capacity to make things happen)? How can that power be used most effectively? The answers to these questions provide the basis for bringing together individuals who are capable of getting things done. In many cases the right coalition may include strange bedfellows. Nevertheless, the mix of people supporting a common objective should not be the primary consideration. Momentary philosophical or personal discomfort can be more than offset by the achievement of a desired outcome.

This guideline is often abandoned or, worse, never even considered, because reformers are not likely to be openminded about the possibility of working with other factions that have the power to bring about change. For example, union leaders can be extremely influential in helping municipal managers accomplish desired results outside of the collective-bargaining context. Yet it is not uncommon to find that county executives or city managers are adamant in their refusal to discuss the value of conducting joint efforts with union leaders. This kind of bureaucratic myopia can adversely affect both the management-union relationship and management effectiveness.

The "I wouldn't work with him if he were the last person on earth" attitude is a barrier to improved performance in all organizations. It is potentially a greater problem in a local government, however, because government employees at all levels have few positive incentives to overcome their personal bias and participate in joint efforts to strengthen the management process and thereby improve performance. The lack of performance standards and the inability to reward individuals for their contribution to better performance (combined with the near-impossibility of firing anyone for lack of performance) allow individuals to place personal pique above needs for cooperation.

Finally, some individuals or groups who possess considerable power are not included in coalition-building efforts because their interests are not accurately interpreted. In many cases, people who have no personal stake in a particular issue may be willing to use their power to achieve a desired result in order to obtain an IOU for support on future issues in which they have a direct interest. On the other hand, if these individuals or groups are not consulted, they may not only withhold their support but even oppose an effort to achieve change in order to demonstrate their power and vent their unhappiness at being ignored.

Creating a sense of due process

This guideline recognizes a fundamental principle of public decision making: the way in which a decision is made often affects the ability to implement it successfully. No matter how much a particular change is needed or desired, efforts to achieve it may be severely undermined if those affected by the proposed change do not perceive that the decision-making process is fair. Including those affected by a decision in the process of making it is what we mean by *due process*.

Giving people an opportunity to be heard cannot be a last-minute or after-the-fact exercise. If a mayor, county executive, or city manager is known to have a closed mind on a particular issue, the process of seeking the views of others will be seen as an attempt to placate potential opposition, not as an honest effort to obtain the reactions of those with different opinions. The result may well be an increase, not a reduction, in opposition to the final decision.

It may be argued that incorporating due process into decision making squanders a top-level manager or political leader's most valuable resource—time. This may be true. It takes time to include people in the decision-making process. However, it should be pointed out that due process does not mean that everyone's view is sought on every issue. If this were the case, little would be accomplished. The successful application of this guideline demands the ability to identify decisions that are likely to generate major opposition or dissent. Due process is crucial only in regard to issues whose final resolution will create clear "winners" and "losers." As a rule, such issues arise with relative infrequency.

Many public officials are hesitant to provide for due process because they are afraid that, once the process of dissent has been established, their freedom to make decisions will be curtailed. In other words, once the genie of participation is out of the bottle, it will never be recaptured or contained. While this is certainly a risk, it may not be so costly as the risk of being tagged as one who believes, "I have the only right answer." Public officials who autocratically decide everything themselves often find that those upon whom successful implementation depends have little enthusiasm for their tasks. Conversely, public officials who try to turn every decision into a popularity contest accomplish little. Finding an appropriate balance between these two extremes is a difficult challenge for elected and appointed government managers.

Successfully meeting this challenge has three important benefits. First, it will ensure that the best cases are made for all points of view. For example, a city council that is attempting to decide whether to construct a new convention center in an area adjacent to a predominantly residential neighborhood will probably find that the best case against the center will be made by those residents who are immediately affected by it. Conversely, business and commercial interests who favor the convention center will probably make the best case for its construction. Neither group should make the decision. Including both groups in the process of deciding what to do, however, will ensure that the most articulate spokesmen are heard and that the best cases for both points of view are presented to council members who must make the final decision.

A second benefit of building due process into decision making is that doing so probably will minimize opposition to the final decision. Common sense tells us that people tend to support that which they have had a role in creating. For example, if a city manager and chief of police actively seek the views of sergeants and patrolmen in developing a neighborhood patrol program, opposition to such a program may be reduced significantly. Patrolmen who do not agree with the ultimate decision will not be able to say "Nobody asked my opinion" or "They just rammed it down our throats!"

Finally, a commitment to due process should result in better decisions. In recent years, it has been popular to initiate major budget reforms within local governments. Too often, such reforms start at the top with the mayor or the city manager and ultimately work down to the operating managers who are most affected by them. Some counties and cities have attempted to reverse this procedure by including operating managers

early in the process, when the budget system and supporting management and financial systems are being defined. When those affected by a budget system have been consulted in its development, the quality of the final product is likely to be higher.

Doing your homework

Simply stated, doing your homework refers to the process of getting the facts about a particular issue or public decision. This guideline is as important to citizens attempting to influence the vote of a board of supervisors or city council as it is to a department head attempting to gain political approval for a high-priority project.

Citizens, community leaders, and public managers are often unwilling to spend the time required to study the facts about an issue because they do not believe that the ultimate political decision will be influenced by facts. This may, of course, be true, but more often it is not. Although the opinions of some may not be affected by facts, these people usually are not the ones who make the final decision. Generally, the real decision makers are those in the middle, who do not have an emotional attachment to either side of a question and whose minds are open to a careful marshaling of facts.

Fact-based analyses may also influence the press, which, in turn, often influences key decision makers. At minimum, a knowledge of the facts about an issue will make it easier to avoid assuming an overdefensive posture in reaction to initial opposition. It is easier to keep your cool in a heated debate if you are confident that your position is based on accurate and pertinent information.

A second explanation for the fact that many people do not do their homework is that it takes considerable time and skill to separate fact from fiction. Citizens and community leaders may become discouraged after months of digging around city hall attempting to obtain information in support of a particular position. Pertinent information often is available only in a form that is difficult to interpret and which requires analytical skills to decipher. In other instances, information is not available or, worse, withheld. Despite these problems, getting the facts and putting them into the right context is one of the most important challenges facing those who are attempting to achieve change within local governments.

Building on a successful track record

The ability to do things as planned depends in large measure on attitude. Successful implementation demands a willingness to take risks and a spirit that seeks to find new and better ways to conduct old business. Individuals, like organizations, go through periods of innovation and creativity as well as periods of stagnation. Therefore, those responsible for the direction of local government should answer two critical questions. How can a climate that is supportive of change be created? How can positive incentives be developed that will increase the willingness to take risks?

These questions are particularly difficult to answer for a public business such as a county or city government. Political leaders and municipal managers can offer few of the traditional rewards to those whose innovative spirits result in superior performance. In many cases, managers cannot hire, fire, promote, or monetarily compensate employees on the basis of perceived merit. Because the compensation awarded to classes of employees is determined by a civil-service system, union contracts, or both, it is difficult to relate financial rewards to individual performance.

Despite such conditions, a climate supportive of change can be created. Using public recognition, assignment of greater responsibility, greater autonomy, and other nonmonetary rewards, public officials can create positive incentives to excel. The critical element in developing such a climate is a demonstrated ability to get things done. An indi-

vidual or institution that has successfully accomplished objectives in the past will develop a positive attitude about its ability to do so again in the future. A successful track record will make it easier for individuals and groups to build the coalitions required to implement larger projects and achieve broader objectives.

The inability to develop a successful track record often results from unwillingness to establish achievable goals and objectives. Just as a swimmer would not attempt to swim the English Channel without successfully completing a number of less-ambitious efforts, both public and private leaders should tailor the things they choose to do to an expanding record of success. Failure to do this reflects both personal impatience and the pressures caused by the electoral process. The fact that community leaders are elected to represent their constituencies for a limited period of time creates the temptation to try to do a lot of things in a hurry. If they are successful, leaders will satisfy constituent expectations and, incidentally, get reelected. It is difficult to persuade constituents that success in achieving limited objectives is preferable to failure at achieving larger ones. Succumbing to the temptation to bite off more than you are able to chew results in a predictable condition: nothing is swallowed, and you run the risk of choking. Thus the rhetoric of change remains just that—words without results.

Recognizing that change takes time

Frustration, disillusionment, and apathy are the products of unrealized expectations. Therefore, it is critical to the success of any action program that both those who are responsible for its implementation and its beneficiaries have accurate expectations about the length of time it will take to achieve intended results.

A practical rule of thumb, developed by those who have experienced the frustration of trying to get things done within a local government, is this: take the amount of time you think would be required to achieve a desired outcome, if you alone had control of all the variables, and multiply it by three. It could be argued that the multiple should be four, five, or even six. The critical point is that public decision making takes time. This fact must be recognized and built into expectations if frustration is to be avoided.

Public decision making is time consuming for a number of reasons. It takes time to build the necessary coalitions. It takes time to develop a track record that will persuade others that you have the capacity to do what you say you will do. It takes time to educate people about the merits of proposed actions. It takes time to coordinate the efforts of all those upon whom successful implementation depends. It takes time to actually carry out all the seemingly unimportant but necessary steps.

There is also a passive dimension to the role of time in accomplishing change within local government. A public decision often requires a gestation period between the introduction of an idea and the final decision. During this period, nothing much seems to happen. It may be that political leaders and municipal managers need this time to adjust their attitudes, to live with an idea for awhile, to see how it feels, to test it out on others, to get a sense of how it will affect other plans, to check the political winds. The more significant the decision or issue, the longer the gestation period.

However, some decisions—often involving millions of dollars of taxpayers' funds— are made almost immediately, with little or no gestation period. The challenge, therefore, for those attempting to influence the final decisions of a board of supervisors or a city council, is how to assess the length of time between the introduction of an issue and its ultimate resolution. Unfortunately, there are no easily discernible standards. How much time is required to make a decision depends on the individuals involved, the past history of the organization making the decision, the credibility of spokesmen

for both sides of the question, the complexity of the issue, and the press of other business.

An important corollary of this guideline is knowing when to stop waiting for a decision and move on to something else. County executives and city managers know that when a legislative body finally decides to act, it may choose to implement only portions of a proposed plan. At this point, it may be better to accept partial defeat and look for new ways of solving the problem until change can be reintroduced at a more propitious time.

Understanding the importance of timing

Timing is a critical ingredient in the equation of getting things done. Knowing when to push for a decision and when to pull back is a skill that characterizes managers who are consistently able to achieve good performance. Often the elements that determine appropriate timing are uncontrollable. The climate in which decisions are made is affected by economic conditions, electoral cycles, and personalities. The difficulty of identifying "an idea whose time has come" should not be underestimated, since the political climate in a city or a county is likely to be variable and unpredictable. The one element that is controllable is the ability and willingness of individuals or institutions to take action when the timing seems appropriate.

In the public sector, the most consistent motivator of change is crisis. Local government officials tend to act only after a problem has reached crisis proportions. For example, a proposal to change a city's budgetary process is not likely to receive a favorable reception while the city has ample resources to carry out its traditional functions. The experience of New York City in 1975 clearly illustrates this point. When the mayor, the Emergency Financial Control Board, and others attempted to determine where excess fat could be lopped off the city budget, they found that their budget system did not give them the information they needed to make these decisions intelligently. At this point they began to be more receptive to recommended changes in the budget system. Budget revision had become "an idea whose time has come."

Another important aspect of selecting the appropriate time to act is an adequate understanding of the tolerance of institutions and individuals for change. Organizations, as well as people, suffer from "future shock"— that is, they can absorb only a finite number of new stimuli within a given period of time before their systems begin to resist or break down. Tolerance for change can critically affect receptivity to new ideas. For instance, if a new city manager takes office in a government that during the past decade has been bombarded with reorganization plans, he or she may be well advised to postpone offering yet another reorganization plan regardless of how badly it is needed. In this case, successful reorganization must wait until the uncertainty and turmoil created by previous attempts have abated and the repercussions of "future shock" have been absorbed.

Experience and judgment are the best tools for determining when organizations or individuals are receptive to initiatives for change (or have reached maximum tolerance for change). Developing the ability to make this determination demands an understanding of organizational behavior as well as of individual psychology. We have personally observed that people seem to be most receptive to change at certain times of the year. In Flint, new programs had the best chance of being approved by the City Council if they were presented in the spring or early summer. Council meetings during the winter months generally lasted much longer than summer meetings. Lacking much else to do, members of the council would examine each proposal in minute detail and with considerable skepticism. With the coming of spring, however, spirits would improve,

council meetings would become shorter, and a more positive attitude toward change would emerge.

Given the pressing needs and high emotions that mark the day-to-day climate of most local governments, it is easy to understand why public officials discount the importance of timing. It is often impossible to wait until events have reached a point favorable to a desired change. Nevertheless, public managers have a much better chance of accomplishing their objectives if they have the patience to wait for the appropriate time to gain the attention and support of key decision makers.

Knowing when to compromise

One of the most oversold and least understood concepts in politics and public management is the notion that getting things done is the art of compromise. If this were literally true, every public decision would represent the arithmetical mean of all the proposals and counterproposals that had been considered. Clearly, this is not the case. Reaching public decisions involves judgments that reflect in some cases considerable compromise and in other cases no compromise at all. Managing a local government successfully depends on the ability to know when to compromise.

Compromise clearly serves a useful purpose when it ensures that public decisions reflect the interests of the majority. Compromise does not serve a useful purpose, however, when it dictates the acceptance of "half a loaf" only to find that the other half was critical. The choice of compromise as the "strategy of first resort" may lead to a serious inability to achieve results.

There is no rule that will help distinguish between acceptable and unacceptable compromises. In making this distinction, a manager must determine the extent to which acceptance of a compromise position would make it impossible to achieve an acceptable proportion of desired objectives. Compromise may not be warranted when a crisis situation has suspended normal procedures, nor when all previous efforts to achieve desired results have failed.

The 1974–1975 financial crisis in New York City illustrates these two points. Following the discovery that the city was almost bankrupt, the Emergency Financial Control Board was given extraordinary powers to improve financial conditions. The board eventually determined that New York's entire financial-management system must be restructured. This drastic recommendation reflected the severity of the financial crisis and the fact that previous (compromise) efforts to improve the system on a piecemeal basis had not been sufficient to correct fundamental problems. In the board's judgment, a no-compromise assault on the existing system was imperative if New York was to regain financial solvency. Nothing short of a total change would solve the problems that the financial crisis had forced on the city.

There are times, of course, when compromise is appropriate. If all individuals and interest groups contending in the political arena refused to compromise, government would degenerate into chaos; nothing would get done. On the other hand, some problems are so serious that compromise will not resolve them. Just as a patient dying of cancer may welcome taking risks that would not be tolerated were the disease less serious, local governments suffering from terminal management problems cannot afford to continue a pattern of compromise that, in part, has produced these problems.

Being a "squeaky wheel"

Textbooks often imply that government decisions are made according to a rational process. This is not always the case. Because decisions are made by people, and people are influenced by other people, the "squeaky wheel" approach to affecting public decisions will always have a chance of working.

Citizens who feel overwhelmed by large, complex government institutions and thus powerless to influence government decisions often do not understand how powerful their individual voices can be. A citizen speaking at a city council meeting (broadcast on the radio, covered on television newscasts, or reported in the newspaper) is likely to present a clear challenge to public officials. "I have a problem," a citizen states, "and I want you to solve it." The ability to do so is a direct test of political performance in that it reveals whether a politician has the willingness and ability to serve his or her constituents.

The "squeaky wheel" approach, of course, does not always work. It works best for individuals or groups outside a local government. Internal dissenters often become labeled "nuisances" whom public officials quickly learn to ignore or reject. Not surprisingly, this approach works best with public officials who are directly dependent on the electorate for their jobs. Moreover, it has the greatest chance of succeeding when it addresses issues or problems that can be resolved quickly. Having inspired a city council, a board of supervisors, or an elected mayor to action, it is important to avoid further consideration. Although "squeaky wheels" can generate considerable emotion in any given meeting, this emotion is quickly dissipated. It is important, therefore, to ensure that the question at issue can be decided without delay and that action can be taken immediately.

In many cases to achieve their ends it is necessary for citizens to document the consequences of failure to act on a recommendation. Consider the following example: a city has adopted a plan to upgrade streetlights over a five- to six-year period. The plan starts with major thoroughfares and then moves to less heavily traveled streets. A citizen group representing a neighborhood that is low on the original schedule wants to have streetlights sooner. Recognizing that it is important to demonstrate the consequences of inaction, the citizens wait until two armed robberies have occurred in unlighted parts of their neighborhood. Then they march down to their city council and "squeak" as loudly as they can. By dramatizing the robberies and their growing fear of walking in their neighborhood after dark, they have a better chance of persuading the city council to revise the streetlight implementation program.

Spreading the credit for success

People are more likely to take risks and attempt to find innovative ways of doing things if they can see something in it for themselves. In a local government, which has few traditional rewards and penalties, the "something in it" is difficult to define. Generally, it means special recognition or public credit for a job well done. If a mayor, city manager, union president, or civic leader takes personal credit for every success that his or her organization achieves, it will not be long before his or her staff stops exerting the extra effort that outstanding performance demands.

Spreading the credit for success (rewarding others for generating and implementing good ideas) is not merely an artificial exercise. Few "new ideas" are really new. Despite the tendency of public officials to describe initiatives as being new or innovative, this is rarely the case. Moreover, the ideas that serve as catalysts for action are rarely implemented. Ideas grow and are nurtured as they receive criticism from those who have different points of view about what should be done. By the time an idea has been translated into a decision, and a decision into action, many people deserve credit for the ultimate outcome.

Related to the importance of giving others the credit for success is knowing when to persuade others to introduce ideas. As most government practitioners know, ideas have a higher probability of being accepted if they are initiated by certain individuals or groups. In state legislatures, sponsors of proposed legislation are carefully selected so as to ensure the greatest possible chance of constructing a coalition able to convert a bill into law. This process is equally important within a local government.

Accepting responsibility for failure may be as important as spreading credit for success. The inability to get something done may be the net result of a number of individual breakdowns. Nevertheless, the person who initiated the program must be prepared to accept total responsibility for failure. This is essential to the maintenance of a leadership role. Willingness to take responsibility for failure contributes to the development of an environment in which risk taking is encouraged. People are reluctant to work under someone whom they know is quick to take credit for success but unwilling to accept responsibility for failure.

Recognizing the importance of follow-up

Public decisions are rarely final. Decisions that are made one day are just as easily unmade the next. Often, a decision is revised slowly, over months or even years, during which time its initial intent may be totally altered. As a result, it is imperative that individuals and institutions trying to get things done within a local government recognize the importance of following the entire course of a particular decision, from initial presentation through final implementation.

Unfortunately, newcomers to the public decision-making process often learn this guideline the hard way. It is not uncommon for neighborhood groups to work energetically to influence a city council decision and then neglect to follow up on the issue after they believe the "final" decision has been made.

The following scenario is typical: an influential developer requests a change in zoning from residential to commercial, and the planning commission schedules several public hearings. Neighbors, alerted by the proposed change, organize themselves and attend the planning-commission meetings to demonstrate their opposition. The planning-commission staff recommends that the developer's request be granted. The planning commision, which generally listens to its staff, concurs and recommends favorable action to the city council. Neighborhood residents, outraged by this decision, urge their supporters to attend the next city council meeting. Unlike the planning commission, which is appointed, the elected city council is more responsive to citizen pressures. After hearing many impassioned speeches from neighborhood residents, the council rejects the planning commission's recommendation. The residents return home, satisfied that they have successfully defeated an unwanted intrusion into their neighborhood.

Three weeks or three months later, the same item is again before the city council. This time there are no citizens in the audience to present their viewpoints. The council, reacting to the sustained lobbying of the developer and the interests he represents, agrees to rehear the zoning case. This time, the council votes to approve the rezoning request. The neighborhood residents have lost their battle.

This scenario—which is repeated in community after community, week after week— underlines the importance of following up on the decision-making process and making sure that public decisions and actions are monitored. Such monitoring will ensure that unexpected changes do not occur, or that, if they do, those affected are made aware of them and have an opportunity to influence the final outcome.

Stepping back to look at the forest

It is easy for people to spend all of their energy reacting to last week's crises and yesterday's problems, never finding the time to examine where local government is going

and whether it is getting there efficiently. Every organization, public and private, suffers from this problem. It is difficult to see the shape of the forest when efforts are totally directed toward counting the trees. Because a local government is constantly bombarded by demands from many different constituencies, it experiences the problem more acutely than does private business, where external demands are more limited and somewhat controllable.

Stepping back periodically to reexamine overall organizational objectives (looking at the forest) will ensure that local-government officials can take advantage of changing conditions. Such an overview might lead to the decision to push harder for a particular objective or wait for more favorable timing. Taking a look at the overall picture also provides an opportunity to reinvigorate and reacquaint people who are working together in pursuit of common ends. This is not an insignificant factor. Achieving change in a local government, as we have indicated throughout this book, requires the cooperation of people working at different levels in different ways. If these individuals or groups lose sight of the objectives that unite their efforts, or lack appreciation of the role each is playing, achievement of common purpose may be jeopardized.

Most people would agree that local-government officials should stop periodically to review government activities in the context of the community conditions they are attempting to address. Why, then, is this guideline not followed in many counties and cities? One explanation is that doing so is time consuming. Because they are so busy reviewing and passing ordinances, responding to citizens' demands, reacting to employee-union requests, and dealing with the backlog of existing problems, local-government officials are seldom willing to take the time required to reassess the overall goals and objectives which, in theory, guide their daily actions.

Furthermore, the political process, by its very nature, is undisciplined. It is extremely difficult to pull together a group of political leaders—who are likely to have major differences of opinion about what a local government should do—to establish common government objectives. Many political leaders refuse to participate in such exercises. For some, this refusal reflects the fear that the press, community leaders, and their constituents will hold them accountable for their contribution. For others, the refusal to assess or periodically reexamine objectives stems from their belief that it cannot be done, that it is too difficult an exercise to attempt, or that citizens don't really care whether it is done or not.

This last point is extremely important. Until citizens—and the news media—demand that elected officials define organizational and community objectives and periodically assess the progress made toward their attainment, politicians will have little incentive to invest the time and effort required to follow this guideline.

CHAPTER 18

Development of Modern Management Tools: A Case Study

At 2:30 p.m. five of Flint's nine council members assembled, an hour and a half late, for an interview with one of a long list of candidates for city manager. Six months earlier the council, led by the mayor, had persuaded the former city manager to resign. Now it was trying to find a replacement—a task made more difficult by the refusal of three council members to consider anyone but the city's former mayor and the allegiance of a fourth councilman to the old city manager. After six months of searching, the five council members were tired of interview rhetoric and were quick to get to the point.

Despite his long wait, the candidate they were interviewing felt composed and well prepared. Having read the past year's editions of the *Flint Journal* and having spent the previous day talking with a number of Flint's community leaders, he felt confident that he could field the toughest questions. He was wrong.

The first councilman began: "Flint looks like hell. The budget is the size of three telephone books; no one can read it, let alone understand it. The city's organization chart looks like a giant spider web; you can't tell who is responsible for what. As a councilman, I do not receive a single report that tells me how our city government is doing. If you

were selected as our next city manager, what would you do about these problems?"

From there on the questions got tougher.

When the interview was concluded, the candidate did not believe he had adequately answered the council members' questions. Nevertheless, the council, after a 5–0 vote, selected him to be the next city manager. On December 7, Pearl Harbor Day, he took office.

Bringing Flint into the twentieth century

Before officially starting his job, the new city manager toured the city with a councilman who was an architect by profession and an astute observer of Flint's problems. As they drove through the city, the councilman pointed out the large number of deteriorating and dilapidated houses and stressed the need for the physical renovation of Flint's inner-city neighborhoods; many of which were not included in the city's urban-renewal program. Driving down Dort Highway, a major city artery, he pointed out the consequences of inadequate land-use planning. Driving around the massive General Motors plants, he explained how the city's dependence on the automobile industry and

its lack of economic diversification was catas-
trophic during times of economic recession.
At the conclusion of this informal tour, the
councilman told the future city manager
that, despite the severe human, economic,
and physical problems of the community,
the most immediate crisis would be found
within Flint's city government. He explained,
"There are no policies or procedures that
guide the activities of the council and its
interaction with top-level managers. We
spend all our time fighting yesterday's fires.
We spend no time looking forward and
deciding what ought to happen. Citizens are
demanding to know what their tax dollars are
buying, and we have no answers." He ended
by saying, "There is no management process
within this city. I hope you will have the
ability to modernize the way this city does its
business and help bring it into the twentieth
century."

Completing a diagnostic study

After being sworn in, the new city manager
initiated a diagnostic evaluation of government operations. He began, routinely
enough, by asking each department head to
submit a memorandum describing the most
critical problems he faced and what actions
he recommended taking to solve them. The
responses to this request were sobering. The
memoranda were short, uninformative, and
unimaginative. Department heads were unwilling or unable to analyze their own operations, identify problems, or propose solutions. After a series of conferences with
these managers, it was clear to the city manager that their responses reflected their inability to identify and articulate problems
and their unwillingness to entertain alternatives to the status quo.

By mid-January the city manager had
developed a list of improvement possibilities
that filled six single-spaced pages. Under the
heading "Improving Management Tools,"
the following entries were listed:

• Replace the sixteen-year-old master plan
  and develop a procedure for keeping the

new plan current.
• Improve the city's operating budget to
  make it more useful.
• Develop a capital-improvement budget
  and a process for keeping it up to date.
• Ensure that financial/management reporting systems are integrated with the new
  budget system.
• Develop a performance-measurement
  system.
• Provide the City Council with periodic
  evaluations of major programs and projects.
• Reorganize government operations.
• Compile a policy and procedures manual.

Similar entries were listed under a number of
other headings.

The manager quickly realized that the key
question was not what should be done but
what should be done *first*. There was a need,
first, to separate the important from the less
important and, second, to identify what
could be accomplished during the remaining two years of the council's term. The
manager turned for assistance to the administrative assistant to Flint's congressman.
This person enjoyed a unique reputation in
Flint because of his knowledge of the community, city government, and key people.
Moreover, his ability to separate the practical
from the impractical could be an invaluable
asset to the new city manager. After discussing the situation with the congressman's
assistant and carefully reviewing the diagnostic evaluation, the city manager decided
that a three-year effort to modernize Flint's
management tools would be one of his major
objectives.

Developing an implementation strategy

Late one evening in February, the city
manager and the recently hired director of
community development outlined a strategy
for improving Flint's management tools. Using a large blackboard, they drew a crude
diagram of the basic management tools they
felt the city needed. A copy of this diagram is
presented in Figure 7.

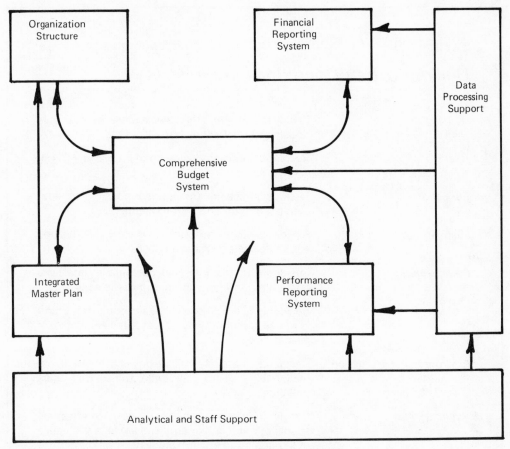

Figure 7. Management tools needed in Flint city government.

An integrated master plan would identify community objectives that public and private institutions should attempt to achieve or advance. This plan would incorporate and interrelate human, social, economic, environmental, and physical needs, and would be organized according to the major conditions that make up the quality of life experienced by citizens in Flint (see Exhibit 94). Within each area, measurable community goals and objectives would be defined along with the policies that should govern their attainment. This plan would serve as a framework for integrating the programs and activities of all segments of the Flint community. It would facilitate interagency coordination and establish a basis for evaluating programs and activities.

One part of this plan would contain objectives that Flint's city government, through its own agencies and departments, would be responsible for achieving. Clearly stating city-government objectives would enable citizens to hold the City Council accountable. In turn, identifying city-government objectives would enable the council to hold its appointed managers accountable for their performance.

A comprehensive budget would identify all city revenues and expenditures and relate them to the organizational units and managers responsible for them. The new budget would ensure that the appropriate managers could be held accountable for both the consumption of resources and performance.

A reorganization of city government

EXHIBIT 94

Desired Urban Conditions in Flint

Housing   Residents of the city have access to adequate housing at prices they can afford.

Health   Residents of the city enjoy good mental and physical health.

Education   Residents have full and equal opportunity for educational growth and development.

Justice   Residents of the city have equal access to a fair and equitable system of justice.

Public safety   Residents of the city feel reasonably safe from crime, fire, and household and traffic accidents.

Recreation   Residents of the city have full and equal opportunity to use community facilities for the enjoyment of leisure time.

Environmental protection   Residents of the city enjoy a physical environment reasonably free from air, water, noise, and visual pollution.

Public utilities   Residents of the city have access to an adequate supply of water and energy and are able to dispose of sewage in an acceptable way.

Transportation   Residents of the city have equal access to an adequate system of transportation.

Employment and economic development   Residents who are physically able and willing to work have equal access to satisfying jobs that provide adequate financial remuneration.

Income maintenance   People's basic needs for food, shelter, and health care are met regardless of their income-earning capacity.

General government   City government is able to use public resources in a productive and effective manner and provide citizens with an equal opportunity to influence the public decisions that affect their lives.

would be necessary to ensure that newly developed management tools were used effectively. Once the City Council had decided where it wanted to go and how much it was willing to spend to get there, it would need to identify the most appropriate way of organizing city-government operations to achieve its objectives. A reorganization effort would address the severe fragmentation of executive authority mandated by the city charter, clarify lines of responsibility within the executive branch, integrate similar functions and activities, develop an adequate balance between line operations and staff support, and designate a reasonable span of control for every key manager.

A *financial-reporting system* tailored to the new budget would be required to ensure adequate management control. Integration of the accounting system, the purchase and encumbrance control system, and the payroll-personnel system with the newly developed budget system would ensure that financial information was provided on an accurate and timely basis.

A *performance-measurement system* would be closely related to the new budget system in order to ensure that managers and members of the council could compare actual results with planned objectives. Establishing such a system would thus create a better basis for making resource-allocation decisions.

To develop and operate these tools, the city would need *improved data-processing support and adequate analytical support.* The former would be necessary to the development of a budget-preparation system as well as to the implementation of financial and performance-reporting systems. The latter would support the development, implementation, and operation of each of the management tools described here.

It was obvious to the manager and the community-development director that the development of all of these tools could not be initiated simultaneously. Weighing political realities, budget and personnel con-

straints, and the limitations on their own time, they developed a three-phase strategy. The first phase was directed toward the development of an integrated master plan and a new budget system. These two efforts would be started simultaneously by different project teams. Recognizing that planning extends from identifying broad community needs to budgeting city-government activities, they designed this two-pronged approach to initiate improvements at both ends of the spectrum. Ultimately, these two efforts would converge. At that point, the city's budget would adequately implement the parts of the integrated master plan for which city government was responsible. It was estimated that Phase 1, which was initiated immediately, would be completed in three years.

Phase 2, which was scheduled to begin the following year, would improve the city's financial and performance-reporting systems and modernize the data-processing system. The final phase, which would not begin until the third year, would address the organization of Flint's city government. Because making many of the proposed organizational changes probably would necessitate changing the city charter, it was felt that this initiative should be delayed.

When the city manager and the community-development director had finished drafting their strategy, they realized that the easy part was over. It had not been difficult to recognize the need for improved management tools or to define what these tools should be and how they should be interrelated. The real problem would be getting them developed and implemented. To accomplish this, the city manager would need to do three things. First, he would need to assemble a staff to be specifically responsible for directing the management-improvement program. Second, he would have to find external funding for the program. (Given the estimated cost of implementing the management-improvement program [approximately $250,000 per year] and the increasing public demand for more and better municipal services, it seemed unlikely that the City Council would divert money to finance such a program.) Finally, he would need to build internal support for the development of new management tools. Convincing department heads and managers that these new tools would help them do their jobs better would be a critical factor in obtaining their support for making changes in the way they went about their business.

In launching Phase 1 of this effort, the manager decided that it would be imprudent to tamper with the existing budget process. He decided to allow the preparation of the fiscal-year 1973 budget to continue. In this way he hoped he would gain a better understanding of how the existing system worked and how its deficiencies affected different users. This knowledge would be invaluable in persuading the City Council to approve the changes he wanted to make.

Creating organizational responsibility

The city manager knew that successfully developing and implementing an integrated master plan and a comprehensive budgeting system would depend on assembling a qualified staff. Although he could provide general direction for these projects, he could not personally do all the work.

Except for some employees in the areas of purchasing, equal opportunity, and human relations, the city manager had no staff members that reported directly to him. Through the assistant city manager, he supervised six of the department heads; the major staff functions of finance, personnel, and planning were directed by independently appointed managers or separate commissions.

In view of this situation, the city manager asked the council to appropriate the funds required to create an office of management and budget. This office would be staffed by four people: a deputy city manager for planning, budgeting, and evaluation; a director of planning and program evaluation; a

budget director; and a director of management services. The annual cost of this office was estimated to be about $150,000.

The City Council initially approved the manager's proposal. They had hired the manager to improve Flint's management process, and they felt they should give him the resources to do it. From the manager's standpoint, it looked as if his program were off on the right foot.

However, his optimism did not last long. Strenuous opposition to the proposal arose from two different sources. The city employee unions attacked the council's decision, arguing that no city manager in Flint's history had ever needed this kind of staff support. Their motivation was unclear. They may have relished the opportunity to publicly take on the manager and thus reaffirm their role in the management of city government, or they may have been afraid that any move to strengthen the city's management represented an attempt by the council to weaken their own power and influence. In any event, the opposition of the unions helped create and foster additional opposition.

Opposition also developed within the City Council. During discussions about the purpose and staffing of the new office, the city manager had let it be known that there were three people in the community whom he thought were qualified to run it. These people were all members of the staff of the county's Model Cities program, which had been at odds with the City Council. Several councilmen reacted negatively to the idea of hiring these people, and they apparently transferred this feeling to the program as a whole.

At a subsequent council meeting, the manager's request was brought up again and tabled. For nearly two months the council discussed the pros and cons of the proposal. Everyone had an opinion about whether the manager should have a staff, and these opinions were expressed again and again at weekly council meetings. Finally a compromise was reached: three, not four, positions would be authorized and funded by the City Council.

But the battle was far from being over. Reacting to union pressure and the recommendations of his own staff technicians, the civil-service director recommended that two of the three positions be filled by city employees, and that only the top position be filled through open competition. The city manager protested this decision vigorously. He told the civil-service director and the Civil Service Commission that if qualified individuals existed within the ranks of city employees, he would have assigned them to this task long ago. It was now the end of April, and, after battling the City Council, the manager was not prepared to fight civil service for another two or three months. After arguing his case personally before the Civil Service Commission, the manager was successful in persuading the commission to allow all three positions to be filled on an open-competitive basis. This approach did not disqualify city employees; it simply forced them to compete with candidates who did not work for the city.

Finally, in August 1972—seven months after the manager had initiated his effort to acquire staff support—two employees joined the city's new Office of Management and Budget. A manager from the county Model Cities staff became budget director, and a recent graduate of the Harvard Graduate School of Business become the director of planning and evaluation. The top position—deputy city manager for planning, budgeting, and evaluation—was never filled. When the leading candidate, the director of the city's community-action program, decided for personal reasons to remove himself from consideration, the city manager faced a difficult problem: under civil-service rules, he was required to hire one of the three highest scorers on the civil-service exam. After sitting in on interviews and evaluating the candidates personally, the manager decided that none of the three finalists could adequately perform the job. Reluctantly, he asked civil service to give another examina-

tion and to prepare another list. Civil service was unable to comply with this request. Under the city charter, the city manager had two options: he could appoint one of the people on the list, or he could wait for a year until the list had expired and then request a new examination. The manager selected the latter option. During the following year the council, reacting to growing fiscal pressures, deleted this position from the budget.

Building internal support

By early spring the city was busy preparing the traditional line-item budget. This was not a difficult exercise. Each department took its budget for the previous year, increased all of the line items, and sent the new request to the Finance Department. After reviewing these requests for consistency and proper form, a staff member in the Finance Department bound them together and passed them on to the city manager. This was the budget process. Budget preparation was not governed by any formal guidelines issued by the City Council or the city manager. There was no review or analysis of budget submissions before they were assembled and passed on to the city manager. The system was inadequate by almost any standard.

The city manager pointed out these deficiencies to the finance director, hoping that he could develop an ally in his efforts to change them. However, the finance director made it clear that he would not participate in efforts to change the budget system. He felt that he alone was responsible for preparing the budget and that he had done an adequate job.

The finance director's opposition to the manager's plan surfaced in early April. Just when it seemed that the council had finally reached a compromise on the city manager's request for new staff positions, the finance director jumped into the argument, indicating that there was no money to pay for these positions. The analysis supporting the manager's request had estimated the total costs but had not indicated in detail the source of funds for paying them. The finance director's opposition held up the council's approval until the manager could find a specific source of funding revenue.

As it turned out, availability of funds was not a problem. The city manager discovered that the General Fund had a $2.5-million unappropriated-fund balance, and that there was a $600,000 unappropriated-fund balance in the Income Tax Fund. Once the existence of this money was brought to the attention of the City Council, the finance director temporarily withdrew his opposition.

Seeking federal assistance

Although the city manager had demonstrated that there was sufficient city money available to finance the management-improvement program, he knew that it would be easier to obtain council approval if he could find some external funding. He discovered, however, that although federal and state money could be found to buy a helicopter, build a hospital, or purchase additional buses, very little money was available to improve the management of the city.

There was one exception—the 701 Planning and Management Assistance Program of the Department of Housing and Urban Development. This program had initially been intended to support local land-use planning, but in recent years its coverage had been expanded to include general management improvements. The city had tried for several years to submit a "701" grant request but had been unable to put together an acceptable application.

In March 1972 the Department of Community Development was in the process of preparing still another "701" grant request. The city manager asked that this request be rewritten and considerably expanded. The modified request called for the federal government to provide $160,000 for a three-year effort to (1) develop a citywide integrated

master plan and (2) develop a comprehensive budget system supported by financial and performance-reporting systems.

HUD officials responded favorably to the city's request. Informal approval was signaled in late May, and official approval eventually arrived in July. The city manager was happy to report to the council that by late summer the city could begin expending "701" funds to implement its management-improvement program.

Increasing reliance on external help

The city manager's initial strategy was to implement the management-improvement program by augmenting his own staff, since outside consultants had a poor reputation in Flint. After the council voted to reduce the staff of the Office of Management and Budget, however, the city manager changed his mind. He realized that if the budget and master plan were to be restructured, external consultants would have to do most of the work. To ensure that knowledge gained in the development effort was not lost, city staff members would work closely with the consultant team.

Having been a management consultant himself for a number of years, the city manager felt particularly well qualified in this area. Armed with council support and federal funds, the city manager proposed that the city contract with two Washington firms to develop the new budgeting and financial-management systems and that a local firm be engaged to develop the integrated master plan. All of the proposed consultants were known personally to the city manager. Anticipating the argument that the contracts should be let by a competitive bidding process, the manager pointed out that, since he alone was accountable to the City Council for the quality of the work produced by the consultants, his knowledge of their skills should be the deciding factor. His argument was sustained.

Unveiling the new budget system

In May 1973, nine months after the effort had begun, the city manager stood before a group of community leaders, reporters, city employees, and council members to unveil the new budget system. Using a metaphor appropriate to Flint, he noted that the previous budget system had resembled a Model T and that the new system "at least represents a 1965 Chevy." Part of the discussion was technical, because this was the manager's first opportunity to fully explain the budget system to the City Council and to the public. Exhibit 95 contains key excerpts from the manager's presentation. Figure 8 shows schematically how Flint's system operated.

Initial reaction to the new budget system was favorable. Some council members commented that the system would be useful in making resource-allocation decisions. Citizen leaders who took the time to review the new budget indicated that it was readable and useful for their purposes. The *Flint Journal* echoed this sentiment in an editorial, observing, "The new budget is understandable and will show residents how their tax dollars are being spent." The editorial went on to contrast the new budget with the old line-item budget, which had been presented annually to the council "in a volume . . . as thick as three telephone directories."

The development of the new budget system had not been achieved without problems. Initially, department heads had been reluctant to become involved in a process that would require considerably more work from them during the annual budget preparation and approval cycle. Moreover, the new system demanded that they have a detailed knowledge of their department operations. As one manager put it, "Digging into department operations and exploring the bowels of the organizations for which we are responsible will force us to come to grips with issues that many of us would just as soon not face." Furthermore, the new system would require cost-center managers to assume expanded and, in some cases, far different roles in the management process. The employee association representing the majority of cost-center managers argued strenuously that these changes should be resisted until the Civil Service Commission was willing to guarantee an increase in compensation which reflected the corresponding increase in responsibility.

Resistance to the new budget did not end with cost-center managers. Some members of the City Council resisted the new budget approach. They had never been convinced that the old system was deficient and that a new one was required.

One councilman, in particular, felt that the new budget system had cost far too much to develop. About a month before the new budget was presented to the council, he asked the finance director to itemize all the costs of preparing the new budget and to compare them with the costs of preparing the old one. The finance director's analysis indicated that the new budget system had cost approximately $187,000; in comparison, the old system had cost $16,000 to prepare. This estimate, he noted, included the value of the time of all the people involved in the development and implementation of the new system as well as in the actual preparation of the following year's budget. He further estimated that at least half of the cost was attributable to the development of the new system and thus would not be incurred in subsequent years.

In a presentation to the City Council, the finance director pointed out that the $187,000 cost represented only .4 percent of the fiscal year 1974 budget. He added, "It is not unreasonable to spend this small percentage of one year's budget planning for the upcoming year. The budget is the primary control document for an entire year. The preparation and review of this document represents the only opportunity for the administration and the council to evaluate the allocation of resources to city functions. This is not a process that should be shortchanged."

EXHIBIT 95

A Comprehensive Budgeting System for the City of Flint

Before a large audience gathered at the Durant Hotel, the city manager described the new budget that was about to be presented to the City Council.

"The key feature of the new budget system is the designation of cost centers," he began. "A cost center is an organizational unit within the city's organizational structure. These centers are the building blocks of the new budget. Each is under the direction of a single manager who can be held accountable for dollars expended and results or services produced. Generally, a cost center is large enough to account for a significant expenditure of resources, yet small enough to be manageable.

"There are two types of cost centers—operating and administrative," he continued. "*Operating cost centers* provide direct services to the public or to other parts of city government. *Administrative cost centers* perform overhead or supervisory functions. Each city employee is assigned to only one cost center.

"Through the cost-center concept, the new budget system solves an exceedingly difficult problem: how to ensure management control, fiduciary control, and political control through a single system. Flint's system solves this problem in this way: Each activity conducted by a cost center is coded so that it can be related to a cost center, to a unique fund, or to the newly developed program structure. Using the computer, an organizational budget, a fund budget, or a program budget can be generated very quickly. In this way, the use of cost centers integrates management control through the organization structure, provides fiduciary control through a fund structure, and allows for political control through a program structure.

"The new budgeting system has additional features as well," the manager explained. "Until now the city has had no formal capital budgeting process; capital project proposals were made to the City Council whenever the need arose. In the new system, a capital budget is included along with the operating budget. This is important, given the close interrelationship between capital and operating budgets. For instance, some cost centers can charge a significant amount of their annual operating costs to capital projects. Similarly, some capital projects may

(continued)

EXHIBIT 95 (cont'd)

have significant operating-cost implications in the future. Under the new system, these implications are clarified and better management control is assured.

"Another feature of the new budget is the distinction between the base budget and the discretionary budget," the city manager pointed out. "In essence, the *base budget* represents last year's business at this year's prices. It presents the anticipated cost of providing the same level of service as that provided the previous year, taking into consideration inflation, salary increases, and changes in work load. The *discretionary budget* presents recommended expenditures for program and service improvements. In both cases, the focus is on a cost center. The final cost-center budget is obtained by adding the discretionary request to the base request.

"Revenues in the new budget system are divided into two categories: operating and nonoperating. *Operating revenue* is defined as revenue generated by the activities of an individual cost center. For instance, the cost center that performs housing inspections generates revenue by charging $20 per inspection. Operating revenue is the responsibility of the cost center that generates it. Other city revenue—property and income taxes, state and federal grants—is considered *nonoperating revenue*. Some cost centers whose annual budgets are financed solely by operating revenue can, under the new system, be managed as if they were separate businesses within city government. That is, they can be required to match expenditures to operating revenue.

"The new budget system projects the future impact of proposed expenditures," the manager went on. "Each cost-center summary contains a five-year forecast of operating revenue and expenditures. This forecast permits the city to compare anticipated expenditures to anticipated revenue in order to identify future financing problems that will be caused by present budget decisions.

"Finally, the process of preparing the new budget has been decentralized. Operational managers will now be responsible for preparing their yearly budget requests and, after receiving the approval of their department heads, justifying these requests before a budget review committee. This approach, which emphasizes the contractual nature of the budget process, has two advantages: it requests information from the manager closest to each activity (who should know the most about it) and it requires the cost-center manager to perform his or her activities during the fiscal year within the constraints imposed by the final budget."

The manager finished his presentation by handing out copies of the new budget document.

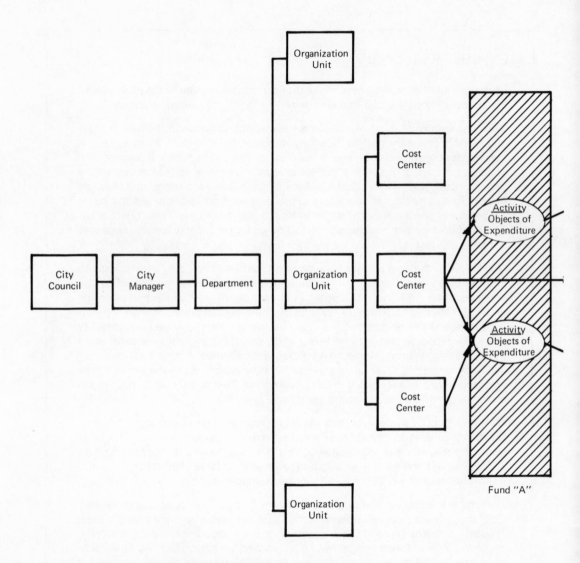

ORGANIZATION

Figure 8. How Flint's new budget system works.

The majority of the City Council agreed with the finance director. So did the *Flint Journal*. In an editorial entitled "Budget Effort Has Great Potential," the *Flint Journal* indicated: "Such an approach should be a continuing benefit to city councils through the years. It should go far toward fixing responsibility, not only for the council's primary task of determining priorities for taxpayer dollars, but also for responsibility for administration in carrying out those priorities."

Developing other management tools

The development and installation of a new budget system was by far the most important

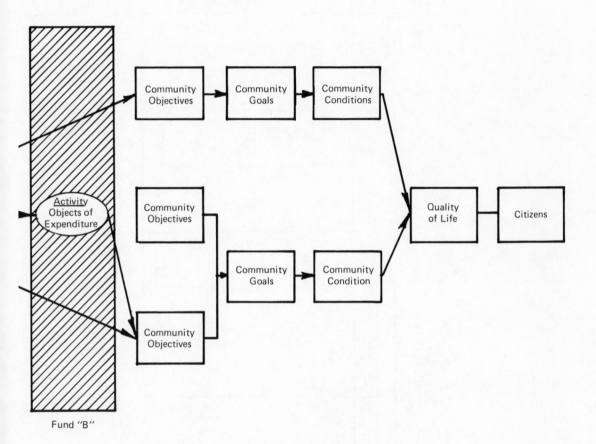

Fund "B"

PROGRAM

step in the overall effort to improve Flint's management. But it was not the only step. During the next three years, Phases 2 and 3 were implemented and additional management tools were developed and introduced. Beginning in late 1973, the city began to implement new financial-reporting procedures tailored to the new budget system. The first such tool was the monthly cost-center reporting system. This system was designed to enable managers to compare actual with projected expenditures for each major line item as well as for each cost-center activity (see Figure 9). By 1974 the city had implemented an automated budget-preparation system and was in the process of modifying the payroll/personnel system and the purchase/encumbrance–control system.

OBJECT/ACTIVITY		EXPENDITURES AND ENCUMBRANCES TO DATE			BUDGET		OVER/UNDER BUDGET TO DATE	UNENCUMBERED BALANCE
CODE	NAME	EXPENDITURES	ENCUMBRANCES	TOTAL	TO DATE	TOTAL		
OBJECT								
100.0	Salaries and Benefits	84		87	90	360	3	273
200.0	Purchased Services	7	5	12	8	16	(4)	4
300.0	Supplies	21		21	22	88	1	67
400.0	Other			0	5	20	5	20
	TOTALS	115	5	120	125	484	5	364
ACTIVITY								
2321	Jail Operations	97	5	102	103	412	1	310
3496	Inmate Evaluation Program	18		18	22	72	4	54
	TOTALS	115	5	120	125	484	5	364

Figure 9. Monthly budget status report.

By the beginning of fiscal year 1975 a performance-measurement system was in place. This system identified standards of performance for each cost center. Targets were then set for each quarter of the fiscal year, thereby creating an overall performance plan for city-government operations. During the year, quarterly reports were prepared which compared actual with anticipated performance (see Figure 10).

Recognizing the importance of data-processing support in the implementation of new systems, in 1973 the City Council adopted a five-year data-processing improvement plan. A new computer system was purchased and installed in 1974. By 1975 a citywide effort was under way to utilize the new data-processing capability.

The final element of the overall management-improvement program was completed in fiscal year 1976, when the new master plan was integrated with Flint's budget system. Then, for the first time, it was possible to relate city-government expenditures and activities to the accomplishment of community objectives as defined by the integrated master plan.

Not all efforts to improve Flint's management tools were successful. In 1973, the city manager presented to the City Council a comprehensive government reorganization plan. After considerable debate, the council approved minor elements of this plan but rejected the rest. The mayor explained, "The City Charter prevents us from organizing Flint's city government in a manner best calculated to meet the needs of the community." The city attorney, arguing that the excessive fragmentation of executive power dictated by the charter expressed the true intent of its drafters, put it this way:

The present charter, adopted by the people on December 2, 1929, does not provide an organization where responsibility for the delivery of major services is clearly defined. To the contrary, and with apparent overt intention, the drafters of the charter disseminated the responsibility and the authority to operate the city by providing for the

appointment of four administrative officials, all independent of one another and all answerable directly to the council.

A majority of the City Council agreed with this opinion. The result was the initiation of a citywide effort to change the city charter. This effort, as Chapter 10 recounts in detail, was successful. In November 1975, Flint's first elected mayor in more than fifty years took office.

Relating management tools to people

After a hotly contested primary and a general election that attracted a larger percentage of voters than had any other local election in recent history, Flint elected its first mayor. He was well known, since he had been the chief of police and had worked for the city for more than thirty years. Immediately after his election, many of Flint's top administrators began to leave. The city manager—who, under the new charter would have assumed responsibility as the chief administrative officer—accepted a similar position in Portland, Oregon. Thus the city lost an administrator with exceptional skills and a demonstrated ability to make things happen. The equal-opportunity director also decided to leave. Because he had developed an outstanding record for including minorities and women in city government, he had made many enemies—including the former chief of police, who did not fully subscribe to the objectives of affirmative action. The equal-opportunity director assumed a similar position in Governor Millikan's office.

For the position of city administrator, the new mayor selected a local businessman with ties to the Mott family. The new city administrator made no secret of his disdain for formal management systems. In 1977 the management tools that had been developed at considerable cost and effort from 1972 to 1976 were no longer being utilized. The data-processing plan was not being implemented on schedule, and improvements in major fi-

DEPARTMENT: Fire

COST CENTER: 2740   Investigation and Inspection
                    Number   Name

RESPONSIBLE MANAGER: Frank Jones

OUTPUT MEASURE	FY 1976 ACTUAL	FY 1977 TARGET	JULY-SEPT. 1976			OCT.-DEC. 1976	
			ACTUAL	TARGET	ACTUAL ÷ TARGET	ACTUAL	TARGET
Fire Cases Investigated	700	800	179	175	102%	181	195
Alarm Cases Investigated	50	50	14	12	117%	12	12
Property Inspections	9,500	11,000	3,279	3,100	106%	3,115	3,000
Weed Abatement Inspections	3,500	3,500	—	—		—	—

Figure 10. Performance-measurement system—annual plan and quarterly report.

nancial-reporting systems had been delayed or cancelled. Most important, information produced by the new budget and management systems was not being used to improve the quality of decisions.

Unlike their predecessors, the new mayor and city administrator had the ability to exert significant control over the expenditure of city resources. However, they chose to place their priorities elsewhere. This state of affairs underlines one important observation: management tools, regardless of their sophistication, are only as valuable as the people who use them.

Applying the Guidelines

Successful implementation of change in such areas as plan formulation, budget preparation, and financial control depends on a thorough knowledge of the strengths and weaknesses of existing systems. In most local governments, these systems have evolved over many years and have been redesigned, patched, and repatched to meet successive waves of requirements. In the process, they are likely to have become extremely complex and fragile. Thus, efforts to replace or modify them must be carried out carefully. In this section, we examine the effort to improve Flint's management tools in the context of the guidelines described in Chapter 17.

RESPONSIBILITY CENTER BUDGET: $252,000

NUMBER OF
AUTHORIZED POSITIONS: 10

| ACTUAL ÷ TARGET | JAN.-MAR. 1977 | | ACTUAL ÷ TARGET | APR.-JUNE 1977 | | ACTUAL ÷ TARGET | FY 1977 TOTAL | ACTUAL ÷ TARGET |
	ACTUAL	TARGET		ACTUAL	TARGET		ACTUAL	TARGET
93%	170	215	79%		215			
100%	11	13	85%		13			
104%	1,307	2,500	53%		2,400			
	709	1,000	71%		2,500			

Understanding the status quo

During his first six months in office, the Flint city manager observed and participated in the traditional budget-preparation process. In this way, he gained a sense of how the existing system responded to the demands of citizens, the City Council, and department managers. In addition, he had an opportunity to understand the effects of the constraints imposed by the state-mandated accounting system, by federal and state funding requirements, and by respective departmental needs. By taking the time to understand existing systems, the manager was able to discover where the "cookie jars" were located. By taking the time to evaluate the personalities of those involved in the budgeting process, he was in a better position to assess how they would react to proposed changes. In fact, not everyone was happy with the existing system; reviewing it with the city manager offered, to many, the opportunity to articulate long-recognized problems. As a result, the manager was able to develop a list of the inadequacies of the existing budget system from the viewpoint of those it was intended to serve.

Recognizing power where it exists

In 1972 the director of finance in Flint had been in his position for more than twenty-five years. He had watched city managers come and go. Since most city managers had shown little interest in financial matters, he had assumed almost total responsibility for the city's budget.

The new city manager, recognizing the finance director's considerable power, at first tried to avoid a confrontation. Ultimately, however, accommodation proved impossible. Challenged by the manager's intent to exercise responsibility for the preparation of the annual budget, the finance director assumed a position of open hostility. He refused to give the city manager a copy of his report showing revenue projections for the following fiscal year, arguing that the manager's job was to spend tax dollars and that his job was to conserve them.

Recognizing that his own power to improve the city's management tools flowed directly from the City Council, the manager took his case privately to council members. The matter was soon resolved. In July, the finance director announced that he would retire the following January.

Incorporating due process

The city manager made use of due process in two ways. First, in designing the budget system, he sought the views of middle- and lower-level managers as well as those of the City Council, department heads, and his own staff. A number of important ideas emerged from this process. For example, the city manager learned that managers did not know the total amount of resources available to them or what they were expected to produce with those resources. Doing something about this situation became the cornerstone of budget-improvement efforts. The contributions of cost-center managers increased substantially during the second year, when the basic pieces of the new system were in place and managers had begun to see what it could do for them.

Second, the city manager incorporated due process into the implementation of the new budget system. Because operating managers formed the link between resource consumption and the provision of services, cost centers became the focus of budget hearings. A budget review committee consisting of the city manager, the finance director, and three department heads asked each cost-center manager to present his own

budget. Together, they explored ways of reducing expenditures and improving services. For example, one manager concluded a review session by saying, "Okay, I need three heavy-duty trucks for winter maintenance operations, and you can take three vacant positions to pay for them." Cost-center managers, for the first time, were involved in the process of determining what resources would be available to them and what they would do with those resources.

Doing your homework

The value of this guideline was most vividly demonstrated in the Flint case by what happened when the city manager failed to do his homework in regard to determining how his proposed office of management and budget would be financed. This oversight, caused by a desire to get the project moving quickly, ended up causing additional delay. When the manager subsequently took the time to do his homework, he found ample resources in the city's unappropriated-fund balances to finance not only this office but also a number of other outstanding projects.

Building on a successful track record

Because Flint's new city manager was an experienced management consultant, he was aware of the importance of introducing change gradually. Thus he adopted an evolutionary approach to systems development and implementation. During the first year, he directed most of his energies toward establishing the basic budget concept implementing the budget-preparation process. Once the new budget system had been made compatible with the city's existing accounting systems, he could improve the budget system by automating the preparation process and refining cost-center classifications and program categories. Then he could work toward integrating other systems with the budget system and developing a performance-measurement system to ensure management control over results. Success in the development of each phase of the budget implementation process made success in the next phase more likely, as both council members and city employees became more confident that the changes proposed by the manager would actually take place.

Realizing that change takes time

Closely related to building a successful track record is the importance of allowing sufficient time for making changes. Initially, the new city manager failed to follow this guideline. He recommended establishing four additional staff positions, with the expectation that his recommendations would quickly be approved and that the new employees would be on the job within several months. In fact, it took almost two months for him to obtain council approval for three of the four positions and an additional seven months for those positions to be filled according to civil-service procedures. This experience made the manager aware that major changes could not take place overnight, and he allocated longer periods of time for the implementation of subsequent proposals.

Recognizing the importance of timing

The city manager's greatest failure resulted from his inability to follow this guideline. In late January and early February 1972 the City Council and the manager were embroiled in a major battle with the city's newspaper over the council's decision to hold executive sessions. The *Flint Journal*, reacting to what it considered a threat to the right of the people to know what was going on in their city government, sued the city and ran a series of scathing editorials and articles. In the middle of all this controversy the city manager introduced his proposal for an office of management and budget. The newspaper, siding

with the city employee unions, attacked the City Council for approving the proposal and the council backed down. Had the city manager waited a few months, allowing tempers to cool and negative feelings to subside, his proposal probably would have received a more favorable reception.

Knowing when to compromise

Compromise was necessary and appropriate when the city manager agreed to accept three new staff positions instead of the four he had requested. In that case, the manager had to choose between a compromise or nothing at all.

In trying to implement the new budget system, however, the manager faced a situation in which compromise was not an appropriate course of action. The issue was this: should cost centers be used as the building blocks of the new budget system? This concept was strenuously opposed by some department heads, who recognized that their responsibilities were not clearly defined and that the cost-center approach might threaten their jobs. It was also opposed by many cost-center managers, who were afraid they might be assigned to new duties without a commensurate increase in compensation.

The city manager refused to accept these arguments. In his view, the main purpose of the new budget system was to ensure direct managerial responsibility for the expenditure of resources and the provision of city services. Backing down on the cost-center concept would have negated this purpose. There was no room for compromise.

The Flint case illustrates other guidelines as well. For example, both the director of finance and the city unions knew when to be *squeaky wheels*. They took their complaints to the City Council and often got results. The importance of follow-up was also recognized. The management-improvement program would not have been implemented successfully if the city manager and his staff had not paid attention to day-to-day details.

On balance, most of the guidelines for successfully getting things done were followed in Flint. By 1976 an integrated master plan was in place, tied to the city's new organization-based budget system. A performance reporting system and financial/management reporting systems had been linked to the budget. A data-processing plan was being implemented, and a new computer had been purchased. Only in the area of analytical assistance had expectations not been realized. Adequate analytical support

had never been achieved. Once the other systems had been completed, this inadequacy was even more apparent. The information provided by better management tools was of little value because it was never analyzed and communicated in a form that could help city administrators make better decisions. In the end, the management-improvement program failed to achieve its ultimate objectives—not because the guidelines listed in Chapter 19 were not followed but because, in the last analysis, people are more important than tools.

CHAPTER 19

Development of an Urban University: A Case Study

On a cold, overcast day in May 1974, federal, state, and local government officials, as well as representatives of almost every special-interest group in Flint, sat on uncomfortable wooden seats in Willson Park listening to the words of Robben Fleming, president of the University of Michigan. President Fleming was thanking all the citizens of Flint for converting a beautiful dream into what promised to be an even more beautiful reality. The occasion was the groundbreaking for the first building of the University of Michigan's new urban campus in Flint. This campus would be located along the Flint River in the heart of downtown. It would cost more than $60 million to construct and would consist of nine major buildings located on nearly forty-two acres of land. When completed, it would provide approximately 10,000 full-time students with the opportunity to pursue their educational goals.

As he watched the first shovelful of dirt lifted from the ground, Flint's city manager said to a friend, "I never thought it would really happen!" In fact, there were few in the audience who, two years before, had honestly believed that this project would ever become a reality. Only yesterday, it seemed, the University of Michigan had been about to construct a new campus on a seventeen-acre site nearby (the East Court Street site) even though the chancellor of the Flint campus had expressed his belief that this site was inadequate and would not serve the university's long-run interests.

Working drawings for one building on the old site had been proposed and bids had been let for construction. Now, two years later, ground was being broken for a major urban university campus on a new site in the heart of downtown. What had happened? Why did the University of Michigan decide to change campus locations? How were the supporters of this change able to obtain agreement and support from a wide variety of individuals and institutions for the idea that this change was best for the community? In short, how did those responsible for this change "get from there to here"?

In the first section of this chapter, we present a case history of the urban campus development project. In the second section, we examine the extent to which the guidelines presented in Chapter 17 were followed in the process.

A Dream Becomes a Reality

"The idea catches the mind"

On Leap Year Day in 1972, Flint's major business and civic leaders gathered in a downtown hotel to hear the bad news. A consulting team, hired by a group of business and community leaders to evaluate the prospects for revitalizing Flint's downtown, was scheduled to present its findings in a report entitled "Centric 80." Even before the carefully prepared slides projected the gloomy statistics on the screen, most people in the room knew the conclusions. Flint—a city that four decades earlier had enjoyed the most rapid population increase in the country, a city that in 1954 had experienced the greatest increase in downtown sales in its history, a city that had been the recipient of the highest per-capita investment of the largest company in the world—was dying.

The indicators of terminal disease were apparent to anyone who looked. From 1960 to 1970 the assessed value of the central business district declined 24 percent, resulting in a major loss of property-tax revenue. Since 1945, only 7 percent of the new office space constructed in Genessee County had been placed downtown, reflecting a major shift of population to the suburbs. During the past decade there had been no growth in retail sales in the downtown area, a condition that resulted from decisions by Sears, Hudson's, Woolworth's, and others to forsake downtown for suburban shopping malls. In fact, from 1965 to 1975, twenty-six businesses left downtown—a reduction of 22 percent— and many other existing downtown businesses were planning to leave because of the deteriorating physical condition of the central business district and the belief that this was no longer a place where one could make a reasonable profit.

Adding to the gloom was the haunting specter of unrealized development dreams. During the previous five years, a number of major development projects had been conceived but never executed. The city's 1960 master plan called for the development of a downtown mall and the closing of major arterial streets to encourage downtown shopping. This had not happened. A plan to construct an automotive hall of fame on an island in the middle of the Flint River had been drawn up by the world-famous architect Minoru Yamasaki, yet this project never got past the talking stage. Even less-ambitious efforts—to persuade the local industrial association to construct its new hockey rink downtown and to persuade the Buick Division of General Motors to locate its new administration building in the central area—had been unsuccessful. In short, dreams and plans to revitalize Flint's central city had failed. Nobody seemed capable of getting from here to anywhere.

As the audience listened to the "Centric 80" report, the gloom began to lift, for yet another idea for the salvation of Flint's central city was being presented. Maybe this was different. People in the back of the room began to listen more attentively as the consultants explained why the University of Michigan should relocate its Flint campus in the heart of downtown, along the Flint River. This project, the consultants asserted, would be a "people generator." It would create a reason for people to live, work, and shop in the downtown area. Moreover, this project would capitalize on Flint's most significant natural feature—its river.

The proposal to locate a major urban university in the center of Flint seemed unblemished by potential liabilities. As one person put it, "This proposal to relocate the University of Michigan campus is not the best alternative to rejuvinate downtown; it is the *only* alternative."

Reaction to the proposed campus relocation was swift and positive. Flint's major newspaper, the *Flint Journal*, described the riverfront campus plan as "an imaginative proposal" that would "put into harmony the needs of the urban university and the needs of the urban center, each helping the other to fulfill its functions." Locating the University of Michigan–Flint campus downtown, the newspaper added, would be "good medicine for the city's ailing heart." The president of the Urban Coalition described the project as "a catalyst that will bring divergent interests of the community together in a common cause." The president of a major retail store, reflecting the views of the business community, described the project as "pennies from heaven." The chairman of the General Neighborhood Redevelopment Project Committee (representing five central city urban-renewal projects) endorsed the project, saying, "This will provide tangible proof that urban renewal works." Then as an afterthought, he added, "People are sick and tired of talk. They want action, and this will provide it." One of Flint's most prominent civic leaders, a former General Motors plant executive, noted that "a vast array of projects in Flint have produced nothing." He cautioned, "We had better not miss the boat this time."

Positive reactions to this idea were not confined to Flint citizens. The director of HUD's area office in Detroit, appearing before Flint's City Council, warmly endorsed the downtown university proposal, saying that it would favorably affect the city's urban-renewal projects. In reacting to the campus relocation proposal, the chancellor of the University of Michigan–Flint captured the spirit of public reaction to the proposal when he observed, "The idea catches the mind." Not everyone favored the idea, however.

Changing horses in the middle of the stream

In reacting to the proposed campus location the president of the Flint Area Conference, Inc. (a group of private business and community leaders united to promote the physical and economic revival of the central area of Flint) pointed out that to implement this proposal the community must convince the University of Michigan to "change horses in the middle of the stream." He was referring to the fact that the university had already begun to execute a plan to build its first classroom-office building on what was now asserted to be an inferior site. The problem was how to stop this effort and to turn campus development plans in a new direction—toward downtown. It was one thing to have an idea, he pointed out, and quite another to execute it.

The first step was to understand thoroughly the existing campus plan. This was not difficult; the plan was minimal. In 1970, the University of Michigan, reacting to an acute shortage of space and to problems imposed by sharing its campus site with a growing community college (more than 10,000 students), accepted a seventeen-acre gift of land from Charles Stewart Mott, president of the Mott Foundation. Without pausing long enough to determine whether this land provided an adequate site on which to expand and develop a campus, university officials initiated a plan to construct three buildings on the site. The land represented a bird in hand that no one wanted to lose by questioning its usefulness.

In almost all respects, the proposed campus site was inadequate. It was broken into three parcels, and, after subtracting unusable land and parking areas from the site, less than half of the seventeen acres remained for campus development. This limitation, in turn, severely limited potential enrollment. A small campus with a capacity for 5,000 full-time-equivalent students would not meet the educational needs of those who lived in the eleven-county region served by the campus. In addition, the site had no expansion potential. It was surrounded by single-family residential neighborhoods on two sides and by major city arteries and an interstate freeway on the other two sides. With this plan, it would be necessary to continue using the existing University of Michigan-Flint campus, forcing students to walk more than five blocks between the old campus and the proposed new one—a hazardous journey which involved crossing a major city artery. Moreover, until parking ramps were constructed, there would be virtually no parking spaces available on the new campus.

Concerned about the inadequacy of the site, Flint's city manager, supported by a wide range of community leaders, began to assemble facts that would provide solid evidence that the downtown riverfront site better served the interests of the University of Michigan, Genessee Community College, and the Flint community. In March 1972, he initiated a series of meetings to present to citizens the best case for the proposed campus relocation.

Stopping the university development in midstream and turning it in a new direction would not be a problem-free process. As the idea began to receive more and more public exposure, its opponents began to show their colors. Some pointed out that the downtown site was almost entirely situated on a flood plain, posing significant construction problems and increased costs. Others noted that a downtown location would separate the campus from the city's cultural area, to which the existing location was connected. Economically minded citizens bemoaned the loss of property-tax revenue that would result from converting land to public use. A student at the University of Michigan pointed out, in a letter to the *Flint Journal*, "Students will not want to enroll in a university located in a crime-infested slum area, next to a dirty, smelly river and crisscrossed by wide streets with heavy traffic." Finally, the president of the NAACP indicated that the downtown campus plan was really "an effort to bail out the downtown merchants" and did not reflect the right prioritization of community needs.

Proponents of the downtown campus attempted to counter each of these objections. They pointed out that the flood-plain location posed design problems but did not prohibit construction. They pointed out that, although the university was a nontaxpaying citizen, expanded campus development would generate increased revenue from sales taxes, appreciation of adjacent property values, and income taxes from both existing

businesses that would be induced to stay downtown and new businesses that would be attracted to the downtown area because of the campus. In answer to the objection to its separation from the cultural center, proponents pointed out that the downtown campus. would ensure proximity to major auditorium facilities, existing parking ramps, an existing outdoor park and recreational facility, a downtown library, and other buildings that could be utilized as temporary space for students and teachers during campus construction.

Downtown campus proponents admitted that the Flint River was dirty. In developing the campus, they argued, incentives would be provided to clean up the river and the environment surrounding the campus. A downtown campus would have a catalytic value in promoting the overall development of the central-city area. Finally, the downtown campus would aid in the completion of several major urban-revewal programs, would stimulate the development of badly needed housing, and would provide a greater opportunity for citizens of all races to attend a high-quality university within reach of their homes and their parents' pocketbooks.

On balance, public and private leaders throughout the community supported moving the University of Michigan campus downtown as representing a unique opportunity. As one leader put it, the campus relocation represented for the city of Flint a "last call to breakfast." Community and civic leaders, however, were not responsible for the final decision about where the university would be located. This responsibility rested with University of Michigan regents. Therefore, it was to the university that the proponents of the campus relocation turned their attention in early March 1972.

Developing "compelling reasons"

On March 9, 1972, ten days after the campus relocation proposal was formally presented, Flint's City Council endorsed the project and appointed eighteen people to serve on a committee charged with the responsibility for converting this idea into reality. The Mayor's Implementation Committee represented almost every facet of the community, ranging from organized labor to General Motors, from urban-renewal project area community members to downtown business owners, from the Human Relations Commission to the Board of Education. The honorary chairman of this committee was Charles Stewart Mott, Flint's philanthropic patriarch, who was entering his ninety-seventh year. The active chairman was George Whyel, president of one of Flint's major banks. Whyel summarized the challenge before the mayor's committee this way: "Our responsibility is to develop 'compelling reasons' that the Board of Regents cannot turn down."

At first glance, the task before this committee did not seem that difficult. Most knowledgeable people agreed that the existing plan for the Flint campus was inadequate and would not serve the university's long-term educational needs or advance community interests. Certainly, the Board of Regents would recognize the overwhelming base of community support for the downtown campus. As one councilman put it, "The Board of Regents cannot ignore an opportunity to construct a first-rate urban campus." The implementation committee had only to marshal the arguments supporting the downtown campus—the merits of the proposal would do the rest.

This assessment was inaccurate. Careful examination of the proposed riverfront campus plan illuminated a vast array of roadblocks standing in the way of the project. These included the needs to amend the city's urban-renewal plans and zoning ordinances, replace downtown parking, remove railroad tracks, close streets, and complete the downtown freeway extension. Removing these obstacles would be time consuming and would require the successful interaction of a vast array of individuals and institutions,

ranging from federal government departments (Housing and Urban Development, Army Corps of Engineers) and state agencies (Bureau of Conservation, Department of Transportation) to the City Council and urban-renewal project area committees.

Successfully solving these problems was important if the Board of Regents was to be persuaded to relocate the campus, but doing so would not guarantee a favorable decision. For the regents, the "compelling reasons" for changing campuses boiled down to two—land and money. The Mayor's Implementation Committee had to find a way to secure the land and to provide the University of Michigan with sufficient financial help to ensure the development of a "first-rate urban campus."

These two requirements were inextricably bound together: to secure the land required money. To determine how much money required an analysis and appraisal of each of the ninety-two separate parcels in the proposed downtown campus area. It would be necessary to determine whether all the land could be acquired, and, if so, when this could be accomplished.

The facts required to answer these questions were not readily available. Recognizing this, and recognizing the importance of the answers in persuading the Board of Regents to accept the proposal, the mayor's committee raised $50,000 to retain McKinsey & Co., a management-consulting firm, to do the analyses. Working quickly, a McKinsey team reviewed every parcel of land and prepared an acquisition schedule that was consistent with the needs and development plans of the university. It also prepared a financial plan geared to the acquisition schedule.

Identifying how much the land would cost was a far easier task than figuring out who would pay for it. Thus, obtaining financial commitments to this project from public and private sources became the committee's principal task.

The first major financial assistance came, surprisingly, from the Flint City Council. On April 24, 1972, the council, after a long debate, offered the University of Michigan $6 million to assist in the relocation of its Flint campus downtown. This commitment would be paid in annual installments of $300,000 for twenty years. The money would be used to acquire land. It would come from the city's Public Improvement Fund and would not require an increase in taxes or a vote of the people. The *Flint Journal,* in somewhat hyperbolic terms, hailed the council's action as "the most important action since reconversion of industry after World War II." The editorial pointed out what all those connected with this project knew: without the council's action, the journey to a downtown campus would have ended before it began.

Armed with this unparalleled financial commitment from the City Council, the implementation committee directed its efforts toward the private sector. Its goal: to raise $10 million by July, just three months away. Summing up the committee's intended effort, its chairman emphasized that he was not going to let anyone off the hook.

By mid-July, the private sector had pledged $7 million to make the downtown campus a reality. This unprecedented response included a $5 million grant from the Mott Foundation, a $1 million grant from the DeWaters Charitable Trust Fund, and $1 million from a large number of private businesses and individuals. Combined with the city's commitment ($6 million), an anticipated $2.5 million contribution from General Motors, and $3.5 million from the anticipated sale of the university's current classroom-office building to the community college, it was estimated that the financial package that would be presented to the University of Michigan would equal $19 million.

On July 1, the Board of Regents met in Ann Arbor to consider the "compelling reasons" offered by the Mayor's Implementation Committee. The challenge presented to the Board of Regents was colorfully expressed by Fred Tucker, a member of the committee and one of the most powerful members of the Flint City Council: "The people of Flint

are saying to you, let's build a real university in Flint. And here's 19 million bucks to do it."

The Board of Regents carefully reviewed McKinsey's land-acquisition analysis and the "financial package" presented by the committee. Following this review, it did what many committees do when they cannot make decisions—they authorized a further study. To ensure that the downtown site was suitable for campus development, the regents felt that a feasibility study must be prepared. Further, they wanted assurances that the needs of students would be met while the downtown campus was being constructed. To accomplish this, the regents suggested that a temporary building be constructed on the present site (a "surge" building) and that the citizens of Flint pay the estimated $700,000 cost of construction.

During the three months following the regents vote to delay a final decision, the implementation committee faced two additional problems: obtaining a financial commitment from General Motors and making sure that the city's initial $6-million pledge could be made legally binding. After eight months of deliberation, the committee experienced its first major setback. General Motors announced in October that it would not contribute to the University of Michigan relocation project. There appeared to be two major reasons for its position: concern about the precedent-setting nature of such a gift and the conviction that General Motors was already providing sufficient support to the University of Michigan in Ann Arbor. The argument that the downtown riverfront project would have a major impact of community development in Flint and that, in the long run, this would serve both the civic and the corporate interests of General Motors had not been persuasive.

On the second front, the implementation committee was more successful. In August 1972, the city of Flint obtained a legal opinion stating that the current City Council could appropriate whatever funds it felt the University of Michigan project warranted during its term of office (1971–73), but that it could not bind future councils to this project. There appeared to be only two ways to bind future councils: the city could finance its contribution through the issuance of bonds, or the present council could contribute the entire $6 million during its term of office. Exercising the first option, it appeared at the time, required a vote of the people; the second required more money than the city had available.

After considerable analysis, Flint's finance director proposed and the City Council agreed that the city's contribution would be increased to $600,000 a year, yielding a total of $1.2 million during the council's term of office. The remaining $4.8 million would be pledged over the remaining eight-year period with the clear understanding that this pledge would not be binding for future councils.

Another major setback involved a decision by the Flint Board of Education to contest the proposed sale of the UM–F's current classroom-office building to the community college. The president of the Board of Education announced that Charles Stewart Mott, who had provided the funds for the building, had stipulated that if it were vacated by UM–F it must be given, not sold, to the community college. By late October this issue was still unresolved.

These events dramatically changed the nature of the financial package being offered the University of Michigan. If the city could legally pledge only $1.2 million, General Motors would not participate at all, and the anticipated $3.5 million from the sale of the classroom building was in doubt, the total guaranteed financial package was reduced from $19 million to approximately $8.2 million. This was not enough. In mid-October, the chancellor of UM–F indicated that it would take a minimum of $9.7 million to convince the Board of Regents to approve the relocation. By implication, the chancellor was saying that anything less would result in a decision that served neither the interests of the university nor the interests of the city.

In the few days remaining before the Board of Regents was to make a final decision, a group of community leaders and institutions made up the $1.5 million balance of the $9.7 million requirement. They did so with the firm understanding that if the city honored its future pledge (beyond $1.2 million), the necessity of their contribution would be removed.

This contribution, along with the study showing that the proposed campus development was feasible, was presented to the Board of Regents. On October 20, 1972, the board voted unanimously to approve the downtown campus proposal, conditional only on the approval of the Joint Capital Outlay Committee of the state legislature. After eight months of intense and dedicated effort, the city of Flint and the members of the Mayor's Implementation Committee had succeeded in presenting the Board of Regents with the "compelling reasons" for developing a first-rate urban university.

Those who felt that victory had been won were premature. Proponents of the downtown riverfront site still had to contend with the Michigan legislature and one of its most prominent members—Senator Garland Lane—the senator from the Flint area.

Coping with neutrality

If you think that the Board of Regents, elected by the citizens of Michigan, should be responsible for determining which campus location would best serve the interests of the University of Michigan, you are right. If you think the Board of Regents has this power, you are wrong. The regents' October 20 decision was not final. Given the political realities in which the university operated, the state legislature still had to approve the plan and appropriate the capital funds to implement it. In the context of this project, the state legislature was one person—Senator Garland Lane.

Senator Lane was elected in 1948 to represent the 29th District, an area that included a major portion of the city of Flint. Building on seven consecutive electoral victories and aided by a rigid seniority system, he had become chairman of the House-Senate Joint Capital Outlay Committee (JCOC). In addition, he was vice-chairman of the Senate Appropriations Committee. The JCOC was responsible for reviewing and recommending to both the House and the Senate an annual capital budget. Therefore, all new building plans, including the proposal to construct a downtown campus in Flint, had to be approved by this committee.

The fact that Senator Lane was chairman of the JCOC made his support for any building program important; the fact that the campus building program was in Flint made his support imperative. In the past, Senator Lane had played a pivotal role in the development of the University of Michigan–Flint campus. Working with C.S. Mott in the 1950's, he had been instrumental in obtaining state funds for the existing campus. The critical question in October 1972 was where the senator stood on the downtown university proposal. Was he for it or against it?

On the surface, the answer was neither. "I am neutral," Senator Lane replied to all those who sought an answer to this question. He quickly added, "And I will remain neutral until all the facts are in." There were few in Flint, however, who agreed with this assessment. In mid-September, Councilman Fred Tucker voiced his feelings when he told the City Council that it was time to call a spade a spade. "Gar Lane," he said, "has been against the move from the start and he's still against it." On the basis of a review of the senator's involvement with this project, it was difficult to disagree with Tucker's assessment.

On March 12, 1972, just two weeks after the announcement of the downtown riverfront campus proposal, Senator Lane sent a list of thirty questions about the proposal to the most influential people in the Flint community and to the Board of Regents. Lane's "nuts and bolts" questions raised important issues. He wondered how much land would be available downtown. He asked when and how it would be acquired and at what cost.

He asked what provision would be made for students during the transition period. Further, he queried whether the city had a plan to control traffic, close streets, and relocate utilities—and who would pay for these. These were all questions that had to be answered if the Board of Regents were to be persuaded that the downtown campus was superior to the one they had previously selected.

Senator Lane's questions did not necessarily represent a negative position on relocation. Some supporters of relocation, however, including the chancellor and a number of Lane's legislative colleagues in Lansing, observed that the questions being asked about the riverfront site had never been asked about the previous site on East Court Street. The chancellor privately pointed out that the current campus development plan, financial plan, and city master plan had been inadequate to guide the development of the old campus. Nevertheless, he believed that such plans were vital to the development of a first-rate campus and should be prepared for the downtown site, regardless of what had happened earlier. He therefore urged the Board of Regents to undertake a feasibility study of the new campus.

From mid-March until September, the Mayor's Implementation Committee diligently attempted to answer the questions that Senator Lane and others had advanced. A management-consulting firm was asked to prepare a land-acquisition and financing plan for the campus development. An engineering firm was engaged to prepare a downtown traffic study, assessing the implications of the university project on existing traffic flow and street systems. A law firm was hired to identify potential legal problems concerning the city's contribution to the University of Michigan and an architectural firm was hired in July to prepare a site-feasibility study.

To ensure that the JCOC was fully informed on this project, the chairman of the Mayor's Implementation Committee invited the entire Joint Capital Outlay Committee to

Flint in late August to view at first hand the proposed site. In addition, he arranged for the management-consulting and architectural firms to prepare a thorough briefing concerning land acquisition, financing, and site feasibility. This meeting, which included a number of state planning officials as well as University of Michigan administrators from Ann Arbor, appeared to be extremely successful. Members of the JCOC left Flint with a much better idea of the potential impact of the downtown campus on the community as well as on the university's intent to construct a campus that would be capable of providing a full curriculum to 10,000 full-time students.

Senator Lane, however, was unpersuaded by the campus briefing. He decided to conduct his own public hearing in Flint in September. According to his administrative assistant, the senator expected this public hearing to reveal the absence of public support for this project.

If this was really the senator's expectation, he was out of touch with the Flint community. In a five-and-a-half-hour session that ended well after midnight, forty-four citizens addressed the senator's committee. Of these, thirty-six voiced support for the downtown project, seven were against it, and one was neutral. Proponents of the downtown campus represented almost every major interest group in the city. Speakers included the president of the community college, the chairman of the UM–F Academic Planning Board, Flint's congressman, the vice-chairman of the Greater Flint AFL–CIO Council, presidents of the urban renewal project area committees, business and civic leaders, and a large number of individual citizens.

Lane still was not satisfied. He told reporters after the meeting, "I want to conduct my own poll through the local media to find out what my constituents want me to do." He added, "The people who testified aren't representative of general public opinion." Concluding a long day, Lane summarized his position by suggesting that project supporters would have to raise $30 million to convince him of this project's practicality.

Senator Lane's professed neutrality began to seem somewhat suspect. A month after the public hearing, U.S. Representative Don Riegle announced the results of a poll he had conducted to determine his constituents' views on the downtown campus proposal. Of those interviewed who expressed an opinion, 64 percent approved the downtown campus move. Again, Senator Lane was unconvinced. He again announced that he would conduct his own poll but would not announce the results until after the Board of Regents' decision on October 20.

It was clear by October that Senator Lane was anything but a neutral actor in the drama surrounding the downtown campus plan. Switching from his earlier role of concerned questioner, Lane began to construct a series of barriers that he apparently hoped would stop the downtown campus momentum. In early October he announced that C.S. Mott was disenchanted with the project and was going to withdraw the Mott Foundation's $5 million commitment. This assertion was immediately denied by Mott's son Harding. Undaunted, Lane announced that GM would not contribute a dime to the project, that Flint's $6 million contribution was illegal, and that a plan to sell the Mott Memorial Building to the community college could not be executed. Then, in a surprise move, Senator Lane announced that there was considerable expansion opportunity near the old campus site. He was referring to twelve acres of land owned by the Board of Education on which five buildings were situated, some of which were major historical landmarks. The Board of Education, in a carefully worded reply to this announcement, indicated that, at a price, the land would be available, but that this price had to include the replacement costs of relocation of the five buildings. In short, it would not be cheap.

Following the regents' unanimous decision on October 20 to accept the downtown proposal, Senator Lane switched the forum of his dissent to the JCOC. Here he wielded unbridled power. This was much in evidence by late October, when the JCOC had scheduled a meeting to finally determine the fate of the downtown campus. University of Michigan officials made a full presentation of the campus plan, supported by a convincing array of evidence indicating why this campus site was in the best interests of the University of Michigan. Five of the eight committee members attended this presentation. Despite the fact that two of the members slept through part of the presentation, a quorum existed that would have been sufficient to settle the matter once and for all. Realizing that he did not have the votes to kill this project, Senator Lane persuaded a colleague to leave the room and then announced that, because of a lack of a quorum, no decision could be made. He summarily ended the meeting, and postponed a final decision until the next meeting in November.

At the November meeting Lane had his votes together. The JCOC voted that it would not make a decision on the project until it had a complete campus development plan. University of Michigan officials attending the meeting indicated that the earliest date by which such a plan could be completed would be February 1973, and estimated that it would cost about $100,000. Lane suggested that the cost be paid by proponents of the downtown campus. In addition, he indicated that construction of the downtown campus would necessitate the construction of a "surge" building that would cost about $400,000, and that this cost would have to be met from privately pledged funds. Robben Fleming, president of the University of Michigan, pressed the senator at this meeting about his true position on the downtown project. "Suppose you see a satisfactory plan on February 1," Fleming asked, "would you then approve this project?" Senator Lane replied, "I don't know what we're doing this work for if we're against it from the start." This didn't answer the question, but he refused to say anything more on the matter.

Following the meeting, Senator Lane gathered reporters together to announce the results of his long-awaited poll. He indicated that his office had sent 9,200 questionnaires

to his constituents to obtain their views on the campus project: of the 14 percent who replied, 687 were against the move, and 599 favored it. In addition, he indicated that he had received thirty-five letters against the campus move and only five in favor of it. He ended his announcement by saying that 95 percent of the people who approached him on the street were against the move.

In early December, the University of Michigan announced that it would hire the firm that prepared the feasibility study to prepare a campus-development plan by February 1. Meanwhile additional pressure was added to the weight of the argument for the downtown campus. The Carnegie Commission on Higher Education issued a report assessing the educational facilities in ninety-nine U.S. metropolitan centers. With respect to Flint, the commission's study indicated that the educational system was "marginally deficient in enrollment capacity given the population served." Adjusting enrollment figures used by the Carnegie Commission staff to reflect the fact that the General Motors Institute had a student body largely made up of out-of-state students, Flint's educational system fell to the bottom ten of the ninety-nine areas studied. This announcement strengthened the argument for a downtown urban university that would provide educational opportunities for nearly twice as many students as the previous site.

By mid-February the stage was set for a final vote on the downtown campus. The campus development plan completed in early February called for the development of a downtown campus at a total cost of about $60 million. Further, it called for the use of the East Court Street site as the location of a temporary "surge" building and as the site for future recreational use and athletic fields. In essence, the University of Michigan wanted the best of both worlds— the downtown area as the site for its main campus and the East Court Street area as the site for ancillary services. On February 16, 1973, the Board of Regents gave its approval of the two-site proposal.

On March 2, 1973—one year after the

downtown campus idea had been announced—the JCOC met to make a decision. Showing a diligence that seemed uncharacteristic, the committee met half-an-hour earlier than the published notice indicated, thereby making the decision behind closed doors in what was later called an "executive session."

After the decision, Lane opened the meeting to the press and the public. At this time, he announced that his committee had approved the site. He then went on to detail a number of stipulations on which its approval was based. Lane demanded that there be no architectural changes in the $6.7 million building formerly planned for the East Court Street site and now to be constructed downtown. He indicated that all utilities and the city's sanitary and storm sewers must be relocated at no cost to the state or to the university. Further, he demanded that improvements to city streets or rerouting of streets outside the campus boundary be done at no cost to the state or to the university, and that the university must buy or obtain long-term options on all publicly owned parcels in the designated campus area within a reasonable period of time. Finally, and most surprisingly, Lane demanded that another campus plan be developed, because he did not think the present one was adequate. He said that a Michigan firm would have to be hired—one that knew how to pronounce Flint's street names. (This reflect-

ed his earlier pique with one of the consultants who had not been able to correctly pronounce the name of a Flint street bisecting the proposed campus site.)

When Lane had finished reading his list of demands, a leading advocate of the downtown riverfront site exuberantly proclaimed, "At last, neutrality has been overcome!"

Postscript

A year later, in May 1974—after architectural drawings had been prepared, zoning maps changed, streets closed and relocated, urban-renewal plans amended, a bond issue sold, and land purchased—ground was finally broken for the downtown riverfront campus. Many believed it inappropriate that Senator Lane was given the honor of inaugurating a project that he had opposed so vigorously for so long.

Following the groundbreaking ceremonies, Lane told a group of supporters that he had not enjoyed the pressure that had been put on him by supporters of this project. He added that he still did not believe the citizens of Flint really supported the project. Apparently he was wrong. Three months later, Senator Lane was soundly defeated in the Democratic primary by a young member of the state House of Representatives—who, incidentally, had strongly supported the project.

Applying the Guidelines

In this section, we reexamine the efforts to develop an urban university in Flint in order to illustrate the importance of following the guidelines presented in Chapter 17.

Understanding the status quo

The failure of campus-relocation proponents to understand why the East Court Street site had been initially selected and

who had a personal interest in its development delayed the decision-making process and nearly caused the defeat of the relocation project. Convinced of the benefits represented by the riverside campus, relocation supporters did not take the time to develop the best case for the East Court Street site. As a result, they were unaware of the importance of Senator Lane's personal commitment to the existing campus site until his position had become solidified.

If more attention had been paid to those who had vested interests in the East Court Street site, relocation supporters would have recognized the power and influence exerted by the architect who had been selected to design the first campus building on the old site. This architect and Senator Lane were close friends and political allies. In retrospect, many people believed that the architect's resistance to the campus relocation, not Senator Lane's opposition, was the major barrier. If this architect had been included in early discussions about the advantages of a downtown campus, his hostility might have been defused, with a corresponding impact on the senator.

Another consequence of not taking the time to understand the status quo was unnecessary opposition from students and faculty who complained that, in the rush to bail out the downtown business interests, no one was considering the interests of the university. Because of the acute shortage of space on the existing University of Michigan–Flint campus and the necessity of sharing parking and building facilities with a growing community college, they found it difficult to accept the prospect of delaying expansion of the East Court Street site. Had this viewpoint been understood during early strategy sessions, greater emphasis could have been placed on solving the interim space needs of students and faculty.

Recognizing power where it exists

With the exception of Senator Lane, campus-relocation proponents had identified and obtained some sort of support from almost every powerful individual and interest group in the Flint community. The implementation committee included representatives from General Motors, the UAW and AFL/CIO municipal employee unions, the newspaper, the Board of Education, the University of Michigan Citizens Advisory Committee, urban-renewal citizen district council representatives, bankers, business owners, members of the Human Relations Commission, members of the City Council, and interested private citizens. With the exception of the NAACP (which was not represented) and the County Board of Supervisors (whose chairman refused to serve) every important interest group was represented on the mayor's committee. While the resultant coalition of interest groups included some strange bedfellows, collectively they had the capacity to get the job done.

In addition to putting together an effective coalition, relocation supporters obtained more than sixty endorsements from influential citizens. These endorsements made it difficult for Senator Lane to argue convincingly that the proposed campus relocation did not have broad-based community support.

The role played by Councilman Fred Tucker provides an excellent illustration of recognizing power where it exists and using it. In developing a strategy to persuade the University of Michigan to relocate its campus to the riverfront site, two critical factors were identified: first, the City Council had to demonstrate its support for the relocation by offering the first financial contribution; and second, the black community had to be convinced that relocating the campus was in the interest of all Flint citizens, not, as the president of the NAACP suggested, "a total distortion of the city's priorities and a sellout to the fat-cat downtown interests."

Recognizing that Tucker, a black and one of the most powerful members of the council, was the key to accomplishing both of these objectives, the city manager and other supporters of the relocation project persuaded the Mayor's Implementation Committee to give him a prominent role. This, as it turned out, was not difficult. An exceptionally effective speaker, Tucker sought every opportunity to advance the case for the downtown campus. His endeavors contributed to the council's decision to pledge $6 million to the move and were largely responsible for the support the relocation plan received from the black community.

If the role of Councilman Tucker illustrates what happens when power is recognized and used, the failure of the relocation supporters to understand the importance of the House–Senate Joint Capital Outlay Committee illustrates the converse. For six months, lobbying efforts were directed almost exclusively toward the University of Michigan, on the assumption that if the Board of Regents determined that the downtown site better served the university, the state legislature would have no recourse but to follow suit. However, as the project proponents belatedly discovered, the legislature actually played the pivotal role in the decision. A more thorough analysis of the decision-making process (and of the institutions and individuals involved in it) could have avoided this misunderstanding and the delay it caused.

Incorporating due process

This guideline is closely related to the first two: without an understanding of who benefits from the status quo and who has power, it is impossible to know what individuals, institutions, and interest groups should be included in the decision-making process. Because relocation proponents failed to recognize that Senator Lane had a personal stake in the East Court Street site and that his power on the JCOC could block the relocation proposal, the views of the Senator and his supporters were not solicited in advance. The consequences of this oversight were significant.

From the perspective of hindsight, it seems possible that proponents of the downtown campus chose an inappropriate strategy for announcing the relocation proposal. The dramatic unveiling of the "Centric 80" report—an event to which relatively few people were invited—may have been a mistake. If the "Centric 80" report had been preceded by a series of discussions with faculty and students, city and county government officials, citizen district council leaders, and other interested parties, the initial reception to the relocation idea might have been even more positive. Certainly, including faculty and students in early discussions

about the riverfront site could have significantly reduced their opposition.

The role of the UM–F chancellor in the relocation effort provides a good illustration of how to involve those upon whom success is dependent. Soon after his arrival in Flint in 1971, the chancellor recognized the inadequacy of the East Court Street site, but he had little power to change the situation. New to the campus and unsure of the political climate, he was hesitant to bring up problems for which there did not appear to be solutions. Therefore, he carefully limited his efforts to asking penetrating questions about the East Court Street site. He met with civic and community leaders, suggesting through his inquiries that the present site was inadequate and that alternative sites might be considered. Although this effort was not entirely successful, he had planted seeds of doubt. The "Centric 80" study, the following year, provided the soil in which those seeds could grow. Without the chancellor's efforts to involve them, however, community leaders might not have been receptive to the "Centric 80" report.

Doing your homework

The careful marshaling of facts, rather than emotions, was a key factor in the success of the downtown campus project. The first public announcement of the campus-relocation proposal was presented in the context of an economic analysis of conditions in Flint. The data in this analysis enhanced the credibility of the university relocation proposal. Following the public presentation of the "Centric 80" report, the city manager held a number of public meetings in which he presented a detailed analysis of the potential benefits a downtown campus could offer for the university, the community college, and Flint residents. This fact-based presentation helped create a favorable public reaction to the proposal.

Outside consultants played an important role in the success of the relocation effort. Their fact-based analyses of various aspects of the proposal were critical to the effort to convince the Board of Regents and the JCOC to relocate the campus. The land-acquisition analysis answered questions about the availability of land and the cost of buying it. The traffic plan and the campus-development plan helped proponents answer hard questions about the feasibility of the move. Using outside expertise lent objectivity and credibility to the proposal. Further, members of the Mayor's Implementation Committee were able to act more assertively because they knew that their conclusions and recommendations were based on facts, not on hopes.

Building on a successful track record

During the 1960s and early 1970s, Flint's civic and community leaders had talked about change but were seldom able to effect it. Multicolored plans were prepared, reviewed, and stored away. Getting things done was the exception, not the rule. As the mayor, City Council, and new city manager examined Flint's development needs in December 1971, they concluded that one of the highest-priority needs was to change this atmosphere, which surrounded city decision makers like a dense fog. Innovative ideas were stifled; risk taking was not rewarded.

Given this climate, the early efforts to persuade government officials and community leaders to relocate the UM–F campus without question violated the "successful track record" guideline. Instead of proposing a small step that was clearly perceived as being doable, the sponsors of the relocation plan asked the community to accept the largest single development project in the city's history. Neither the chancellor of the university, the newly elected City Council, nor the recently hired local-government officials had acquired a track record in the community on which to build expectations that they could successfully implement a

project of this magnitude. However, there are exceptions to every rule, and knowing when to make an exception is as important as knowing all the rules. The campus relocation seemed so important to its proponents that, despite their lack of an established track record, they believed it was worth undertaking.

The success of the campus-relocation project generated a new climate and a new set of expectations in Flint. Following the state legislature's approval of the riverfront campus in February 1973, important changes began to take place: citizens voted to replace the city's outdated charter, a multimillion-dollar river beautification and flood-control project was financed and initiated, and the Mott Foundation subsidized the development of a low- and moderate-income housing project in an urban-renewal area adjacent to the new university campus. In addition, the foundation gave the city $1.8 million to develop an industrial park in one of the poorest areas of the city. There can be no better illustration of the adage that success breeds success: the success of the campus-relocation effort produced an environment in Flint in which other things began to happen.

Realizing that change takes time

The University of Michigan relocation project provided some vivid examples of the truism that achieving change in the public sector is a time-consuming process. The Mayor's Implementation Committee failed to achieve a single one of its objectives on time. The financial inducement package was to be delivered to the Board of Regents by April 1, 1972; it was not completed until July. The regents were to make a final decision on the campus relocation in July; this did not occur until October. The Joint Capital Outlay Committee was to make a decision on the university project in early November 1972;

the JCOC did not decide the matter until the following February. These delays reflected overoptimistic target dates that did not take into account the complexity of the proposal, the time required to develop the necessary information about it, and, perhaps most important, the reluctance of the Board of Regents and the JCOC to make controversial decisions.

The UM–F chancellor realized that a major public decision often requires a gestation period, so that people can digest a proposal and get used to the idea of change. He applied this guideline in his attempt to change the site of the downtown campus.

Flint's city manager and community-development director had initially identified a kidney-shaped thirty-acre site along the Flint River. This site was composed in large part of urban-renewal land already owned by the city, and it would have required a minimal disturbance of city streets and utilities. Its main disadvantage was its shape—a poor configuration for a campus. Moreover, the fact that it was almost entirely on the Flint River flood plain would have imposed significant limitations on construction.

The chancellor had believed from the beginning that this proposed location was not the best alternative in the downtown area. Instead of confronting the issue directly and thereby running the risk of jeopardizing the entire project, he queried key decision makers about ways to improve the proposed site. As the city manager, the community-development director, and other government officials responded to his questions and examined some of the problems associated with the initial site, they began to reconsider their decision.

The site ultimately chosen for the new University of Michigan–Flint campus bears little resemblance to the one originally selected. The final plan shows more than forty acres of land in a square shape, most of it outside the flood plain. By recognizing the importance of allowing time for local-government officials to come to their own conclusions, the chancellor successfully influenced a critical decision about the downtown campus.

Recognizing the importance of timing

Throughout the two-year effort to relocate the campus, proponents of the idea were aware of this guideline. Recognizing that the City Council's initial reaction to the proposal was favorable and that a financial contribution from the city was imperative, the Mayor's Implementation Committee capitalized on this momentum by directing its initial strategy toward the council. The committee's recognition of the importance of timing paid a major dividend: the council pledged $6 million for the downtown campus only two months after the idea was announced. This initial pledge was a primary factor in making the relocation plan credible and in persuading others to make financial contributions.

Knowing when to compromise

The relocation effort was characterized throughout by willingness to compromise. Its proponents did everything possible to satisfy the demands made by the Board of Regents and the Joint Capital Outlay Committee. Flint community leaders paid more than $100,000 in consulting fees, and the university itself spent more than $60,000 to ensure that the regents and Senator Lane's committee had sufficient information to make the relocation decision. Supporters of the downtown campus financed the $400,000 "surge" building required to meet the interim needs of students. In resolving issues related to parking, land acquisition, utility relocation, street closing, and urban-renewal plan amendments, everything possible was done to find a common ground that would be satisfactory to everyone who had an interest in the outcome. While there clearly were points on which the Mayor's Implementation Committee would not compromise, in the end its willingness to seek a mutually acceptable solution to every problem wore down resistance and contributed significantly to the success of the project.

To a lesser extent, the successful relocation of the UM–F campus reflects the application of other guidelines. For example, the *squeaky wheels* received considerable oil during the two-year decision-making period. Furthermore, every effort was made to *spread the credit* for the initial success of this project to individuals and institutions whose support and enthusiasm would be critical to realizing the final objective. Finally, the university's campus planning staff and the city of Flint's Department of Community Development monitored and *followed up* on every

critical step in the process of converting the downtown campus from rhetoric to reality. Few loose ends remained untied for long. In addition, proponents of the project periodically took the opportunity to step back and *reexamine objectives* and the assumptions on which they were based. By holding regular strategy meetings with the university, the city, and the private sector, they made sure that there was a common understanding of what had to be done and who was responsible for doing it.

The accomplishment of the University of Michigan–Flint relocation was a major public undertaking. This case demonstrates that a variety of people representing a variety of interests can unite to accomplish an important community objective. It also demonstrates that getting from here to there is not easy.

CHAPTER 20

A Concluding Note

Improving local-government performance is increasingly important to the economic and social health of our nation. As more than 39,000 units of local government employ an increasing percentage of the civilian work force, consume an increasing quantity of resources, and provide an increasing quantity of goods and services, their contribution to economic growth and prosperity will increase. If local governments' expenditures increase without a corresponding increase in the quality and the quantity of the goods and services they provide, the result will be a potential source of inflation and a continuing drag on economic growth and prosperity.

Twenty years ago, local governments served primarily as "public housekeepers" responsible for maintenance functions. Today, local governments are responsible for housing, the environment, transportation, health care, employment, and a full range of economic and social services. Traditionally, local governments were considered too small, too corrupt, and too inefficient to meet the human needs of local citizens; yet meeting such needs is increasingly their responsibility. If this responsibility is to be met, local governments must be managed for performance.

The importance of government performance goes beyond questions of costs and responsibilities to the fundamental issue of citizen confidence in government. The way a local government conducts the public's business in large part shapes citizens' views of government in general. If local-government officials can't get the job done, citizens' confidence in the ability of state and federal government officials will decline correspondingly. Conversely, improving the performance of local government can restore citizen confidence in the fundamental capabilities of government. At present, most local citizens do not know what their tax dollars are buying, and they generally believe that they aren't getting their money's worth. This perception, combined with increasing allegations of mismanagement and corruption at all levels of government, perpetuates a feeling that local government is beyond redemption: it isn't working and it can't work. The result is an increase in public cynicism, alienation, and apathy. This trend can be reversed, and public confidence in government can be restored, if local governments strengthen their capacity to translate available resources into services that meet public needs.

The essential premise underlying President Nixon's policy of New Federalism was correct: local governments are in the best

383

position to meet locally determined needs in accordance with locally determined policies and priorities. Fulfilling the promise embodied in this national policy, however, depends on the capacity of local-government officials to allocate and manage existing resources in an efficient and responsive manner. In the short run, the growing gap between expenditures and revenue may be closed only by cutting costs and services, increasing taxes, or both. In the long run, however, local governments must address a third alternative: the development and implementation of active programs that will improve the capacity of public officials to satisfy community needs more efficiently and effectively. This third alternative may well pose the most significant challenge facing American government as it enters its third century.

In this book we have tried to simplify an extremely complex subject and at the same time present it systematically and comprehensively. In so doing, we may have implied that our approach to understanding and improving the process of managing a local government for improved performance is precise, or that it is the only way to address this subject. Neither implication is intended. By its very nature, the process of improving performance is imprecise. In our society, government—especially local government—is everybody's business. In essence, a county or city government represents a combination of values, attitudes, and ideas generated within a highly pluralistic community. Each local government reflects a unique combination of environmental constraints, historical events, and personal decisions. Hence there is no one right answer to the question of how to manage a city, or other municipality, for improved performance.

The essential need, in our judgment, is to provide local-government officials, civic and community leaders, and private citizens with a conceptual framework that will allow them to diagnose their own local conditions and reach their own decisions about how best to improve the performance of their local government. It is to the task of developing and applying such a diagnostic tool that this book has been dedicated. Using the tool to "get from here to there" is a task for the readers to undertake.

Glossary

Glossary

Accountability. The process by which local-government employees are held responsible for results produced or tasks completed. To hold managers or employees accountable, desired results or duties must be clearly defined and there must be an appropriate balance between responsibility and authority. *Responsibility* refers to assigned functions or duties. *Authority* describes the latitude that is given to people in the performance of these duties or functions. If individuals have responsibility but do not have authority, they cannot be held accountable.

Activity. A discrete operation or function performed by one or more organizational units which requires an expenditure of resources. A group of activities constitute a *project* or a *program*.

Budget. A financial and operational plan for a particular period of time, generally one year.

Budgeting. The process of relating planned resource expenditures to the results they are expected to achieve and of relating both to responsible managers. Budgeting is the last stage in the planning process.

Capital expenditures. Dollars expended on capital projects. Capital expenditures can

also include dollars expended on items of equipment.

Capital project. A project which results in the acquisition or construction of fixed assets of a local government which are of a long-term and permanent nature. Such assets include land, buildings and related improvements, streets and highways, bridges, sewers, and parks.

Cash management. The process of managing monies of a local government in order to ensure maximum cash availability and maximum yield from the investment of idle cash.

Charter. An enactment that delegates the governing powers of a state to a local government. Practically, a charter is a document that contains the powers, rights, and obligations of a local government and describes the manner in which these powers are to be exercised.

Citizen involvement. The process of providing all residents of a local government a full and equal opportunity to influence those government decisions that affect the quality of their lives. The term *residents* refers to ordinary citizens who are generally not represented by established interest groups or private institutions. *Decisions* refers to the final policies and programs adopted by polit-ical leaders that determine what a local gov-ernment will do with tax dollars and how it will do it. *Full and equal opportunity* means that all residents should have the same op-portunity to influence government deci-sions, regardless of their social, economic, or corporate status.

Data processing. The collection and dissem-ination of information from a variety of sources to a variety of users, usually by means of a computer and related systems.

Delegation. The process of assigning ap-propriate responsibilities to subordinates.

Effectiveness. The degree to which a stated community condition or organizational ob-jective is achieved or maintained. Effective-ness is measured by comparing planned to actual levels of achievement.

Efficiency. The quantity of resources ex-pended to produce a unit of output or to achieve a specific result.

Evaluation. The third phase of the manage-ment process which answers these ques-tions: Did a local government do what it said it would do? Were results produced and resources consumed as planned? In other words, the process of relating what was intended to be done to what was actually done.

Exogenous elements. External forces and conditions, such as geography, location, chance, and natural disasters, which affect the ability of public officials to get things done within a local government or which constrain the potential for improving its per-formance.

Factor. A force, institution or element that affects the ability of public officials to use available resources to get things done effi-ciently and effectively. A factor may be inter-nal or external. *Internal* factors are those which exist within the legal, political, and administrative structure of a local govern-ment. *External* factors exist outside this struc-ture.

Financing and financial practices. The sys-tems and methods by which a local govern-ment obtains financial resources and con-trols or restricts their use.

Fund. An independent fiscal and account-ing entity with a self-balancing set of ac-counts. These accounts record cash and other assets together with all related liabili-ties, obligations, reserves, and equities. Funds are segregated so that revenues will be used only for the purpose of carrying out specific activities in accordance with special regulations, restrictions, or limitations.

Goal. The broadest end toward which effort is directed. Goals are normally stated in terms of the fulfillment of broad public needs, the preservation of fundamental prin-ciples, or the solution of major problems. Characteristically, goals are statements of purposes often not attainable in the short term and frequently incapable of expression in quantifiable terms. *Community goals* are broad ends toward which a local govern-ment and other public and private institu-tions direct their efforts. *Organizational goals* are the ends toward which a specific organization directs its efforts. They are ex-pressed in terms of specific organizational levels (overall local-government goals, de-partment goals, division goals). A depart-ment goal must be broad enough to include the goals of its constituent divisions. Similar-ly, within this hierarchy the achievement of an organizational goal should advance a community goal.

Implementation. The second phase of the management process, which addresses this question: How will a local government do what it has decided to do? A local-govern-ment budget represents a series of contracts wherein responsible managers agree to pro-duce specified results with budgeted resour-ces. Implementation is the process of execut-ing these contracts. Accordingly, it involves organizing (relating people, functions, and activities), staffing (putting the right people in the right jobs), determining productivity standards (identifying the results that should be obtained per unit of resource consumed), and supervising and controlling work (directing day-to-day activity to ensure that resources are spent and results are produced according to plan).

Intergovernmental relationships. The assignment of responsibilities to, and the conduct of functions by, levels of government, and the relationships among these levels.

Internal government structure. The formal (legal) relationships among individuals and functions of a local government, as established by a charter, state legislation, or administrative regulations.

Judicial system. The branch of government entrusted with the responsibilities of interpreting constitutions, laws, and charters, and of resolving differences among levels and other branches of government.

Management by exception. The process by which a manager involves himself only when problems cannot be resolved at a subordinate level or when performance deviates from predetermined limits or standards. This concept is related closely to *delegation.* Effective delegation of responsibility and authority to subordinates, if accompanied by a clear definition of the results expected, allows managers to manage by exception.

Management process. The way in which public officials translate community needs into community objectives; develop strategies and programs to achieve those objectives with available resources; implement the programs, producing desired results with budgeted resources; and evaluate results, making adjustments as necessary. The management process consists of three major phases: *planning, implementation,* and *evaluation.*

Management tools. Methods, systems, and devices used to generate and interpret the information required by political leaders, municipal managers, and citizens in order to make public decisions.

Municipal employees. Local-government personnel who are not categorized as political leaders or municipal managers.

Municipal employee unions. Organizations that represent municipal employees in the collective-bargaining process.

Municipal managers. Nonelected full-time professional personnel who have significant management responsibilities, as determined by the number of employees they supervise, amount of money they control, or importance of their functions.

News media. Private organizations and individuals engaged in the collection and dissemination of news and public information. Generally, the news media consist of newspapers, television stations, radio stations, and periodicals.

Objective. The specific, attainable end toward which effort is directed. When achieved, objectives represent significant and measurable progress toward the attainment of broader, longer-range goals. Characteristically, objectives are subordinate to goals, are narrower and shorter-range in nature, are measurable and quantifiable, and have a reasonable probability of attainment within specified time periods. *Community objectives* are measurable conditions within the community that can be realized by a specific point in time. Responsibility for the achievement of community objectives need not necessarily be that of a local government. When achieved, community objectives represent measurable progress toward the attainment of community goals. *Organizational objectives* are precise statements of desired achievements that will result from the implementation of organizational programs. The achievement of organizational objectives is a necessary step toward the attainment of an organizational goal.

Organizational structure. The relationship among people, functions, and activities within an organization. There are both line and staff organizations within a local government. *Line organizations* are responsible for the delivery of services directly to citizens. *Staff organizations* are responsible for the delivery of support services to other government operations.

Output measure. A standard for measuring the results produced by an organizational unit of a local government. These results include work load, effectiveness, productivity, and quality.

Performance. The extent to which objectives are achieved with the least expenditure of resources. Optimum performance must combine effectiveness (achieving a stated objective) with efficiency (achieving a stated objective at least cost). Performance is both doing the rights things and doing things right. *Local-government performance* is the extent to which public officials are able to achieve stated economic, social, or environmental conditions within a community with a minimum expenditure of resources. *Organizational performance* is the ability of organizational units within a local government to produce specific results with a minimum expenditure of resources.

Performance measurement. An evaluation of the degree to which a community objective or desired community condition has been achieved.

Planning. The first phase of the management process. It involves four steps: (1) determining what to do (the translation of community needs into community objectives), (2) determining how to do it (the identification of required means [programs, strategies, projects] to achieve stated objectives), (3) identifying responsible managers (the identification of who will be held accountable for carrying out specific programs or projects), and (4) allocating resources (the development of a budget for each program and each responsible manager).

Policy. A rule, principle, constraint, or guideline affecting action in prescribed circumstances. Generally, policies influence the selection of the ends (goals and objectives) toward which government activity is directed and limit the means available to achieve the selected ends.

Political leaders. Elected local officials and political appointees to independent boards, commissions, and authorities.

Priority. The assigned order of importance given the attainment or maintenance of community purposes, goals, and objectives. Priorities are the basis for allocating resources.

Private-interest groups. Civic associations, banks or branches of larger banks, consumer organizations, foundations, universities, private corporations, associations of local business executives, and other for-profit organizations and institutions that have the power to influence decisions of public officials.

Procedure. Specified steps to be taken in carrying out a policy.

Productivity. The relationship between the quantity of results produced (output) and the quantity of resources (labor, capital, energy, time) required to produce them. Changes in productivity are measured by relating changes in the real volume of goods and services produced to changes in the quantities of input associated with their production. Productivity is not coterminous with performance. Productivity is a measure of efficiency. As such, increasing productivity is necessary but not sufficient to ensure improved performance.

Program. An ongoing effort, under the direction of a responsible manager, that consumes resources and produces results. A program, by itself or in conjunction with other programs, represents the means to accomplish both organizational and community objectives. A program may be internally made up of discrete activities and projects, each of which is under the direction of a responsible manager and produces identifiable results.

Project. A one-time or time-limited expenditure of resources, which combined with other projects and/or activities is required in the execution of a program.

Quality of life. A comprehensive evaluation of the living experience within a community. Maintaining and improving the quality of life is the ultimate purpose of a local government. To make this concept manageable, the quality of life may be divided into a number of desired community conditions in such areas as housing, transportation, health, justice, public safety, environmental protection, and education.

Resources. Assets consumed by a program, a project, or an activity in producing results. These include dollars, time, material, and capital (plant and equipment). Characteristically, available resources are not sufficient to accomplish all the desired goals and conditions in a community.

Resource allocation. The process of assigning resources to programs, projects, and activities.

Responsibility center. The unit of a local government's organizational structure that represents the most appropriate level for management. Generally, a responsibility center is large enough to account for a significant expenditure of resources, yet small enough to be manageable, with a limited range of activities directed toward the same principal objective. Each responsibility center is under the direction of a single manager who is responsible for the dollars expended and results produced by that responsibility center.

Revenue. Money that flows into a local government. Revenue is *recurring* if it is received on a consistent and periodic basis (e.g., sales-tax revenue, property-tax revenue), or *nonrecurring* (e.g., a federal grant).

Supervisor. A municipal manager who has the power to direct the work of others and who exercises on behalf of management one or more of the following functions: hiring, promotion, transfers, suspensions, discharges, adjudication of employee grievances. The exercise of these responsibilities is not routine, but rather requires the exercise of independent judgment.

Appendixes

A Profile of Conditions in Flint

The purpose of this appendix is to present a profile of conditions in Flint. This profile is organized according to desired urban conditions. A *desired urban condition* represents a general statement of a social, economic, or physical condition that describes the city of Flint as a desirable place to live. In total, desired urban conditions constitute the ends toward which Flint's city-government programs and policies should be directed. Operationally, desired urban conditions break down the totality of the urban environment or quality of life into somewhat more-definitive and manageable categories. As with any such categorizations of an abstract whole, the categories chosen are arbitrary and somewhat overlapping.

The ten desired urban conditions selected for Flint are these:

- Residents of the city have an adequate standard of living.
- Residents of the city have access to adequate housing.
- Residents of the city live in a desirable physical environment.
- Residents and users of the city are safe.
- Residents of the city are healthy.
- Residents have access to a fair and equitable system of justice.
- Residents of the city have full and equal opportunity for educational growth and development.
- Residents of the city have full and equal opportunity for the enjoyment of leisure time.
- Residents of the city have access to an adequate system of transportation.
- Residents of the city have full and equal opportunity to influence the decisions that affect their lives.

Given the development of indicators that are used to measure the current status of each respective urban-condition area, we present a composite profile of the quality

The material presented in this appendix was developed by Ward McAllister under contract to the city of Flint for the development of an integrated master plan.

of life in Flint. Where possible, we compare conditions in Flint with conditions in other, comparable cities in the United States. Selection of other cities for comparison was based on similarity in present population, population change between 1960 and 1970, and economic characteristics.

An Analysis of Urban Conditions in Flint

Adequate Standard of Living

An *adequate standard of living* is defined as an annual income of at least $7,214 for a family of four (the recommendation of the Michigan Governor's Welfare Study Commission), adjusted for family size and based on 1971 cost-of-living figures.

Families below 1.99 poverty level
Multiplying the federally designated poverty-level income ($3,745 for a family of four) by 1.99 yields a rough approximation of the adequate standard of living defined by the welfare study commission. *Condition:* In 1970, 26 percent of all families in Flint fell below this standard (21 percent of all white families; 41 percent of all black families). *Change:* This percentage represents a 5-percent decrease since 1960. *Ranking:* In 1970, Flint had the third-highest percentage of nine selected cities of people with adequate standards of living (see Figure 11).

Families below federal poverty level
The percentage of families below the federal poverty level indicates the most-severe condition of inadequate standard of living. *Condition:* In 1970, 10 percent of all families had incomes below this level (6 percent of all white families; 18 percent of all black families). *Change:* This figure reflects a 3-percent decrease since 1960. *Ranking:* In 1970, Flint ranked fourth among nine cities in percentage of population above this level (see Figure 12).

Access to Adequate Housing

Adequate housing is defined as safe, healthful, uncrowded housing. *Access* is defined as the availability of adequate housing to all residents of the city without racial or economic barriers.

Supply of adequate housing
The number of nondeteriorated housing units compared to the total number of households in Flint is a gross indication of the sufficiency of adequate housing, without considering size or price of housing units. *Condition:* In 1972 Flint showed a deficit of 4.4 percent in the gross supply of adequate housing.

Degree of overcrowding
Inadequate space fosters unhealthy living conditions. United States Census Bureau standards (1.01 persons per room) were used to determine the degree of overcrowding in Flint. *Condition:* In 1970, almost 9 percent of housing in the city was

Figure 11

PERCENTAGE OF FAMILIES HAVING AN INADEQUATE STANDARD OF LIVING
COMPARISON WITH SELECTED SIMILAR CITIES

Explanation: Adequate standard of living is $7,214 for a family of four (adjusted for family size). The actual figures presented here relate the percentage of families with incomes below $7,490 (adjusted for family size). Lower percentages mean fewer people have inadequate standards of living.

CITY	Percentage
Worcester	24.7%
Des Moines	24.9%
FLINT	25.9%
Dayton	29.1%
Syracuse	29.8%
Spokane	30.8%
Salt Lake City	31.5%
Gary	32.1%
Providence	34.5%
AVERAGE:	29.3%

Source: U.S. Bureau of the Census — 1970

overcrowded. *Change:* This figure represents a 3-percent reduction since 1960. *Ranking:* In 1970, Flint ranked eighth of nine cities (see Figure 13).

Economic barriers
Comparison of the rents paid by Flint residents with the rents they can afford to pay, on the basis of their incomes, provides a measure of the economic barriers people encounter in securing adequate housing. The federally accepted standard of maximum housing cost is a figure less than or equal to 25 percent of family income. *Condition:* In 1970, most renters could afford to pay higher gross rents than they were actually paying.

Racial barriers
The racial composition of census tracts is a direct indication of integration in housing. *Condition:* In 1970, 94 percent of blacks in Flint lived in 43 percent of the city's census tracts.

Figure 12

PERCENTAGE OF FAMILIES WITH INCOMES BELOW POVERTY LEVEL

COMPARISON WITH OTHER CITIES

Explanation: Poverty level income is $3,745 for a family of four (adjusted for family size).
Lower percentages mean less incidence of poverty.

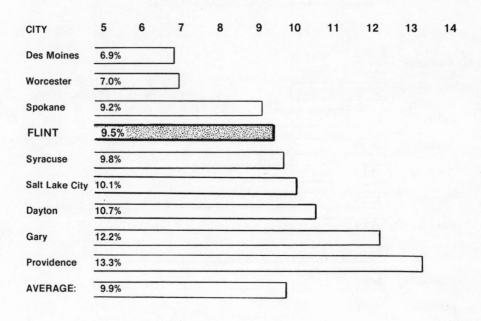

CITY										
	5	6	7	8	9	10	11	12	13	14
Des Moines	6.9%									
Worcester	7.0%									
Spokane	9.2%									
FLINT	9.5%									
Syracuse	9.8%									
Salt Lake City	10.1%									
Dayton	10.7%									
Gary	12.2%									
Providence	13.3%									
AVERAGE:	9.9%									

Source: U.S. Bureau of the Census — 1970

Desirable Physical Environment

A *desirable physical environment* is defined as a healthful and visually appealing
physical setting designed to provide residents with convenient access to the basic
facilities and services which they use in their daily lives.

Air pollution

Air quality affects the health of city residents. The 1975 Federal Air Quality
Standards were used as a basis for determining the general quality of air in Flint.
Condition: In 1970, air quality met or exceeded federal standards, except in the
north-central sector. *Ranking:* In 1972, air quality in Flint's central business district
was better than that in seven similar cities (see Figure 14).

Water pollution

Water is a natural resource that should be kept clean for present and future
enjoyment. Michigan water-quality standards were used as a basis for determining

Figure 13

PERCENTAGE OF OVERCROWDED HOUSING UNITS

COMPARISON WITH OTHER CITIES

Explanation: The Federal definition for overcrowding is used. It constitutes 1.01 persons or more per room in living quarters. Lower percentages mean less overcrowding.

CITY		0	2	4	6	8	10	12	14	16
Spokane		4.3%								
Syracuse		4.5%								
Providence		5.4%								
Worcester		5.6%								
Des Moines		5.8%								
Salt Lake City		6.3%								
Dayton		7.5%								
FLINT		8.8%								
Gary		15.8%								
AVERAGE:		7.1%								

Source: U.S. Bureau of the Census — 1970

the general condition of the Flint River. *Condition:* In 1970, water leaving the city did not meet state standards.

Well-maintained housing

The exterior condition of housing structures affects the general appearance of an area. Standards and data from the Project Echo 1972 Environmental Block Appraisal were used in determining the percentage of well-maintained housing structures. *Condition:* In 1972, 83 percent of housing structures in Flint were well maintained. *Change:* This figure represents a 5-percent increase since 1970.

Parks and playgrounds

Adequate and convenient open space and recreational facilities permit enjoyment of the outdoors. This index is based on park acreage (3.5 acres per 1,000 people is considered adequate) and pedestrian accessibility to parks. *Condition:* In 1970, 50 percent of Flint's census tracts did not meet this standard.

Figure 14
AIR QUALITY
COMPARISON WITH OTHER CITIES*

Explanation: The 1975 Federal Air Quality Standards state that the annual geometric mean for suspended particulates shall not exceed 75 micrograms/cubic meter. This standard was used for comparison with other cities; the figures cited are for the air sampling stations closest to the respective downtown areas. In Flint, the station is located on top of City Hall. Lower values mean less pollution.

CITY	0	25	50	75	100	125	150	175	200	225
FLINT	66									
Spokane	85									
Worcester	86									
Dayton	87									
Salt Lake City	94									
Syracuse	94									
Providence	102									
Gary	122									
AVERAGE:	92									

Source: Air pollution control personnel in the respective cities — 1972 data.

*Data for Des Moines not available

Grocery and drug stores

Evaluation of the accessibility of grocery and drug stores indicates whether residents can conveniently obtain the necessities of daily life. *Condition:* In 1970 such accessibility was generally adequate.

Safety of Residents

Safety is defined as freedom from the threat of injury and/or loss of property resulting from physical assault, hazardous conditions, and accidents.

Total crimes

The FBI Crime Index was used to measure both total crimes committed and levels of specific types of crimes. *Condition and change:* Between 1971 and 1972, Flint experienced a 2.3-percent increase in major crimes. *Ranking:* This was the second-highest increase among eight selected cities (see Figure 15). *Condition and change:* Between 1971 and 1972, there was a 9.5-percent increase in violent crimes in Flint.

Figure 15

RATE OF MAJOR CRIMES (1972 FBI CRIME INDEX)

COMPARISON WITH OTHER CITIES*

Explanation: The Crime Index is a composite of the following crimes: murder and non-negligent manslaughter, forcible rape, robbery, aggravated assault, burglary, breaking or entering, larceny $50 and over, and auto theft. The number of crimes reported are added together, and the total is then reported out per 100,000 population, so that comparisons may be made. Lower rates reflect fewer crimes. The figure in parenthesis shows the percent change between 1971 and 1972.

CITY	2000 2500 3000 3500 4000 4500 5000 5500 6000 6500 7000 7500
Des Moines	2972 (–9.1%)
Syracuse	3098 (–11.1%)
Spokane	3425 (–2.3%)
Salt Lake City	5718 (–1.0%)
Providence	5778 (–13.5%)
FLINT	5854 (+2.3%)
Gary	6433 (–3.7%)
Worcester	7302 (+2.7%)
AVERAGE:	5072 (–4.5%)

Source: "Uniform Crime Reporting," (1972 Preliminary Annual Release)
United States Department of Justice
Federal Bureau of Investigation

*1972 data for Dayton not available. Rates were arrived at by using 1970 Census figures for population.

Ranking: Flint had the third-highest increase of eight cities (see Figure 16). *Condition and change:* Between 1971 and 1972, the city saw a 1.5-percent decrease in property crimes. *Ranking:* Flint had the seventh-greatest reduction of eight cities (see Figure 17).

Residential burglaries

Residential burglary is a hazard to the safety of citizens' property and possessions. *Condition and change:* Between 1970 and 1971, Flint experienced a 31.7-percent increase in residential burglaries. *Ranking:* In 1971, Flint ranked fourth-highest among nine cities in number of residential burglaries per 100,000 population (see Figure 18).

Traffic fatalities

The hazards of living in the city include the risk of being injured or killed in a traffic accident. *Condition:* In 1972, Flint had 12 traffic fatalities per 100,000 population. *Change:* This figure represents a 16-percent increase between 1970 and 1972. *Ranking:* Flint ranked fifth of nine cities (see Figure 19).

Figure 16

RATE OF SELECTED VIOLENT CRIMES — 1972

COMPARISON WITH OTHER CITIES*

Explanation: The crimes are those reported by the FBI: aggravated assault, murder, forcible rape, and robbery. The number of crimes reported are added together and the total is then reported out per 100,000 population so that comparisons may be made. Lower rates reflect fewer crimes. The figure in parenthesis shows the percent change between 1971 and 1972.

CITY		200	400	600	800	1000	1200	1400
Des Moines	216 (−27.5%)							
Spokane	230 (+ 4.3%)							
Syracuse	359 (−17.3%)							
Worcester	462 (+ 15.8%)							
Salt Lake City	504 (+ 13.6%)							
Providence	560 (−15.1%)							
Gary	1108 (−1.4%)							
FLINT	1137 (+ 9.5%)							
AVERAGE:	572 (−2.3%)							

Source: "Uniform Crime Reporting," (1972 Preliminary Annual Release)
    Federal Bureau of Investigation
    U.S. Department of Justice

*1972 data for Dayton not available. Rates were arrived at by using 1970 Census figures for population.

Residential fires

Fires reflect hazardous conditions. The safety of city residents can be gauged in part by the rate of occurrence of home fires. *Condition:* In 1971, there was 1 fire per 105 occupied dwellings in Flint. *Change:* Between 1970 and 1971 Flint realized a 4-percent decrease in home fires.

Health of Residents

Health is defined as physical health: the absence of preventable physical disabilities and the ability to lead a functional life. (The lack of a generally accepted definition of mental health makes it difficult to assess this component.)

Figure 17

RATE OF SELECTED PROPERTY CRIMES — 1972

COMPARISON WITH OTHER CITIES*

Explanation: The crimes are those reported by the FBI, burglary, larceny $50 and over, auto theft. The number of crimes reported are added together, and the total is then reported out per 100,000 population so that comparisons may be made. Lower rates reflect fewer crimes. The figure in parenthesis shows the percent change between 1971 and 1972.

CITY	2500 3000 3500 4000 4500 5000 5500 6000 6500 7000
Syracuse	2739 (−10.2%)
Des Moines	2756 (−7.3%)
Spokane	3195 (−2.7%)
FLINT	4718 (− 1.5%)
Salt Lake City	5214 (−11.8%)
Providence	5218 (−14.3%)
Gary	5325 (−4.1%)
Worcester	6840 (+ 1.9%)
AVERAGE:	4501 (−6.3%)

Source: "Uniform Crime Reporting," (1972 Preliminary Annual Release)
        Federal Bureau of Investigation
        U.S. Department of Justice

*1972 data for Dayton not available. Rates were arrived at by using 1970 Census figures for population.

Projected life span

The relative health of a population subgroup may be evaluated in part by measuring the median age range at time of death. *Condition:* In 1970, the median age range at death was 70–74 for whites in Flint and 50-54 for blacks.

Infant mortality

Infant-mortality rates indicate the general level of health of mothers as well as of infants. Comparing rates by race reveals the relative healthiness of each racial group. *Condition:* In 1968, there were 22.4 deaths per 1,000 live births in Flint (19 per 1,000 for whites; 39 per 1,000 for blacks). *Ranking:* Flint's total rate was the second-highest of nine selected cities (see Figure 20).

Figure 18

RATE OF RESIDENTIAL BURGLARIES — 1971*

COMPARISON WITH OTHER CITIES

Explanation: Residential burglaries are reported out per 100,000 population, so that comparisons may be made. Lower rates reflect fewer burglaries. The figures in parenthesis show the percent change between 1971 and 1970.

CITY	200	500	800	1100	1400	1700	2000
Des Moines	496 (+ 14.6%)						
Syracuse	805 (+ 5.4%)						
Spokane	1056 (+20.6%)						
Salt Lake City	1347 (+ 3.9%)						
Providence	1409 (+ 11.7%)						
FLINT	1638 (+ 31.7%)						
Dayton	1720 (−7.9%)						
Worcester	1811 (+ 24.2%)						
Gary	2021 (+ 53.8%)						
AVERAGE:	1367 (+ 17.6%)						

Source: Uniform Crime Reporting Division, Federal Bureau of Investigation, United States Department of Justice

*It should be noted that the other comparisons relating to safety are based on 1972 figures. The figures here do not reflect the significant change which occurred in 1972. These 1971 figures are based on reports from agencies submitting supplemental information for 1970 and 1971. Rates were arrived at by using 1970 Census figures for population.

Childhood inoculations

In addition to revealing the measures taken to avoid preventable illness, the inoculation rate also serves as a general indicator of the quality of a city's preventive health practices, since inoculations are usually administered during routine medical checkups. *Condition:* In 1971, approximately 10 percent of Flint's elementary-school children had not received necessary inoculations. *Change:* This figure represents a 4-percent increase since 1967.

Equitable System of Justice

An *equitable system of justice* is defined as the equal application of civil and criminal law and the ability to secure equal treatment and protection before the law.

Figure 19

RATE OF AUTOMOBILE ACCIDENT FATALITIES — 1972

COMPARISON WITH OTHER CITIES

Explanation: The number of automobile fatalities are reported out per 100,000 population so that comparisons may be made. Lower rates reflect fewer fatalities.

CITY		9	10	11	12	13	14	15	16	17	18	19	20
Worcester	7												
Providence	9												
Syracuse	9												
Des Moines	9												
FLINT	12												
Dayton	15												
Gary*	17												
Salt Lake City	17												
Spokane	20												
AVERAGE:	14.4												

Source: National Safety Council, Detroit, Michigan

*Gary data were for 11 months. For comparison purposes, the data were projected and reported out for 12 months. Rates were arrived at by using 1970 Census figures for population.

Time between arrest and sentencing

The length of time between arrest and sentencing indicates the degree of hardship experienced by persons suspected of criminal behavior. (A speedy trial is guaranteed to all citizens by the U.S. Constitution.) *Condition:* In 1970, 6 percent of those arrested and subsequently tried for armed robbery waited more than one year before being brought to trial; the median time was six months.

Arrests and convictions by race

Comparing the rates of arrests and convictions of different racial groups indicates whether the judicial process is applied equally and equitably. *Condition:* In 1970, 37 percent of blacks arrested for armed robbery were ultimately tried and convicted; the rate was 17 percent for whites arrested for armed robbery.

Opportunity for Educational Growth

Opportunity for educational growth is defined as open access to an educational system that provides the assistance necessary for each student to realize his full potential for learning.

Figure 20

RATE OF INFANT MORTALITY — 1968

COMPARISON WITH OTHER CITIES

Explanation: The figures are for Standard Metropolitan Statistical Areas. They reflect the
number of infant deaths per 1,000 live births. Lower rates reflect fewer deaths.

CITY	16	17	18	19	20	21	22	23	24	25	26	27	28
Syracuse	17.8%												
Salt Lake City	17.9%												
Des Moines	19.2%												
Spokane	19.6%												
Dayton	19.7%												
Worcester	21.3%												
Providence	22.3%												
FLINT	22.4%												
Gary	26.7%												
AVERAGE:	20.8%												

Source: Vital Statistics of the United States, National Center for Health Statistics,
U.S. Department of Health, Education and Welfare, Vols. I and II.

Per-pupil expenditure

The amount spent per pupil for instructional costs is one indication of the
adequacy of elementary and secondary educational services. Variations in per-pupil
expenditures among schools are an indication of nonequal access to educational
resources. *Condition:* In 1970, the Flint school system spent $425-$864 per pupil,
with most schools in economically deprived areas falling at the high end of the
range. *Ranking:* Flint's average per-pupil expenditure ($720) was higher than the
state average ($525).

Adult educational level

The percentage of adults who have completed high school is a general indication
of a city's educational level and of the need for adult high-school completion
services. *Condition:* In 1970, 48.6 percent of Flint residents twenty-five and older had
completed high school. *Ranking:* Flint ranked sixth-highest of nine cities (see Figure
21).

College enrollment

The standard for local college enrollment developed by the Carnegie Commission on Higher Education was used to indicate the overall adequacy of resources for
higher education in Flint. *Condition:* In 1970, the Carnegie Commission termed Flint
"marginally deficient" because less than 2.5 percent of the city's population was
enrolled in a local college or university.

Figure 21

PERCENT OF ADULTS 25 YEARS AND OLDER WHO HAVE COMPLETED HIGH SCHOOL
COMPARISON WITH OTHER CITIES

CITY		
Des Moines	65.3	
Salt Lake City	64.5	
Spokane	64.0	
Syracuse	52.4	
Worcester	49.8	
FLINT	48.6	
Dayton	44.8	
Gary	42.7	
Providence	40.6	

Source: U.S. Bureau of the Census — 1970

School dropout rates

Most students who do not complete high school have not realized their full educational potential. *Condition:* In the early 1970s, 10 percent of all secondary-level students in Flint dropped out each year; approximately 25 percent of all tenth-grade students failed to graduate. *Ranking:* Flint's dropout rate was lower than the rates in fifteen other cities in Michigan, but higher than the state average (6 percent).

Pupil achievement scores

One indicator of educational growth and development is performance on standardized achievement tests administered to elementary and secondary school pupils. The Michigan Assessment Program scores of schoolchildren in the Flint system provided these data. *Ranking:* During the 1971-1972 school year, Flint fourth-graders ranked in the 8th percentile among all fourth-graders in the state of Michigan and in the 45th percentile among all fourth-graders in metropolitan areas in the state; Flint seventh-graders ranked in the 6th percentile in Michigan and in the 50th percentile of city pupils at that grade level.

Opportunity for the Enjoyment of Leisure Time

Opportunity for the enjoyment of leisure time is defined as the ability to pursue a variety of active or passive recreational activities at locations convenient to people's homes and at a reasonable cost.

Figure 22

PERCENT OF ELIGIBLE VOTERS VOTING IN 1972 PRESIDENTIAL ELECTION

COMPARISON WITH OTHER CITIES

CITY	35	40	45	50	55	60	65	70	75	80

Salt Lake City 85.6%

Des Moines 84.0%

Spokane 78.2%

Dayton 73.0%

Syracuse 72.5%

FLINT 71.5%

Providence 69.6%

Gary 66.2%

Worcester 41.5%

AVERAGE: 71.3%

Source: Congressional Research Service, Washington, D.C.

Enrollment in extended community school services

The degree of participation in the extended community school programs indicates to what extent these programs meet the needs of residents of individual neighborhoods and of the city as a whole. *Condition:* In 1970, 7 percent of Flint's population participated in these programs; of this number, 24 percent were blacks—a percentage roughly equal to black representation in the total population.

Adequacy of parks and playgrounds

See page 399.

Adequate System of Transportation

An *adequate system of transportation* is defined as one that allows residents to move within and around the city in a safe and convenient manner, and which permits residents to travel easily from the city to destinations outside the city.

Road conditions

The majority of intercity and intracity travel in Michigan is accomplished in automobiles. This index assesses road conditions in Flint on the basis of improvements needed in the city's major traffic arteries, as determined by the State Department of Highways. *Condition:* In 1972, 80 percent of recommended improvements of statewide arteries and roads in Flint had been implemented; the balance was expected to be completed by 1980.

Traffic safety
See page 401.

Bus service
The city bus system is the principal means of transportation for residents who do not drive. Evaluating the accessibility and convenience of bus service between residential areas and major activity centers provides an indication of the quality of public transportation in Flint. *Condition:* In 1974, bus service was provided, on the average, every thirty minutes to all shopping centers and residential areas.

Air travel facilities
The number and frequency of commercial airline flights to and from major destinations indicate the convenience of air travel for Flint residents. *Condition:* In 1970, daily flights were available to and from Detroit, Chicago, and Cleveland.

Opportunity for Citizens to Influence Community Decisions

The *opportunity to influence decisions* is defined as open and equal access to the decision-making process and to city decision makers.

Participation in elections
Voter turnout is an indication of the interest and confidence which citizens have in the governmental process, and thus, perhaps, is also an indicator of the extent to which citizens view themselves as significant participants in public decision making. *Condition:* In the 1970 local and national election, 63 percent of Flint's registered electors voted. The charter-revision election drew a 6-percent turnout; 7 percent voted in the 1971 school board election. In the 1972 presidential election, 72 percent of those eligible voted—the sixth-highest percentage of nine selected cities (see Figure 22).

Evaluation Criteria for Identifying Opportunities To Improve Performance

Internal Factors

Political Leaders

- Do elected officials demonstrate the willingness to lead?
- Are political leaders able to translate community needs into community objectives?
- Are political leaders willing to delegate to municipal managers authority and responsibility for achieving community objectives?
- Do political leaders have the ability to marshal external support and resources required to achieve community objectives?
- Can political leaders gain and maintain the respect and confidence of the people they represent?

Municipal Managers

Criteria for evaluating the impact of municipal managers on performance is divided into two areas.

Competence
- Do municipal managers individually and collectively have the requisite management skills?
- Are municipal managers promoted primarily on the basis of their ability to perform in higher-level positions?
- Are municipal managers provided opportunities to improve their management skills?

Motivation
- Do political leaders provide requisite support to municipal managers?
- Do municipal managers know what they are expected to achieve, and can they be held accountable for their performance?

- Is compensation of municipal managers based on performance?
- Are municipal managers residents of the community for which they have public responsibility?
- Do municipal managers view themselves as professionals?

Municipal Employees and Employee Unions

Criteria for evaluating the impact of municipal employees and employee unions on performance are divided into three areas.

Competence
- Are the best-qualified people able to compete for all government positions on an equal basis, without artificially created barriers?
- Are tests for local-government positions job-related?
- Are promotion decisions job-related?
- Are educational and training opportunities available?

Motivation
- Do employees have reasonable job security?
- Is employee compensation equitable and based on job performance?
- Are employees adequately supervised?
- Do employees have an opportunity to advance commensurate with their interests and skills?
- Is there a fair and timely procedure for handling employee grievances?
- Are employees satisfied with their jobs?

Balance between management responsibilities and union rights
- Is union representation limited to nonmanagement personnel?
- Is management's responsibility for collective bargaining clearly established and professionally administered?
- Is the scope of bargaining clearly established?
- Is the length of the negotiation process defined, and is the contractual period of reasonable length?
- Does management develop a strategy prior to the initiation of the collective-bargaining process?
- Are both public officials and union leaders accountable for the consequences of an impasse situation?
- Is management prepared to continue government services in the event of an employee strike or work stoppage?
- Are negotiated union contracts adequately administered?

Management Tools

Criteria for evaluating the impact of management tools on performance are shown with respect to the five most important management tools and the analytical assistance required to use them.

Planning process
- Is planning realistic?
- Is the plan comprehensive?
- Does the plan consider unique community conditions?
- Is the planning process integrated with related functions?
- Does the planning process bring together essential public and private interests?
- Are citizens involved in the planning process?
- Is the final master plan understandable?
- Is the master plan continuously updated to reflect changing conditions?

Budgeting system
- Is the budgeting process integrated with the planning process?
- Is the budget comprehensive?
- Are resources related to results and to responsible managers?
- Does the budget reflect the future consequences of current budget decisions?
- Is the budget understandable and usable?

Performance-measurement system
- Does the performance-measurement system establish performance standards and targets for all governmental operations?
- Is the performance-measurement system integrated with planning, budgeting, and control systems?
- Is performance-measurement information used by a wide variety of people?

Organizational structure
- Does the organizational structure capitalize on the strengths of present personnel?
- Does the organizational structure clearly define responsibility and authority for achieving objectives?
- Does the organizational structure provide managers with a reasonable span of control?
- Does the organizational structure facilitate delegation of authority and responsibility to the lowest level where it can be exercised well?
- Is the organizational structure flexible?

Data-processing system
- Is data-processing support available to all departments of a local government?
- Is the data-processing function centralized at the appropriate level?
- Is there a data-processing plan based on governmentwide user needs?
- Is the data-processing system designed to be flexible?

Analytical assistance
- Is the existing analytical staff adequate both in skills and in number?
- Are consultants and other outside experts used appropriately?
- Is analytical assistance provided at appropriate organizational levels?

Financing and Financial Practices

Criteria for assessing the impact of financing and financial practices on performance may be divided into four areas.

Assessing financial health
- Does a local government know the full costs of the services it provides?
- Are the individual and corporate citizens of a local government capable of paying the full costs of current and future services?
- Does a local government provide comparable and consistent information concerning its financial health?

Raising and spending financial resources
- Is revenue received related to services provided?
- Does the local government have access to debt financing?
- Are there unnecessary restrictions on the raising and using of financial resources?

Providing financial information for decision-making
- Is the finance and accounting system uniform, and is it integrated with other management systems?
- Is finance and accounting information useful and usable?

Meeting fiduciary responsibilities
- Are financial assets professionally managed?
- Is an audit of financial statements and accounting records conducted annually?

Internal Government Structure

- Are the branches of government clearly separated, with appropriate powers and responsibilities assigned and adequate checks and balances assured?
- Are the lines of authority within the executive branch of government clearly established?
- Are the interests of the entire city as well as of its discrete geographical areas adequately represented?
- Is the structure of government clearly defined, and is it understandable to all citizens?
- Can the structure of a local government be adjusted easily to meet changing needs and requirements?

Intergovernmental Relationships

- Is a local government responsible for an appropriate mix of government functions and activities?
- Do government officials have the authority and the responsibility required to manage assigned functions and activities?
- Do regulations and red tape imposed by other levels of government restrict the ability of local-government officials to do their jobs?
- Do separate units of local government cooperate in the achievement of common community objectives?

Citizen Involvement

- Do citizens actively participate in the election process?
- Do citizens want to be involved in the decision-making process of their elected officials?
- Are public officials committed to a participatory process?
- Is the role and responsibility of citizens clearly defined?
- Is there a formal mechanism to involve citizens in the decision-making process?
- Does the city have the administrative capacity to respond to citizen requests?

The News Media

- Is reporting accurate and fair?
- Are both sides of controversial issues presented in media reports?
- Do reporters explain why things happen as well as what happened?
- Do editors take public positions on important community issues, and is editorial opinion clearly identified as such?
- Do the news media attempt to provide a forum for public information?

Private-Interest Groups

- Are private interests willing to make sacrifices for a community purpose?
- Do public officials and private interests share information?
- Do private interests conduct public business publicly?
- Do private interests provide resources for projects that benefit the public?

The Judiciary

- Do judges assume legislative and executive responsibilities?
- Do judges accurately identify the costs and financial consequences of their decisions?
- Are judicial decisions influenced by political pressures?
- Is the judicial system free from undue dependence on legislative and executive decisions?
- Do judicial decisions support law-enforcement activities?
- Does the judicial system operate efficiently?

Notes

Notes

Introduction

1. See Peter F. Drucker, *Management*, Harper and Row, Inc., New York, 1973.

2. Alfred P. Sloan, Jr., *My Years With General Motors*, Doubleday & Company Inc., New York, 1964, p. 4.

Chapter 1

1. These statements are taken from two of President Nixon's speeches to Congress on the subject of revenue-sharing. The citations are as follows: Richard M. Nixon, "Federal Revenue Sharing With the States," 91st Congress 1st Session, House of Representatives, August 13, 1969, Document no. 91-148; Richard M. Nixon, "Revenue Sharing," 92nd Congress 1st Session, House of Representatives, February 4, 1971, Document no. 92-44. These two speeches are contained in a thorough review of the revenue sharing program in a book entitled *Revenue Sharing* edited by William Willner and John P. Nichols, Propaln International Ltd., Inc., Washington, D.C., 1973.

2. This quote was taken from a special issue of *The Public Interest*, no. 34 (Winter 1974), in which guest editors Eli Ginzberg and Robert Solow evaluate the federal policies of "social intervention" that marked the 1960s.

3. See Floyd J. Fowler, Jr., *Citizen Attitudes Toward Social Government Services and Taxes* (Cambridge, Massachusetts, Ballinger Publishing Company, 1974). This work examines citizen perceptions about city government in 10 major cities, noting that in all cities but one more than 50 percent of the people did not feel that they got a dollar's worth of service for each tax dollar—a fact that 30 percent attributed to spending money on the wrong things (poor priorities) and 26 percent felt was the result of poor administration (the process of collecting taxes and delivering services).

4. On Tuesday, August 10, the *Los Angeles Times* noted that "opposition to local tax proposals has stiffened greatly since the early 1960s. According to a national study, the percentage of proposed school bond issues approved in elections dropped from 72.4 percent in 1962 to 51.4 percent last year. In California, the percentage of school tax increases approved dropped from 82 percent in 1962 to 47.4 percent last year. The nadir of support for new borrowing may have been reached in November of 1975 when—by value—93 percent of all bond proposals submitted to the electorate were rejected."

Chapter 2

1. Peter F. Drucker, *Management*, Harper and Row, New York, 1973, p. 141.

419

Chapter 4

1. Richard Hébert, *The Politics of City Transportation,* The Bobbs-Merrill Company, New York, 1972, p. 5.

Chapter 5

1. See Jeffrey Pressman, *Preconditions of Mayoral Leadership,* Institute of Urban and Regional Development, University of California, Berkeley, p. 16-20.

2. *Flint Journal,* February 22, 1973.

Chapter 6

1. *Flint Journal,* November 15, 1973.

2. Marvin Bower, *The Will to Manage,* McGraw-Hill, New York, 1966, p. vi.

Chapter 7

1. Our description of the impact of civil service and its characterization as a "meritless" system parallels the thinking and writing of E. S. Savas. For an excellent description of the impact of civil service on the city of New York, see E. S. Savas and Sigmund G. Ginsberg, "The Civil Service: A Meritless System?," *Good Government,* vol. 92, no. 1 (Winter 1974). See also, for a description of civil service and well-reasoned thoughts for coping with it, "Municipal Monopoly— Uncivil Servants: There Are No Culprits, Only Scapegoats," *Harper's,* December 1971, pp. 55-60.

2. The percentage of full-time employees belonging to an employee association by function is as follows: education, 67 percent; highways, 34 percent; public welfare, 47 percent; hospitals, 32 percent; police protection, 56 percent; local fire protection, 74 percent; sanitation other than sewage, 50 percent; and all other functions, 38 percent. See *Labor-Management Relations in State and Local Governments: 1974,* Special Studies no. 75, U.S. Department of Commerce and U.S. Department of Labor, February 1976.

3. See Walker Fogel and Herbert Lewin, "Wage Determination in the Public Sector,"

Industrial and Labor Relations Review, vol. 27 (April 1974), for an analysis that concludes that public-sector wages now "exceed those paid in the private sector for all occupations except high-level managers and professionals."

4. *Los Angeles Times,* August 26, 1975.

5. Frederick O'R. Hayes, "Collective Bargaining and the Budget Director," in Sam Zagoria, ed., *Public Workers and the Public Unions,* Prentice Hall, Englewood Cliffs, N.J., 1972, p. 99.

6. David T. Stanley, *Managing Local Government under Union Pressure,* Brookings Institution, Washington, D.C., 1972, pp. 1-6.

7. In 1974 Flint's city hospital employed roughly the same number of employees as the city (approximately 2,000), all of whom were covered by civil service, including the director. The Board of Education, which was completely independent of city government, consisted of seven members, elected at large. The Board of Education employed more people (2,500) than either the hospital or the city. Despite the fact that the Board of Education did not have a civil service system, it appointed one of the commission members that determined the personnel policies and procedures of Flint's city government.

8. It is interesting to note that the National Civil Service League, which played a key role in the adoption of civil service systems at the turn of the century, officially recommended in 1970 that all personnel functions be vested in the executive branch and that independent civil service commissions be given only a watchdog role.

Chapter 9

1. See Committee on Governmental Accounting and Auditing, *Industry Audit Guide: Audits of State and Local Governmental Units,* American Institute of Certified Public Accountants, New York, 1974.

2. National Committee on Governmental Accounting, *Governmental Accounting, Auditing and Financial Reporting,* Municipal Finance Officers Assn., Chicago, Ill., 1968.

3. See the *Los Angeles Times,* Sunday, May 16, 1976, for a review of "City Financial Emergencies," a report prepared by Philip Dearborn for the Advisory Commission on Intergovernmental Relations.

Chapter 11

1. These issues are discussed in a report prepared by the Advisory Commission on Intergovernmental Relations entitled "American Federalism: Toward a More Effective Partnership" (Washington, D.C., 1975). This document contains a report of and papers from the National Conference of American Federalism in Action, held in Washington, D.C., February 20-22, 1975.

2. Ibid, p. 8.

3. See "Strengthening Public Management in the Intergovernmental System," a report prepared for the Office of Management and Budget by the Study Committee on Policy Management Assistance, Executive Office of the President (Washington, D.C., 1975), p. 8.

4. Ibid, p. 27.

5. Ibid, p. 5.

6. This quotation was taken from an early draft of "Strengthening Public Management in the Intergovernmental System," p. 8.

7. Mitchell Gordon, *Sick Cities,* Penguin Books, New York, 1966.

8. Advisory Commission on Intergovernmental Relations, "American Federalism," p. 1.

9. Ibid, p. 9.

10. This quotation appears in an article written by David M. Halpern in *Newsweek,* December 15, 1975.

11. This quotation was taken from a White House transcript presentation by Governor Daniel J. Evans to the Public Forum on Domestic Policy held in Los Angeles, December 9, 1975.

12. This quotation was taken from an early draft of "Strengthening Public Management in the Intergovernmental System," p. 114.

13. The Committee for Economic Development, in its most recent publication, *Improving Productivity in State and Local Government,* notes that the federal government has a history of making its grants contingent upon meeting specific standards (e.g., installation of civil service systems as a requirement for financing state employment services in the 1930s, development of a hospital construction plan as a requirement for receiving Hill-Burton funds, and preparation of "workable programs" as a requirement for receiving urban-renewal grants). This report also notes that in the late 1960s, Senators Hubert Humphrey and Henry Ruess suggested that bloc grants be given to state and local governments that developed "modern government programs" specifying how the management process would be improved.

Chapter 12

1. Elliot L. Richardson, "Significant Individual Participation: The New Challenge in American Government," the C. R. Musser lecture delivered at the University of Chicago Law School on April 26, 1967. This lecture is reprinted in the University of Chicago's *Law School Record,* vol. 15 (Autumn 1967), pp. 36-44.

2. The Lou Harris poll quoted was conducted for the Senate Committee on Governmental Operations in late 1973. The results of this poll are contained in Elliot Richardson, *The Creative Balance,* Holt, Reinhart and Winston, New York, 1976, p. 88.

3. General Motors Institute, *Survey of Citizen Opinions and Citizen Involvement,* Flint, Mich., May 1974.

4. This material was taken from a WJRT-TV editorial that appeared on October 22, 1973, in Flint.

5. This was taken from a report entitled "Flint Area Attitude and Opinion Survey," prepared by the Flint Environmental Action Team in November 1973.

6. See Barbara Jordan, Keynote Address to the 1976 Democratic National Convention held in New York on July 12, 1976, p. 2.

Chapter 13

1. Justice Potter Stewart, "Or of the Press," Sesquicentennial Address to the Yale Law School, November 2, 1974.

2. Quoted by Henry Grunwald, "Don't Love the Press, But Understand It," *Time Magazine*, July 8, 1974.

3. Quoted in *Fortune Magazine*, "The New Concerns About the Press," April 1975, p. 121.

4. Elliot Richardson, *The Creative Balance*, Holt, Reinhart and Winston, New York, 1976, p. 116.

5. *Los Angeles Times*, December 14, 1976.

6. Quoted by Henry Grunwald, "Covering Watergate: Success and Backlash," *Time Magazine*, July 8, 1976, p. 68.

7. Ibid, p. 69.

8. *Flint Journal*, May 13, 1973.

9. Richardson, *The Creative Balance*, p. 121.

Chapter 14

1. *Flint Journal*, July 14, 1974.

Chapter 15

1. Nathan Glazer, "Toward an Imperial Judiciary?," *The Public Interest*, Fall 1975, pp. 104-123.

2. Quoted by Jerrold K. Footlick, "Too Much Law?," *Newsweek*, January 10, 1977, p. 45.

3. See "The Power of Our Judges: Are They Going Too Far?," *U.S. News and World Report*, January 19, 1976, p. 30.

4. Ibid, p. 30.

5. Ibid, p. 33.

6. Ibid, p. 31.

7. Ibid, p. 34.

8. See *Los Angeles Times*, "Activist Judges Expand Power of the Bench," December 22, 1976, for an excellent summary of the judicial impact on the achievement of law-enforcement objectives as well as a general discussion of the growing power of the judiciary in legislative and executive affairs.

Chapter 16

1. Richardson, *The Creative Balance*, p. 136.